Shojo Beat

BABY & Me

Vol. 15

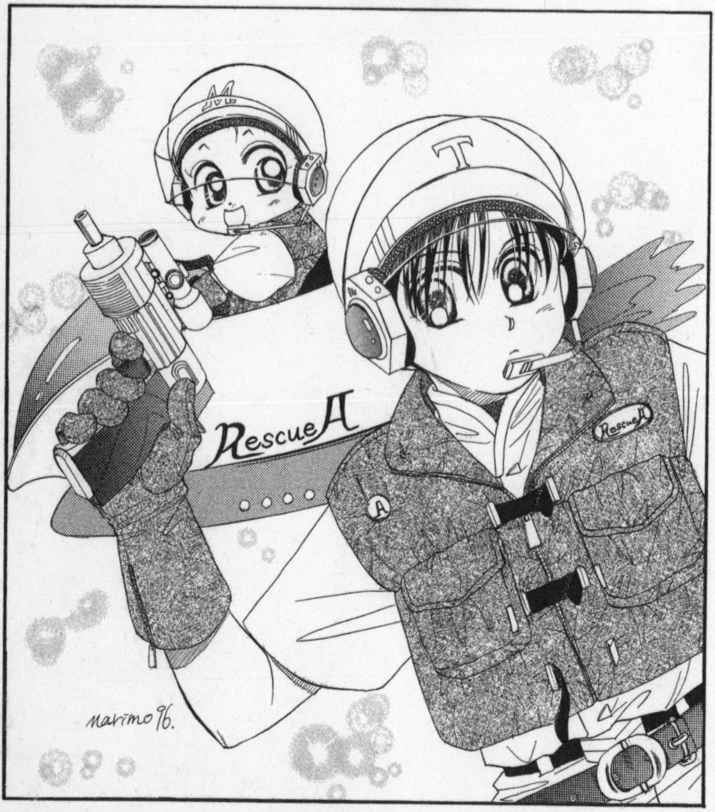

Rescue A
marimo 96.

Story & Art by Marimo Ragawa

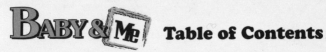

BABY & Me Table of Contents

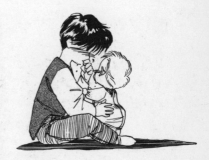

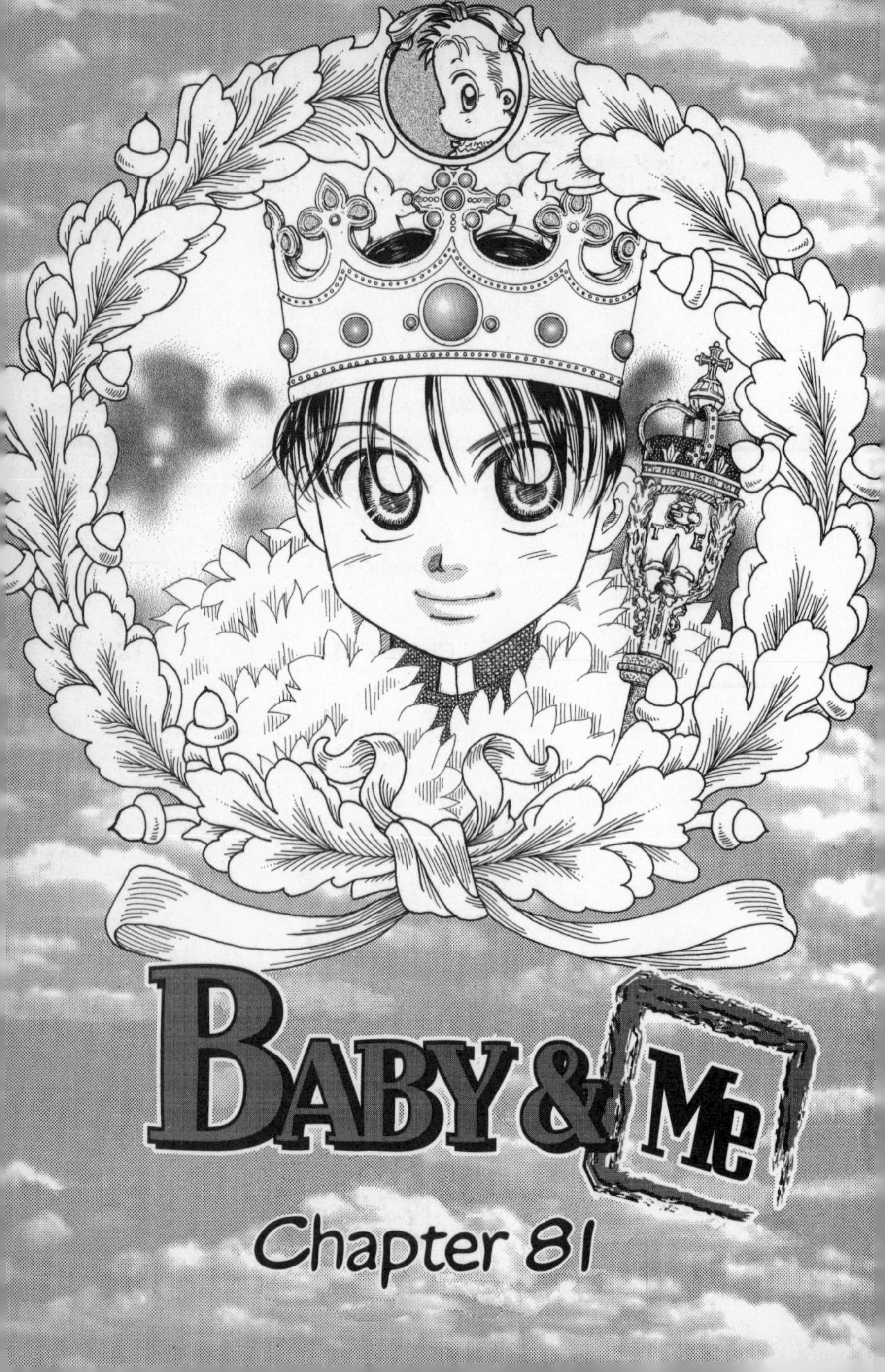

BABY & Me

Chapter 81

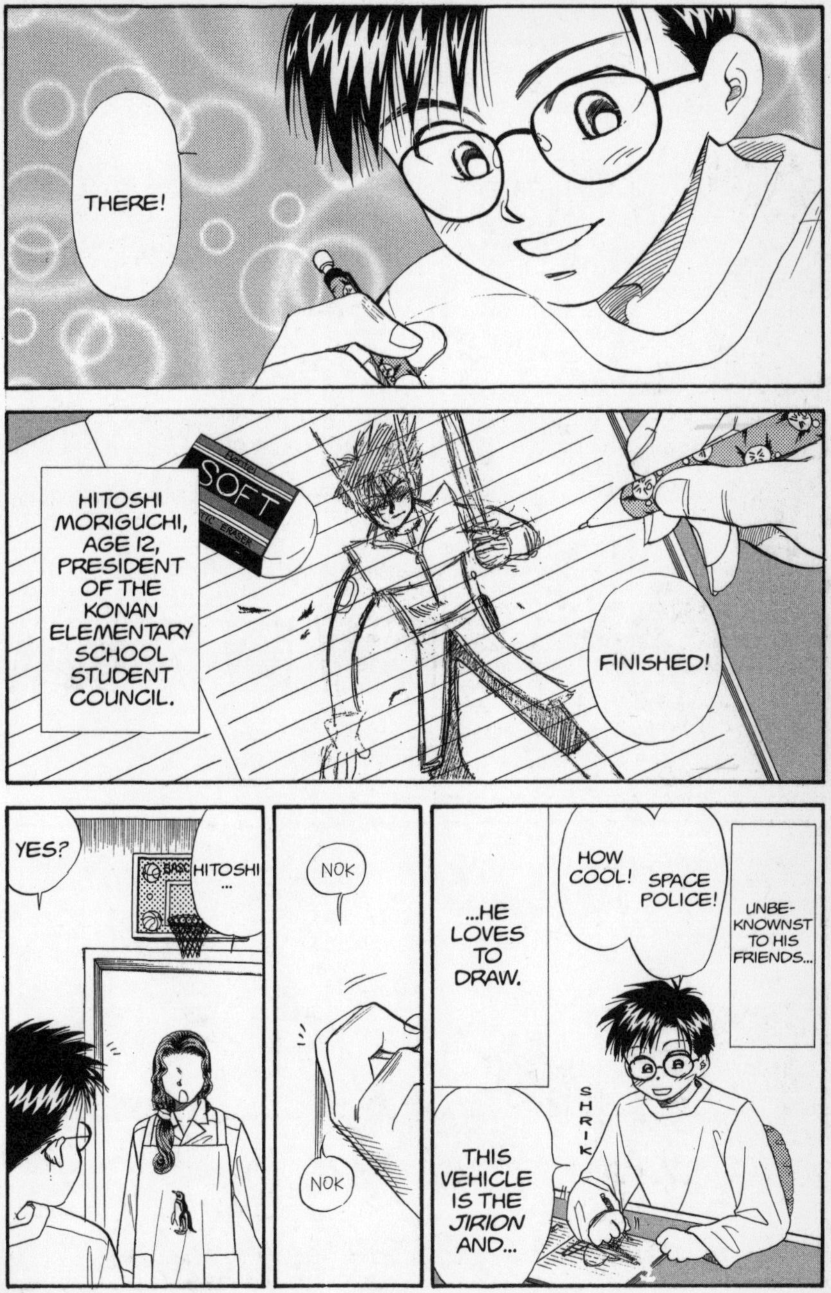
THERE!
FINISHED!
HITOSHI MORIGUCHI, AGE 12, PRESIDENT OF THE KONAN ELEMENTARY SCHOOL STUDENT COUNCIL.
UNBE-KNOWNST TO HIS FRIENDS...
SPACE POLICE!
HOW COOL!
...HE LOVES TO DRAW.
SHRIK
THIS VEHICLE IS THE *JIRION* AND...
NOK
NOK
HITOSHI ...
YES?

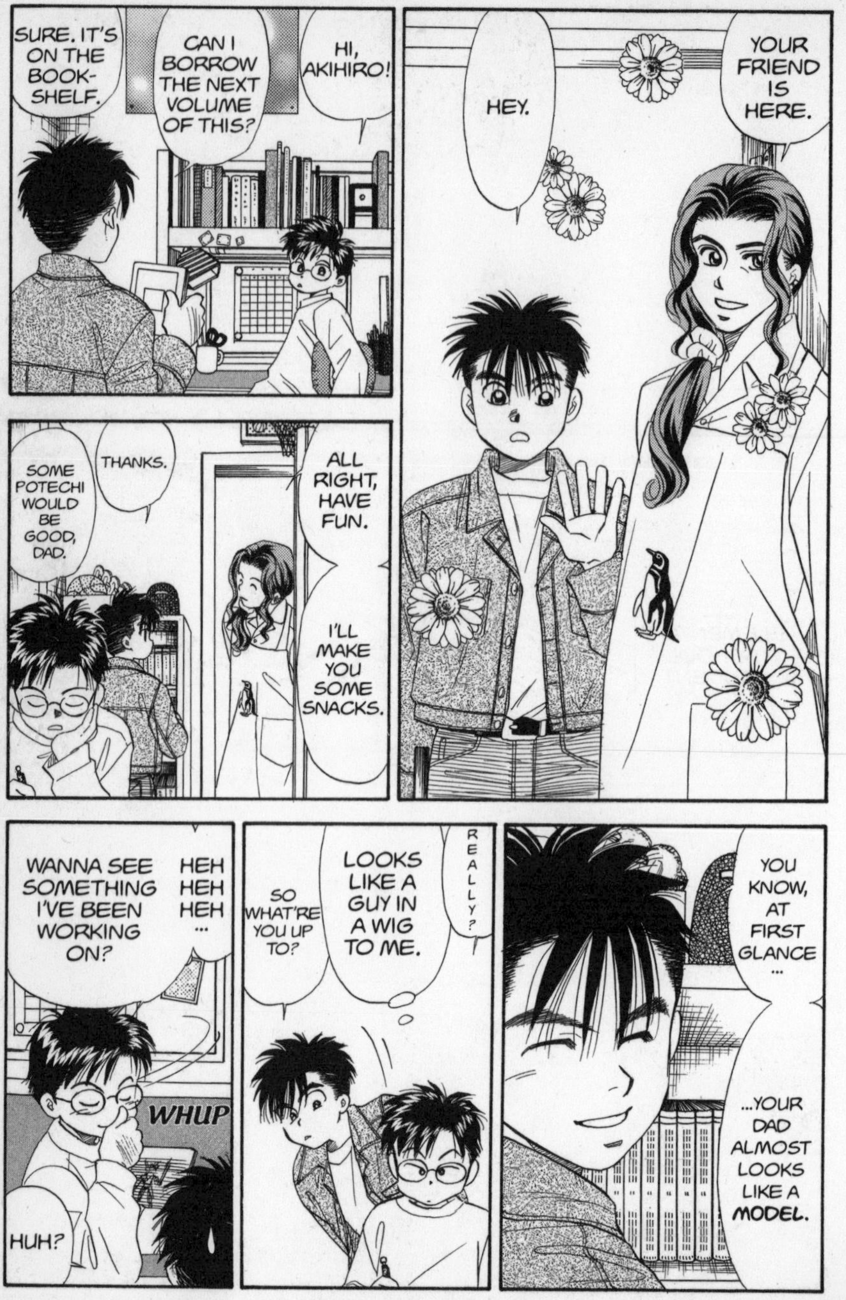
YOUR FRIEND IS HERE.
HEY.
HI, AKIHIRO!
CAN I BORROW THE NEXT VOLUME OF THIS?
SURE. IT'S ON THE BOOK-SHELF.
ALL RIGHT, HAVE FUN.
I'LL MAKE YOU SOME SNACKS.
THANKS.
SOME POTECHI WOULD BE GOOD, DAD.
YOU KNOW, AT FIRST GLANCE...
...YOUR DAD ALMOST LOOKS LIKE A **MODEL**.
REALLY?
LOOKS LIKE A GUY IN A WIG TO ME.
SO WHAT'RE YOU UP TO?
HEH HEH HEH...
WANNA SEE SOMETHING I'VE BEEN WORKING ON?
WHUP
HUH?

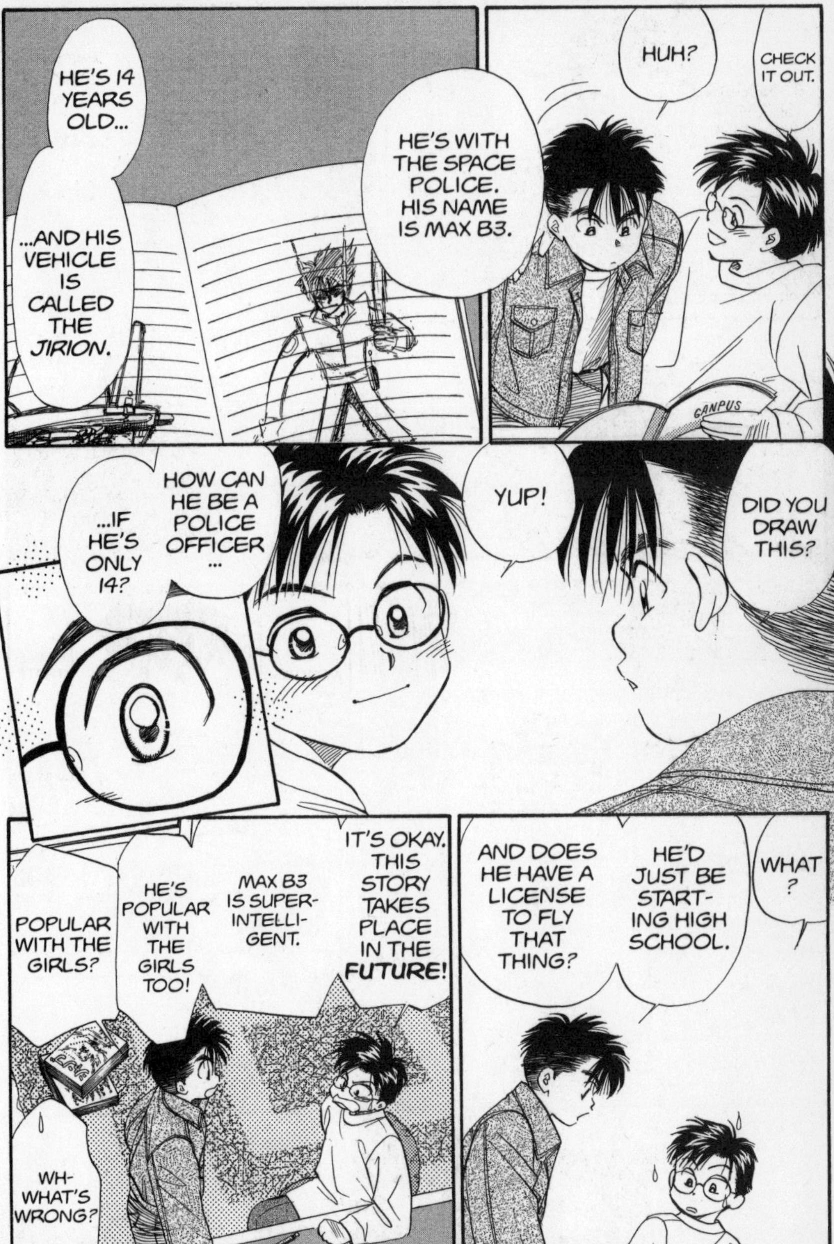
CHECK IT OUT.
HUH?
HE'S WITH THE SPACE POLICE. HIS NAME IS MAX B3.
GANPUS
HE'S 14 YEARS OLD...
...AND HIS VEHICLE IS CALLED THE JIRION.
DID YOU DRAW THIS?
YUP!
HOW CAN HE BE A POLICE OFFICER...
...IF HE'S ONLY 14?
WHAT?
HE'D JUST BE START-ING HIGH SCHOOL.
AND DOES HE HAVE A LICENSE TO FLY THAT THING?
IT'S OKAY. THIS STORY TAKES PLACE IN THE **FUTURE**!
MAX B3 IS SUPER-INTELLI-GENT.
HE'S POPULAR WITH THE GIRLS TOO!
POPULAR WITH THE GIRLS?
WH-WHAT'S WRONG?

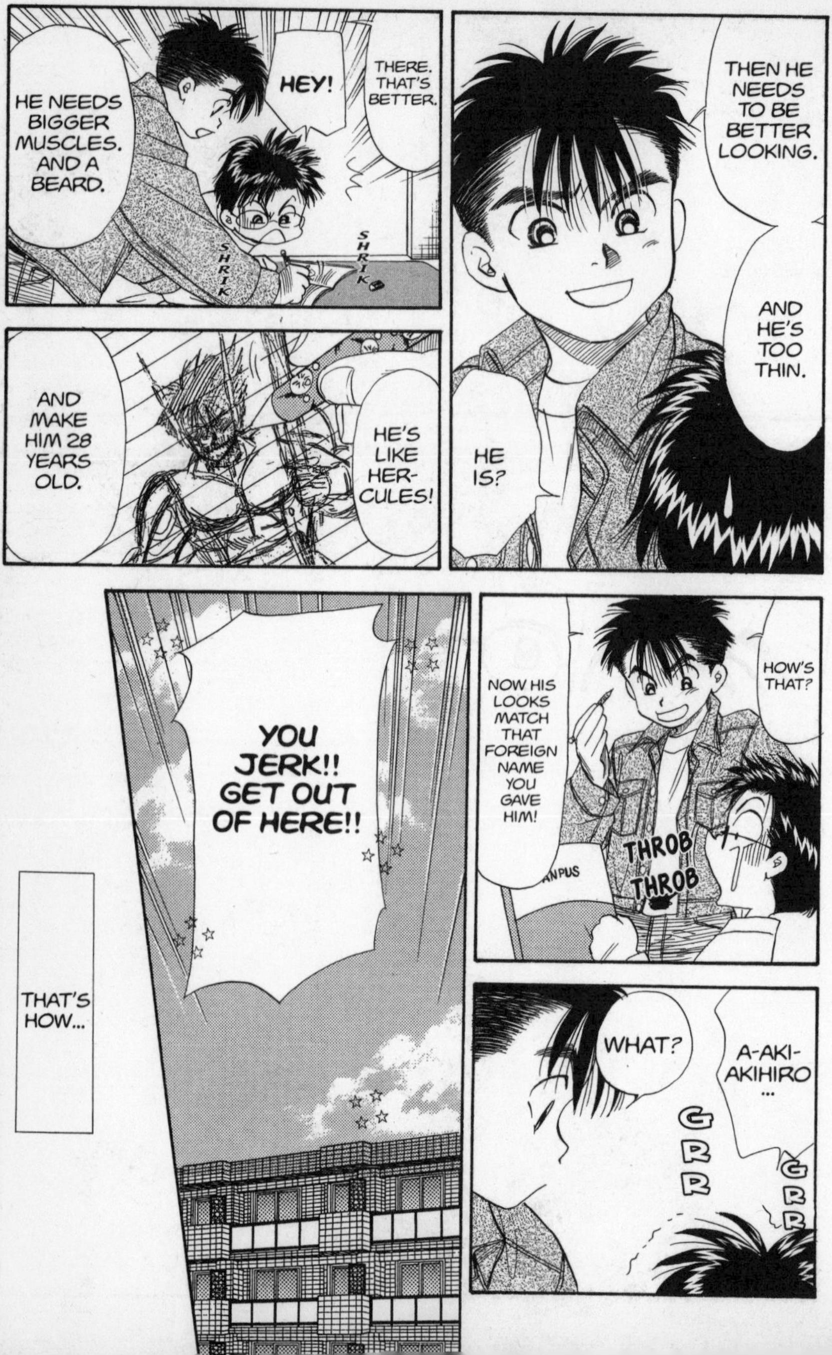
THEN HE NEEDS TO BE BETTER LOOKING.
AND HE'S TOO THIN.
HE IS?
THERE. THAT'S BETTER.
HEY!
HE NEEDS BIGGER MUSCLES. AND A BEARD.
SHRIK
SHRIK
HE'S LIKE HER-CULES!
AND MAKE HIM 28 YEARS OLD.
HOW'S THAT?
NOW HIS LOOKS MATCH THAT FOREIGN NAME YOU GAVE HIM!
THROB THROB
ANPUS
A-AKI-AKIHIRO...
WHAT?
GRR
GRR
YOU JERK!! GET OUT OF HERE!!
THAT'S HOW...

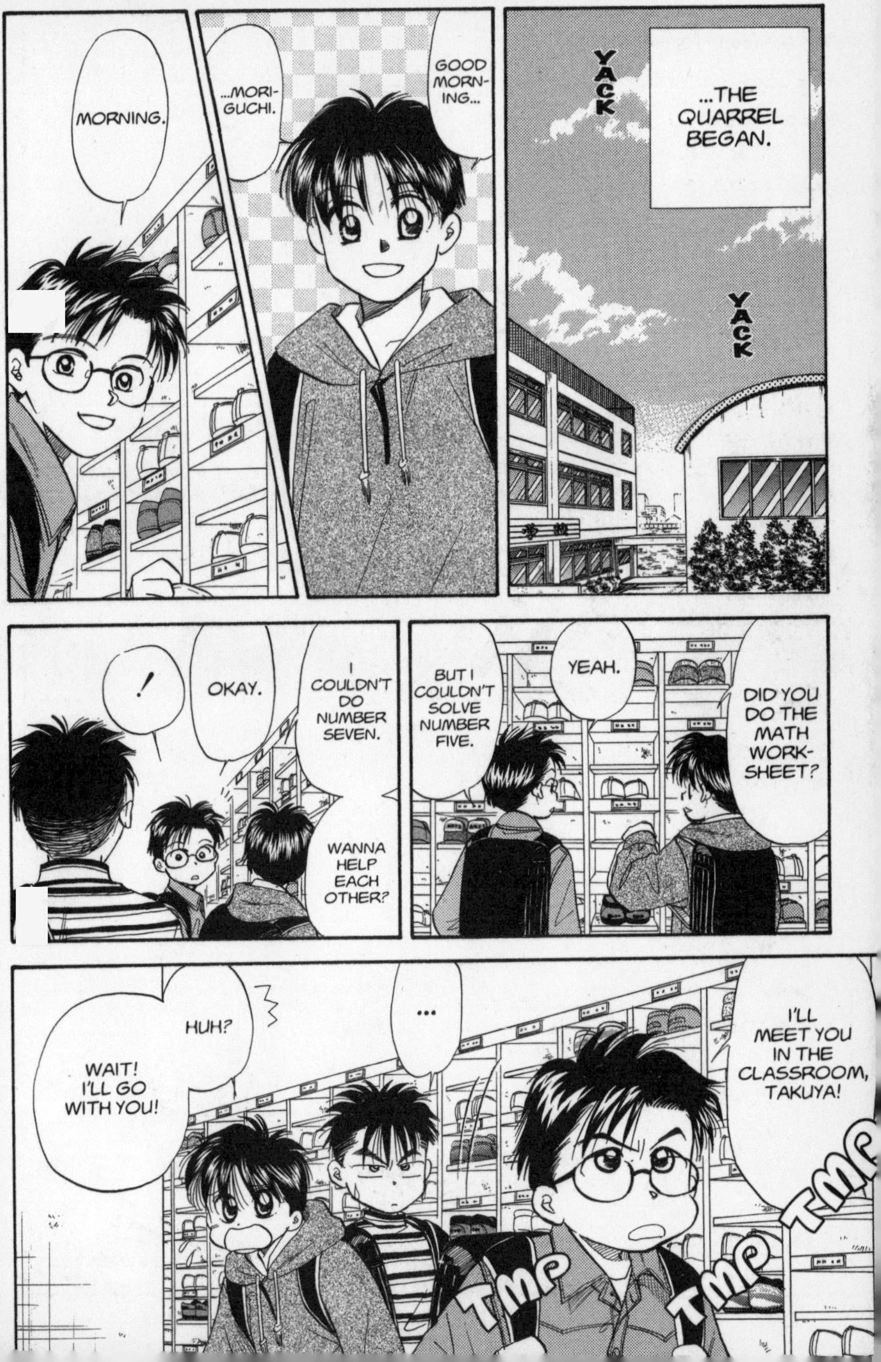
...THE QUARREL BEGAN.
YACK
YACK
GOOD MORNING...
...MORIGUCHI.
MORNING.
DID YOU DO THE MATH WORKSHEET?
YEAH.
BUT I COULDN'T SOLVE NUMBER FIVE.
I COULDN'T DO NUMBER SEVEN.
WANNA HELP EACH OTHER?
OKAY.
!
I'LL MEET YOU IN THE CLASSROOM, TAKUYA!
TMP TMP TMP TMP
...
HUH?
WAIT! I'LL GO WITH YOU!

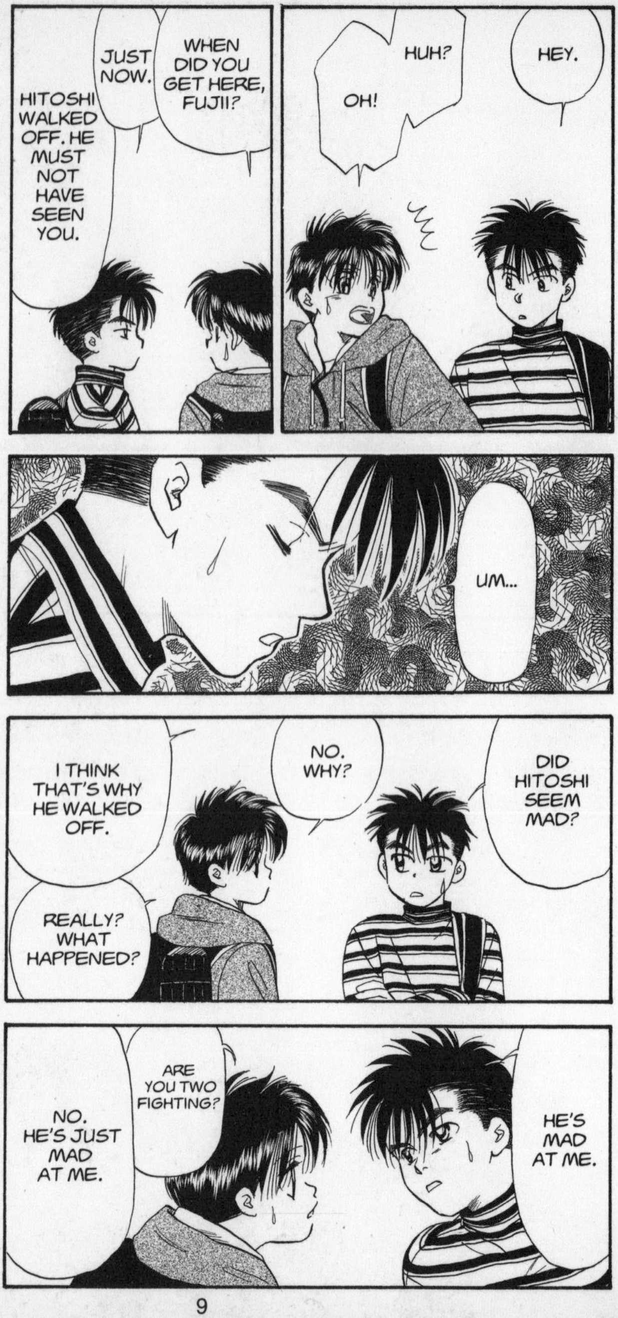
HEY.
HUH?
OH!
WHEN DID YOU GET HERE, FUJII?
JUST NOW.
HITOSHI WALKED OFF. HE MUST NOT HAVE SEEN YOU.
UM...
DID HITOSHI SEEM MAD?
NO. WHY?
I THINK THAT'S WHY HE WALKED OFF.
REALLY? WHAT HAPPENED?
HE'S MAD AT ME.
ARE YOU TWO FIGHTING?
NO. HE'S JUST MAD AT ME.

Author's Note: Part 1

Hi, everybody. Marimo Ragawa here. In this volume, two of my assistants, my sister and Devil F, will be helping me with my Author's Notes. I'm having a hard time coming up with things to write about. I really appreciate their help!

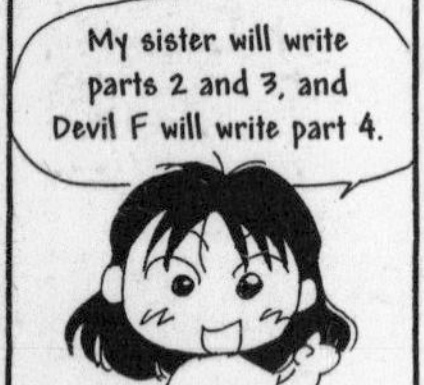
My sister will write parts 2 and 3, and Devil F will write part 4.

The History of Hayami Kasuga's Hairstyles

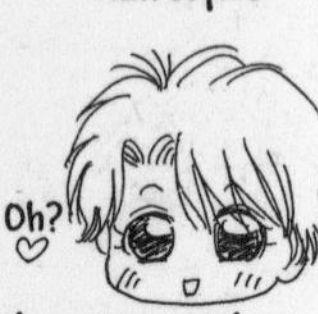
Oh?

Hayami in Volume 14

Before

↓

Hayami in Volume 15

After

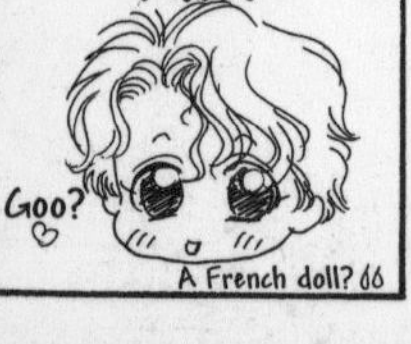
Goo?
A French doll?

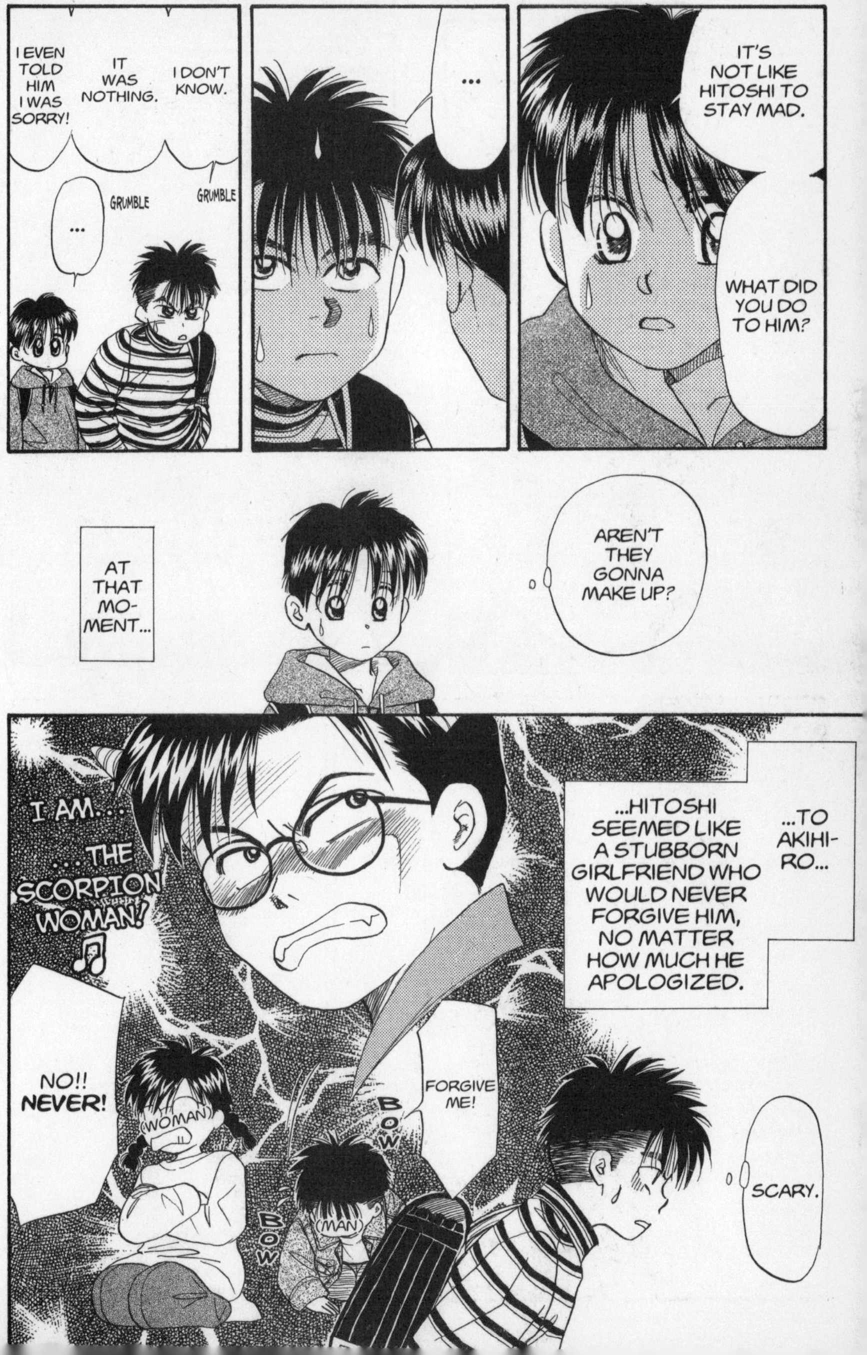
IT'S NOT LIKE HITOSHI TO STAY MAD.
WHAT DID YOU DO TO HIM?
...
I DON'T KNOW.
IT WAS NOTHING.
I EVEN TOLD HIM I WAS SORRY!
GRUMBLE
GRUMBLE
...
AREN'T THEY GONNA MAKE UP?
AT THAT MO-MENT...
...TO AKIHI-RO...
...HITOSHI SEEMED LIKE A STUBBORN GIRLFRIEND WHO WOULD NEVER FORGIVE HIM, NO MATTER HOW MUCH HE APOLOGIZED.
I AM... ...THE SCORPION WOMAN! ♫
SCARY.
FORGIVE ME!
BOW
BOW
(MAN)
NO!! **NEVER!**
(WOMAN)

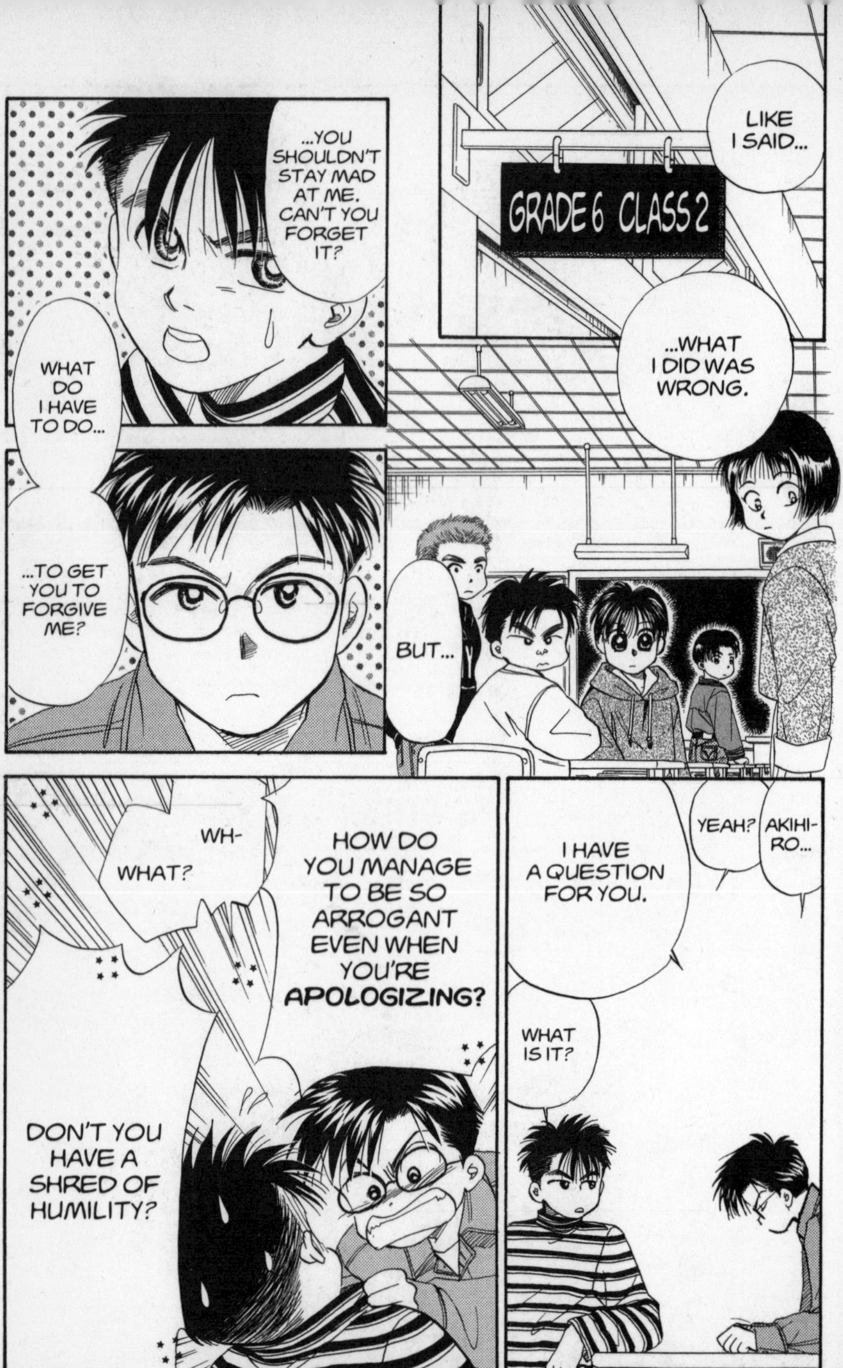
LIKE I SAID...
GRADE 6 CLASS 2
...WHAT I DID WAS WRONG.
BUT...
...YOU SHOULDN'T STAY MAD AT ME. CAN'T YOU FORGET IT?
WHAT DO I HAVE TO DO...
...TO GET YOU TO FORGIVE ME?
AKIHI-RO...
YEAH?
I HAVE A QUESTION FOR YOU.
WHAT IS IT?
HOW DO YOU MANAGE TO BE SO ARROGANT EVEN WHEN YOU'RE APOLOGIZING?
WH- WHAT?
DON'T YOU HAVE A SHRED OF HUMILITY?

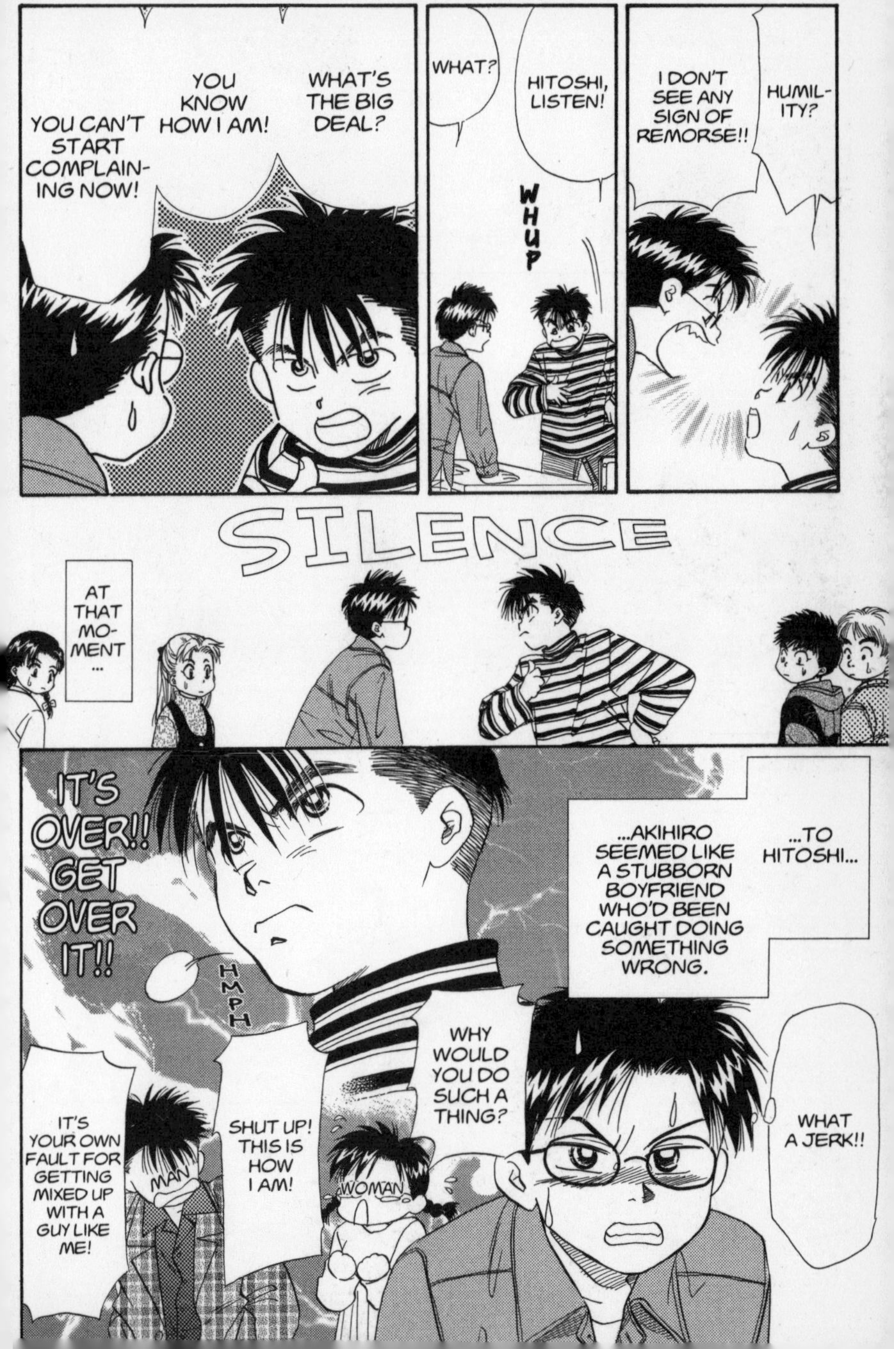
HUMIL-ITY?
I DON'T SEE ANY SIGN OF REMORSE!!
HITOSHI, LISTEN!
WHAT?
WHUP
WHAT'S THE BIG DEAL?
YOU KNOW HOW I AM!
YOU CAN'T START COMPLAIN-ING NOW!
SILENCE
AT THAT MO-MENT...
...TO HITOSHI...
...AKIHIRO SEEMED LIKE A STUBBORN BOYFRIEND WHO'D BEEN CAUGHT DOING SOMETHING WRONG.
WHAT A JERK!!
WHY WOULD YOU DO SUCH A THING?
WOMAN
SHUT UP! THIS IS HOW I AM!
IT'S YOUR OWN FAULT FOR GETTING MIXED UP WITH A GUY LIKE ME!
MAN
IT'S OVER!! GET OVER IT!!
HMPH

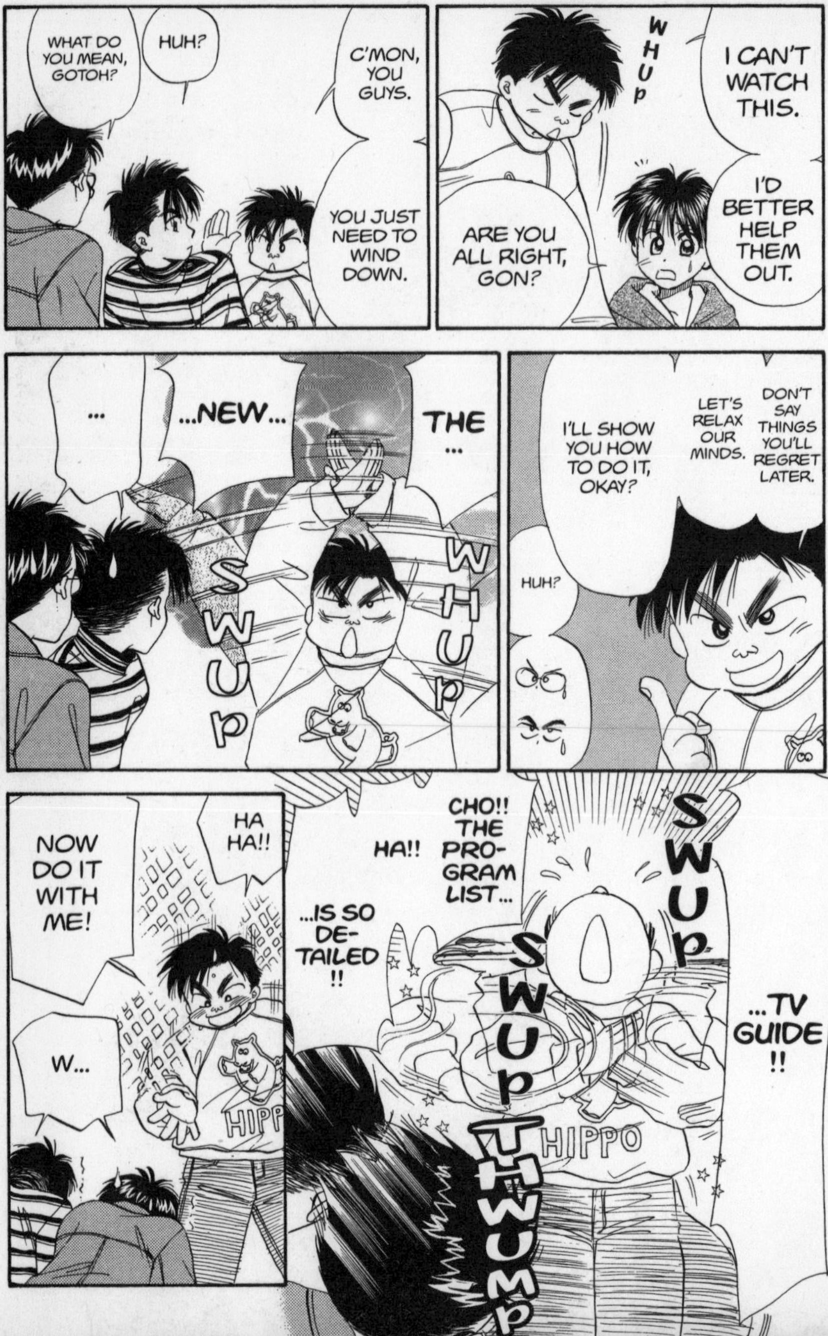
WHUp
I CAN'T WATCH THIS.
I'D BETTER HELP THEM OUT.
ARE YOU ALL RIGHT, GON?
C'MON, YOU GUYS.
YOU JUST NEED TO WIND DOWN.
HUH?
WHAT DO YOU MEAN, GOTOH?
DON'T SAY THINGS YOU'LL REGRET LATER.
LET'S RELAX OUR MINDS.
I'LL SHOW YOU HOW TO DO IT, OKAY?
HUH?
THE...
WHUp
...NEW...
...
SWUp
SWUp
CHO!! THE PRO-GRAM LIST...
HA!!
...IS SO DE-TAILED!!
...TV GUIDE!!
SWUp
SWUp
THWUMP
HIPPO
HA HA!!
NOW DO IT WITH ME!
W...
HIPP

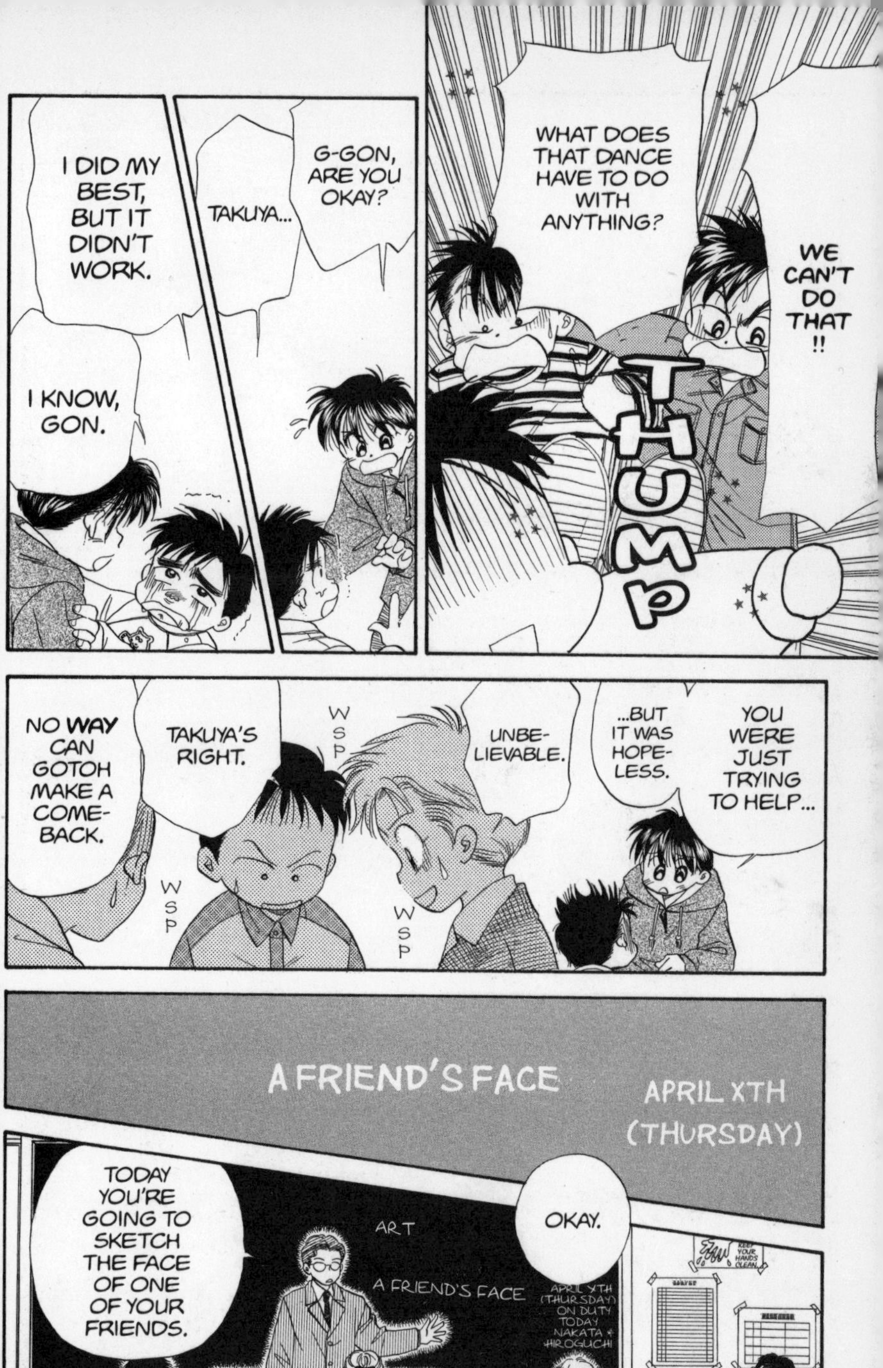
WHAT DOES THAT DANCE HAVE TO DO WITH ANYTHING?
WE CAN'T DO THAT!!
THUMP
G-GON, ARE YOU OKAY?
TAKUYA...
I DID MY BEST, BUT IT DIDN'T WORK.
I KNOW, GON.
YOU WERE JUST TRYING TO HELP...
...BUT IT WAS HOPELESS.
UNBE-LIEVABLE.
WSP
TAKUYA'S RIGHT.
WSP
WSP
NO **WAY** CAN GOTOH MAKE A COME-BACK.
APRIL XTH (THURSDAY)
A FRIEND'S FACE
OKAY.
KEEP YOUR HANDS CLEAN.
APRIL XTH (THURSDAY) ON DUTY TODAY NAKATA + HIROGUCHI
ART
A FRIEND'S FACE
TODAY YOU'RE GOING TO SKETCH THE FACE OF ONE OF YOUR FRIENDS.

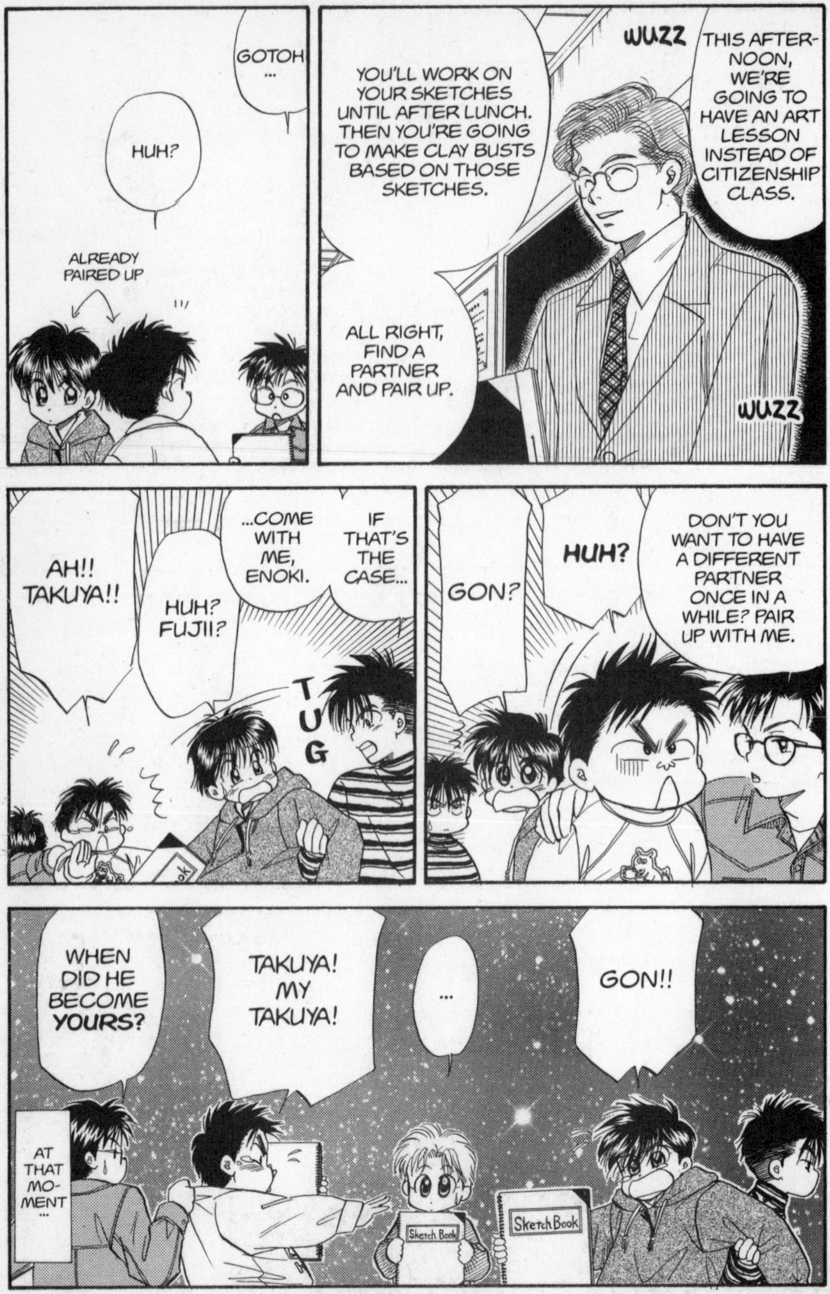
THIS AFTER-NOON, WE'RE GOING TO HAVE AN ART LESSON INSTEAD OF CITIZENSHIP CLASS.
WUZZ
YOU'LL WORK ON YOUR SKETCHES UNTIL AFTER LUNCH. THEN YOU'RE GOING TO MAKE CLAY BUSTS BASED ON THOSE SKETCHES.
ALL RIGHT, FIND A PARTNER AND PAIR UP.
WUZZ
GOTOH ...
HUH?
ALREADY PAIRED UP
DON'T YOU WANT TO HAVE A DIFFERENT PARTNER ONCE IN A WHILE? PAIR UP WITH ME.
HUH?
GON?
IF THAT'S THE CASE...
...COME WITH ME, ENOKI.
TUG
HUH? FUJII?
AH!! TAKUYA!!
GON!!
...
TAKUYA! MY TAKUYA!
WHEN DID HE BECOME YOURS?
AT THAT MO-MENT ...
Sketch Book
Sketch Book

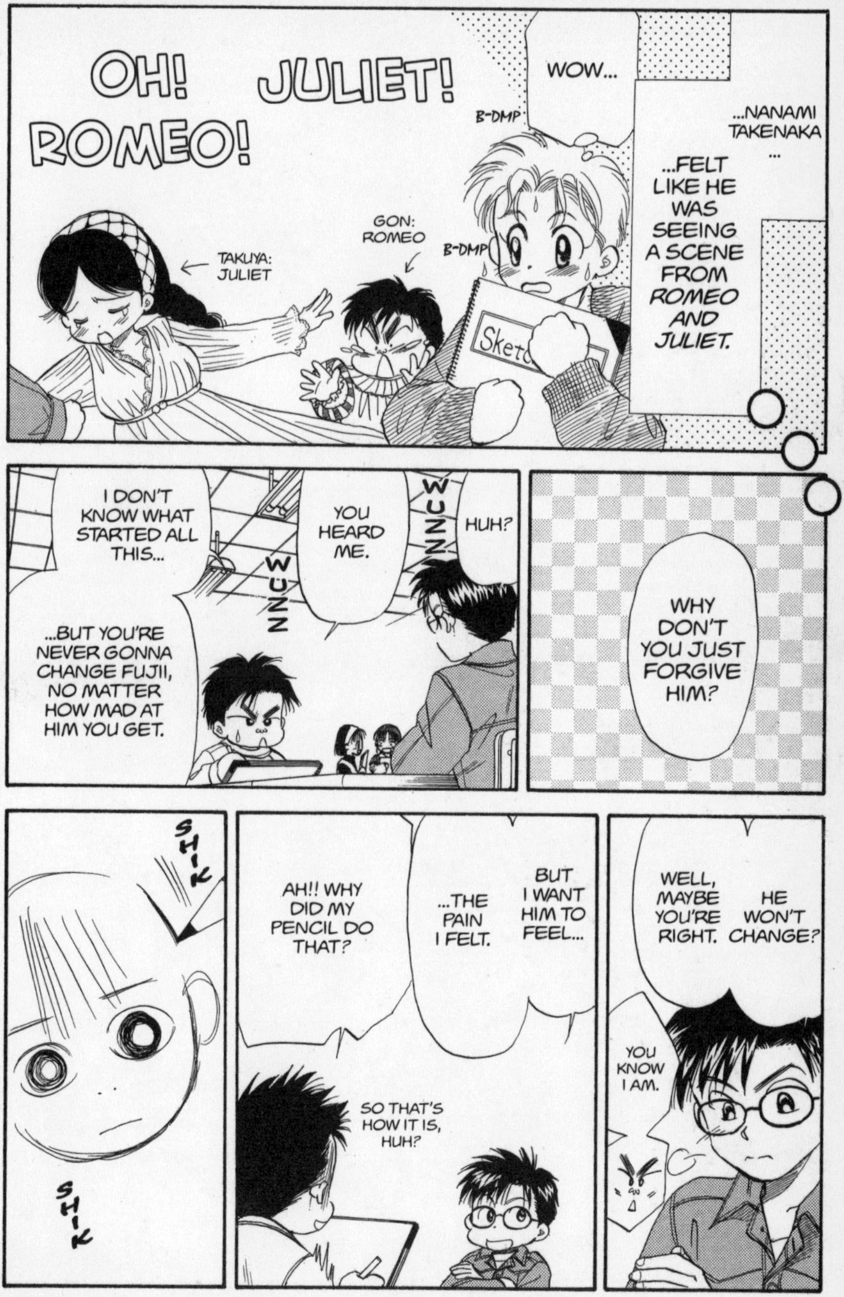
...NANAMI TAKENAKA ...
...FELT LIKE HE WAS SEEING A SCENE FROM ROMEO AND JULIET.
WOW...
B-DMP
B-DMP
GON: ROMEO
JULIET!
OH!
ROMEO!
TAKUYA: JULIET
WHY DON'T YOU JUST FORGIVE HIM?
HUH?
WUZZ
YOU HEARD ME.
WUZZ
I DON'T KNOW WHAT STARTED ALL THIS...
...BUT YOU'RE NEVER GONNA CHANGE FUJII, NO MATTER HOW MAD AT HIM YOU GET.
HE WON'T CHANGE?
WELL, MAYBE YOU'RE RIGHT.
YOU KNOW I AM.
BUT I WANT HIM TO FEEL...
...THE PAIN I FELT.
AH!! WHY DID MY PENCIL DO THAT?
SO THAT'S HOW IT IS, HUH?
SHIK
SHIK

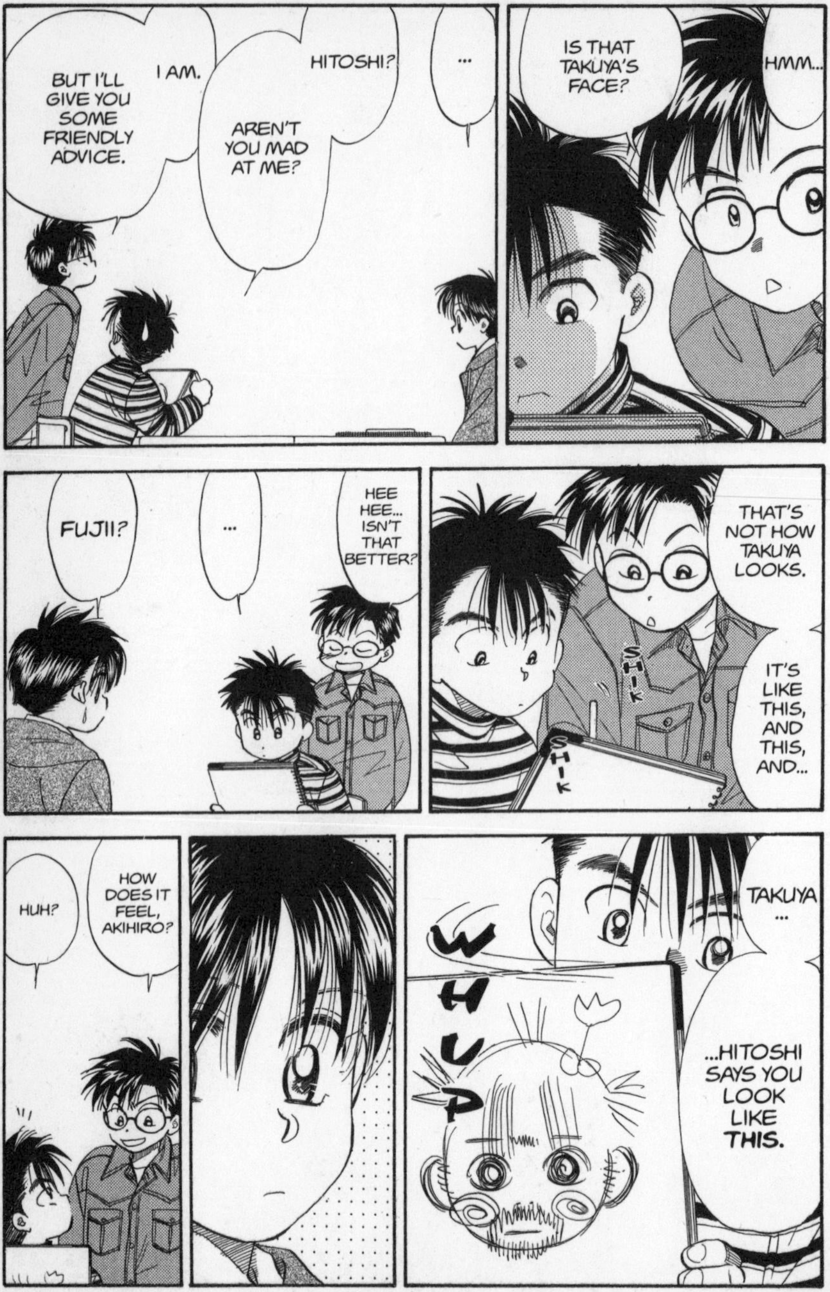
HMM...
IS THAT TAKUYA'S FACE?
...
HITOSHI?
AREN'T YOU MAD AT ME?
I AM.
BUT I'LL GIVE YOU SOME FRIENDLY ADVICE.
THAT'S NOT HOW TAKUYA LOOKS.
SHIK
IT'S LIKE THIS, AND THIS, AND...
SHIK
HEE HEE... ISN'T THAT BETTER?
...
FUJII?
TAKUYA...
WHUP
...HITOSHI SAYS YOU LOOK LIKE **THIS.**
HOW DOES IT FEEL, AKIHIRO?
HUH?

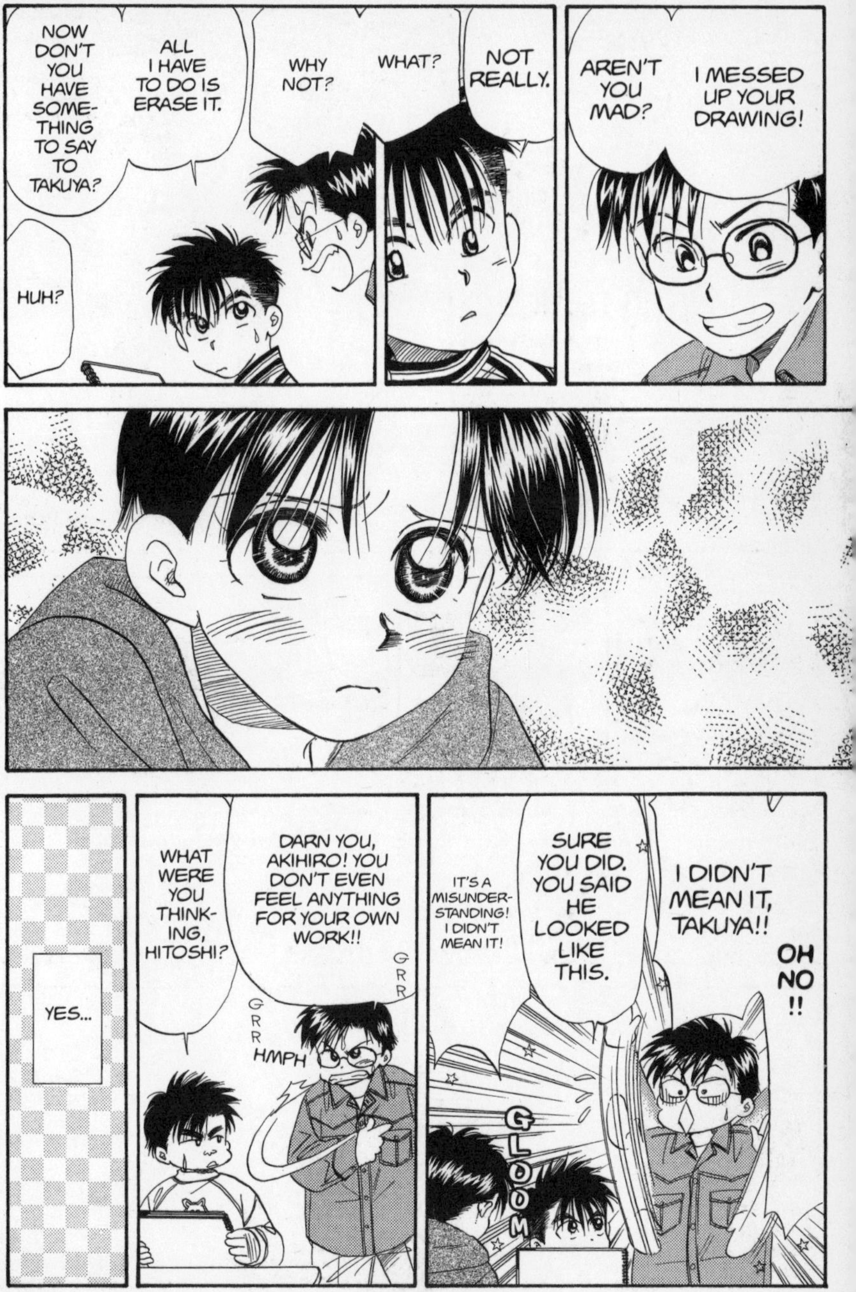
I MESSED UP YOUR DRAWING!
AREN'T YOU MAD?
NOT REALLY.
WHAT?
WHY NOT?
ALL I HAVE TO DO IS ERASE IT.
NOW DON'T YOU HAVE SOMETHING TO SAY TO TAKUYA?
HUH?
OH NO!!
I DIDN'T MEAN IT, TAKUYA!!
SURE YOU DID. YOU SAID HE LOOKED LIKE THIS.
IT'S A MISUNDERSTANDING! I DIDN'T MEAN IT!
GLOOM
DARN YOU, AKIHIRO! YOU DON'T EVEN FEEL ANYTHING FOR YOUR OWN WORK!!
GRR
WHAT WERE YOU THINKING, HITOSHI?
GRR
HMPH
YES...

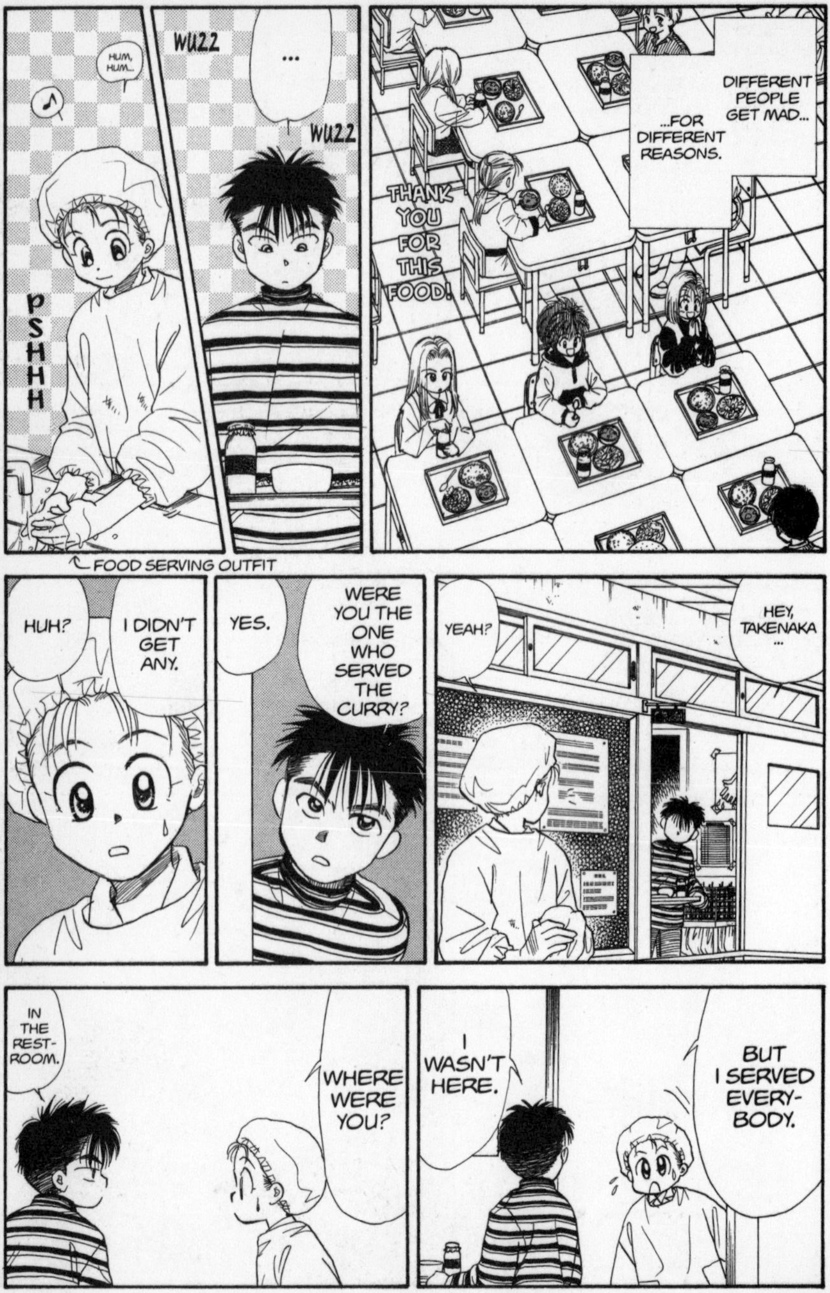
DIFFERENT PEOPLE GET MAD...
...FOR DIFFERENT REASONS.
THANK YOU FOR THIS FOOD!
WUZZ
...
WUZZ
HUM, HUM...
♪
PSHHH
FOOD SERVING OUTFIT
HEY, TAKENAKA ...
YEAH?
WERE YOU THE ONE WHO SERVED THE CURRY?
YES.
I DIDN'T GET ANY.
HUH?
BUT I SERVED EVERYBODY.
I WASN'T HERE.
WHERE WERE YOU?
IN THE REST-ROOM.

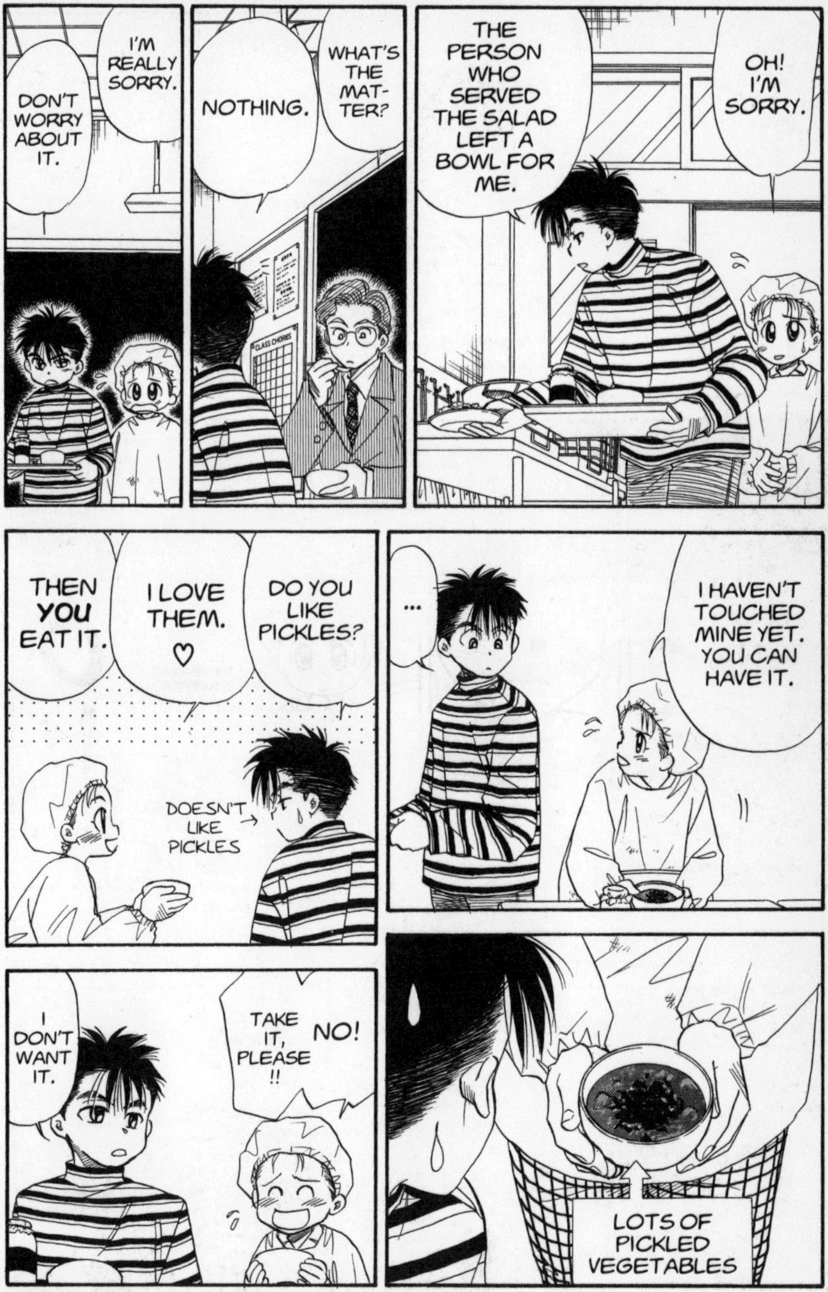
OH! I'M SORRY.
THE PERSON WHO SERVED THE SALAD LEFT A BOWL FOR ME.
WHAT'S THE MAT-TER?
NOTHING.
CLASS CHORES
I'M REALLY SORRY.
DON'T WORRY ABOUT IT.
I HAVEN'T TOUCHED MINE YET. YOU CAN HAVE IT.
...
DO YOU LIKE PICKLES?
I LOVE THEM. ♡
THEN **YOU** EAT IT.
DOESN'T LIKE PICKLES
LOTS OF PICKLED VEGETABLES
NO!
TAKE IT, PLEASE !!
I DON'T WANT IT.

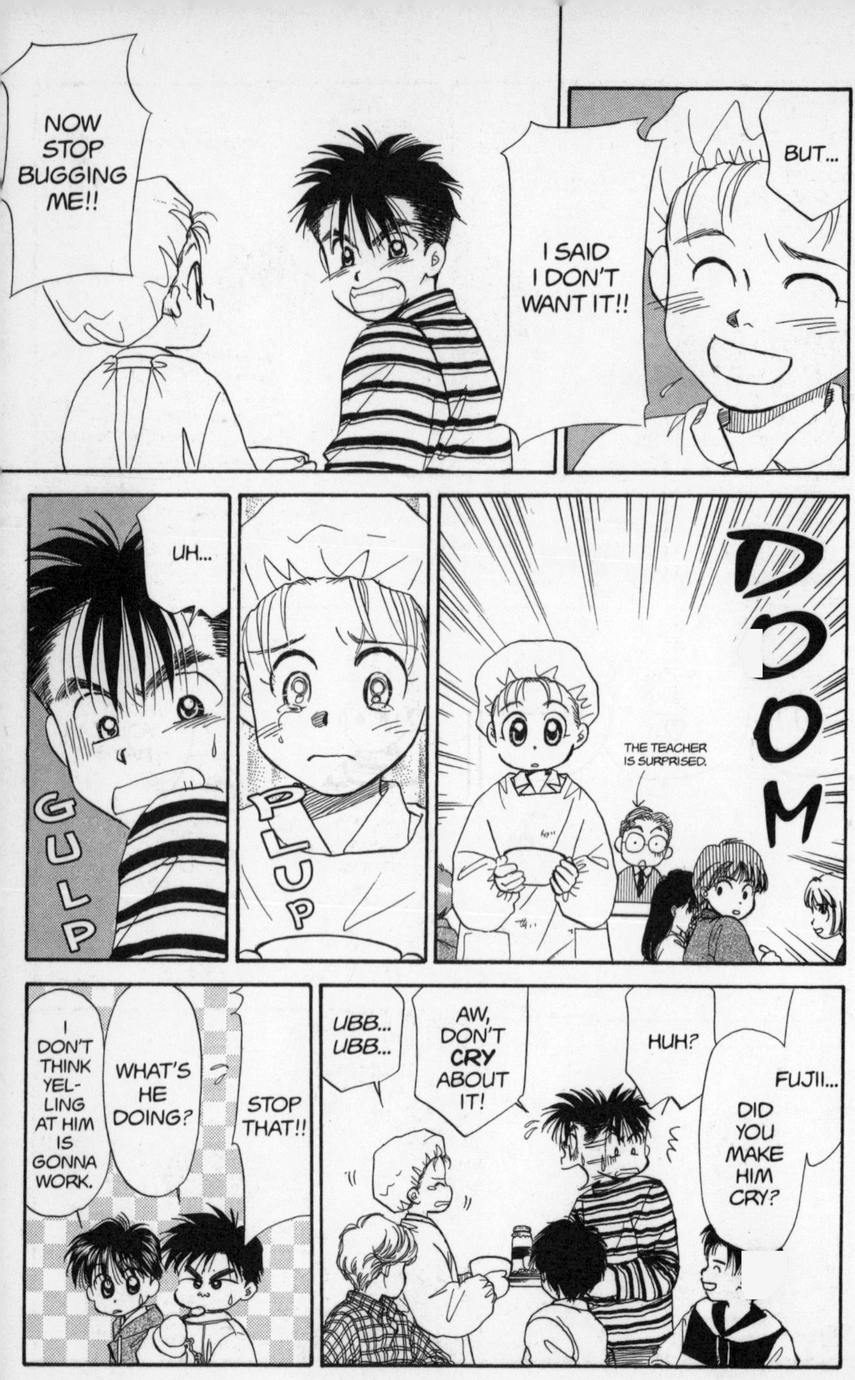

BUT...
I SAID I DON'T WANT IT!!
NOW STOP BUGGING ME!!
DOOM
THE TEACHER IS SURPRISED.
PLUP
UH...
GULP
FUJII... DID YOU MAKE HIM CRY?
HUH?
AW, DON'T CRY ABOUT IT!
UBB... UBB...
STOP THAT!!
WHAT'S HE DOING?
I DON'T THINK YEL-LING AT HIM IS GONNA WORK.

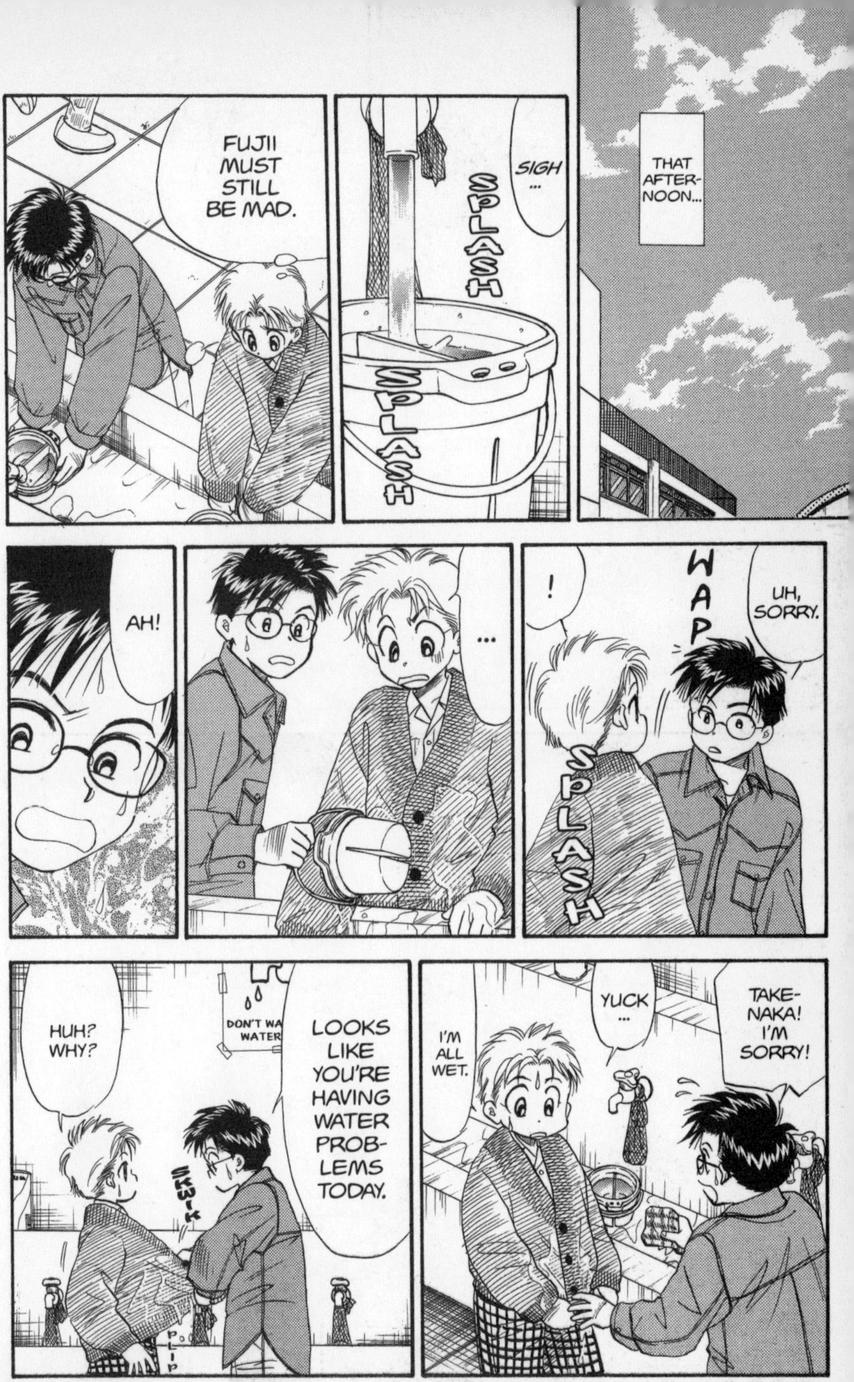
THAT AFTER-NOON...
SIGH ...
SPLASH
SPLASH
FUJII MUST STILL BE MAD.
WAP
UH, SORRY.
!
SPLASH
...
AH!
TAKE-NAKA! I'M SORRY!
YUCK ...
I'M ALL WET.
LOOKS LIKE YOU'RE HAVING WATER PROB-LEMS TODAY.
SKWIK
HUH? WHY?
PLIP

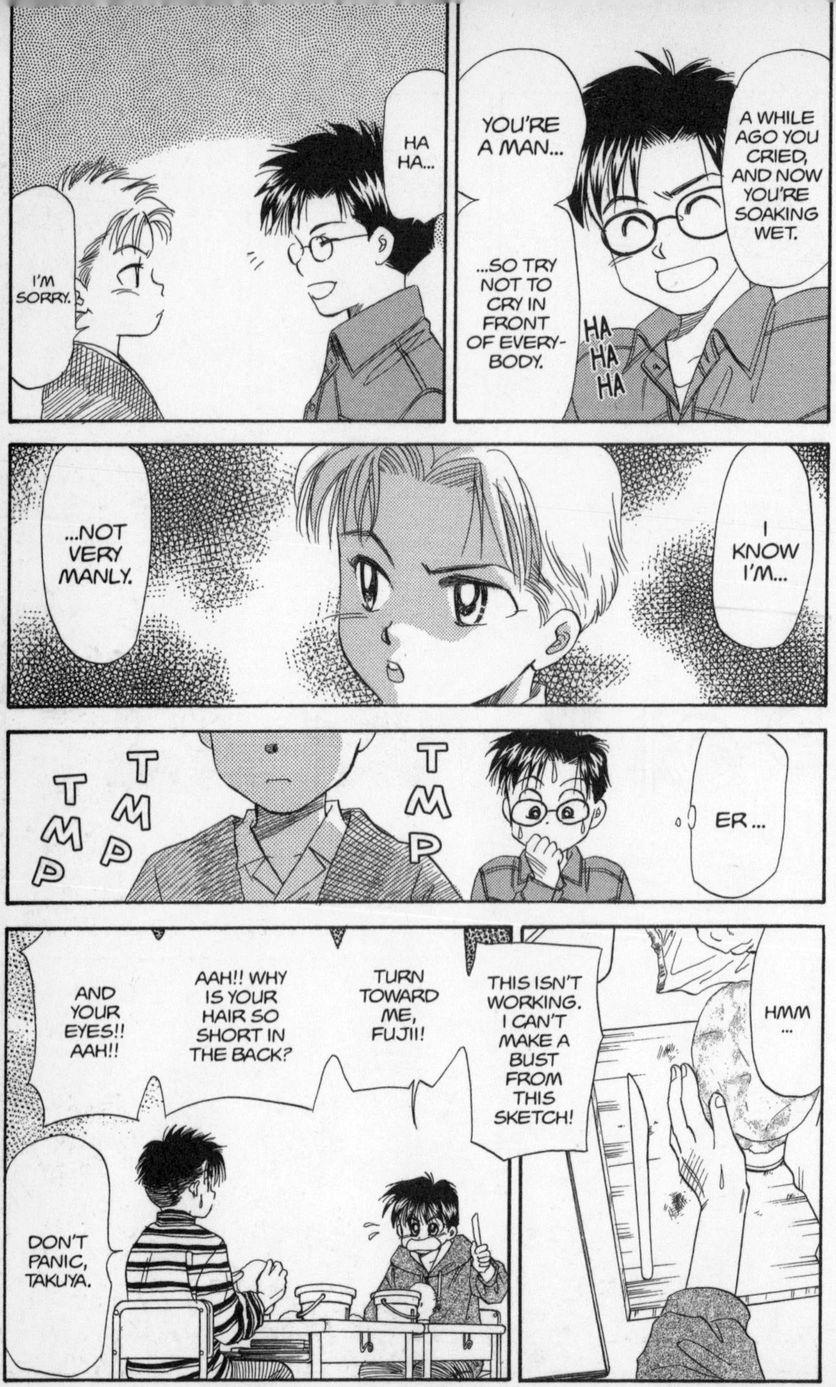
A WHILE AGO YOU CRIED, AND NOW YOU'RE SOAKING WET.
HA HA HA
YOU'RE A MAN...
...SO TRY NOT TO CRY IN FRONT OF EVERY-BODY.
HA HA...
I'M SORRY.
I KNOW I'M...
...NOT VERY MANLY.
ER...
TMP
TMP
TMP
HMM ...
THIS ISN'T WORKING. I CAN'T MAKE A BUST FROM THIS SKETCH!
TURN TOWARD ME, FUJII!
AAH!! WHY IS YOUR HAIR SO SHORT IN THE BACK?
AND YOUR EYES!! AAH!!
DON'T PANIC, TAKUYA.

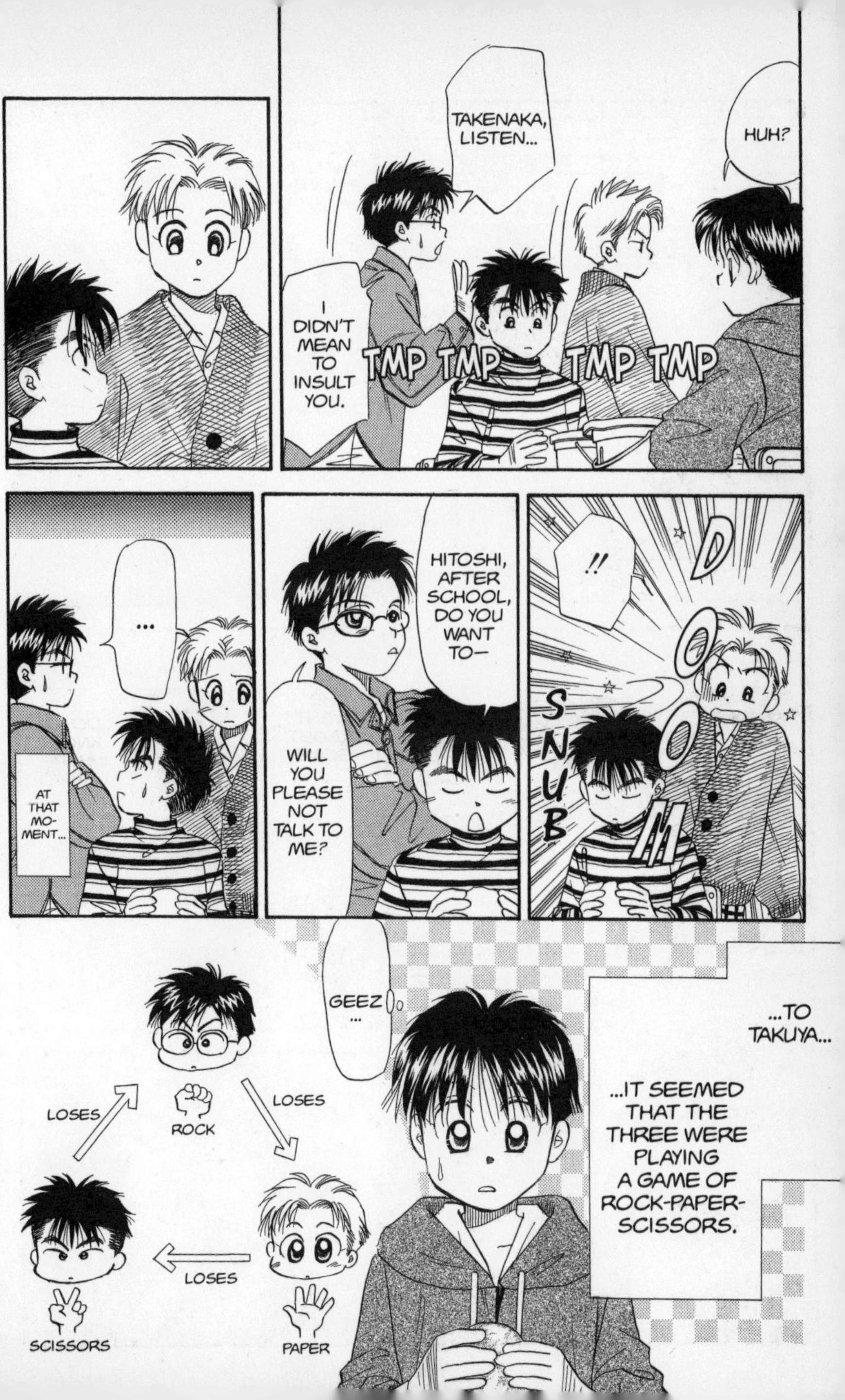
TAKENAKA, LISTEN...
HUH?
I DIDN'T MEAN TO INSULT YOU.
TMP TMP TMP TMP
!!
DOOM
SNUB
HITOSHI, AFTER SCHOOL, DO YOU WANT TO—
WILL YOU PLEASE NOT TALK TO ME?
...
AT THAT MO-MENT...
...TO TAKUYA...
...IT SEEMED THAT THE THREE WERE PLAYING A GAME OF ROCK-PAPER-SCISSORS.
GEEZ...
ROCK
LOSES
LOSES
PAPER
LOSES
SCISSORS

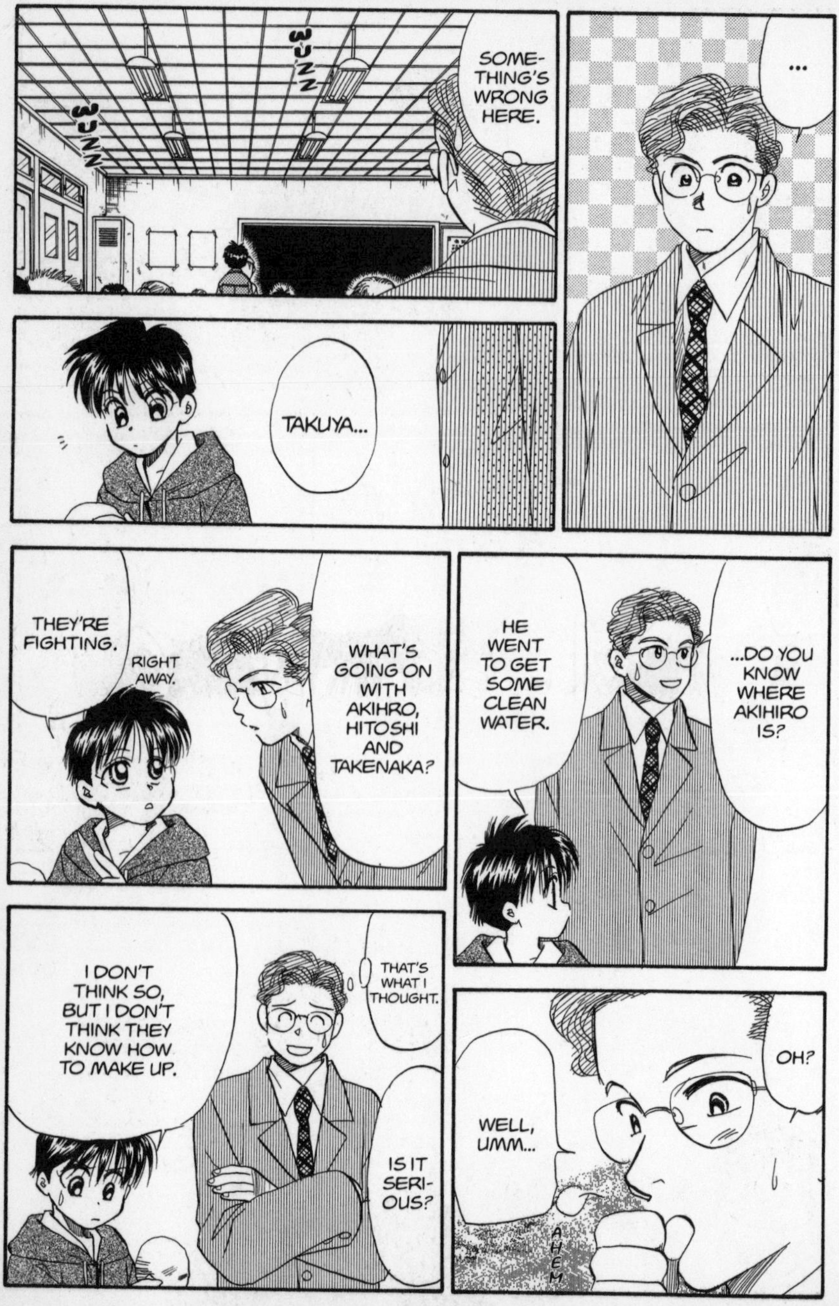
...
WUZZ
WUZZ
SOME-THING'S WRONG HERE.
TAKUYA...
...DO YOU KNOW WHERE AKIHIRO IS?
HE WENT TO GET SOME CLEAN WATER.
WHAT'S GOING ON WITH AKIHIRO, HITOSHI AND TAKENAKA?
THEY'RE FIGHTING.
RIGHT AWAY.
OH?
WELL, UMM...
AHEM
THAT'S WHAT I THOUGHT.
IS IT SERIOUS?
I DON'T THINK SO, BUT I DON'T THINK THEY KNOW HOW TO MAKE UP.

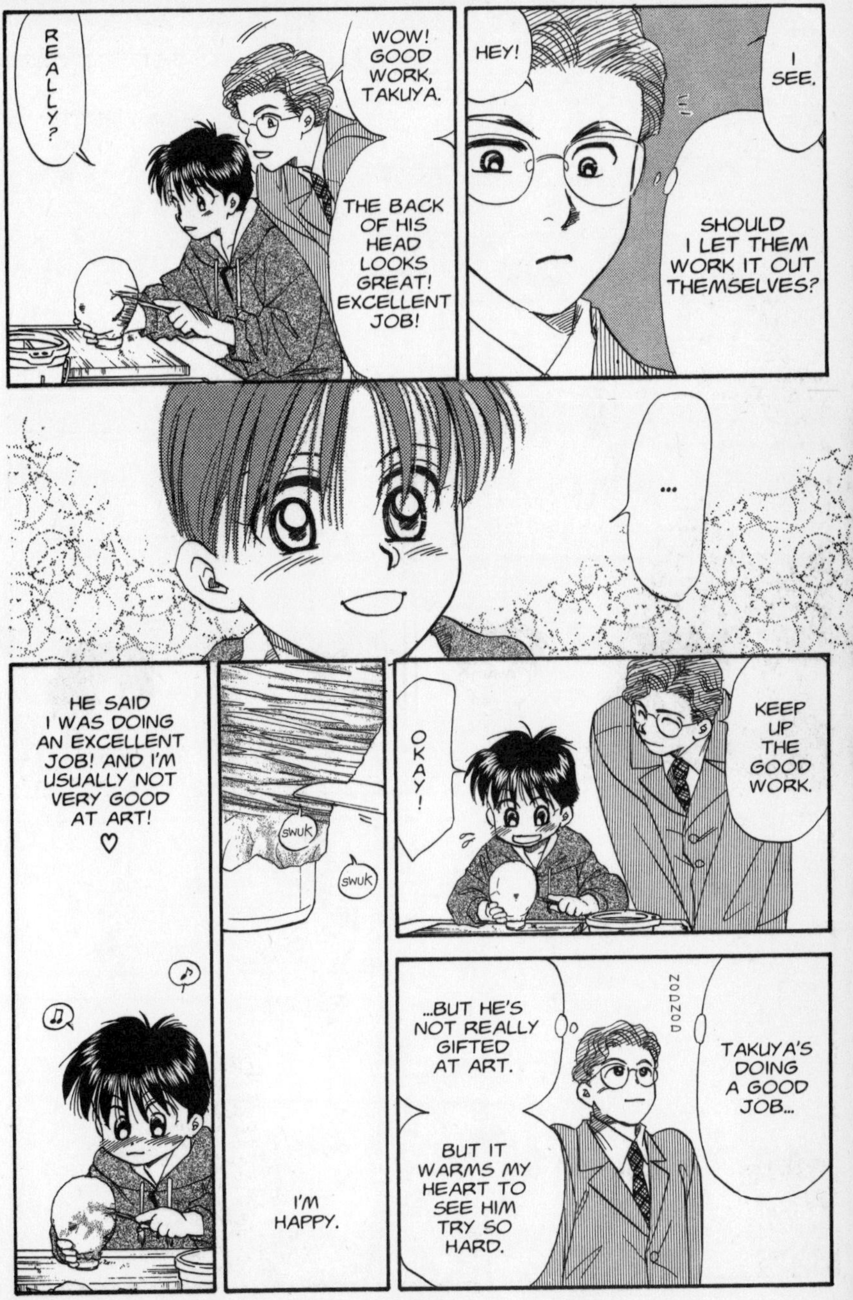
I SEE.
HEY!
SHOULD I LET THEM WORK IT OUT THEMSELVES?
WOW! GOOD WORK, TAKUYA.
THE BACK OF HIS HEAD LOOKS GREAT! EXCELLENT JOB!
REALLY?
...
KEEP UP THE GOOD WORK.
OKAY!
TAKUYA'S DOING A GOOD JOB...
NODNOD
...BUT HE'S NOT REALLY GIFTED AT ART.
BUT IT WARMS MY HEART TO SEE HIM TRY SO HARD.
SWUK
SWUK
I'M HAPPY.
HE SAID I WAS DOING AN EXCELLENT JOB! AND I'M USUALLY NOT VERY GOOD AT ART! ♡
♪
♪

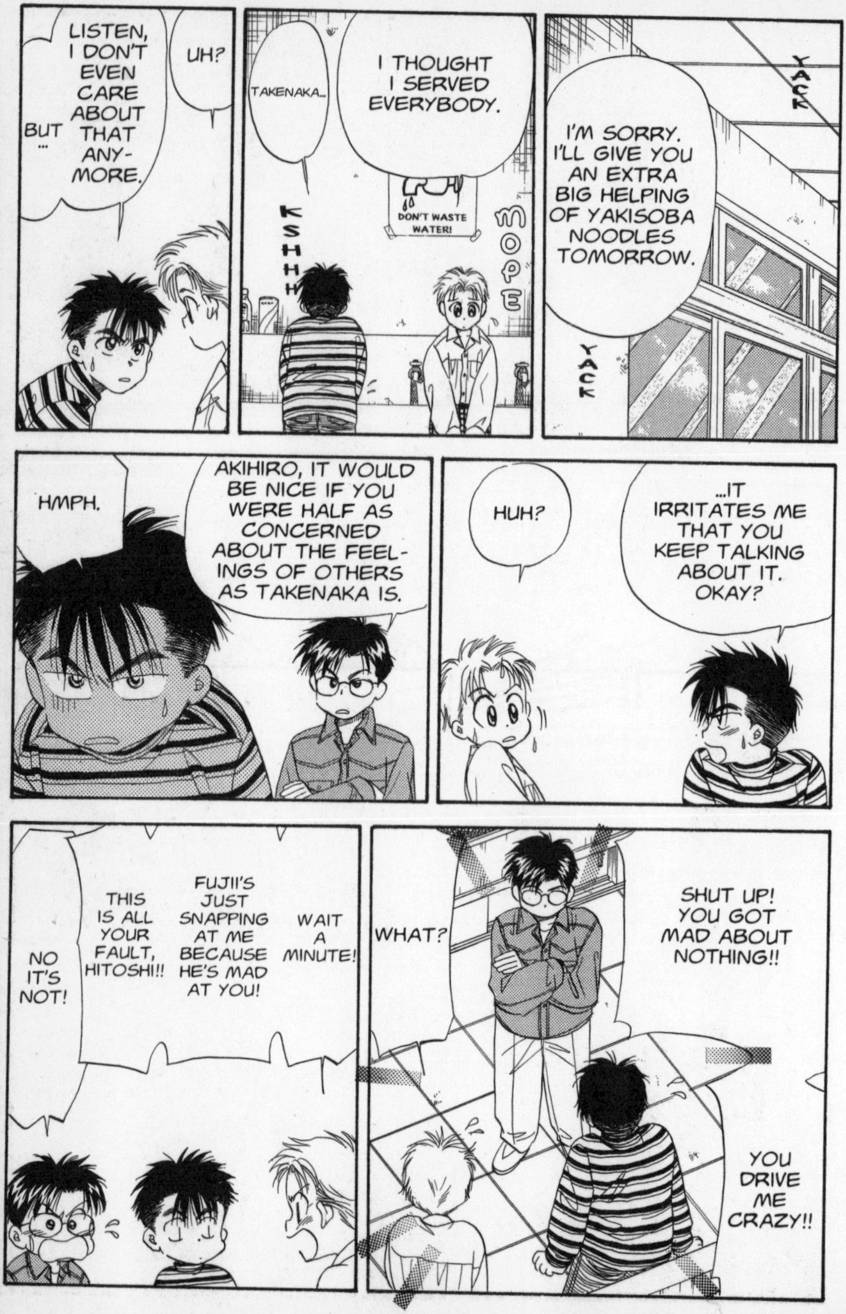
I'M SORRY. I'LL GIVE YOU AN EXTRA BIG HELPING OF YAKISOBA NOODLES TOMORROW.
YACK
YACK
I THOUGHT I SERVED EVERYBODY.
TAKENAKA...
DON'T WASTE WATER!
MOPE
KSHHH
UH?
LISTEN, I DON'T EVEN CARE ABOUT THAT ANYMORE.
BUT ...
...IT IRRITATES ME THAT YOU KEEP TALKING ABOUT IT. OKAY?
HUH?
AKIHIRO, IT WOULD BE NICE IF YOU WERE HALF AS CONCERNED ABOUT THE FEELINGS OF OTHERS AS TAKENAKA IS.
HMPH.
SHUT UP! YOU GOT MAD ABOUT NOTHING!!
YOU DRIVE ME CRAZY!!
WHAT?
WAIT A MINUTE!
FUJII'S JUST SNAPPING AT ME BECAUSE HE'S MAD AT YOU!
THIS IS ALL YOUR FAULT, HITOSHI!!
NO IT'S NOT!

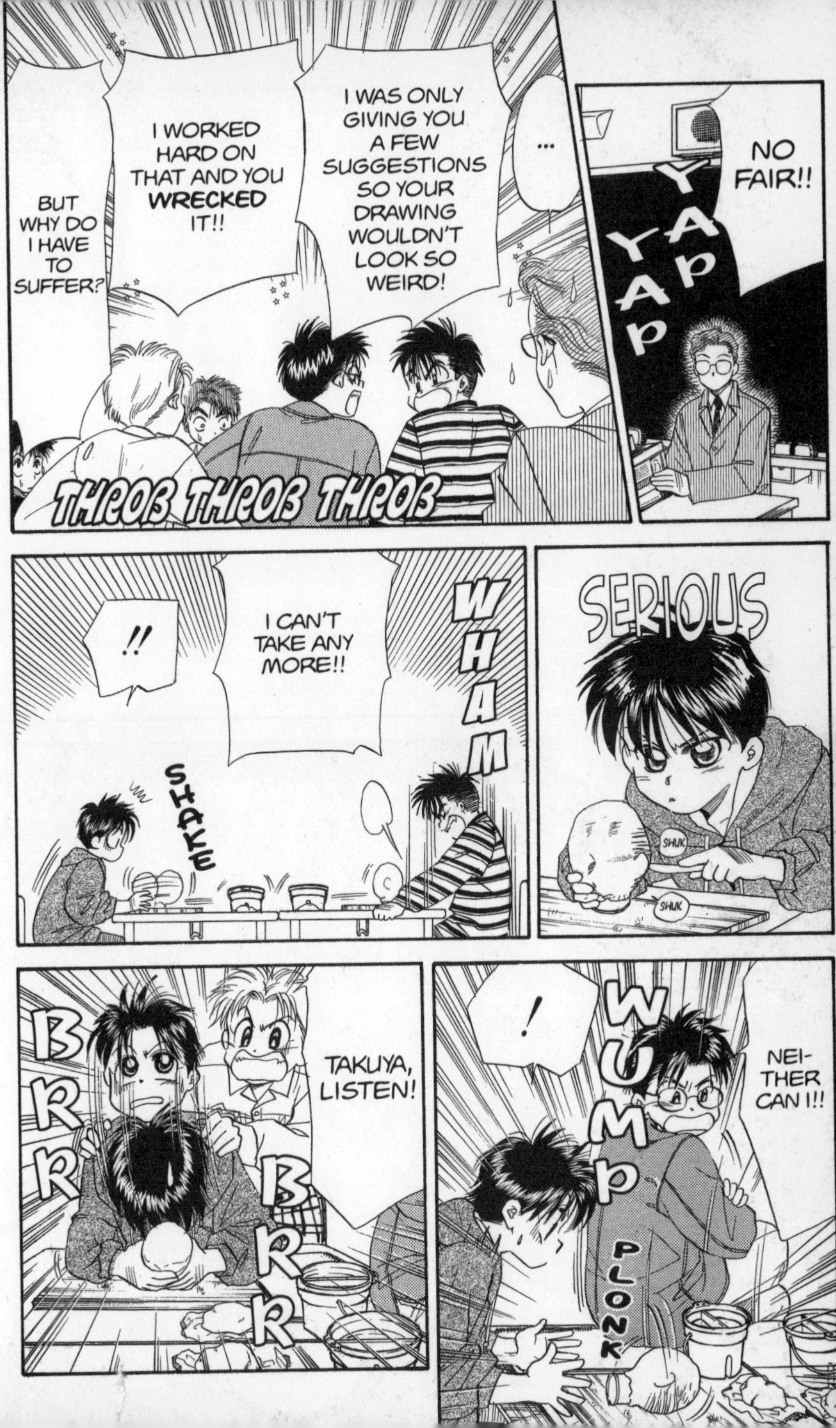
NO FAIR!!
YAP YAP YAP
...
I WAS ONLY GIVING YOU A FEW SUGGESTIONS SO YOUR DRAWING WOULDN'T LOOK SO WEIRD!
I WORKED HARD ON THAT AND YOU **WRECKED** IT!!
BUT WHY DO I HAVE TO SUFFER?
THROB THROB THROB
SERIOUS
SHUK
SHUK
WHAM
I CAN'T TAKE ANY MORE!!
!!
SHAKE
NEI-THER CAN I!!!
WUMP
!
PLONK
TAKUYA, LISTEN!
BRR
BRR

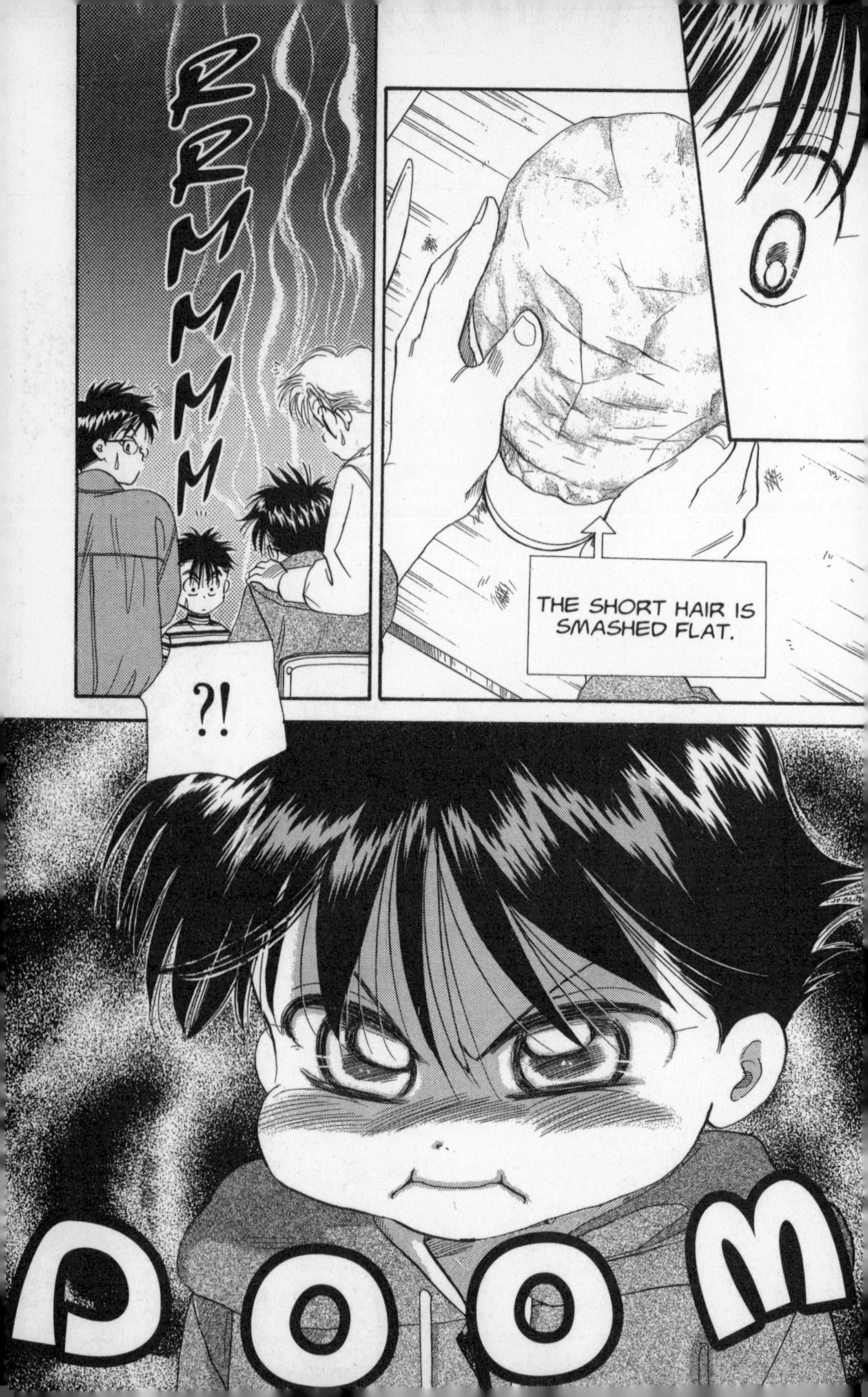
THE SHORT HAIR IS SMASHED FLAT.
RRMMMM
?!
DOOM

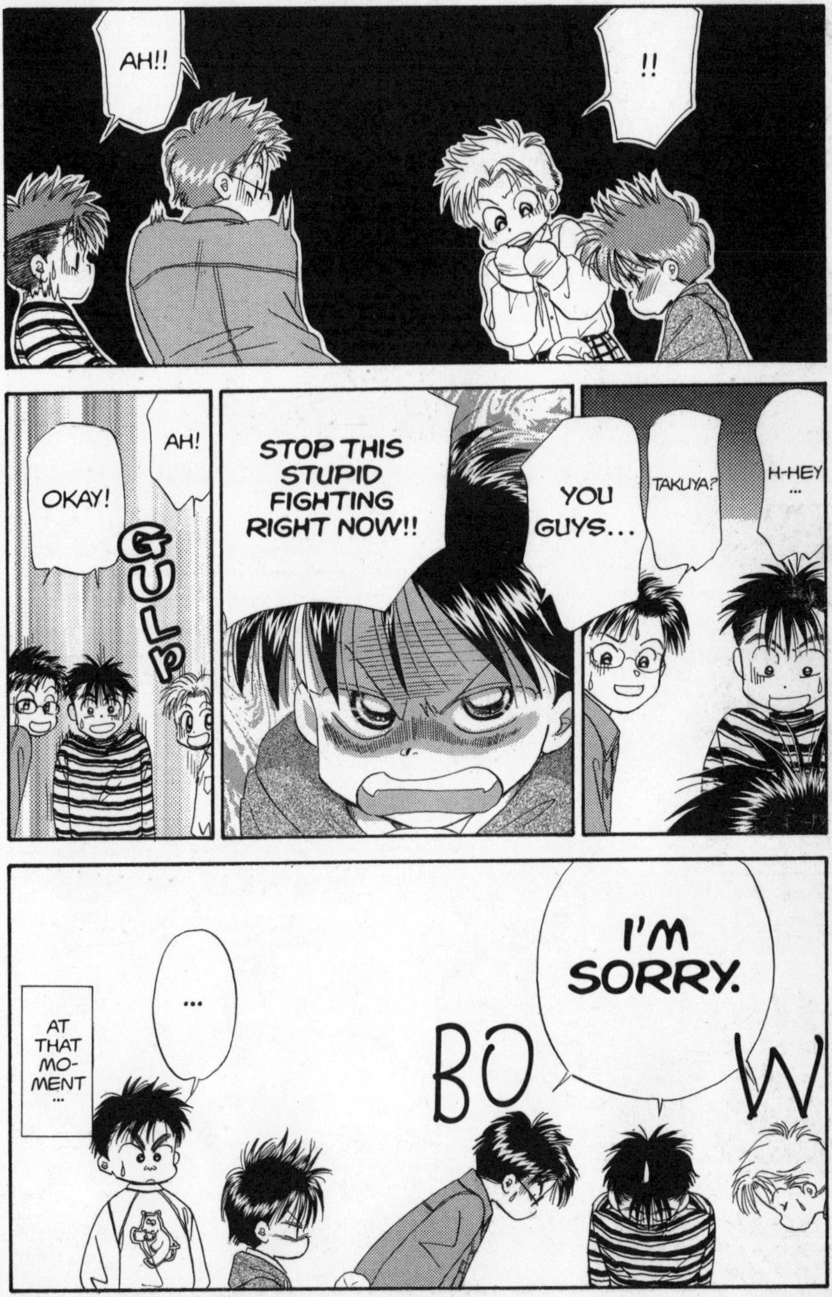
!!
AH!!
H-HEY ...
TAKUYA?
YOU GUYS...
STOP THIS STUPID FIGHTING RIGHT NOW!!
AH!
OKAY!
GULP
I'M SORRY.
BOW
...
AT THAT MO-MENT ...

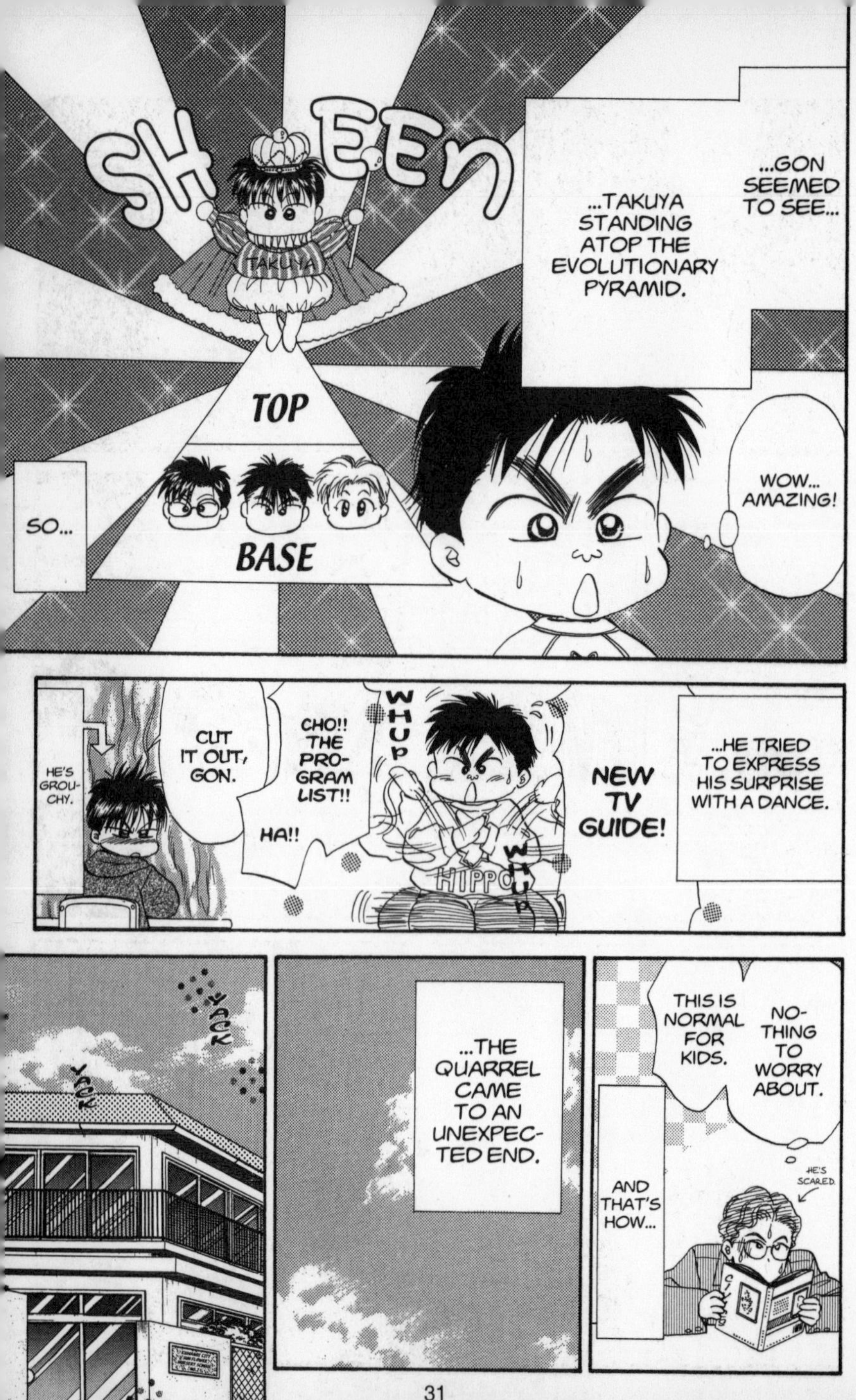
...GON SEEMED TO SEE...
...TAKUYA STANDING ATOP THE EVOLUTIONARY PYRAMID.
WOW... AMAZING!
SHEEN
TAKUYA
TOP
BASE
SO...
...HE TRIED TO EXPRESS HIS SURPRISE WITH A DANCE.
NEW TV GUIDE!
WHUP
WHUP
HIPPO
CHO!! THE PRO-GRAM LIST!!
HA!!
CUT IT OUT, GON.
HE'S GROU-CHY.
NO-THING TO WORRY ABOUT.
THIS IS NORMAL FOR KIDS.
HE'S SCARED.
AND THAT'S HOW...
...THE QUARREL CAME TO AN UNEXPEC-TED END.
YACK
YACK

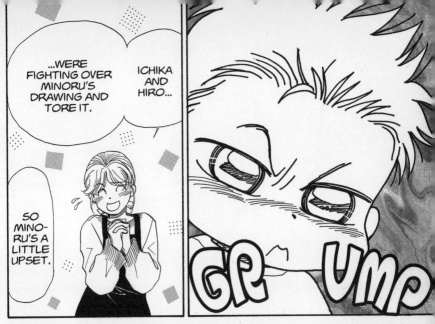

...WERE FIGHTING OVER MINORU'S DRAWING AND TORE IT.

ICHIKA AND HIRO...

SO MINORU'S A LITTLE UPSET.

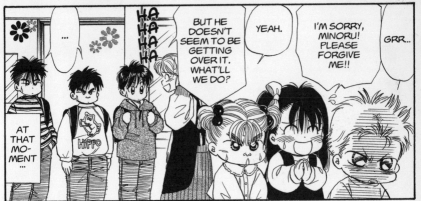

...

BUT HE DOESN'T SEEM TO BE GETTING OVER IT. WHAT'LL WE DO?

YEAH.

I'M SORRY, MINORU! PLEASE FORGIVE ME!!

GRR...

AT THAT MOMENT...

...IT WAS PLAIN TO EVERYBODY THAT TAKUYA AND MINORU WERE BROTHERS.

Chapter 81 / The End

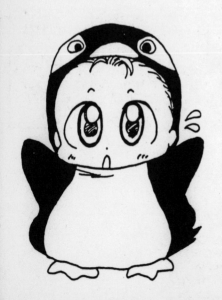

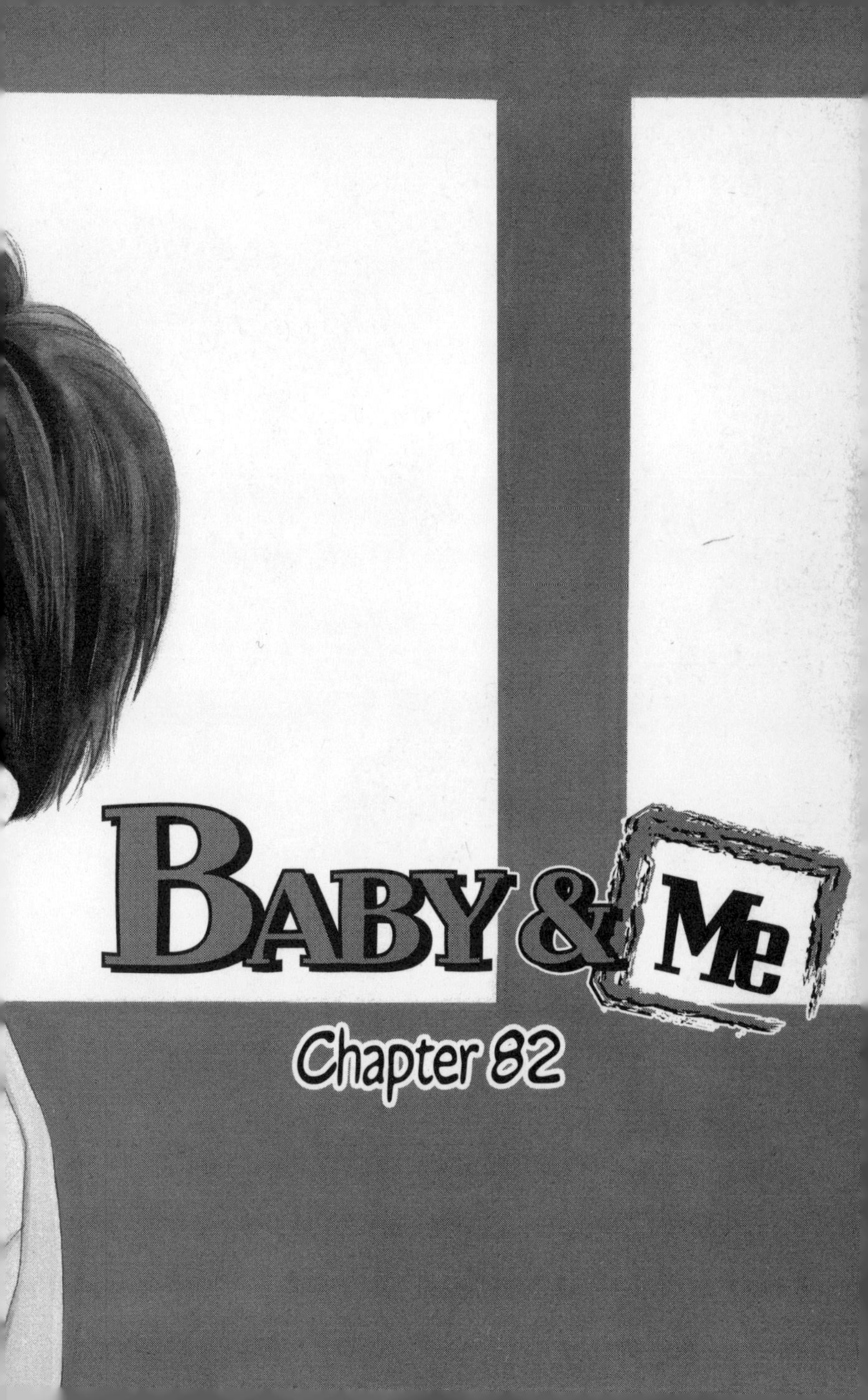
BABY & Me
Chapter 82

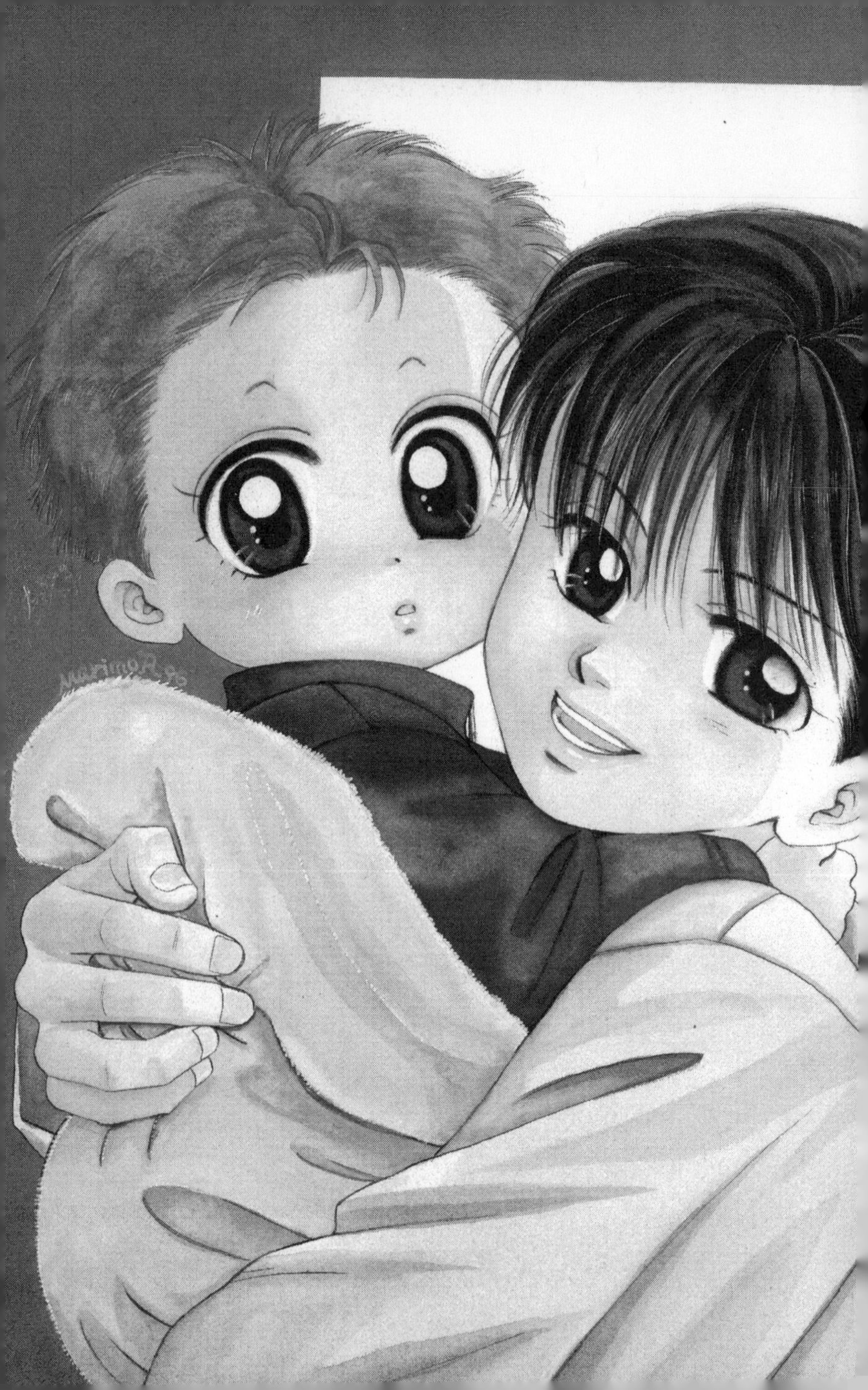

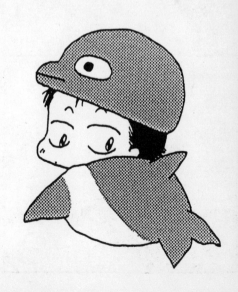

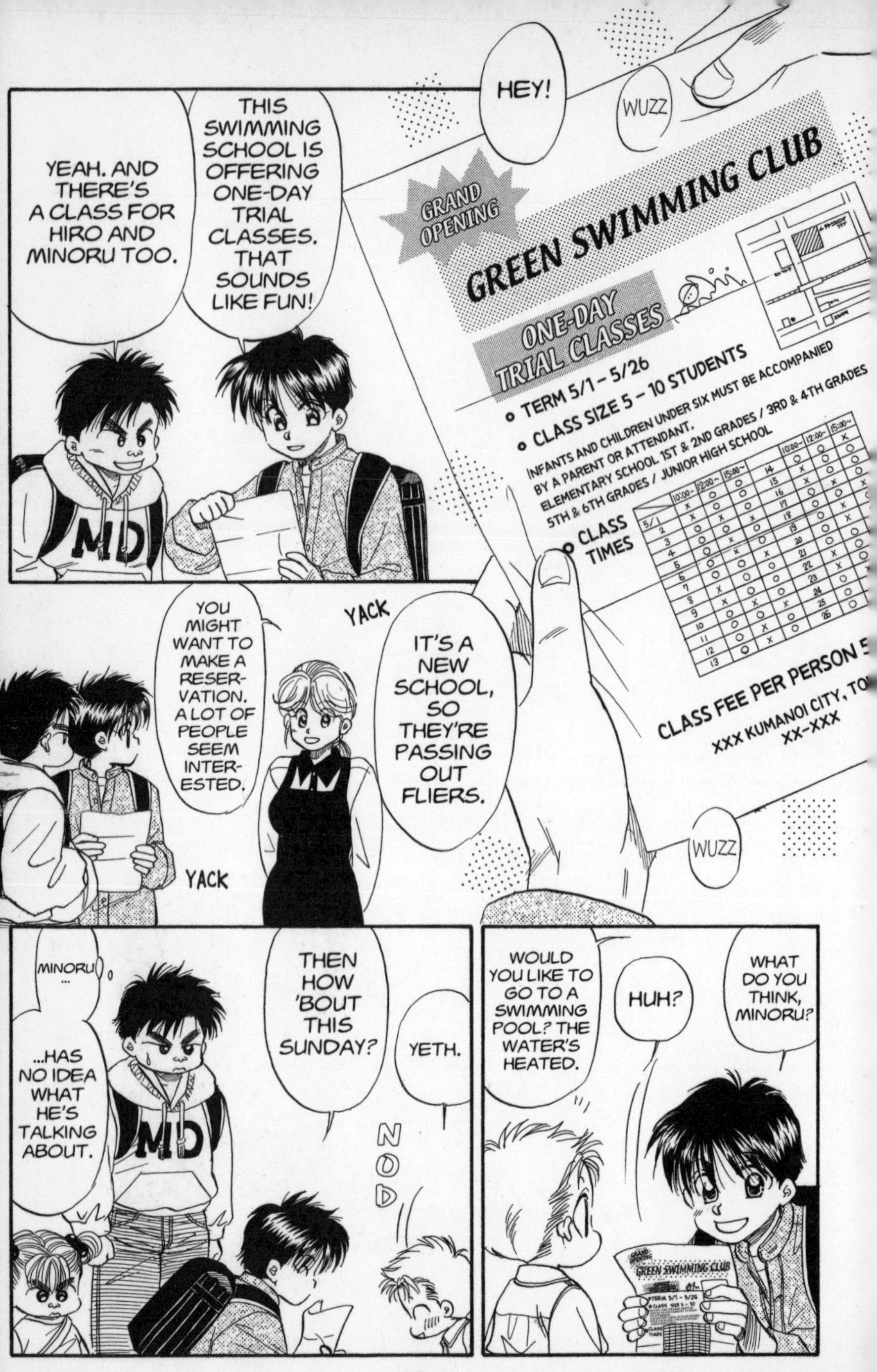
HEY!
WUZZ
GRAND OPENING
GREEN SWIMMING CLUB
ONE-DAY TRIAL CLASSES
TERM 5/1 – 5/26
CLASS SIZE 5 – 10 STUDENTS
INFANTS AND CHILDREN UNDER SIX MUST BE ACCOMPANIED BY A PARENT OR ATTENDANT.
ELEMENTARY SCHOOL 1ST & 2ND GRADES / 3RD & 4TH GRADES
5TH & 6TH GRADES / JUNIOR HIGH SCHOOL
CLASS TIMES
CLASS FEE PER PERSON 5
XXX KUMANOI CITY, TO
XX-XXX
WUZZ
THIS SWIMMING SCHOOL IS OFFERING ONE-DAY TRIAL CLASSES. THAT SOUNDS LIKE FUN!
YEAH. AND THERE'S A CLASS FOR HIRO AND MINORU TOO.
IT'S A NEW SCHOOL, SO THEY'RE PASSING OUT FLIERS.
YACK
YOU MIGHT WANT TO MAKE A RESERVATION. A LOT OF PEOPLE SEEM INTERESTED.
YACK
WHAT DO YOU THINK, MINORU?
HUH?
WOULD YOU LIKE TO GO TO A SWIMMING POOL? THE WATER'S HEATED.
GREEN SWIMMING CLUB
YETH.
NOD
THEN HOW 'BOUT THIS SUNDAY?
MINORU ...
...HAS NO IDEA WHAT HE'S TALKING ABOUT.

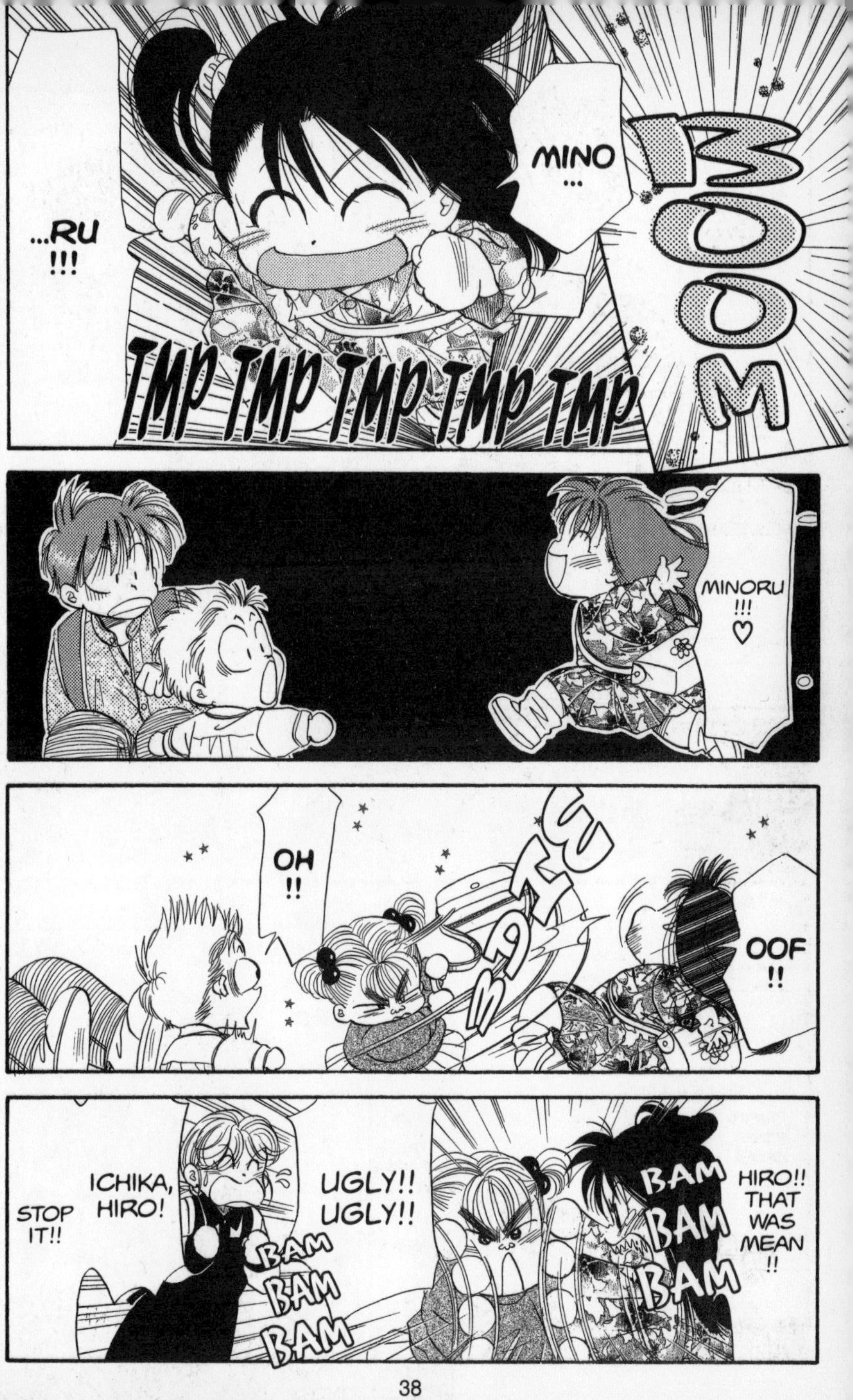
BOOM
MINO ...
...RU !!!
TMP TMP TMP TMP TMP
MINORU !!! ♡
OOF !!
OH !!
HIRO!! THAT WAS MEAN !!
BAM BAM BAM
UGLY!! UGLY!!
BAM BAM BAM
ICHIKA, HIRO!
STOP IT!!

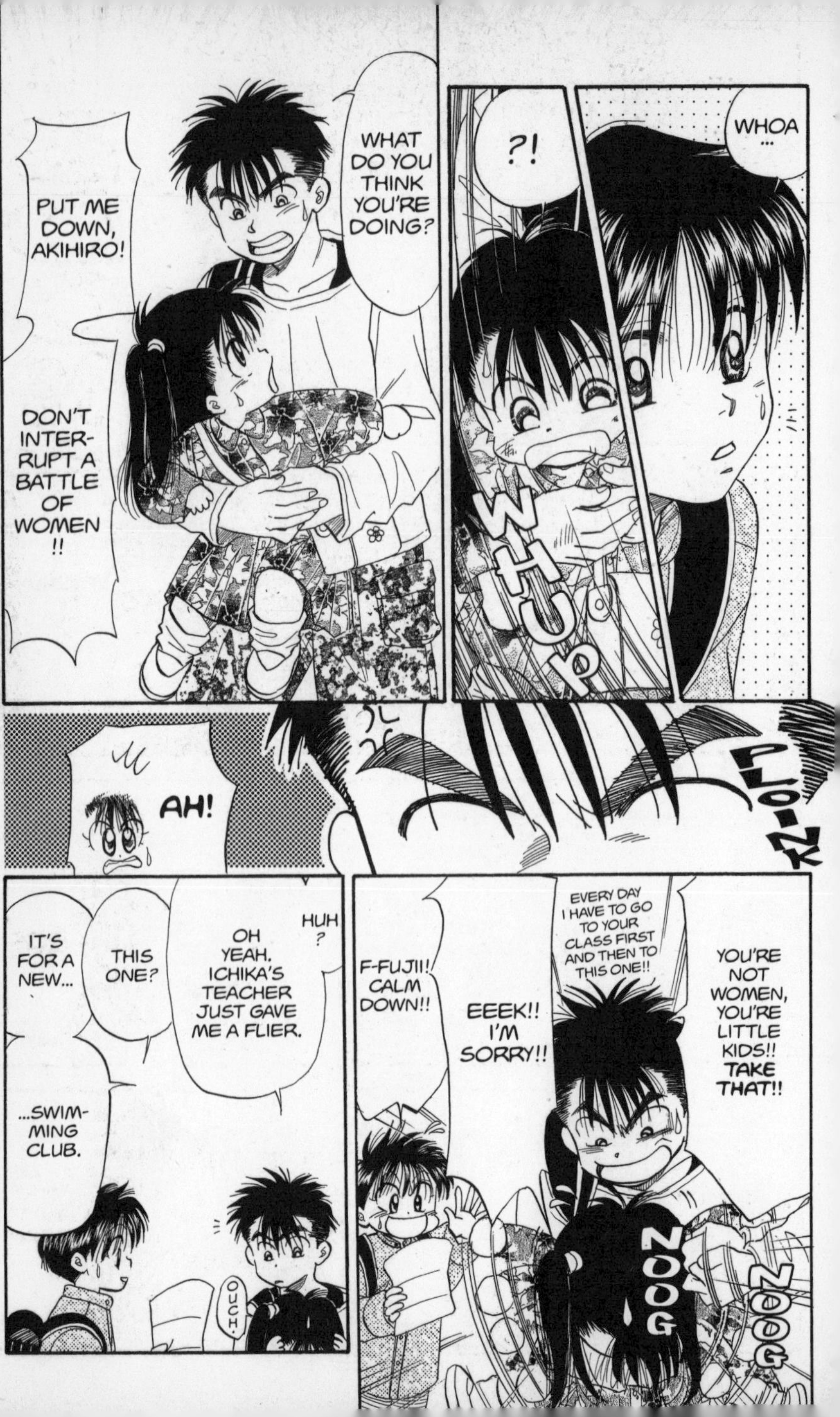
WHOA ...
?!
WHUP
WHAT DO YOU THINK YOU'RE DOING?
PUT ME DOWN, AKIHIRO!
DON'T INTER-RUPT A BATTLE OF WOMEN!!
PLOINK
AH!
YOU'RE NOT WOMEN, YOU'RE LITTLE KIDS!! TAKE THAT!!
EVERY DAY I HAVE TO GO TO YOUR CLASS FIRST AND THEN TO THIS ONE!!
EEEK!! I'M SORRY!!
F-FUJII! CALM DOWN!!
NOOG
NOOG
HUH?
OH YEAH. ICHIKA'S TEACHER JUST GAVE ME A FLIER.
THIS ONE?
IT'S FOR A NEW...
...SWIM-MING CLUB.
OUCH.

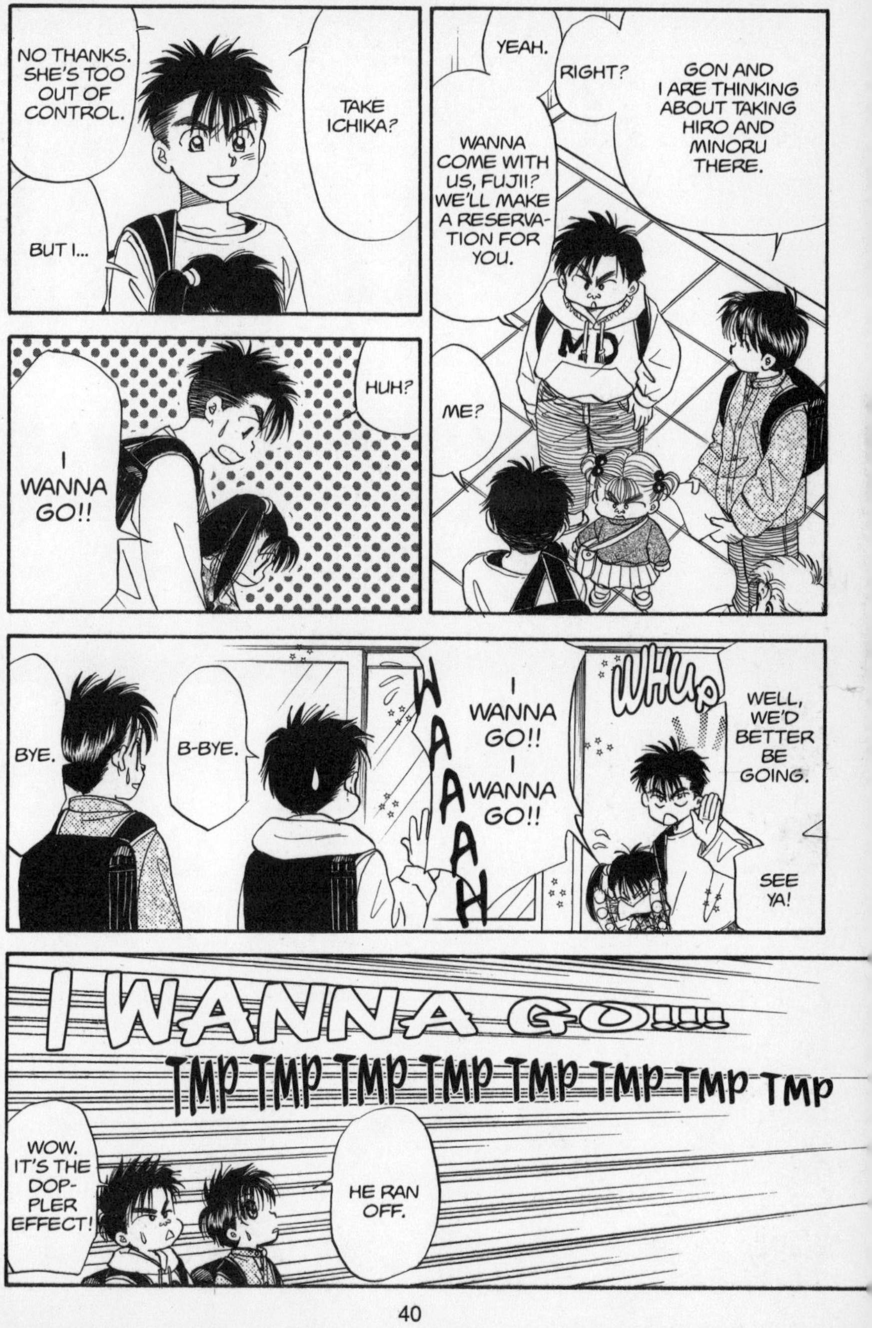
GON AND I ARE THINKING ABOUT TAKING HIRO AND MINORU THERE.
RIGHT?
YEAH.
WANNA COME WITH US, FUJII? WE'LL MAKE A RESERVATION FOR YOU.
ME?
TAKE ICHIKA?
NO THANKS. SHE'S TOO OUT OF CONTROL.
BUT I...
HUH?
I WANNA GO!!
WELL, WE'D BETTER BE GOING.
WHUP
SEE YA!
I WANNA GO!! I WANNA GO!!
WAAAAH
B-BYE.
BYE.
I WANNA GO!!!
TMP TMP TMP TMP TMP TMP TMP TMP
HE RAN OFF.
WOW. IT'S THE DOPPLER EFFECT!

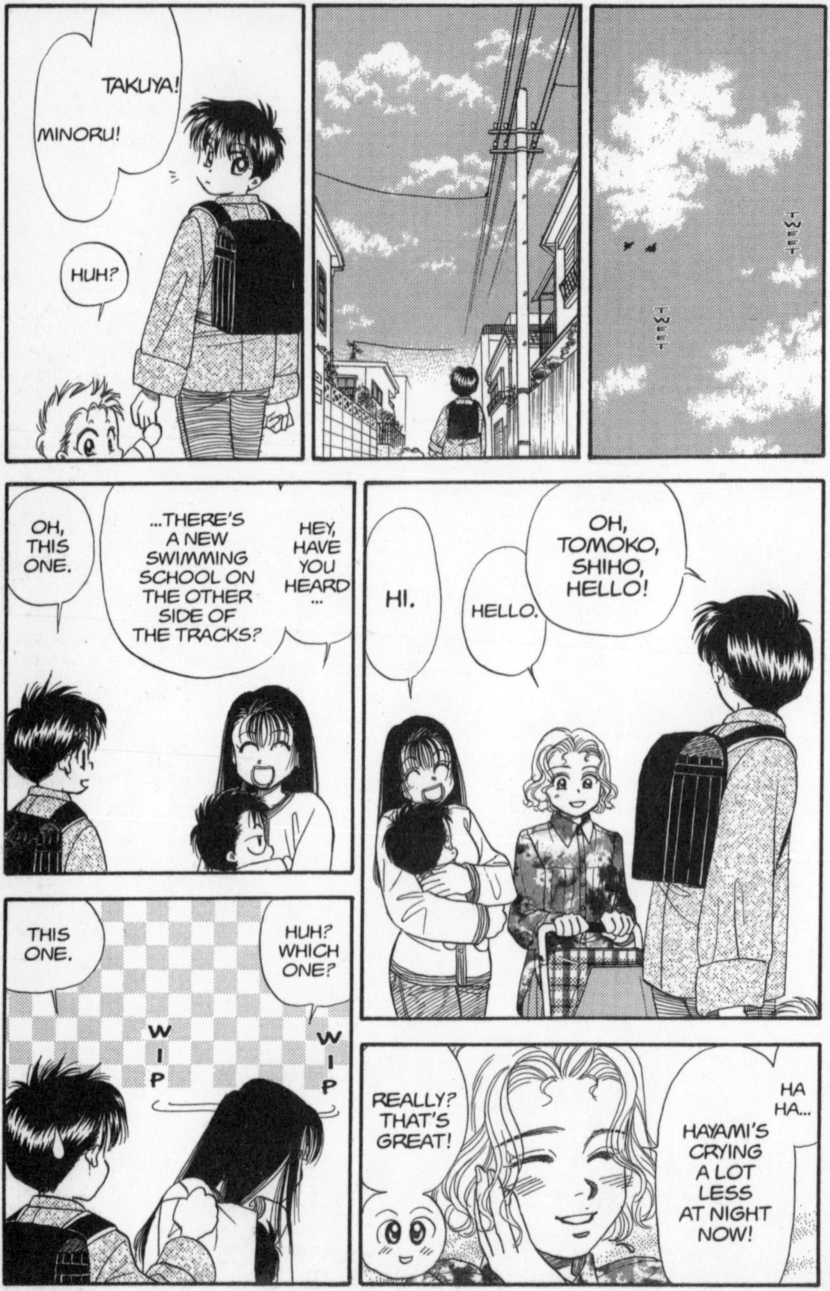
TWEET
TWEET
TAKUYA!
MINORU!
HUH?
OH, TOMOKO, SHIHO, HELLO!
HELLO.
HI.
HA HA...
HAYAMI'S CRYING A LOT LESS AT NIGHT NOW!
REALLY? THAT'S GREAT!
HEY, HAVE YOU HEARD...
...THERE'S A NEW SWIMMING SCHOOL ON THE OTHER SIDE OF THE TRACKS?
OH, THIS ONE.
HUH? WHICH ONE?
WIP
WIP
THIS ONE.

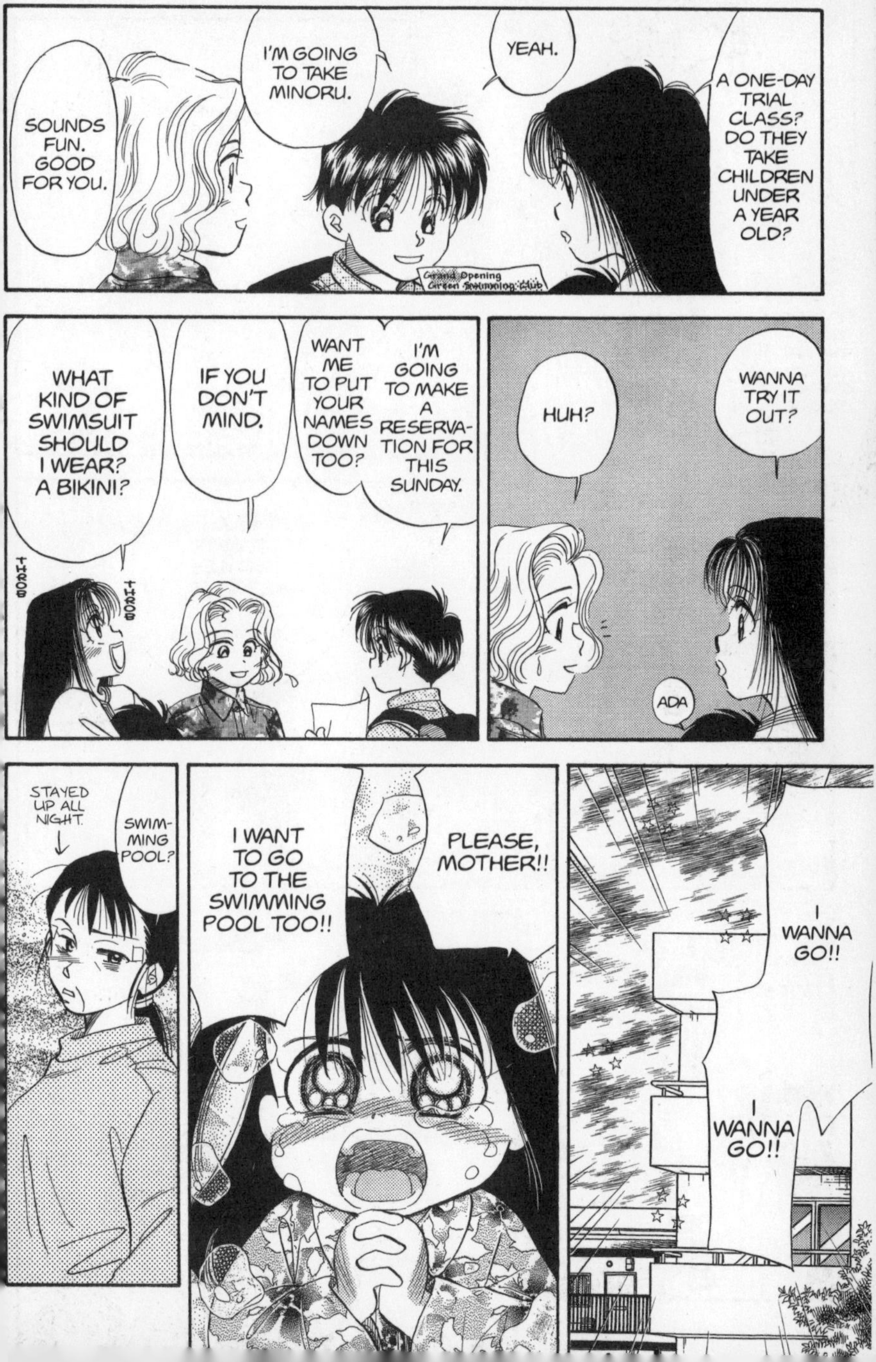
A ONE-DAY TRIAL CLASS? DO THEY TAKE CHILDREN UNDER A YEAR OLD?
YEAH.
I'M GOING TO TAKE MINORU.
Grand Opening Green Swimming Club
SOUNDS FUN. GOOD FOR YOU.
WANNA TRY IT OUT?
HUH?
ADA
I'M GOING TO MAKE A RESERVATION FOR THIS SUNDAY.
WANT ME TO PUT YOUR NAMES DOWN TOO?
IF YOU DON'T MIND.
WHAT KIND OF SWIMSUIT SHOULD I WEAR? A BIKINI?
THROB
THROB
I WANNA GO!!
I WANNA GO!!
PLEASE, MOTHER!!
I WANT TO GO TO THE SWIMMING POOL TOO!!
SWIMMING POOL?
STAYED UP ALL NIGHT.

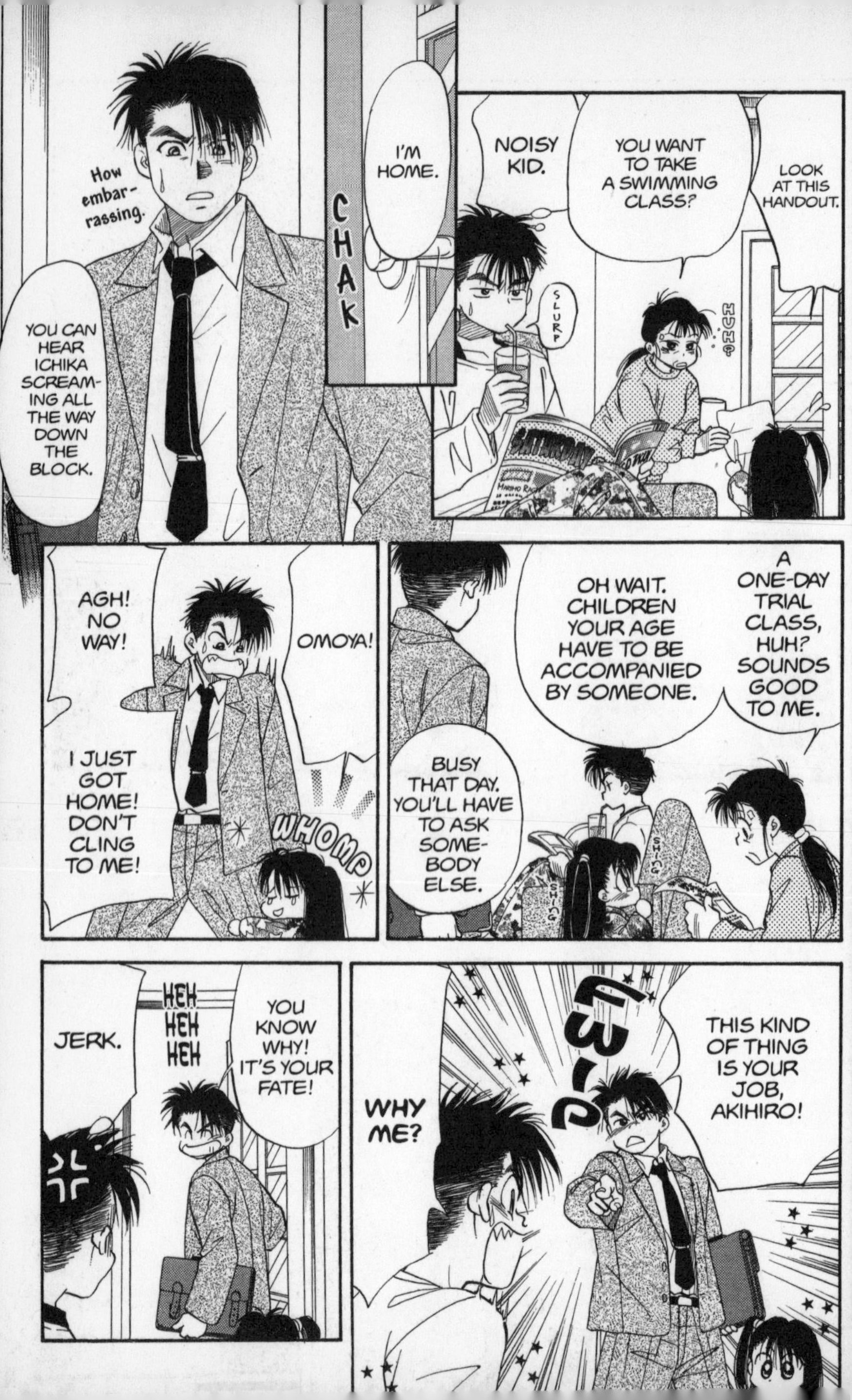
LOOK AT THIS HANDOUT.
YOU WANT TO TAKE A SWIMMING CLASS?
HUH?
NOISY KID.
SLURP
I'M HOME.
CHAK
How embarrassing.
YOU CAN HEAR ICHIKA SCREAMING ALL THE WAY DOWN THE BLOCK.
A ONE-DAY TRIAL CLASS, HUH? SOUNDS GOOD TO ME.
OH WAIT. CHILDREN YOUR AGE HAVE TO BE ACCOMPANIED BY SOMEONE.
BUSY THAT DAY. YOU'LL HAVE TO ASK SOMEBODY ELSE.
SHING
SHING
OMOYA!
AGH! NO WAY!
I JUST GOT HOME! DON'T CLING TO ME!
WHOMP
THIS KIND OF THING IS YOUR JOB, AKIHIRO!
WHY ME?
YOU KNOW WHY! IT'S YOUR FATE!
HEH HEH HEH
JERK.

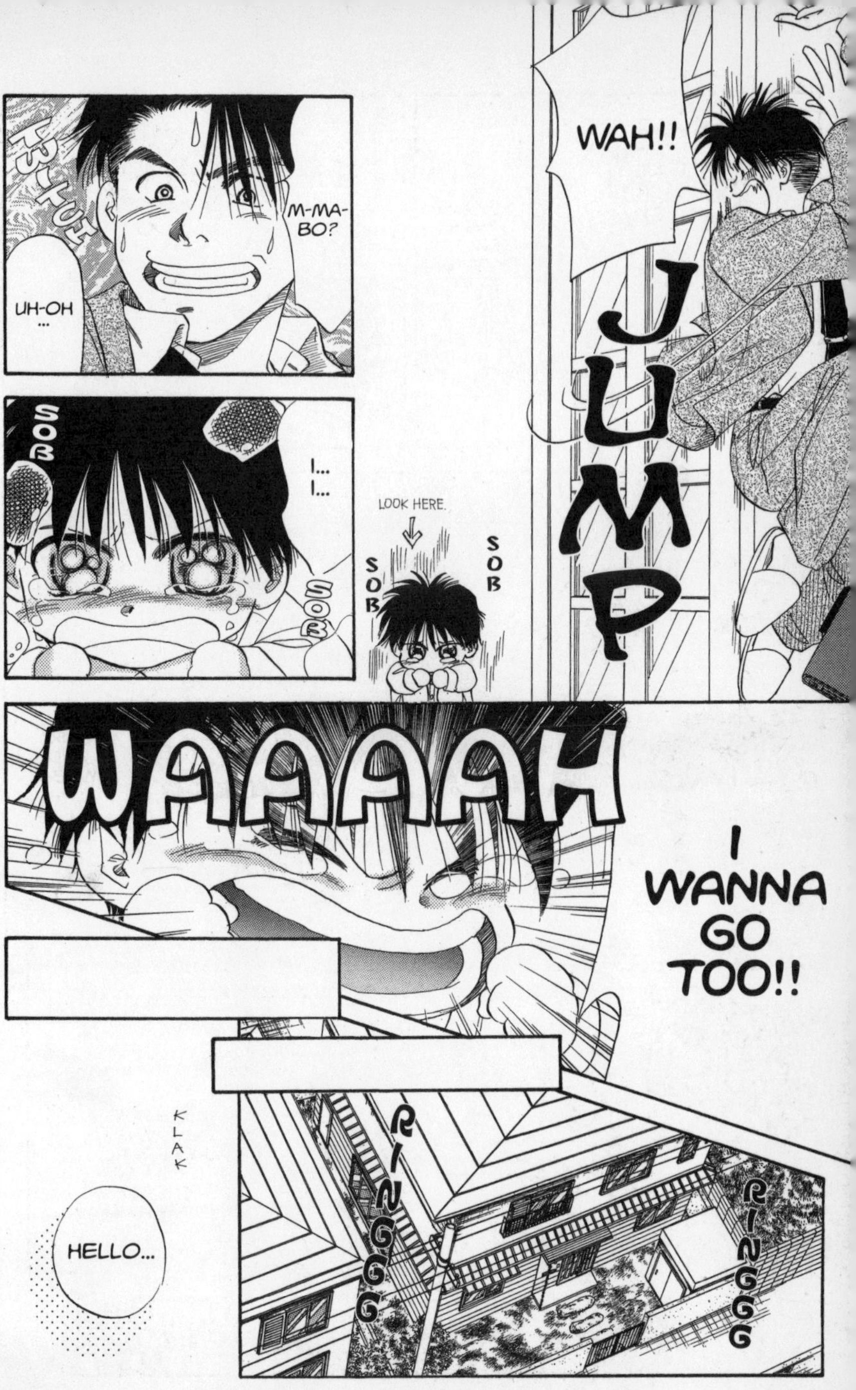
WAH!!
JUMP
M-MA-BO?
UH-OH ...
I... I...
SOB
SOB
LOOK HERE.
SOB
SOB
I WANNA GO TOO!!
WAAAAAH
RINGGG
RINGGG
KLAK
HELLO...

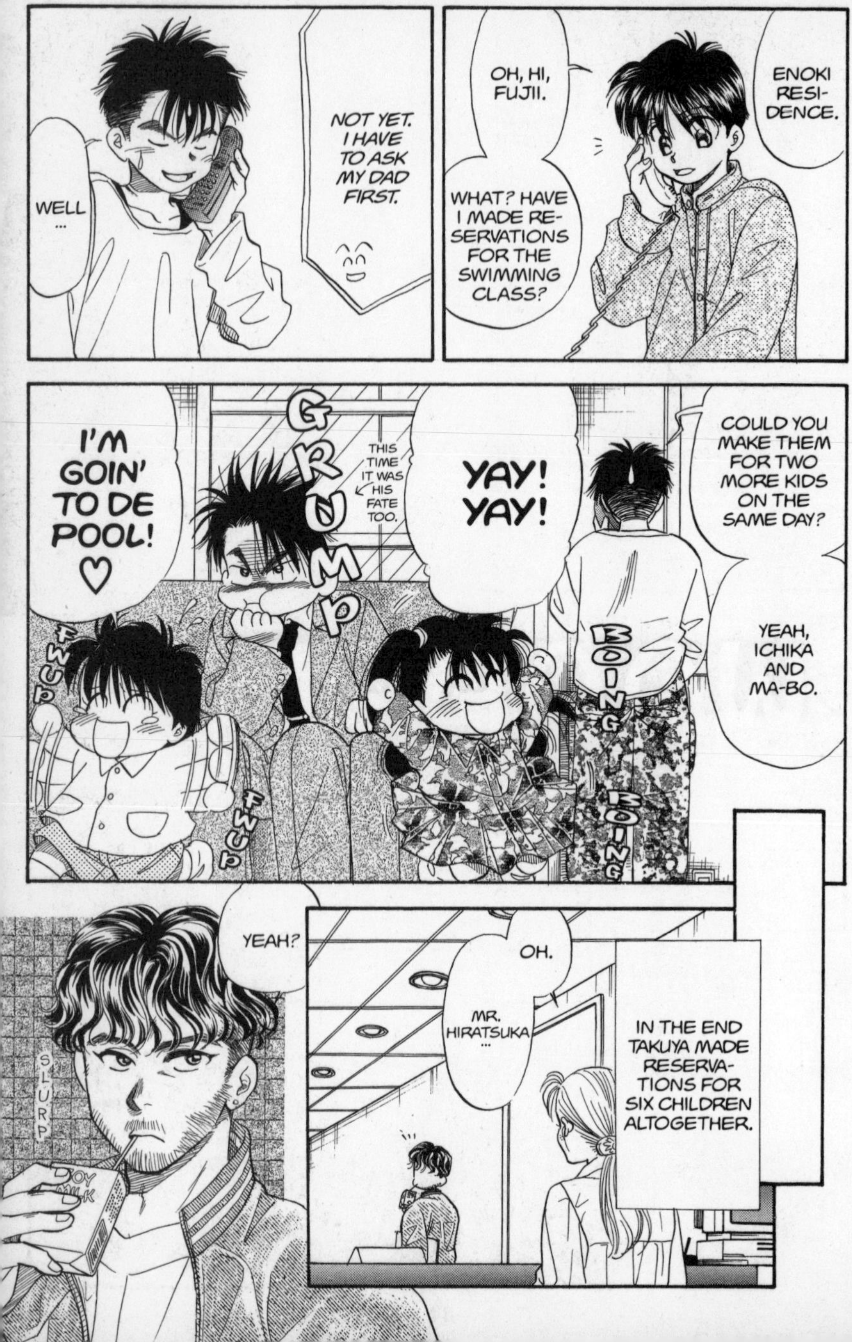

ENOKI RESI-DENCE.
OH, HI, FUJII.
WHAT? HAVE I MADE RE-SERVATIONS FOR THE SWIMMING CLASS?
NOT YET. I HAVE TO ASK MY DAD FIRST.
WELL...
COULD YOU MAKE THEM FOR TWO MORE KIDS ON THE SAME DAY?
YEAH, ICHIKA AND MA-BO.
BOING
BOING
YAY! YAY!
GRUMP
THIS TIME IT WAS HIS FATE TOO.
I'M GOIN' TO DE POOL! ♡
FWUP
FWUP
IN THE END TAKUYA MADE RESERVA-TIONS FOR SIX CHILDREN ALTOGETHER.
OH.
MR. HIRATSUKA...
YEAH?
SLURP
SOY MILK

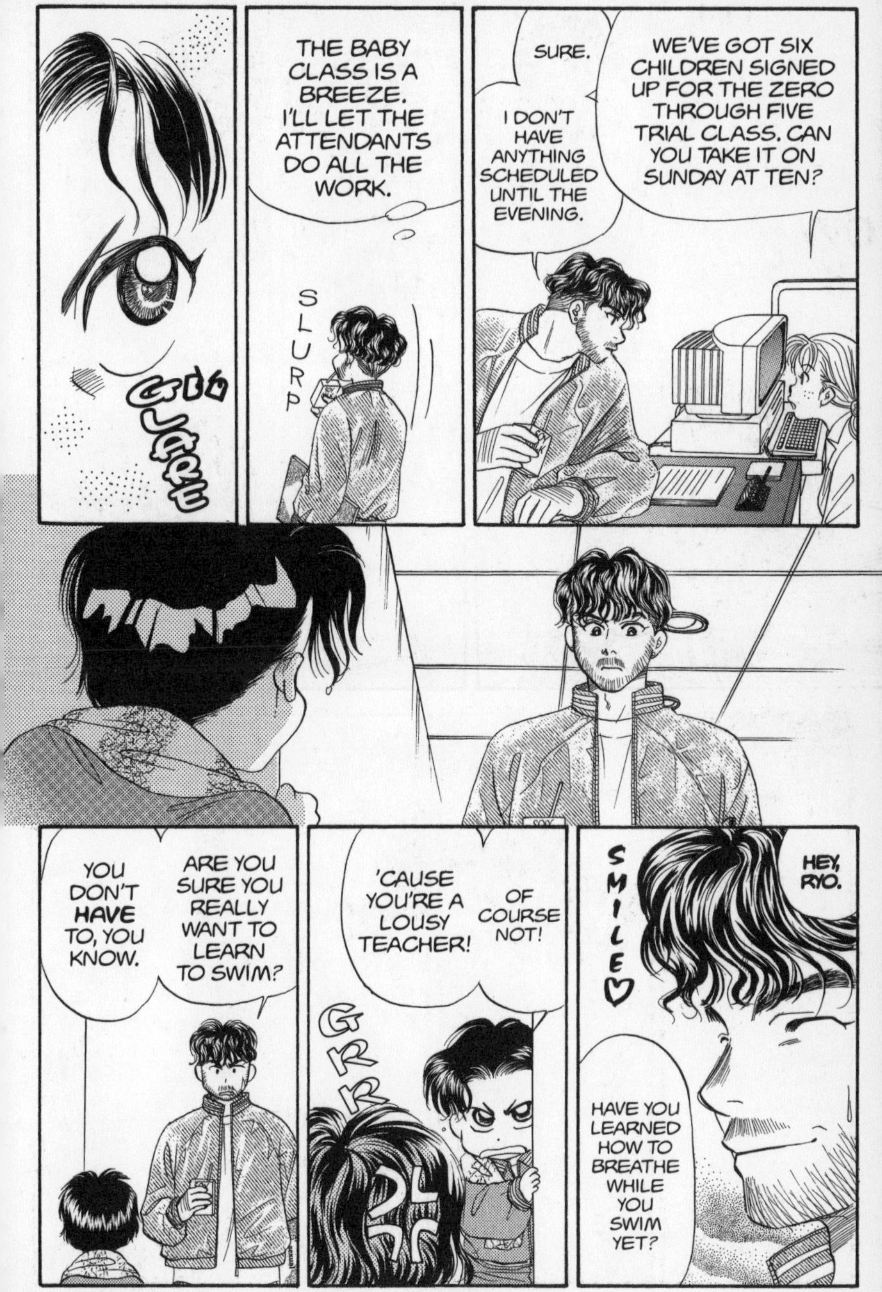
WE'VE GOT SIX CHILDREN SIGNED UP FOR THE ZERO THROUGH FIVE TRIAL CLASS. CAN YOU TAKE IT ON SUNDAY AT TEN?
SURE.
I DON'T HAVE ANYTHING SCHEDULED UNTIL THE EVENING.
THE BABY CLASS IS A BREEZE. I'LL LET THE ATTENDANTS DO ALL THE WORK.
SLURP
GLARE
SMILE♡
HEY, RYO.
HAVE YOU LEARNED HOW TO BREATHE WHILE YOU SWIM YET?
OF COURSE NOT!
'CAUSE YOU'RE A LOUSY TEACHER!
GRR
ARE YOU SURE YOU REALLY WANT TO LEARN TO SWIM?
YOU DON'T **HAVE** TO, YOU KNOW.

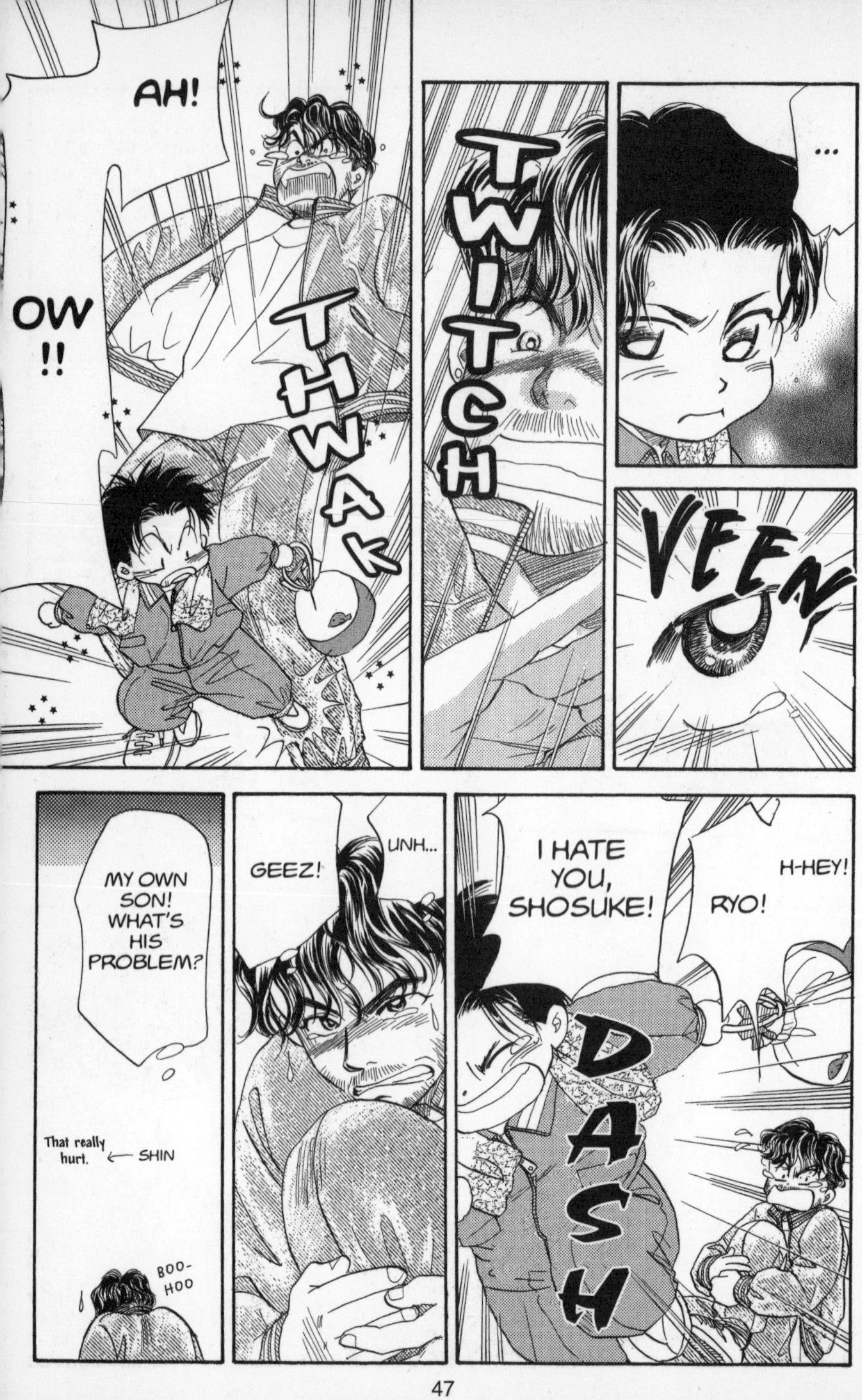
...
VEEN
TWITCH
AH!
THWAK
OW !!
H-HEY! RYO!
I HATE YOU, SHOSUKE!
DASH
UNH...
GEEZ!
MY OWN SON! WHAT'S HIS PROBLEM?
That really hurt. ← SHIN
BOO-HOO

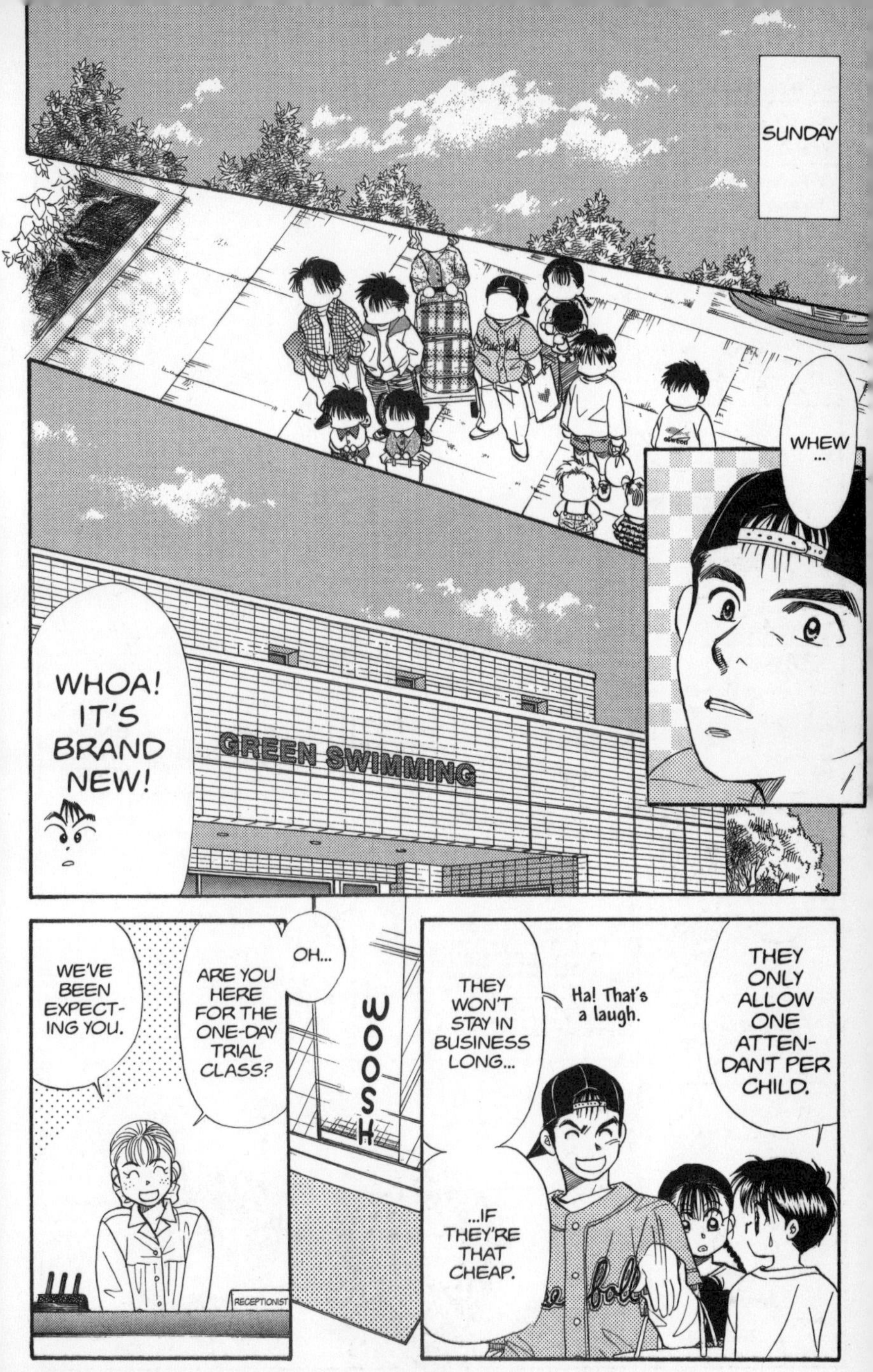
SUNDAY
WHEW...
WHOA! IT'S BRAND NEW!
GREEN SWIMMING
THEY ONLY ALLOW ONE ATTENDANT PER CHILD.
Ha! That's a laugh.
THEY WON'T STAY IN BUSINESS LONG...
...IF THEY'RE THAT CHEAP.
OH...
WOOSH
ARE YOU HERE FOR THE ONE-DAY TRIAL CLASS?
WE'VE BEEN EXPECTING YOU.
RECEPTIONIST

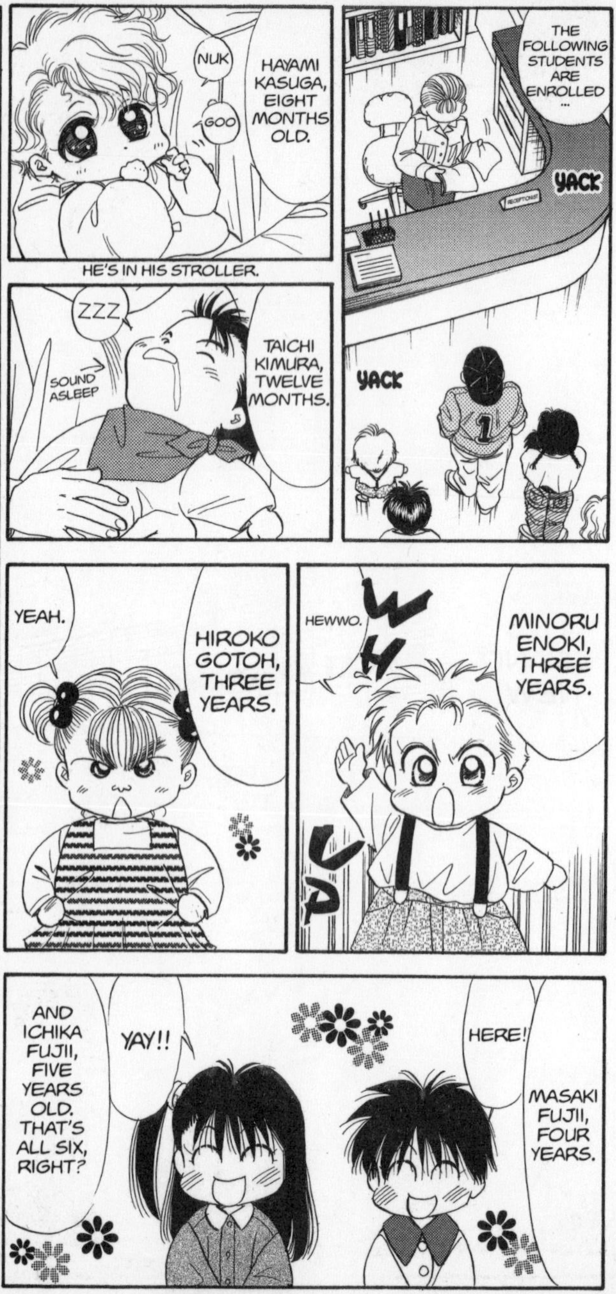
THE FOLLOWING STUDENTS ARE ENROLLED ...
YACK
YACK
HAYAMI KASUGA, EIGHT MONTHS OLD.
NUK
GOO
HE'S IN HIS STROLLER.
TAICHI KIMURA, TWELVE MONTHS.
ZZZ
SOUND ASLEEP
MINORU ENOKI, THREE YEARS.
WHUP
HEWWO.
HIROKO GOTOH, THREE YEARS.
YEAH.
MASAKI FUJII, FOUR YEARS.
HERE!
AND ICHIKA FUJII, FIVE YEARS OLD. THAT'S ALL SIX, RIGHT?
YAY!!

Author's Note: Part 2

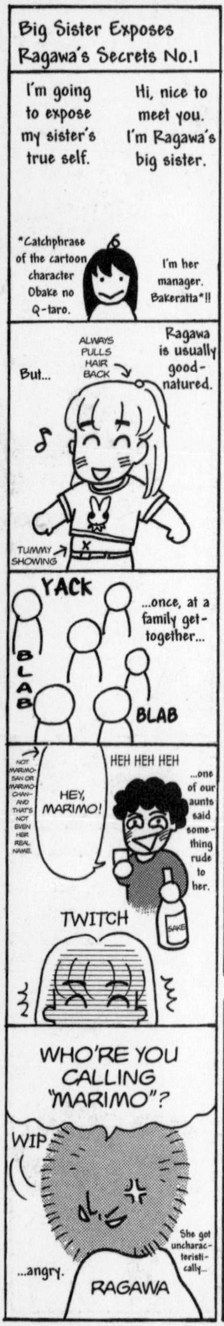
Big Sister Exposes Ragawa's Secrets No.1
Hi, nice to meet you. I'm Ragawa's big sister.
I'm going to expose my sister's true self.
I'm her manager. Bakeratta*!!
*Catchphrase of the cartoon character Obake no Q-taro.
Ragawa is usually good-natured.
ALWAYS PULLS HAIR BACK
But...
TUMMY SHOWING
...once, at a family get-together...
YACK
BLAB
BLAB
...one of our aunts said something rude to her.
HEH HEH HEH
HEY, MARIMO!
NOT MARIMO-SAN OR MARIMO-CHAN—AND THAT'S NOT EVEN HER REAL NAME.
SAKE
TWITCH
WHO'RE YOU CALLING "MARIMO"?
WIP
She got uncharacteristically...
...angry.
RAGAWA

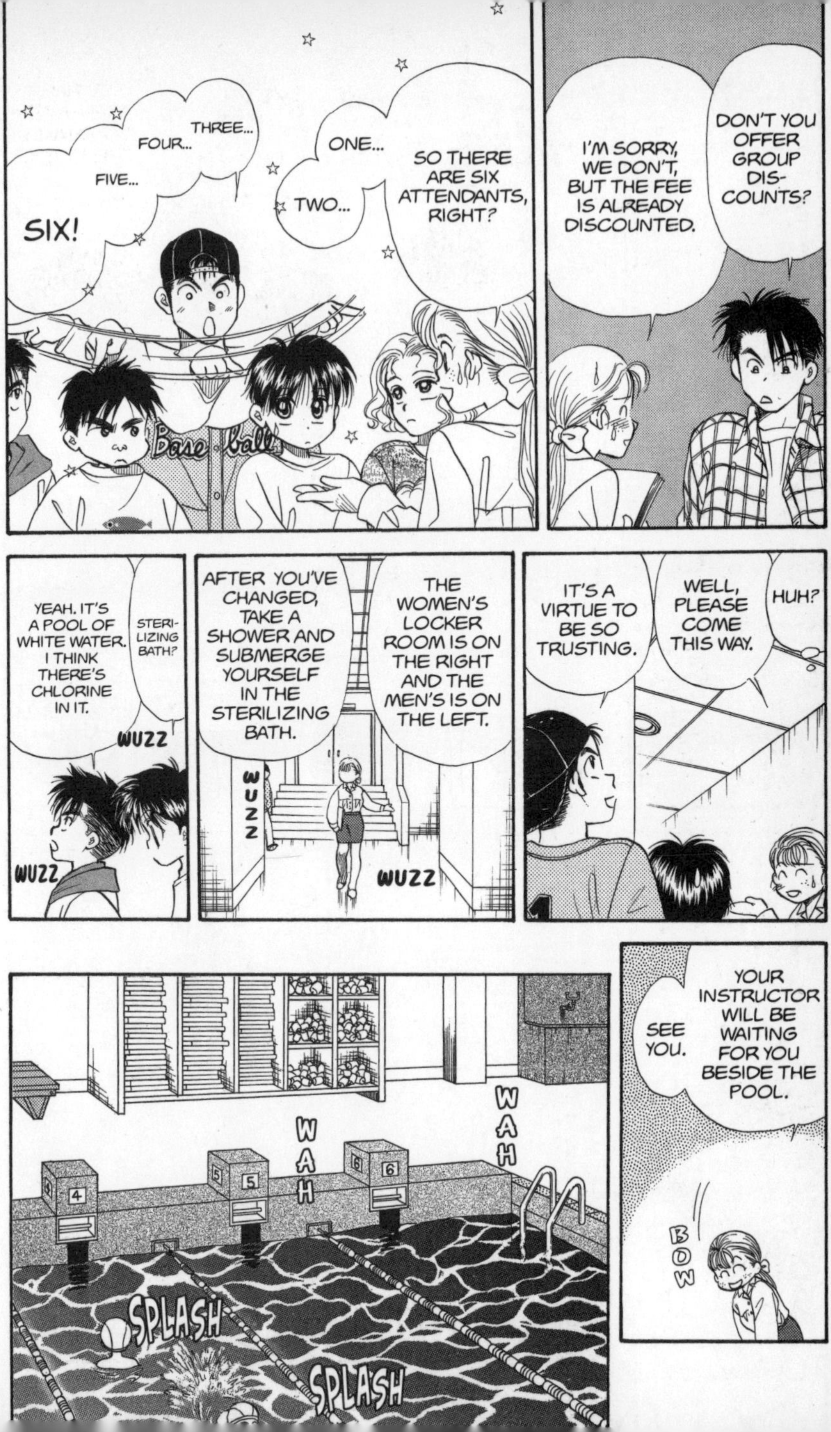
DON'T YOU OFFER GROUP DISCOUNTS?
I'M SORRY, WE DON'T, BUT THE FEE IS ALREADY DISCOUNTED.
SO THERE ARE SIX ATTENDANTS, RIGHT?
ONE...
TWO...
THREE...
FOUR...
FIVE...
SIX!
HUH?
WELL, PLEASE COME THIS WAY.
IT'S A VIRTUE TO BE SO TRUSTING.
THE WOMEN'S LOCKER ROOM IS ON THE RIGHT AND THE MEN'S IS ON THE LEFT.
AFTER YOU'VE CHANGED, TAKE A SHOWER AND SUBMERGE YOURSELF IN THE STERILIZING BATH.
WUZZ
WUZZ
STERILIZING BATH?
YEAH. IT'S A POOL OF WHITE WATER. I THINK THERE'S CHLORINE IN IT.
WUZZ
WUZZ
YOUR INSTRUCTOR WILL BE WAITING FOR YOU BESIDE THE POOL.
SEE YOU.
BOW
WAH
WAH
SPLASH
SPLASH

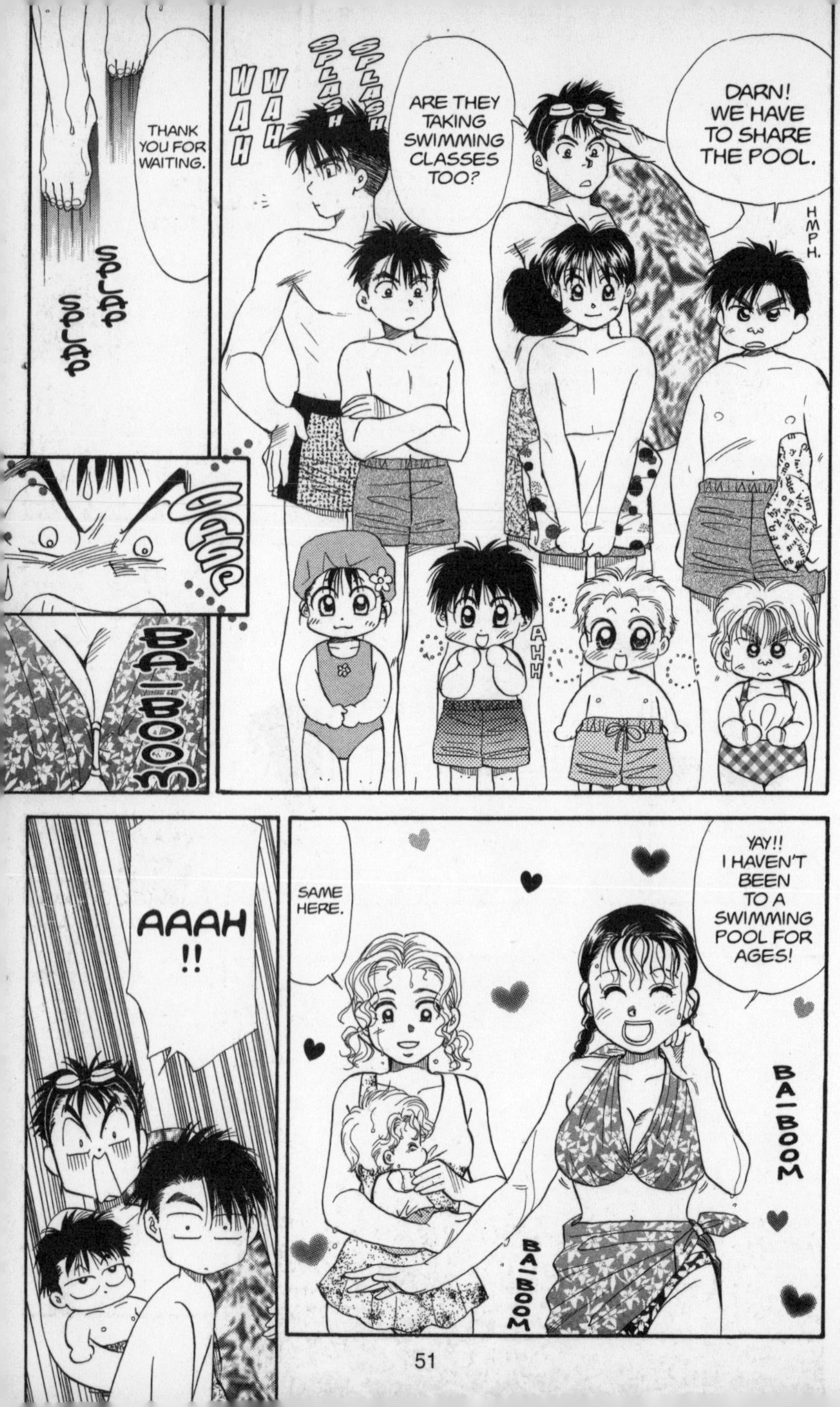
DARN! WE HAVE TO SHARE THE POOL.
HMPH.
ARE THEY TAKING SWIMMING CLASSES TOO?
SPLASH SPLASH
WAH WAH
THANK YOU FOR WAITING.
SPLAP SPLAP
BA-BOOM
AHHH
YAY!! I HAVEN'T BEEN TO A SWIMMING POOL FOR AGES!
SAME HERE.
BA-BOOM
BA-BOOM
AAAH !!

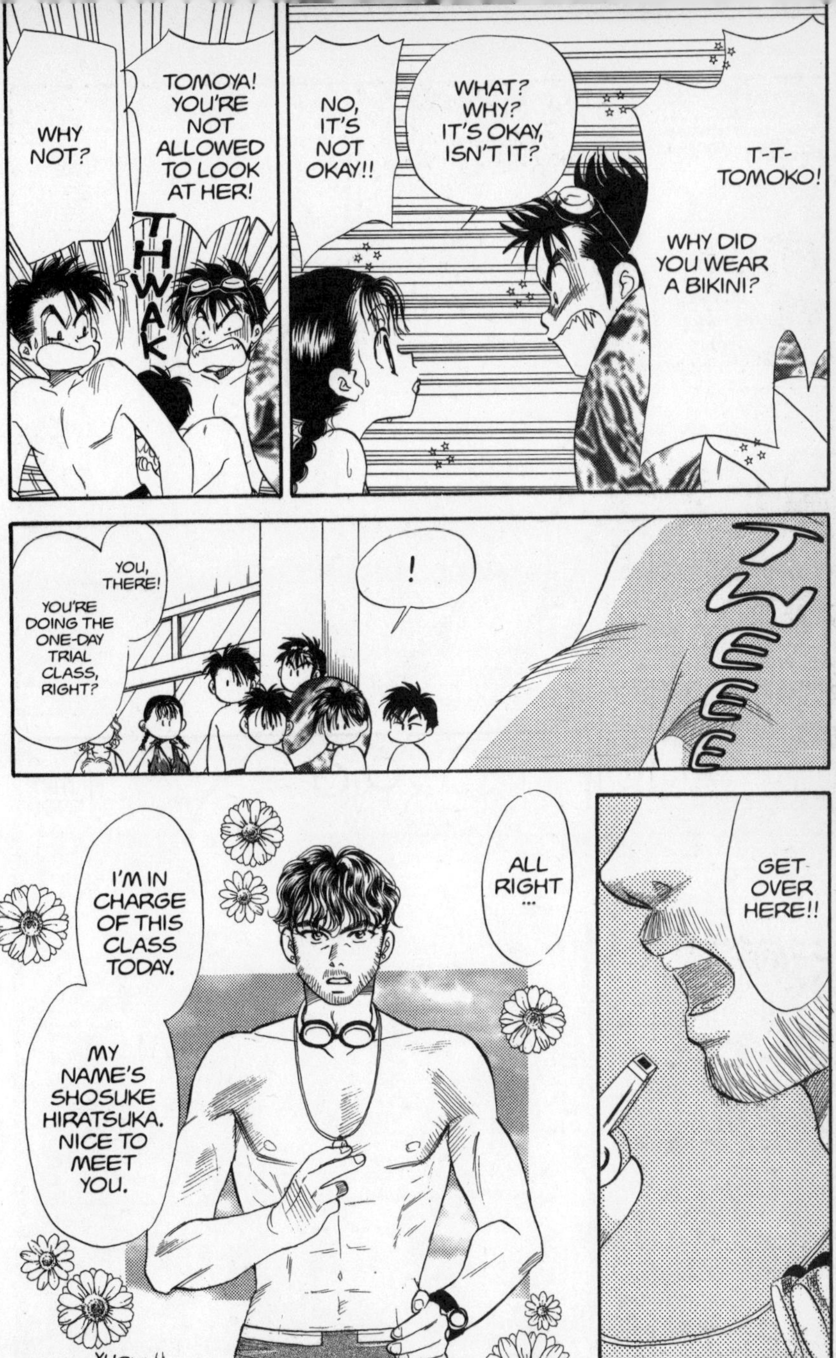
T-T-TOMOKO!
WHY DID YOU WEAR A BIKINI?
WHAT? WHY? IT'S OKAY, ISN'T IT?
NO, IT'S NOT OKAY!!
TOMOYA! YOU'RE NOT ALLOWED TO LOOK AT HER!
THWAK
WHY NOT?
TWEEE
!
YOU, THERE! YOU'RE DOING THE ONE-DAY TRIAL CLASS, RIGHT?
GET OVER HERE!!
ALL RIGHT ...
I'M IN CHARGE OF THIS CLASS TODAY.
MY NAME'S SHOSUKE HIRATSUKA. NICE TO MEET YOU.
YUCK!

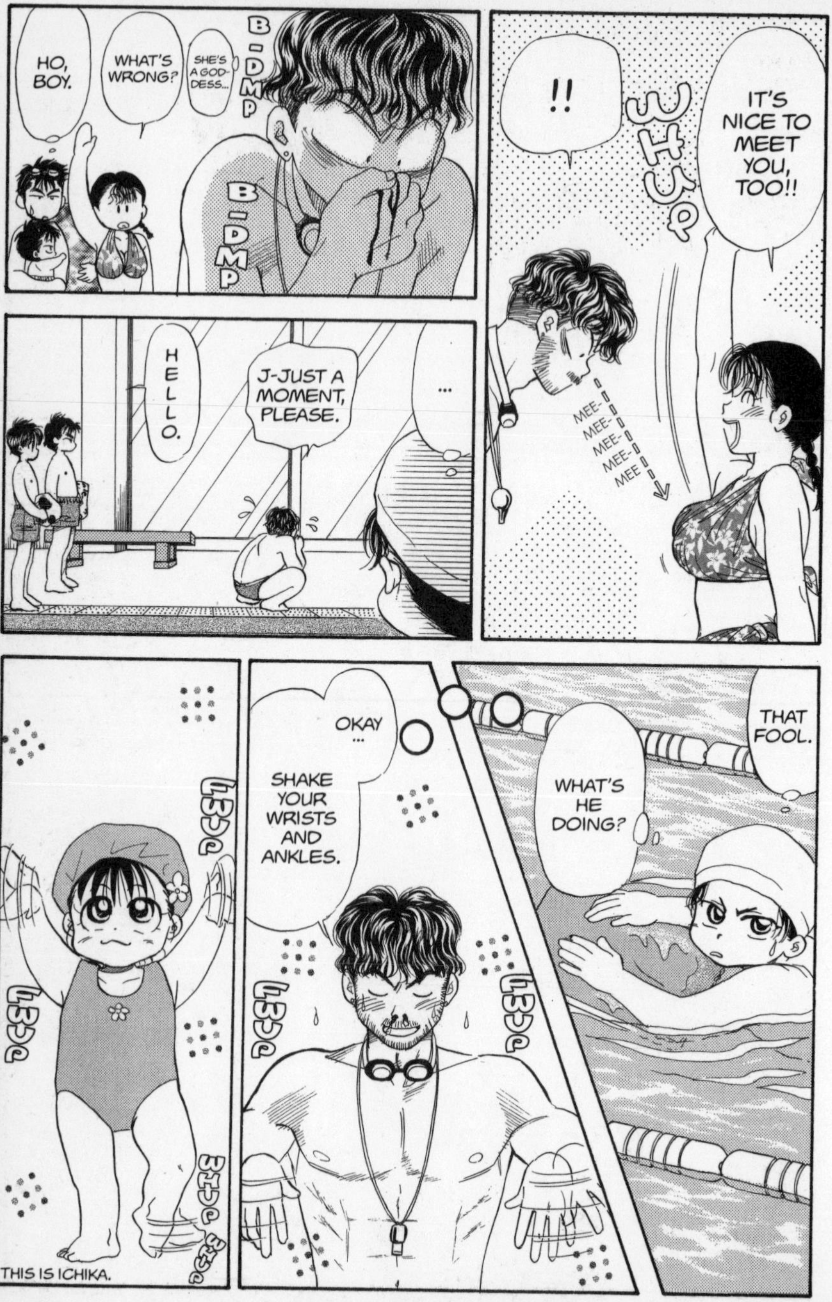
IT'S NICE TO MEET YOU, TOO!!
WHUP
!!
MEE-MEE-MEE-MEE-MEE
B-DMP
B-DMP
SHE'S A GODDESS...
WHAT'S WRONG?
HO, BOY.
...
J-JUST A MOMENT, PLEASE.
HELLO.
THAT FOOL.
WHAT'S HE DOING?
OKAY ...
SHAKE YOUR WRISTS AND ANKLES.
THIS IS ICHIKA.

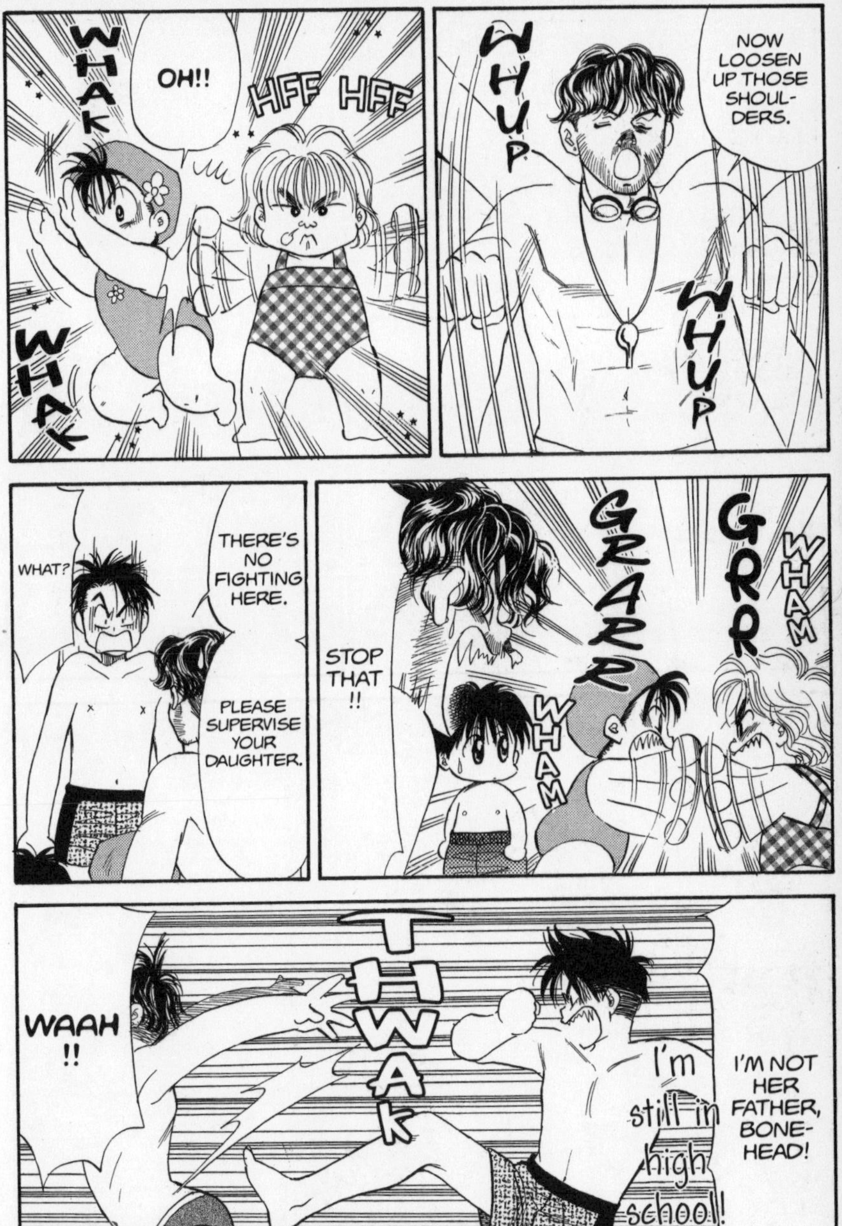
NOW LOOSEN UP THOSE SHOUL-DERS.
WHUP
WHUP
WHAK
OH!!
HFF HFF
WHAK
GRR
WHAM
GRARR
STOP THAT!!
WHAM
THERE'S NO FIGHTING HERE.
PLEASE SUPERVISE YOUR DAUGHTER.
WHAT?
I'M NOT HER FATHER, BONE-HEAD!
I'm still in high school!
THWAK
WAAH!!

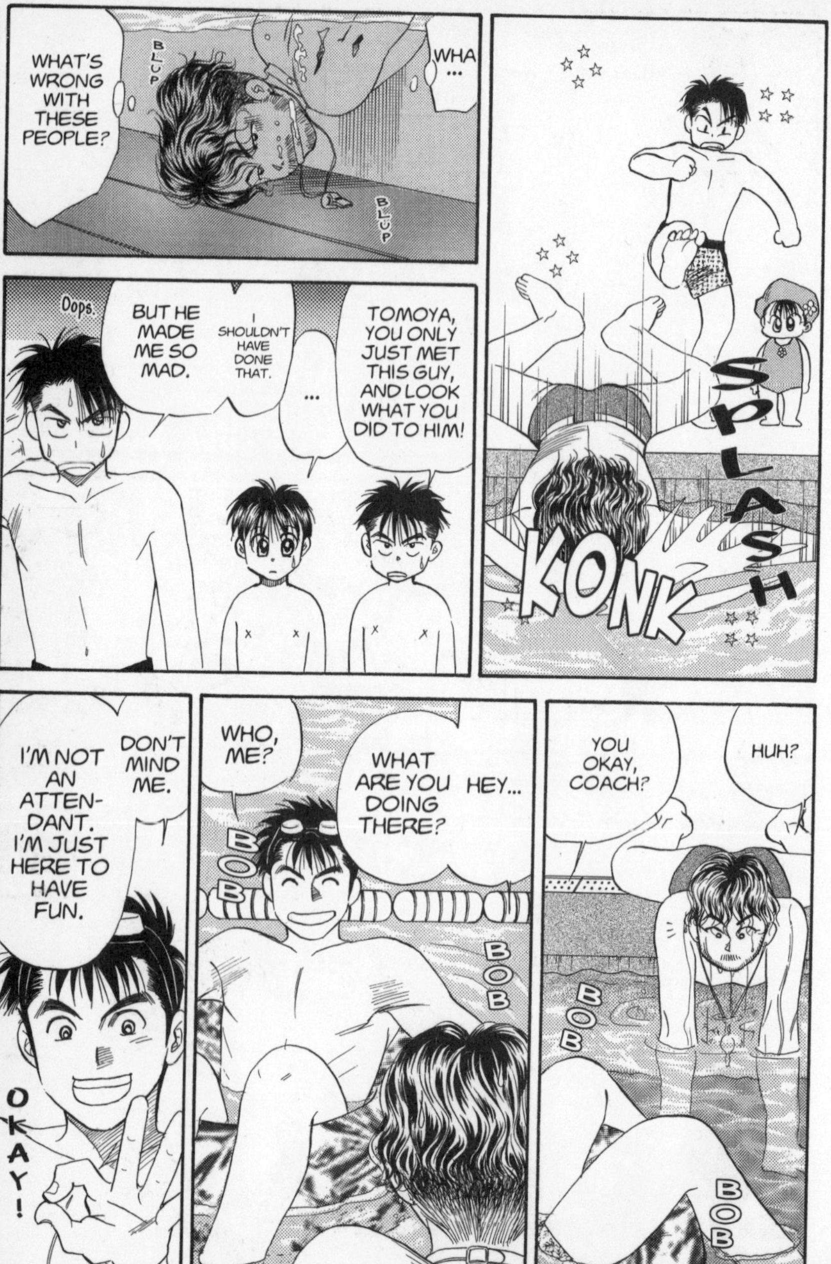
SPLASH
KONK
WHA ...
BLUP
BLUP
WHAT'S WRONG WITH THESE PEOPLE?
TOMOYA, YOU ONLY JUST MET THIS GUY, AND LOOK WHAT YOU DID TO HIM!
...
I SHOULDN'T HAVE DONE THAT.
BUT HE MADE ME SO MAD.
Oops.
HUH?
YOU OKAY, COACH?
BOB
BOB
HEY...
WHAT ARE YOU DOING THERE?
WHO, ME?
BOB
BOB
BOB
DON'T MIND ME.
I'M NOT AN ATTEN-DANT. I'M JUST HERE TO HAVE FUN.
OKAY!

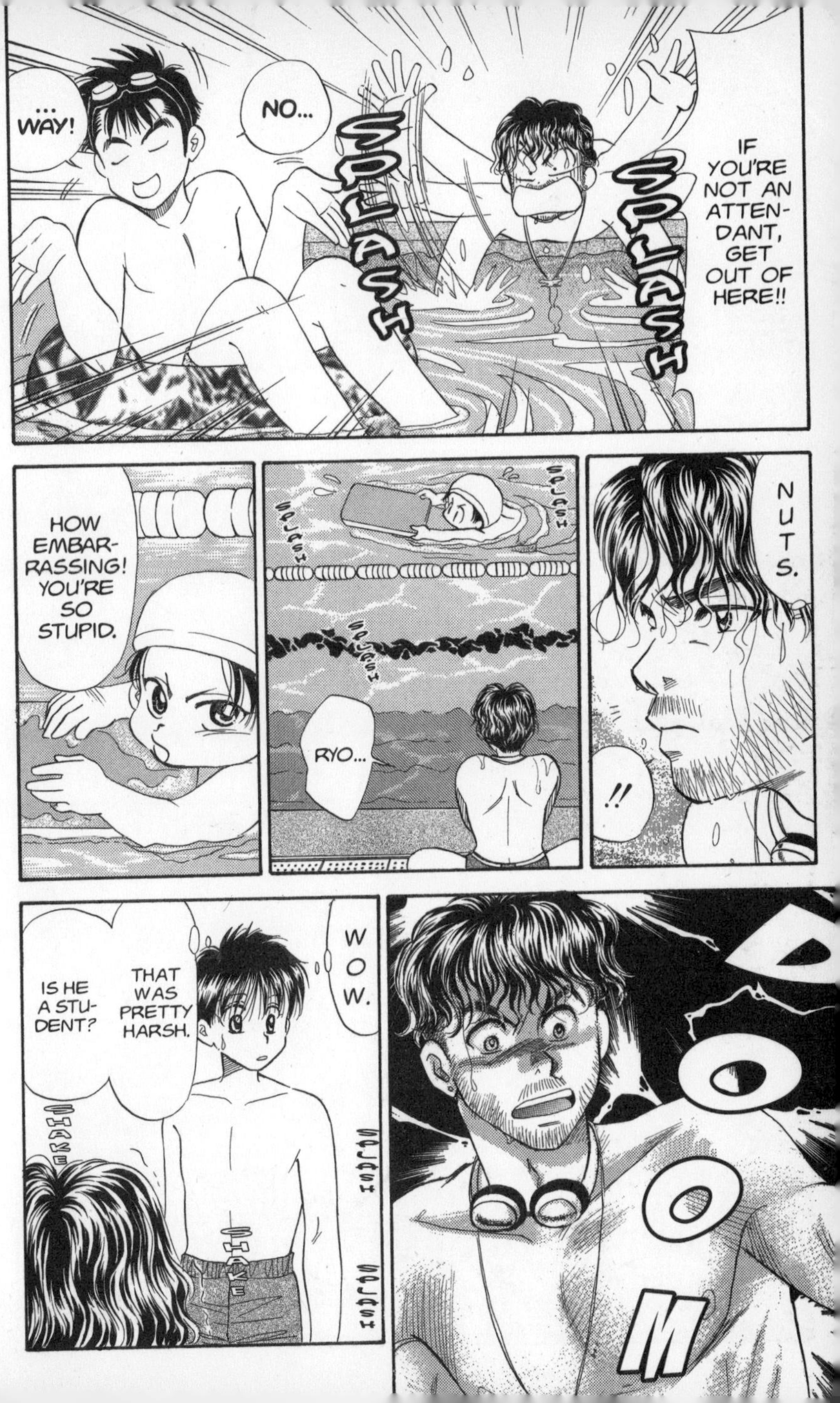
IF YOU'RE NOT AN ATTENDANT, GET OUT OF HERE!!
SPLASH
SPLASH
NO...
... WAY!
NUTS.
!!
SPLASH
SPLASH
SPLASH
RYO...
HOW EMBARRASSING! YOU'RE SO STUPID.
DOOM
WOW.
THAT WAS PRETTY HARSH.
IS HE A STUDENT?
SHAKE
SHAKE
SPLASH
SPLASH

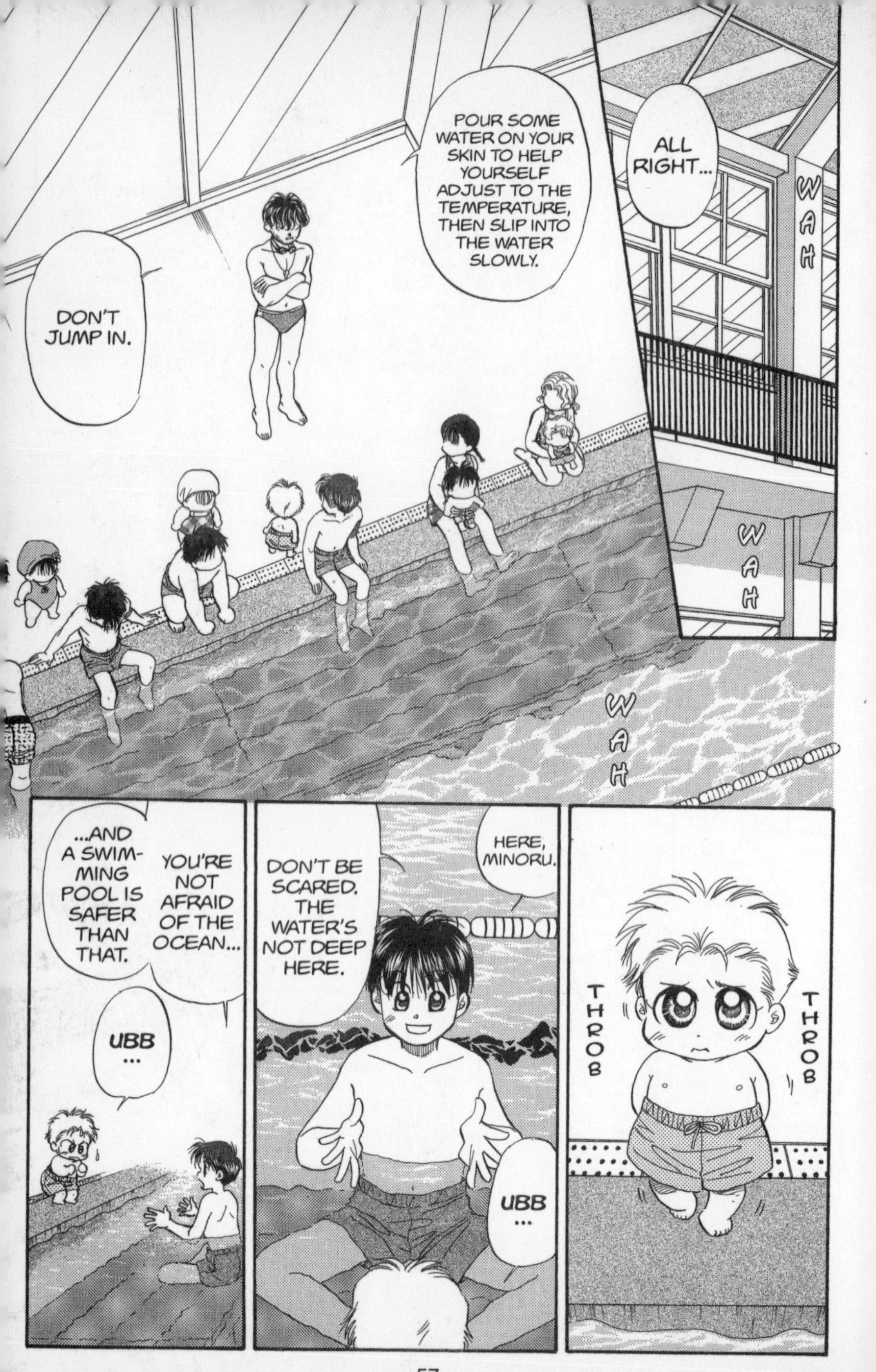
ALL RIGHT...
WAH
WAH
WAH
POUR SOME WATER ON YOUR SKIN TO HELP YOURSELF ADJUST TO THE TEMPERATURE, THEN SLIP INTO THE WATER SLOWLY.
DON'T JUMP IN.
THROB
THROB
HERE, MINORU.
DON'T BE SCARED. THE WATER'S NOT DEEP HERE.
UBB ...
YOU'RE NOT AFRAID OF THE OCEAN...
...AND A SWIMMING POOL IS SAFER THAN THAT.
UBB ...

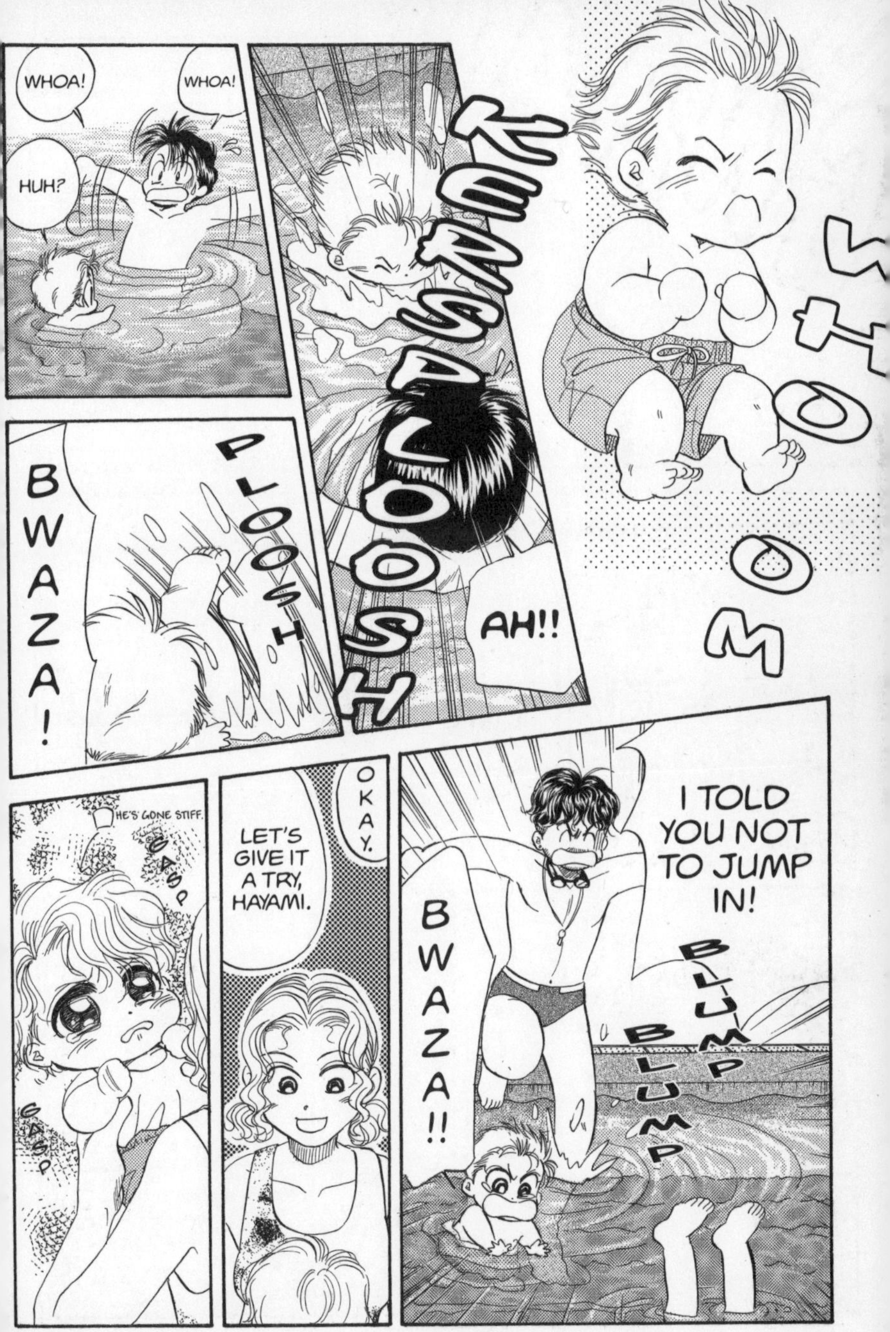
WHOOOM
KERSPLOOSH
AH!!
WHOA!
WHOA!
HUH?
PLOOSH
BWAZA!
I TOLD YOU NOT TO JUMP IN!
BLUMP
BLUMP
BWAZA!!
OKAY.
LET'S GIVE IT A TRY, HAYAMI.
HE'S GONE STIFF.
GASP
GASP

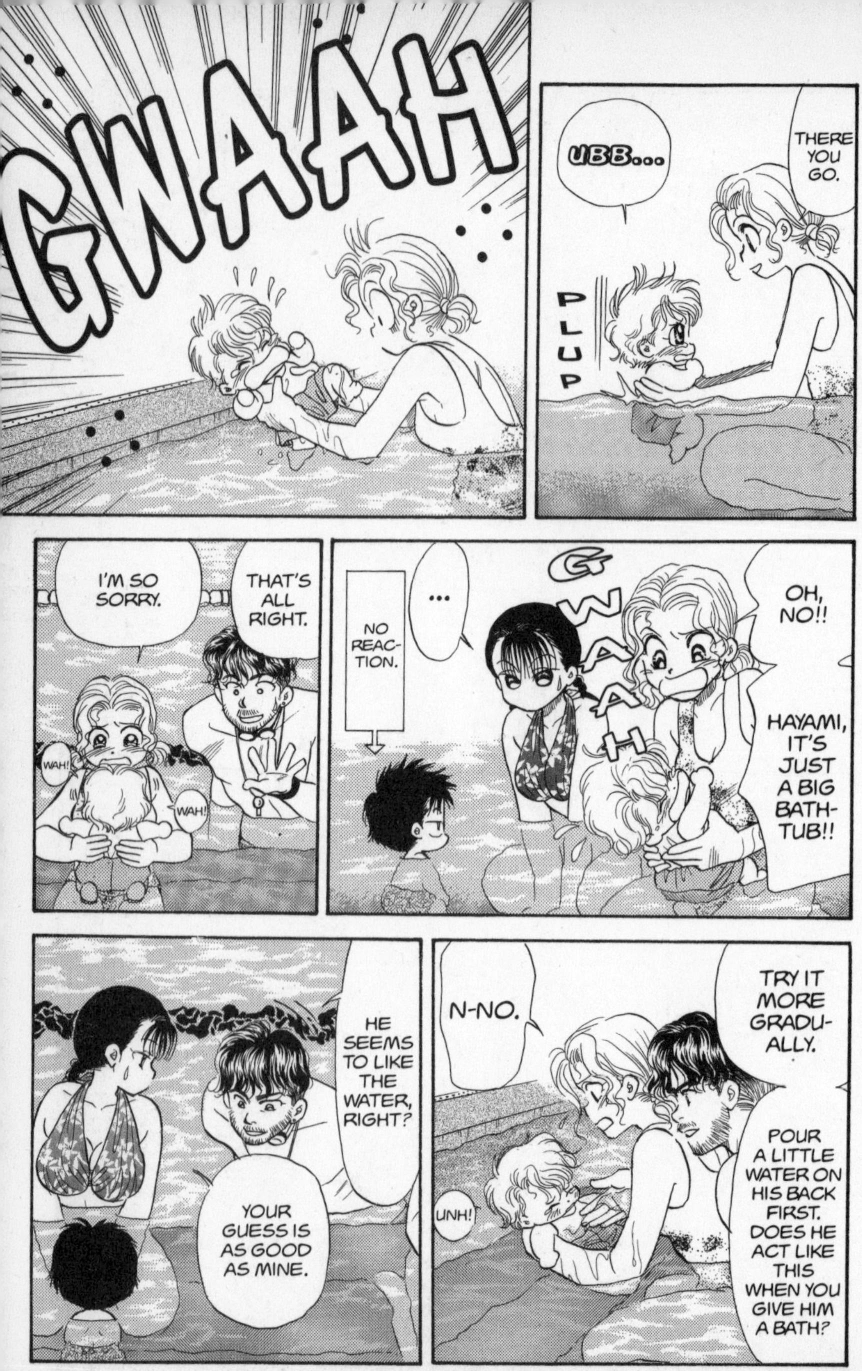
THERE YOU GO.
UBB...
PLUP
GWAAH
OH, NO!!
HAYAMI, IT'S JUST A BIG BATH-TUB!!
GWAAH
...
NO REAC-TION.
THAT'S ALL RIGHT.
I'M SO SORRY.
WAH!
WAH!
TRY IT MORE GRADU-ALLY.
N-NO.
POUR A LITTLE WATER ON HIS BACK FIRST. DOES HE ACT LIKE THIS WHEN YOU GIVE HIM A BATH?
UNH!
HE SEEMS TO LIKE THE WATER, RIGHT?
YOUR GUESS IS AS GOOD AS MINE.

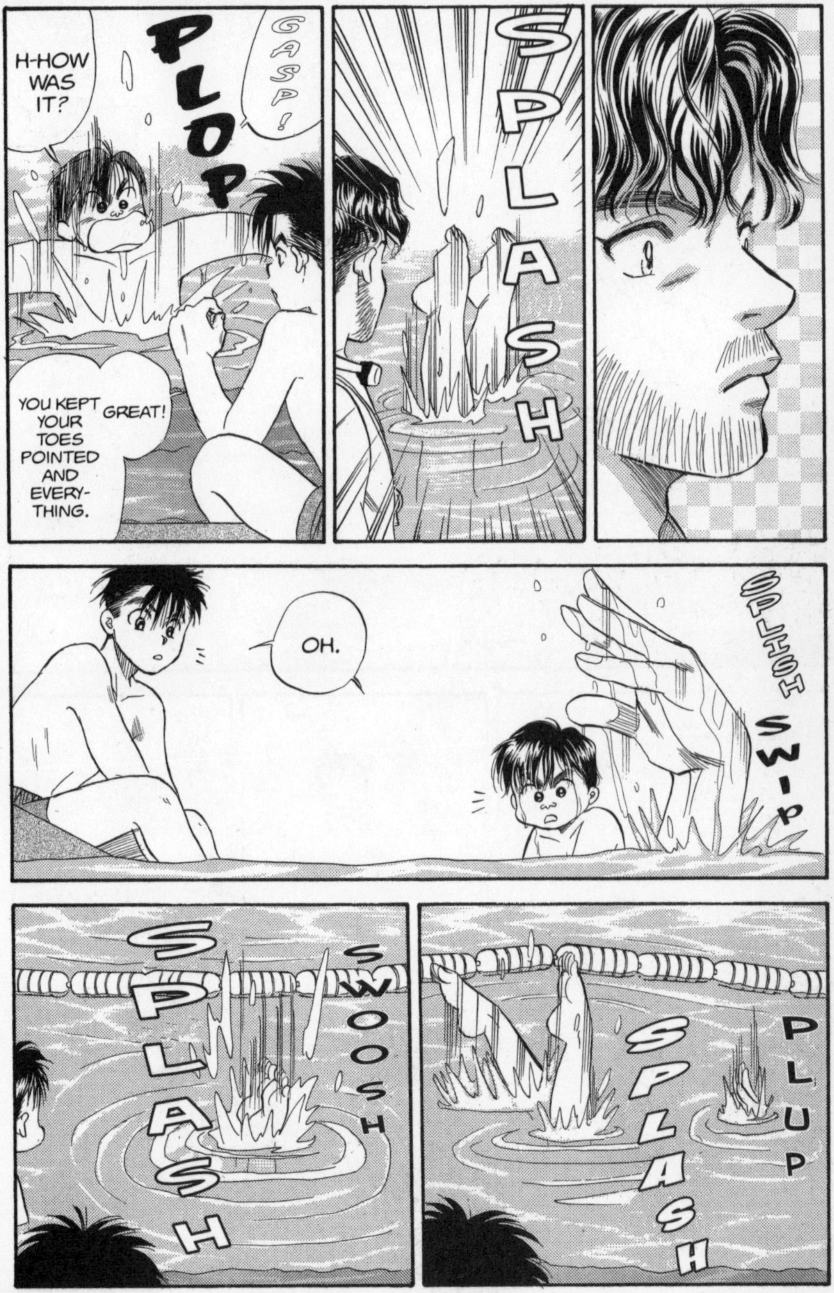
SPLASH
GASP!
PLOP
H-HOW WAS IT?
GREAT!
YOU KEPT YOUR TOES POINTED AND EVERYTHING.
SPLISH
SWIP
OH.
PLUP
SPLASH
SWOOSH
SPLASH

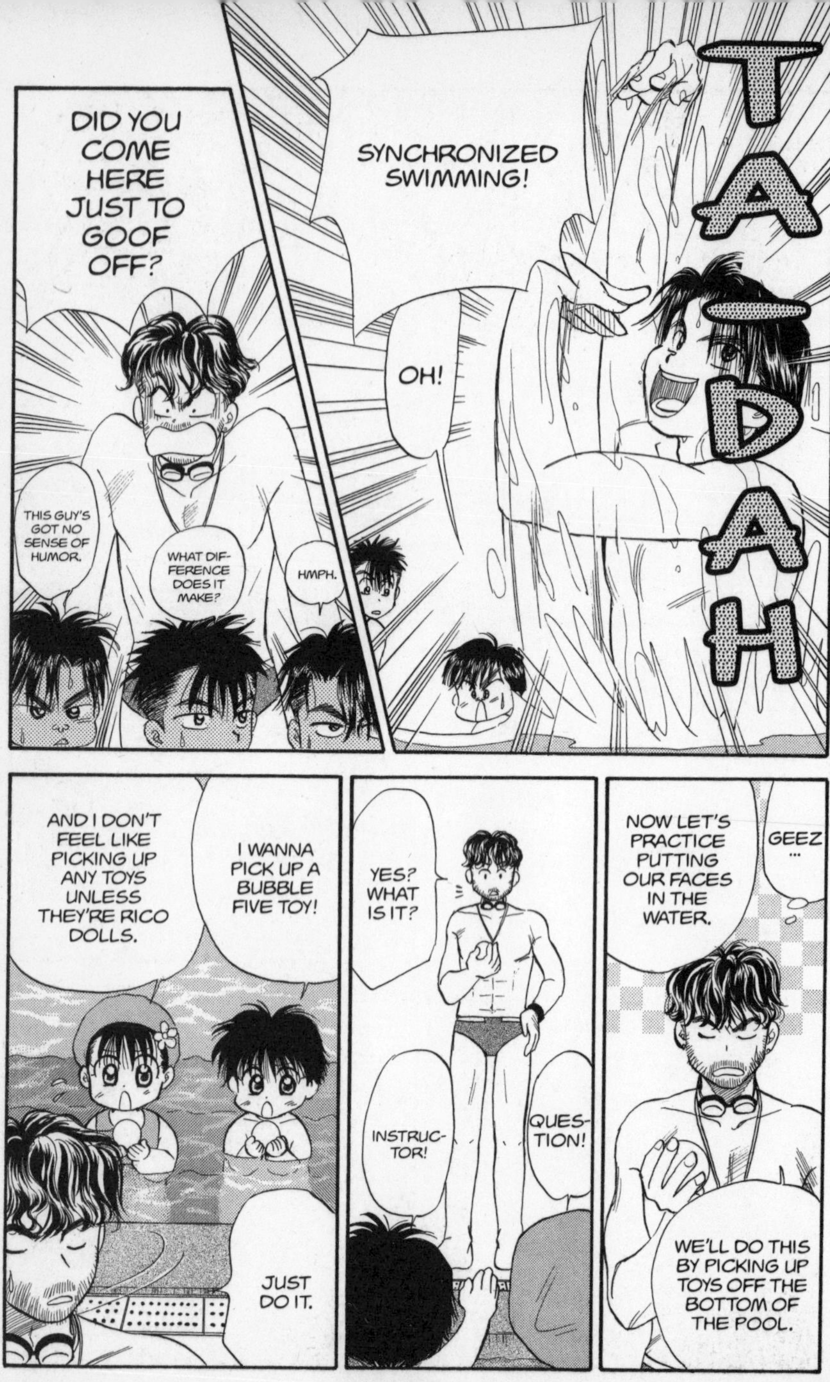
SYNCHRONIZED SWIMMING!
TA-DAH
OH!
DID YOU COME HERE JUST TO GOOF OFF?
HMPH.
WHAT DIF-FERENCE DOES IT MAKE?
THIS GUY'S GOT NO SENSE OF HUMOR.
GEEZ ...
NOW LET'S PRACTICE PUTTING OUR FACES IN THE WATER.
WE'LL DO THIS BY PICKING UP TOYS OFF THE BOTTOM OF THE POOL.
YES? WHAT IS IT?
QUES-TION!
INSTRUC-TOR!
I WANNA PICK UP A BUBBLE FIVE TOY!
AND I DON'T FEEL LIKE PICKING UP ANY TOYS UNLESS THEY'RE RICO DOLLS.
JUST DO IT.

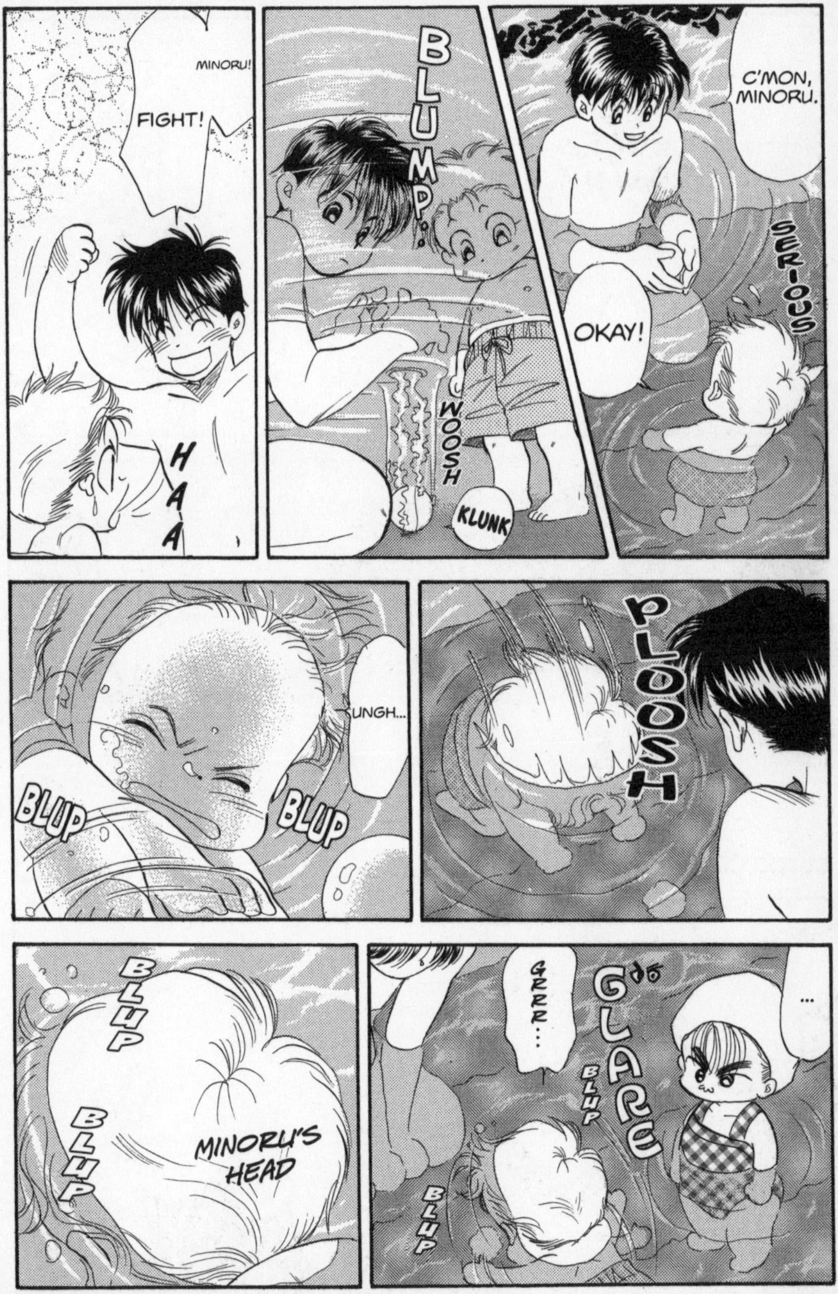
C'MON, MINORU.
OKAY!
SERIOUS
BLUMP..
WOOSH
KLUNK
MINORU!
FIGHT!
HAA
PLOOOSH
UNGH...
BLUP
BLUP
...
GLARE
GRRR...
BLUP
BLUP
BLUP
BLUP
MINORU'S HEAD

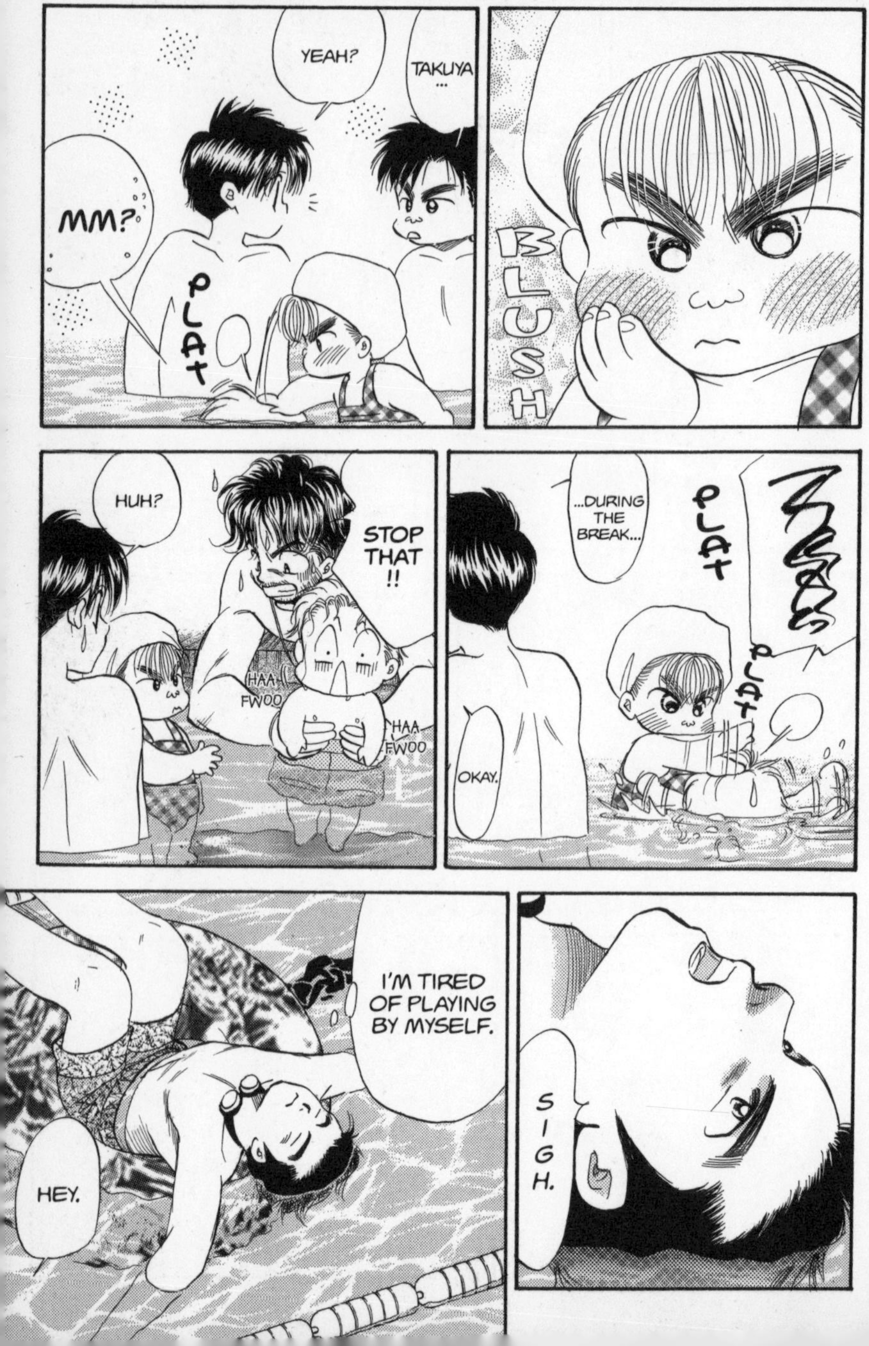
BLUSH
TAKUYA...
YEAH?
MM?
PLAT
...DURING THE BREAK...
PLAT
PLAT
OKAY.
STOP THAT!!
HUH?
HAA FWOO
HAA FWOO
SIGH.
I'M TIRED OF PLAYING BY MYSELF.
HEY.

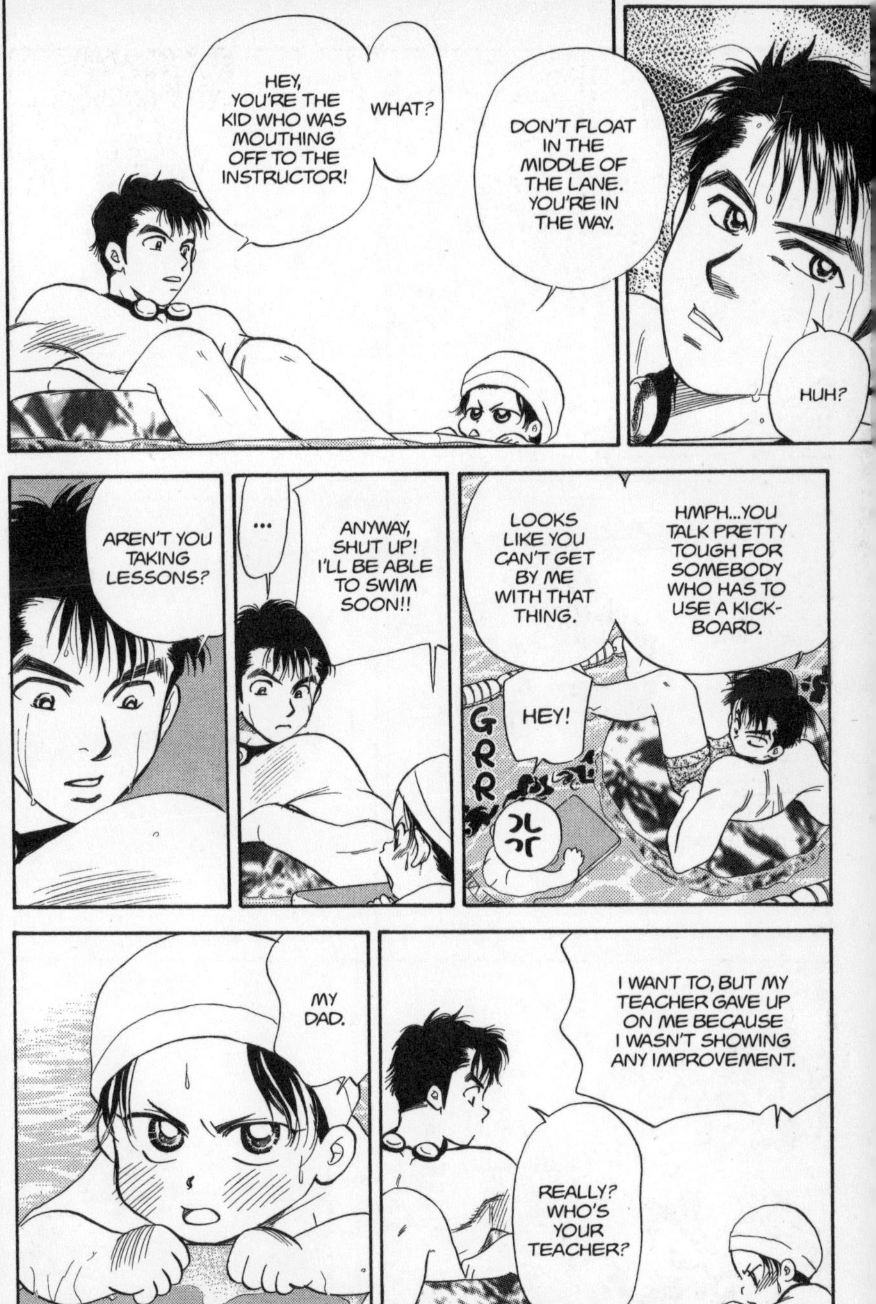
HUH?
DON'T FLOAT IN THE MIDDLE OF THE LANE. YOU'RE IN THE WAY.
WHAT?
HEY, YOU'RE THE KID WHO WAS MOUTHING OFF TO THE INSTRUCTOR!
HMPH...YOU TALK PRETTY TOUGH FOR SOMEBODY WHO HAS TO USE A KICK-BOARD.
LOOKS LIKE YOU CAN'T GET BY ME WITH THAT THING.
HEY!
GRR
ANYWAY, SHUT UP! I'LL BE ABLE TO SWIM SOON!!
...
AREN'T YOU TAKING LESSONS?
I WANT TO, BUT MY TEACHER GAVE UP ON ME BECAUSE I WASN'T SHOWING ANY IMPROVEMENT.
REALLY? WHO'S YOUR TEACHER?
MY DAD.

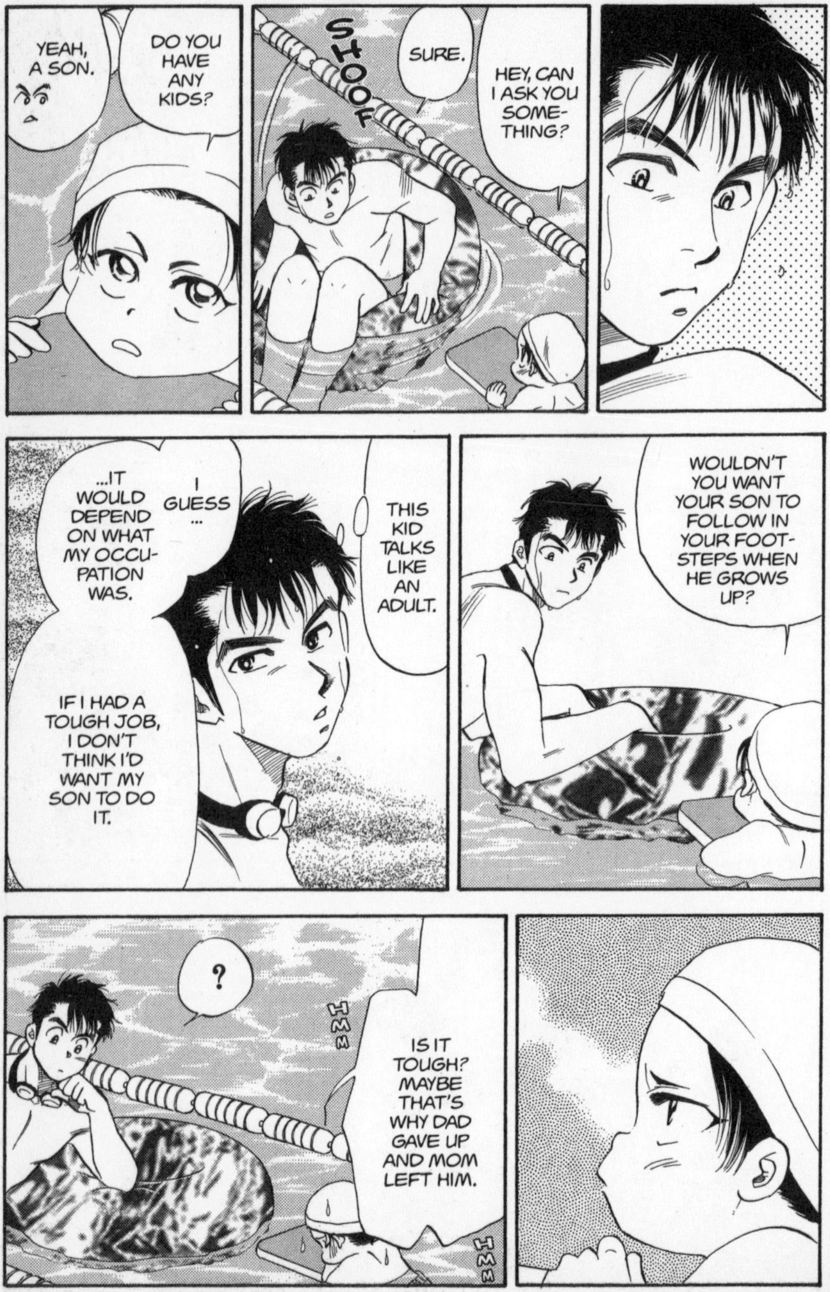
HEY, CAN I ASK YOU SOMETHING?
SURE.
SHOOF
DO YOU HAVE ANY KIDS?
YEAH, A SON.
WOULDN'T YOU WANT YOUR SON TO FOLLOW IN YOUR FOOTSTEPS WHEN HE GROWS UP?
THIS KID TALKS LIKE AN ADULT.
I GUESS...
...IT WOULD DEPEND ON WHAT MY OCCUPATION WAS.
IF I HAD A TOUGH JOB, I DON'T THINK I'D WANT MY SON TO DO IT.
HMM
IS IT TOUGH? MAYBE THAT'S WHY DAD GAVE UP AND MOM LEFT HIM.
HMM
?

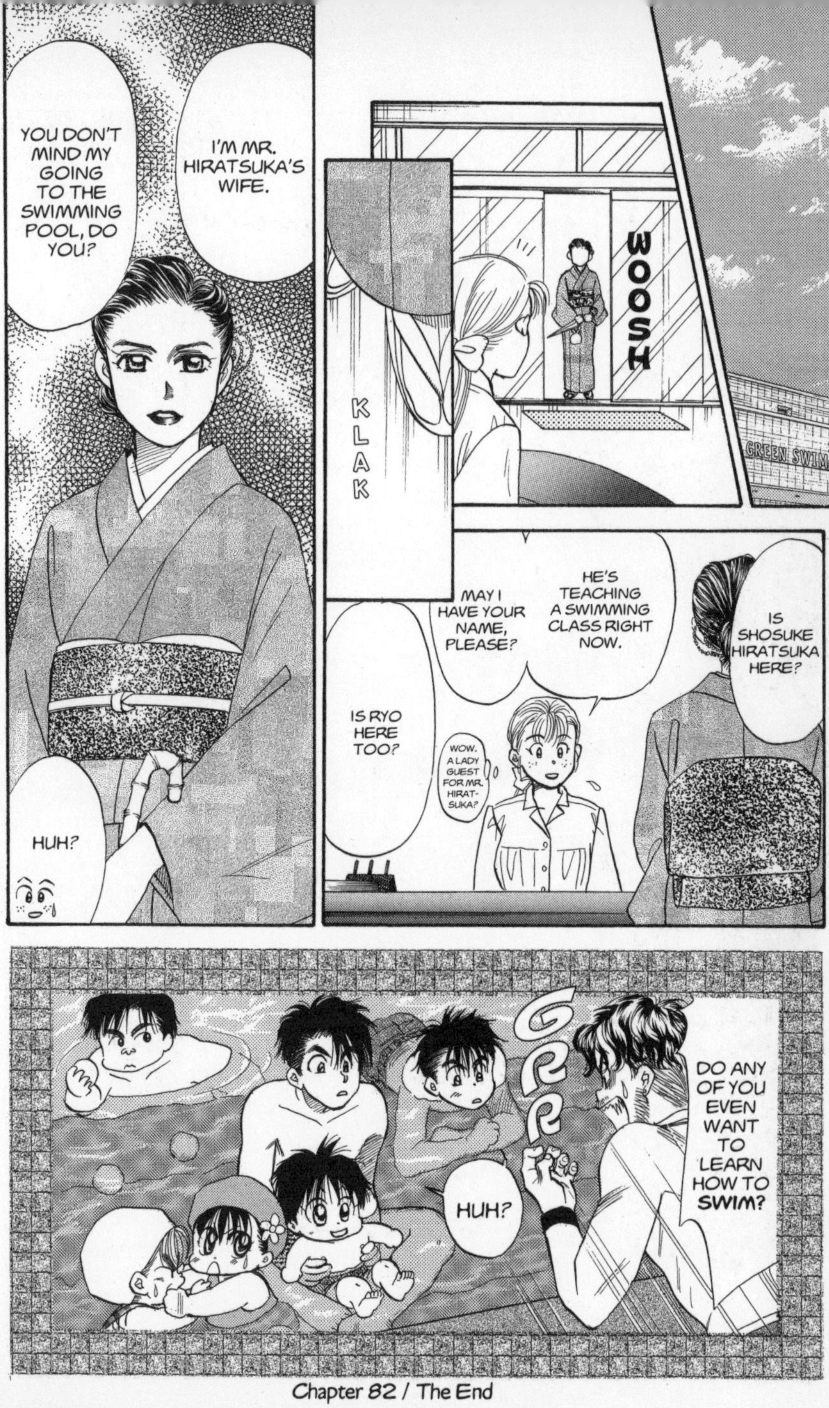
GREEN SWIMMIN
WOOSH
KLAK
IS SHOSUKE HIRATSUKA HERE?
HE'S TEACHING A SWIMMING CLASS RIGHT NOW.
MAY I HAVE YOUR NAME, PLEASE?
WOW, A LADY GUEST FOR MR. HIRATSUKA?
IS RYO HERE TOO?
I'M MR. HIRATSUKA'S WIFE.
YOU DON'T MIND MY GOING TO THE SWIMMING POOL, DO YOU?
HUH?
DO ANY OF YOU EVEN WANT TO LEARN HOW TO **SWIM**?
GRR
HUH?

Chapter 82 / The End

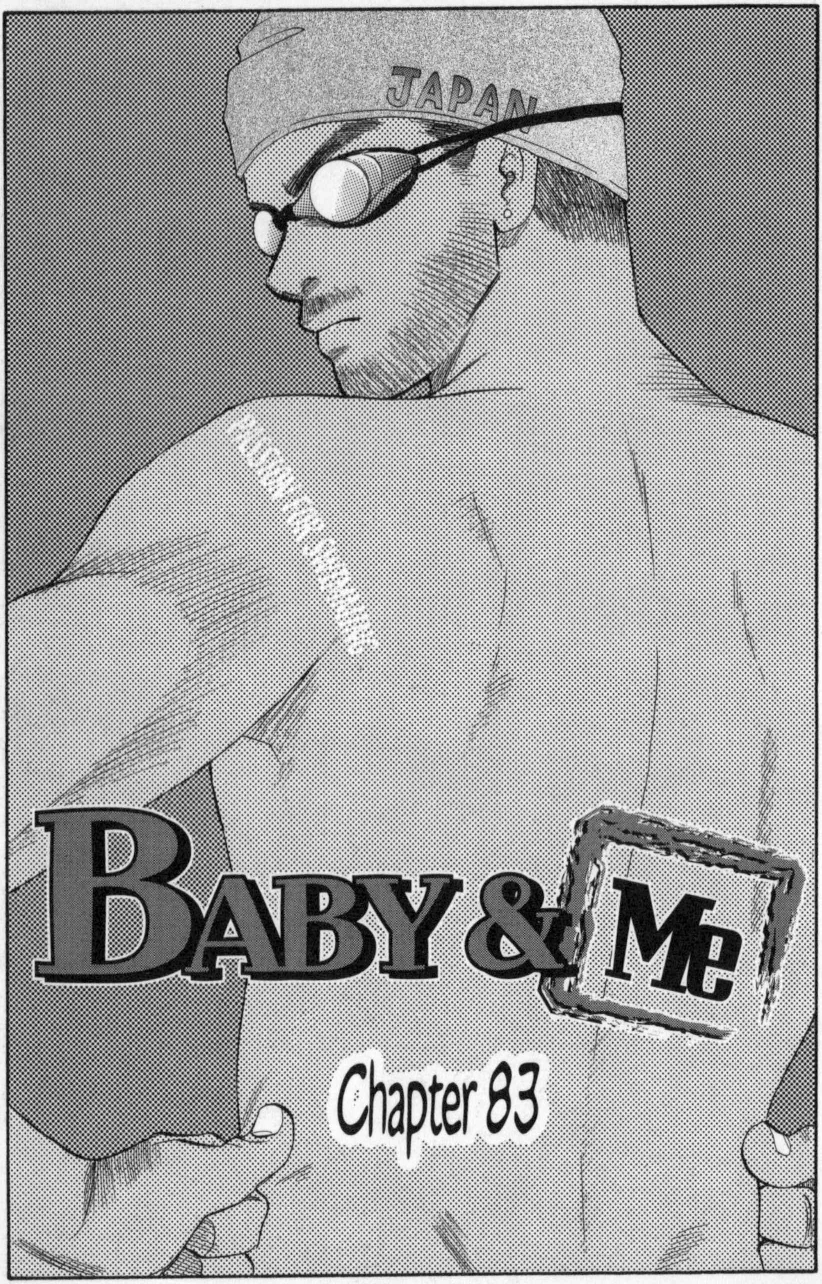
JAPAN
BABY & Me
Chapter 83

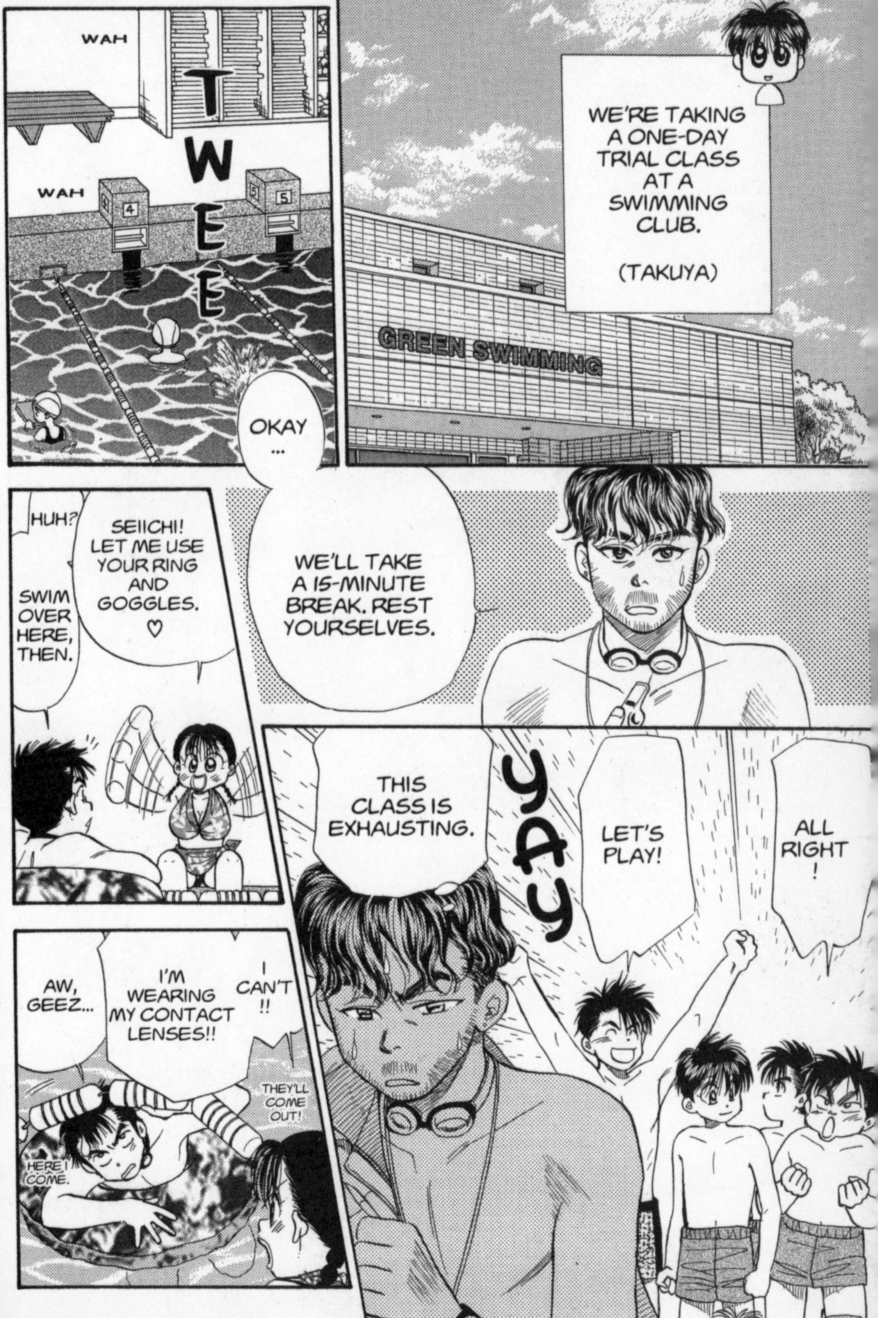
WE'RE TAKING A ONE-DAY TRIAL CLASS AT A SWIMMING CLUB.
(TAKUYA)
GREEN SWIMMING
WAH
TWEE
WAH
OKAY ...
WE'LL TAKE A 15-MINUTE BREAK. REST YOURSELVES.
SEIICHI! LET ME USE YOUR RING AND GOGGLES. ♡
HUH?
SWIM OVER HERE, THEN.
ALL RIGHT!
LET'S PLAY!
YAY
THIS CLASS IS EXHAUSTING.
MINORU
I CAN'T!!
I'M WEARING MY CONTACT LENSES!!
THEY'LL COME OUT!
AW, GEEZ...
HERE I COME.

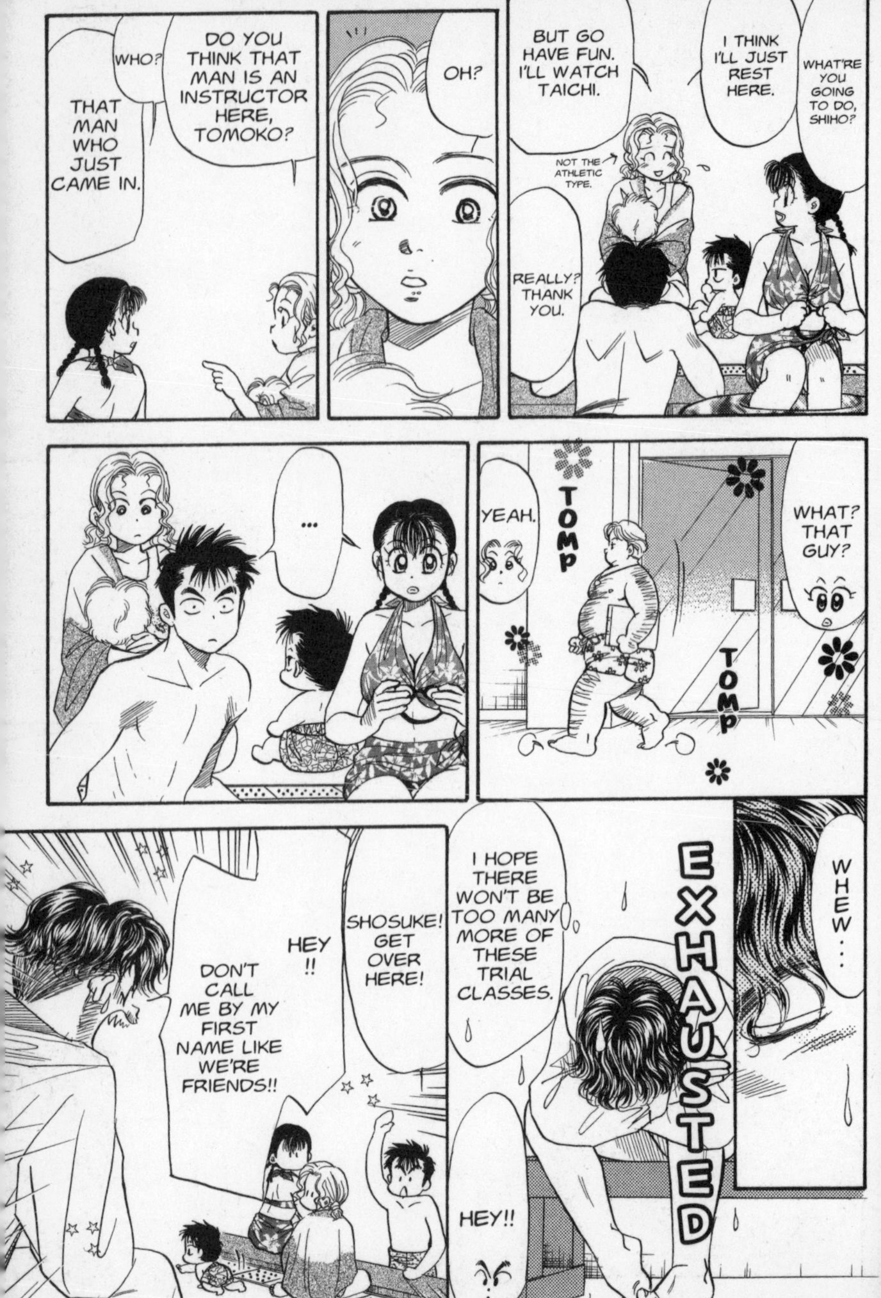
WHAT'RE YOU GOING TO DO, SHIHO?
I THINK I'LL JUST REST HERE.
BUT GO HAVE FUN. I'LL WATCH TAICHI.
NOT THE ATHLETIC TYPE.
REALLY? THANK YOU.
OH?
DO YOU THINK THAT MAN IS AN INSTRUCTOR HERE, TOMOKO?
WHO?
THAT MAN WHO JUST CAME IN.
WHAT? THAT GUY?
TOMP
TOMP
YEAH.
...
WHEW...
EXHAUSTED
I HOPE THERE WON'T BE TOO MANY MORE OF THESE TRIAL CLASSES.
HEY!!
SHOSUKE! GET OVER HERE!
HEY!!
DON'T CALL ME BY MY FIRST NAME LIKE WE'RE FRIENDS!!

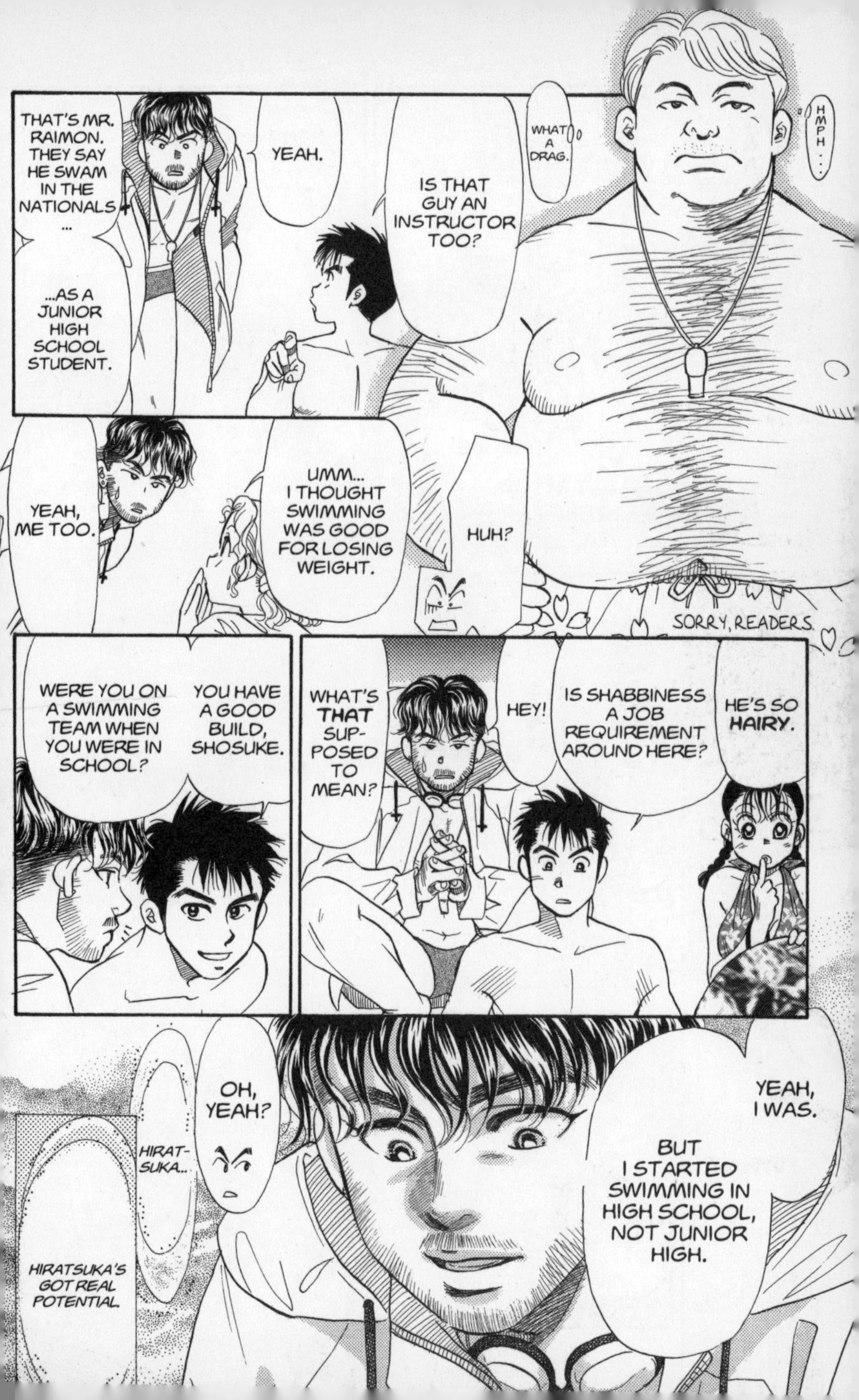
HMPH...
WHAT A DRAG.
SORRY, READERS.
IS THAT GUY AN INSTRUCTOR TOO?
YEAH.
THAT'S MR. RAIMON. THEY SAY HE SWAM IN THE NATIONALS...
...AS A JUNIOR HIGH SCHOOL STUDENT.
HUH?
UMM... I THOUGHT SWIMMING WAS GOOD FOR LOSING WEIGHT.
YEAH, ME TOO.
HE'S SO **HAIRY**.
IS SHABBINESS A JOB REQUIREMENT AROUND HERE?
HEY!
WHAT'S **THAT** SUP-POSED TO MEAN?
YOU HAVE A GOOD BUILD, SHOSUKE.
WERE YOU ON A SWIMMING TEAM WHEN YOU WERE IN SCHOOL?
YEAH, I WAS.
BUT I STARTED SWIMMING IN HIGH SCHOOL, NOT JUNIOR HIGH.
OH, YEAH?
HIRAT-SUKA...
HIRATSUKA'S GOT REAL POTENTIAL.

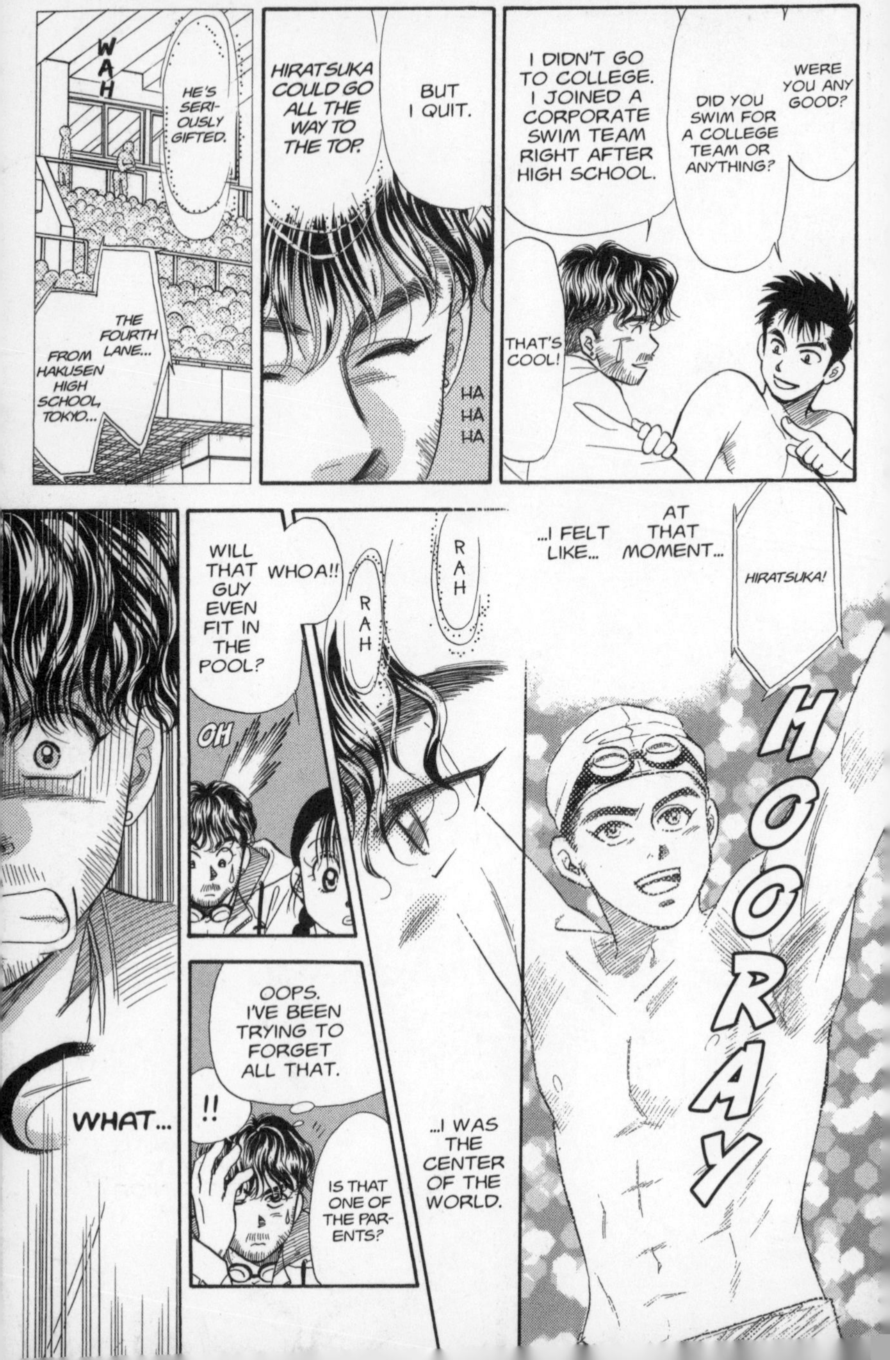
WERE YOU ANY GOOD?
DID YOU SWIM FOR A COLLEGE TEAM OR ANYTHING?
I DIDN'T GO TO COLLEGE. I JOINED A CORPORATE SWIM TEAM RIGHT AFTER HIGH SCHOOL.
THAT'S COOL!
BUT I QUIT.
HIRATSUKA COULD GO ALL THE WAY TO THE TOP.
HA HA HA
WAH
HE'S SERI-OUSLY GIFTED.
THE FOURTH LANE...
FROM HAKUSEN HIGH SCHOOL, TOKYO...
HIRATSUKA!
AT THAT MOMENT...
...I FELT LIKE...
HOORAY
...I WAS THE CENTER OF THE WORLD.
RAH
RAH
WHOA!!
WILL THAT GUY EVEN FIT IN THE POOL?
OH
OOPS. I'VE BEEN TRYING TO FORGET ALL THAT.
IS THAT ONE OF THE PAR-ENTS?
!!
WHAT...

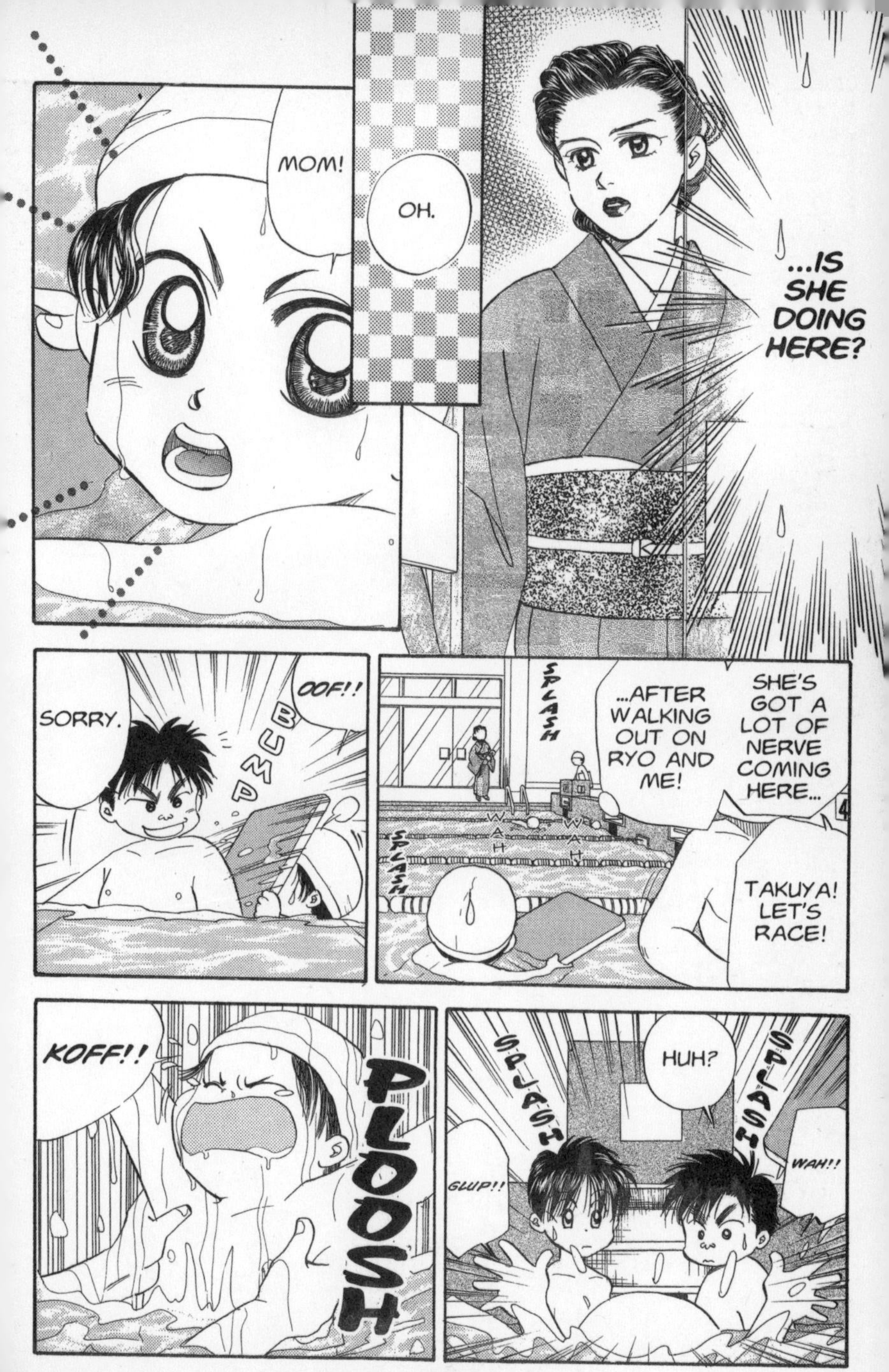
...IS SHE DOING HERE?
OH.
MOM!
SHE'S GOT A LOT OF NERVE COMING HERE...
...AFTER WALKING OUT ON RYO AND ME!
SPLASH
WAH
WAH
SPLASH
TAKUYA! LET'S RACE!
OOF!!
BUMP
SORRY.
SPLASH
HUH?
SPLASH
WAH!!
GLUP!!
PLOOSH
KOFF!!

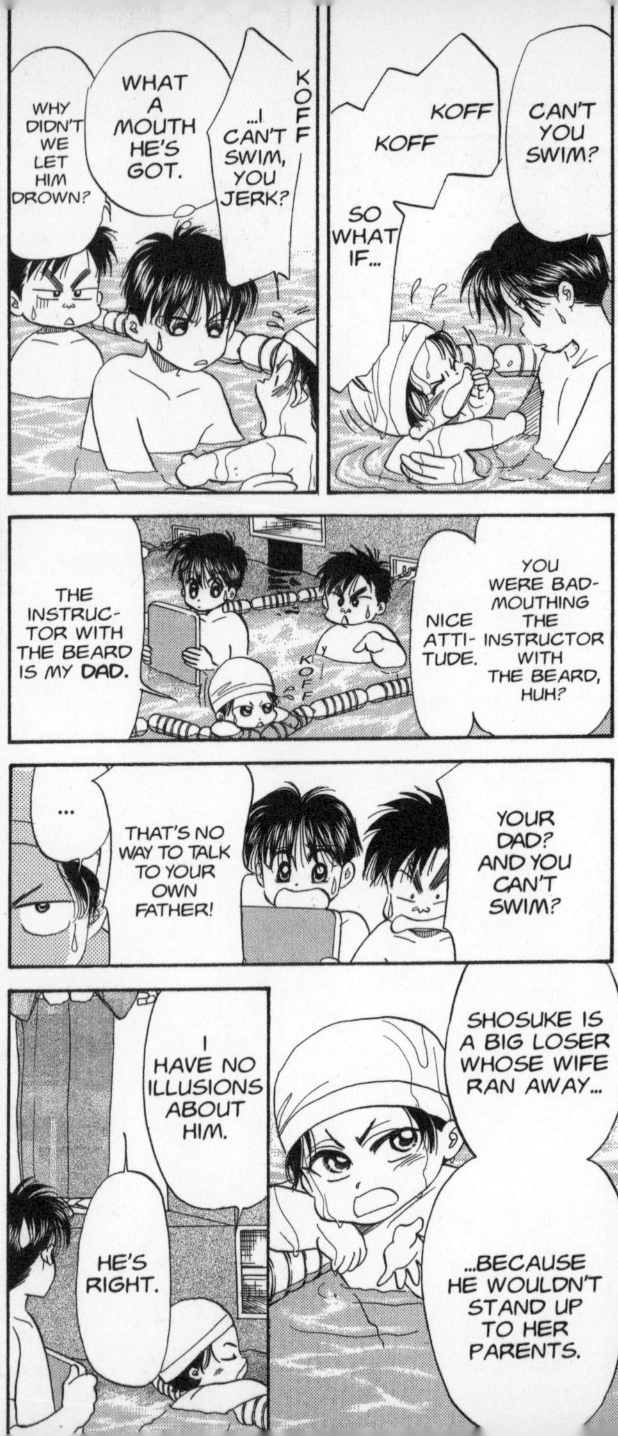
CAN'T YOU SWIM?
KOFF
KOFF
SO WHAT IF...
KOFF
...I CAN'T SWIM, YOU JERK?
WHAT A MOUTH HE'S GOT.
WHY DIDN'T WE LET HIM DROWN?
YOU WERE BAD-MOUTHING THE INSTRUCTOR WITH THE BEARD, HUH?
NICE ATTI-TUDE.
KOFF
THE INSTRUCTOR WITH THE BEARD IS MY **DAD**.
YOUR DAD? AND YOU CAN'T SWIM?
THAT'S NO WAY TO TALK TO YOUR OWN FATHER!
...
SHOSUKE IS A BIG LOSER WHOSE WIFE RAN AWAY...
...BECAUSE HE WOULDN'T STAND UP TO HER PARENTS.
I HAVE NO ILLUSIONS ABOUT HIM.
HE'S RIGHT.

Author's Note: Part 3

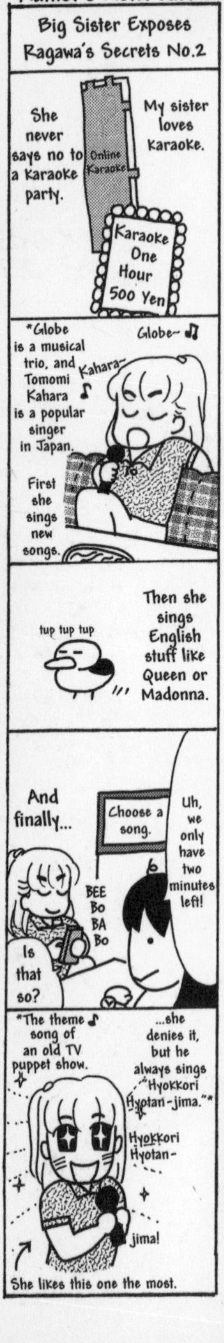
Big Sister Exposes Ragawa's Secrets No.2
My sister loves karaoke.
She never says no to a karaoke party.
Online Karaoke
Karaoke One Hour 500 Yen
Globe~
Kahara~
*Globe is a musical trio, and Tomomi Kahara is a popular singer in Japan.
First she sings new songs.
Then she sings English stuff like Queen or Madonna.
tup tup tup
And finally...
Choose a song.
Uh, we only have two minutes left!
BEE Bo BA Bo
Is that so?
...she denies it, but he always sings "Hyokkori Hyotan-jima."*
*The theme song of an old TV puppet show.
Hyokkori Hyotan-
jima!
She likes this one the most.

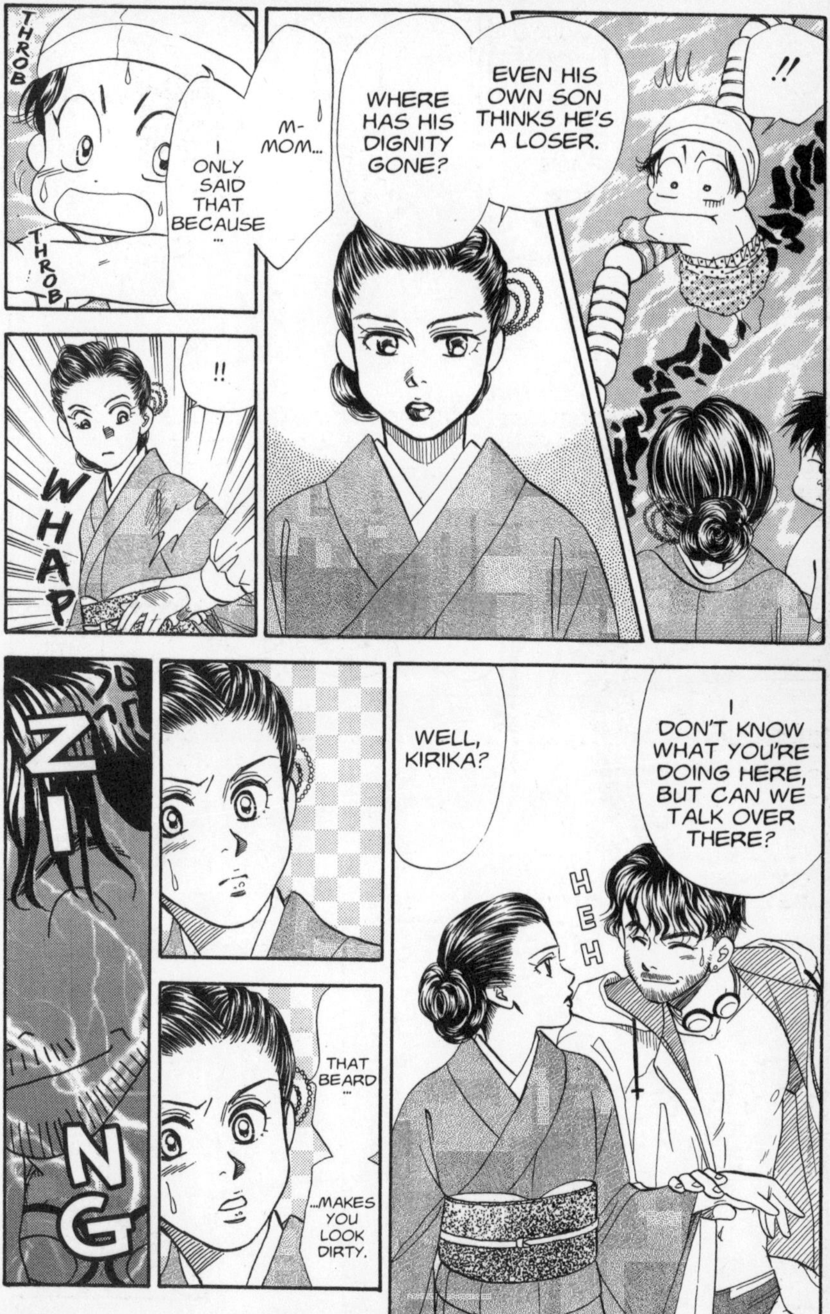
!!
EVEN HIS OWN SON THINKS HE'S A LOSER.
WHERE HAS HIS DIGNITY GONE?
M-MOM...
I ONLY SAID THAT BECAUSE ...
THROB
THROB
!!
WHAP
I DON'T KNOW WHAT YOU'RE DOING HERE, BUT CAN WE TALK OVER THERE?
WELL, KIRIKA?
HEH
THAT BEARD ...
...MAKES YOU LOOK DIRTY.
ZI
NG

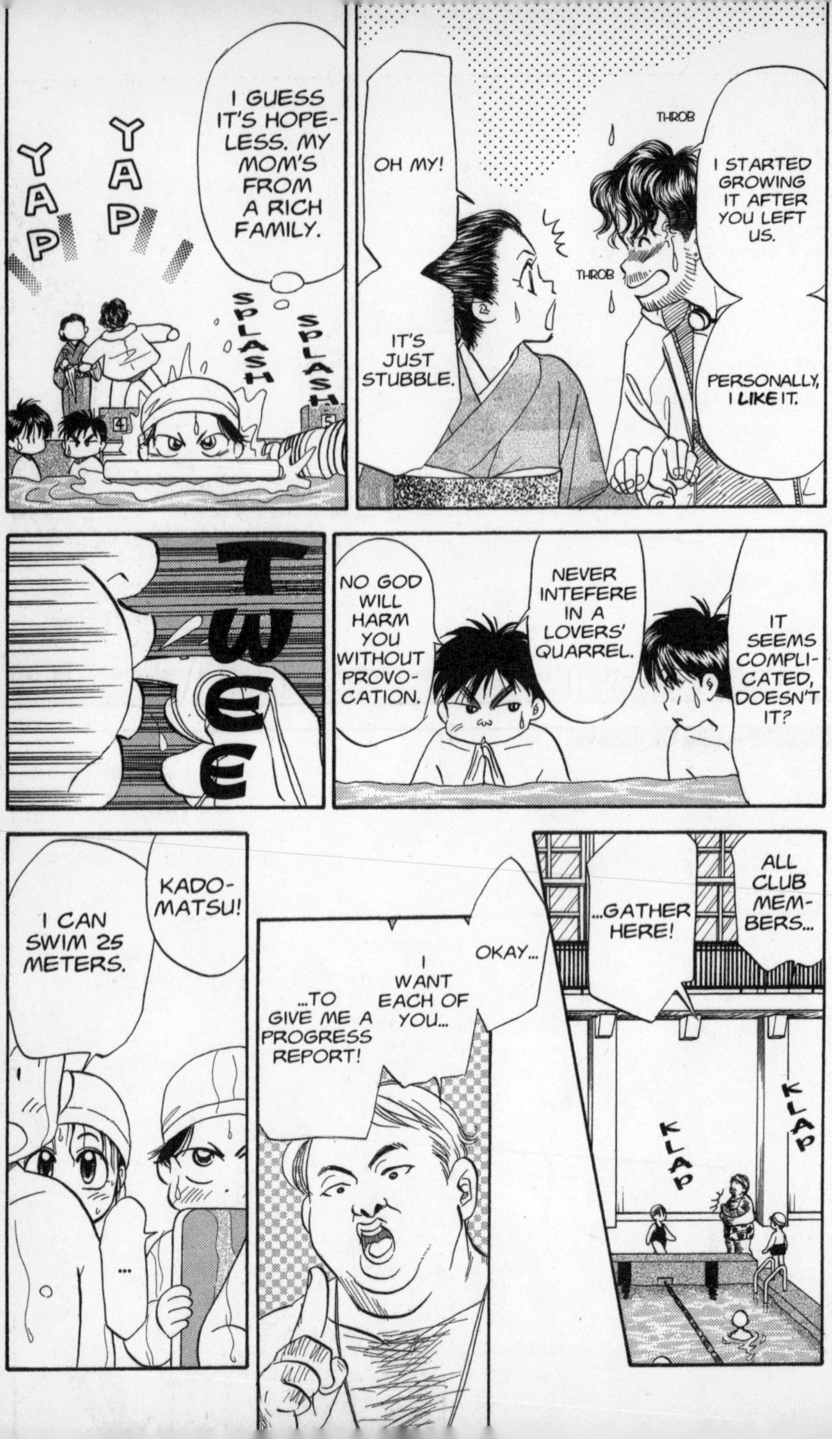
THROB
I STARTED GROWING IT AFTER YOU LEFT US.
OH MY!
THROB
PERSONALLY, I **LIKE** IT.
IT'S JUST STUBBLE.
I GUESS IT'S HOPE-LESS. MY MOM'S FROM A RICH FAMILY.
YAP
YAP
SPLASH
SPLASH
IT SEEMS COMPLI-CATED, DOESN'T IT?
NEVER INTEFERE IN A LOVERS' QUARREL.
NO GOD WILL HARM YOU WITHOUT PROVO-CATION.
TWEE
ALL CLUB MEM-BERS...
...GATHER HERE!
KLAP
KLAP
OKAY...
I WANT EACH OF YOU...
...TO GIVE ME A PROGRESS REPORT!
KADO-MATSU!
I CAN SWIM 25 METERS.
...

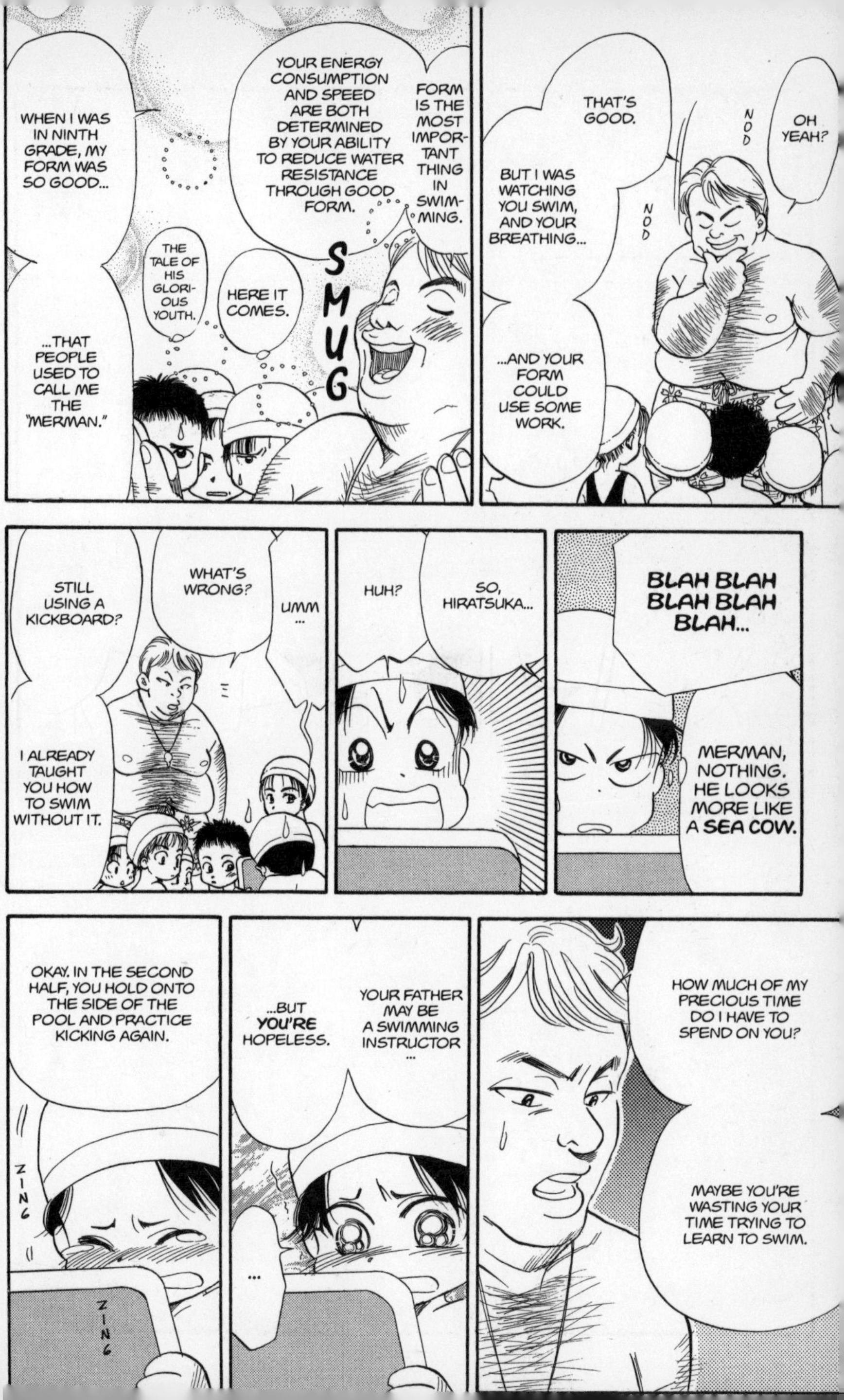
OH YEAH?
NOD NOD
THAT'S GOOD.
BUT I WAS WATCHING YOU SWIM, AND YOUR BREATHING...
...AND YOUR FORM COULD USE SOME WORK.
FORM IS THE MOST IMPORTANT THING IN SWIMMING.
YOUR ENERGY CONSUMPTION AND SPEED ARE BOTH DETERMINED BY YOUR ABILITY TO REDUCE WATER RESISTANCE THROUGH GOOD FORM.
WHEN I WAS IN NINTH GRADE, MY FORM WAS SO GOOD...
SMUG
HERE IT COMES.
THE TALE OF HIS GLORIOUS YOUTH.
...THAT PEOPLE USED TO CALL ME THE "MERMAN."
BLAH BLAH BLAH BLAH BLAH...
MERMAN, NOTHING. HE LOOKS MORE LIKE A SEA COW.
SO, HIRATSUKA...
HUH?
UMM...
WHAT'S WRONG?
STILL USING A KICKBOARD?
I ALREADY TAUGHT YOU HOW TO SWIM WITHOUT IT.
HOW MUCH OF MY PRECIOUS TIME DO I HAVE TO SPEND ON YOU?
MAYBE YOU'RE WASTING YOUR TIME TRYING TO LEARN TO SWIM.
YOUR FATHER MAY BE A SWIMMING INSTRUCTOR...
...BUT YOU'RE HOPELESS.
...
OKAY. IN THE SECOND HALF, YOU HOLD ONTO THE SIDE OF THE POOL AND PRACTICE KICKING AGAIN.
ZING
ZING

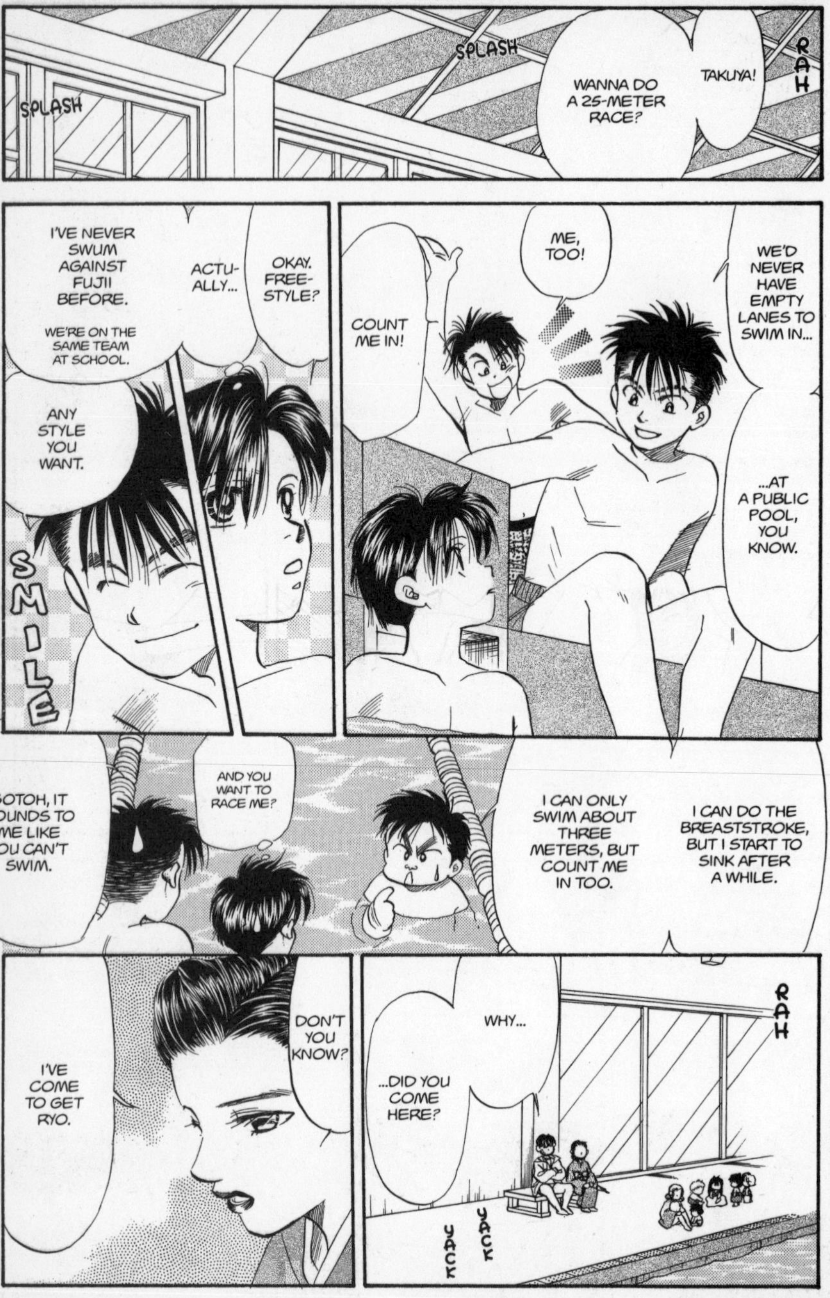
RAH
TAKUYA!
WANNA DO A 25-METER RACE?
SPLASH
SPLASH
WE'D NEVER HAVE EMPTY LANES TO SWIM IN...
...AT A PUBLIC POOL, YOU KNOW.
ME, TOO!
COUNT ME IN!
OKAY. FREE-STYLE?
ACTU-ALLY...
I'VE NEVER SWUM AGAINST FUJII BEFORE.
WE'RE ON THE SAME TEAM AT SCHOOL.
ANY STYLE YOU WANT.
SMILE
I CAN DO THE BREASTSTROKE, BUT I START TO SINK AFTER A WHILE.
I CAN ONLY SWIM ABOUT THREE METERS, BUT COUNT ME IN TOO.
AND YOU WANT TO RACE ME?
GOTOH, IT SOUNDS TO ME LIKE YOU CAN'T SWIM.
RAH
WHY...
...DID YOU COME HERE?
YACK
YACK
DON'T YOU KNOW?
I'VE COME TO GET RYO.

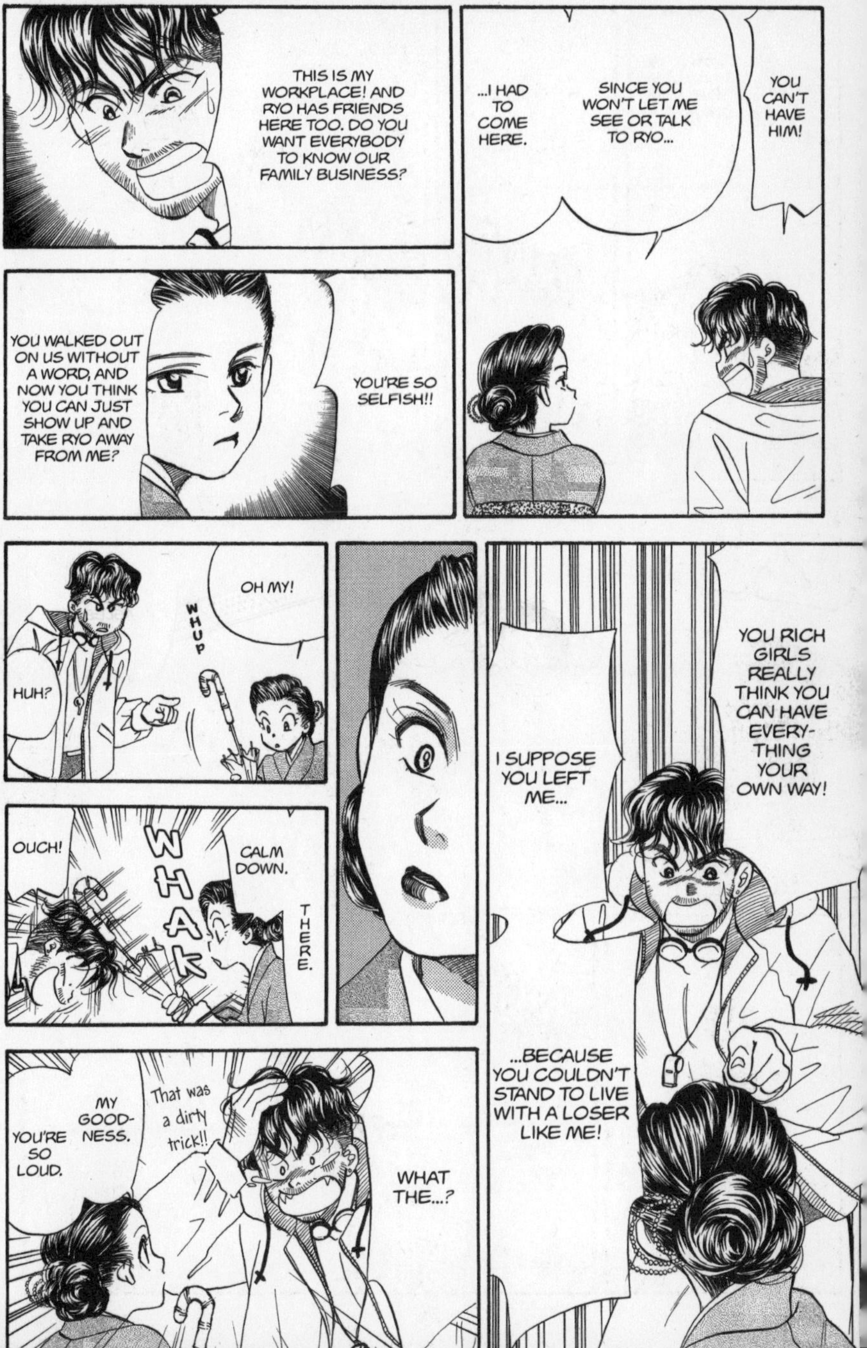
YOU CAN'T HAVE HIM!
SINCE YOU WON'T LET ME SEE OR TALK TO RYO...
...I HAD TO COME HERE.
THIS IS MY WORKPLACE! AND RYO HAS FRIENDS HERE TOO. DO YOU WANT EVERYBODY TO KNOW OUR FAMILY BUSINESS?
YOU'RE SO SELFISH!!
YOU WALKED OUT ON US WITHOUT A WORD, AND NOW YOU THINK YOU CAN JUST SHOW UP AND TAKE RYO AWAY FROM ME?
YOU RICH GIRLS REALLY THINK YOU CAN HAVE EVERY-THING YOUR OWN WAY!
I SUPPOSE YOU LEFT ME...
...BECAUSE YOU COULDN'T STAND TO LIVE WITH A LOSER LIKE ME!
OH MY!
WHUP
HUH?
THERE.
CALM DOWN.
WHAK
OUCH!
WHAT THE...?
That was a dirty trick!!
MY GOOD-NESS.
YOU'RE SO LOUD.

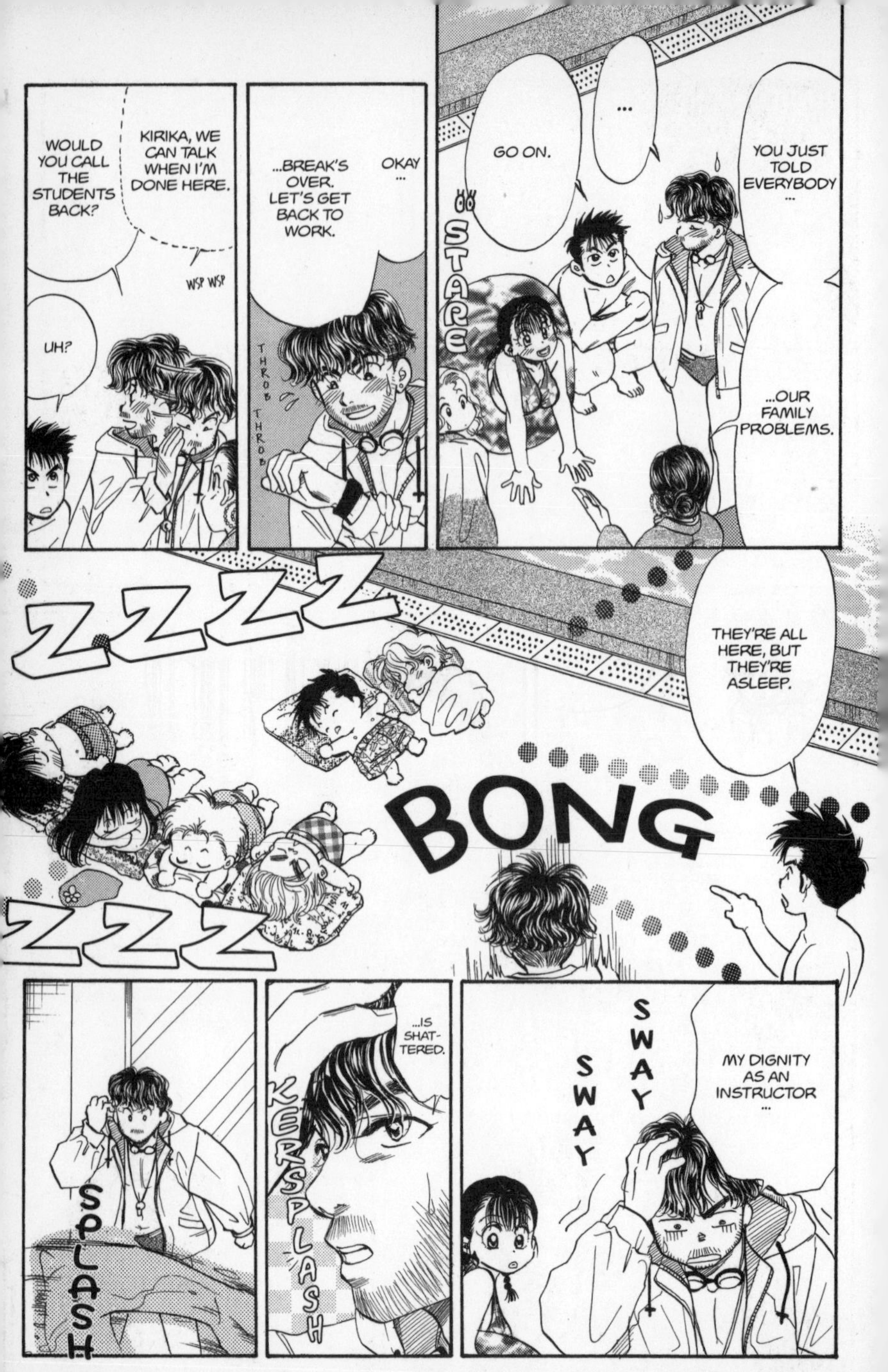
YOU JUST TOLD EVERYBODY ...
...
GO ON.
STARE
...OUR FAMILY PROBLEMS.
OKAY ...
...BREAK'S OVER. LET'S GET BACK TO WORK.
THROB THROB
KIRIKA, WE CAN TALK WHEN I'M DONE HERE.
WOULD YOU CALL THE STUDENTS BACK?
WSP WSP
UH?
THEY'RE ALL HERE, BUT THEY'RE ASLEEP.
BONG
ZZZZ
ZZZ
MY DIGNITY AS AN INSTRUCTOR ...
SWAY SWAY
...IS SHAT-TERED.
KERSPLASH
SPLASH

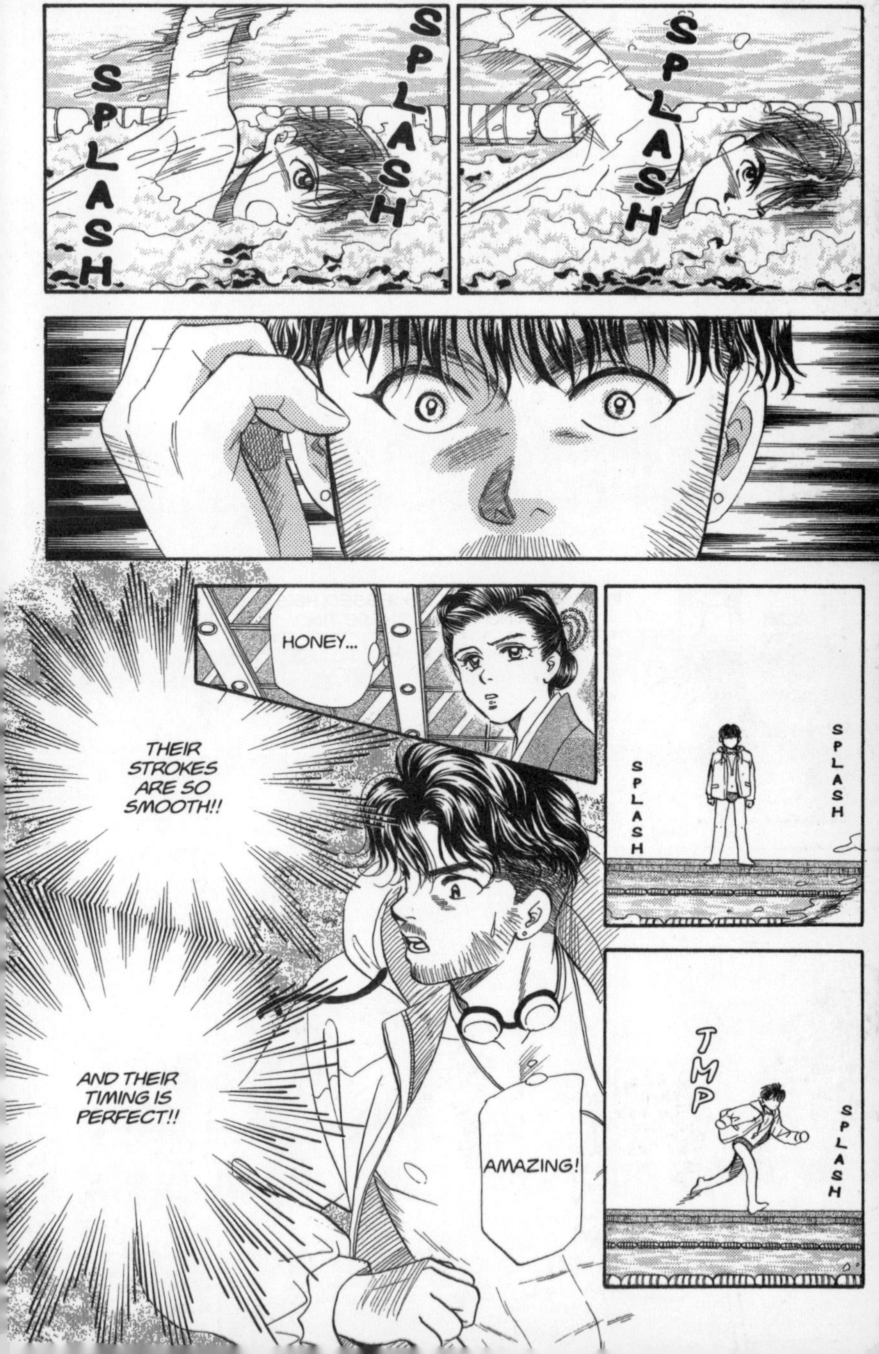
SPLASH
SPLASH
SPLASH
SPLASH
SPLASH
TMP
SPLASH
HONEY...
THEIR STROKES ARE SO SMOOTH!!
AND THEIR TIMING IS PERFECT!!
AMAZING!

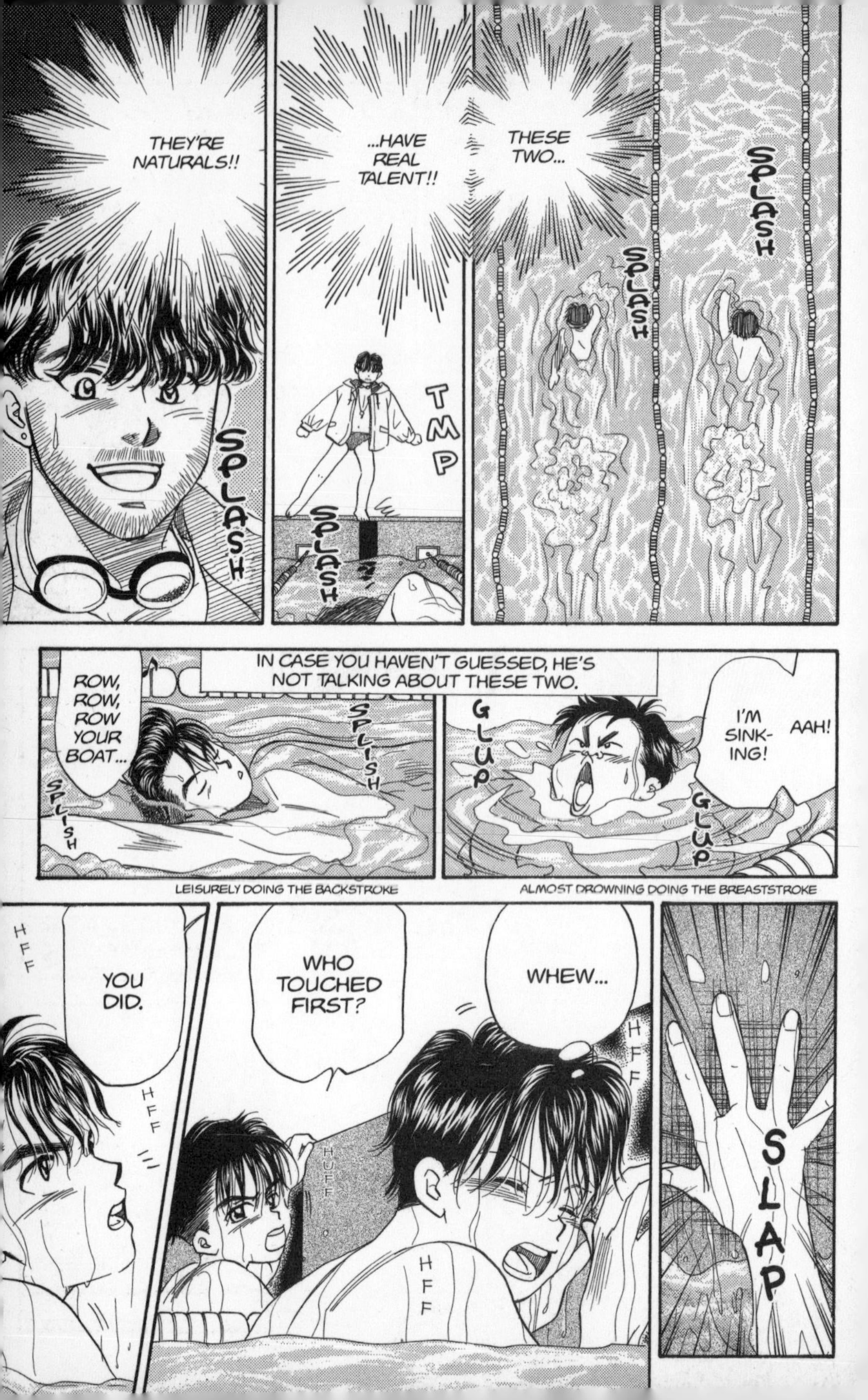
THESE TWO...
SPLASH
SPLASH
...HAVE REAL TALENT!!
TMP
SPLASH
THEY'RE NATURALS!!
SPLASH
IN CASE YOU HAVEN'T GUESSED, HE'S NOT TALKING ABOUT THESE TWO.
AAH!
I'M SINKING!
GLUP
GLUP
ALMOST DROWNING DOING THE BREASTSTROKE
ROW, ROW, ROW YOUR BOAT...
SPLISH
SPLISH
LEISURELY DOING THE BACKSTROKE
SLAP
WHEW...
HFF
WHO TOUCHED FIRST?
HUFF
HFF
YOU DID.
HFF
HFF

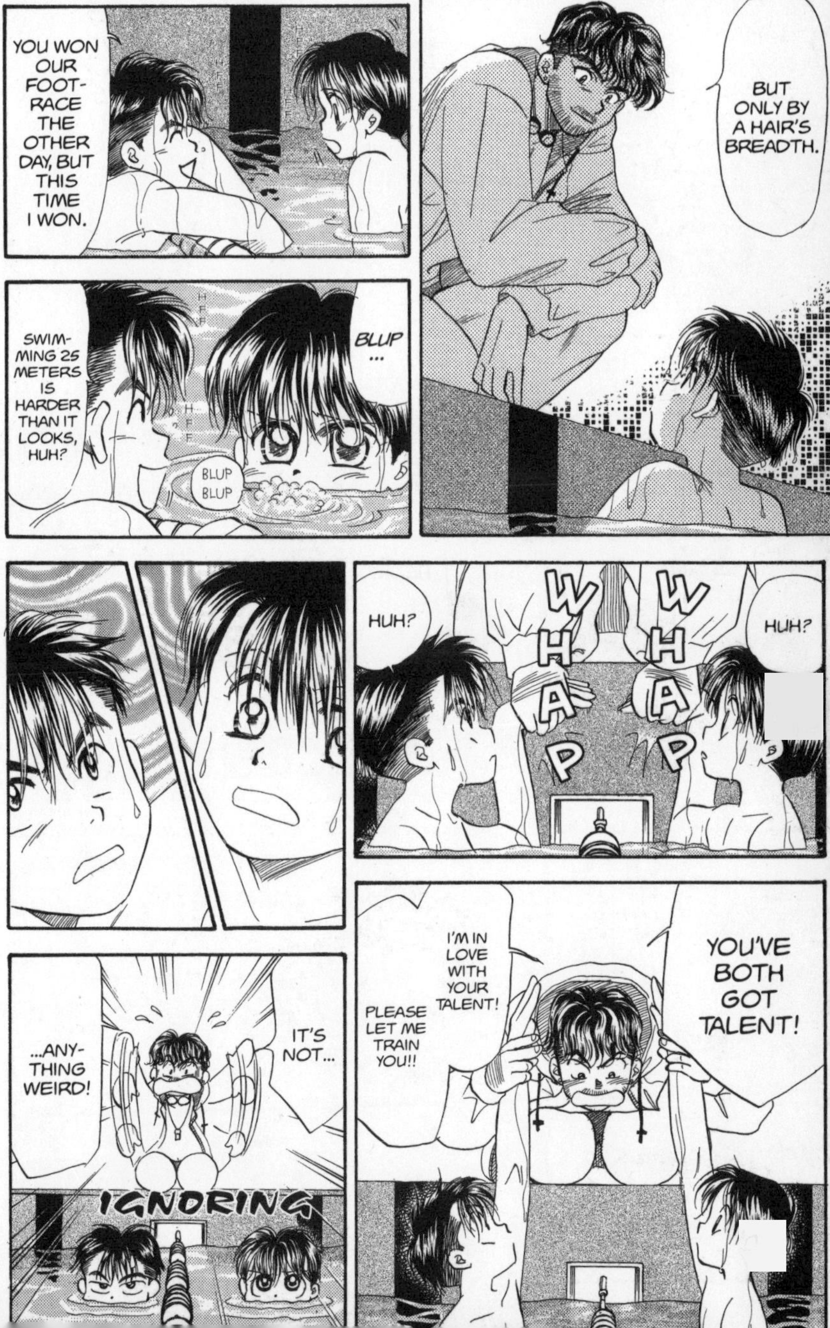
BUT ONLY BY A HAIR'S BREADTH.
YOU WON OUR FOOT-RACE THE OTHER DAY, BUT THIS TIME I WON.
BLUP...
SWIMMING 25 METERS IS HARDER THAN IT LOOKS, HUH?
BLUP BLUP
HUH?
WHAP
WHAP
HUH?
YOU'VE BOTH GOT TALENT!
I'M IN LOVE WITH YOUR TALENT!
PLEASE LET ME TRAIN YOU!!
IT'S NOT...
...ANY-THING WEIRD!
IGNORING

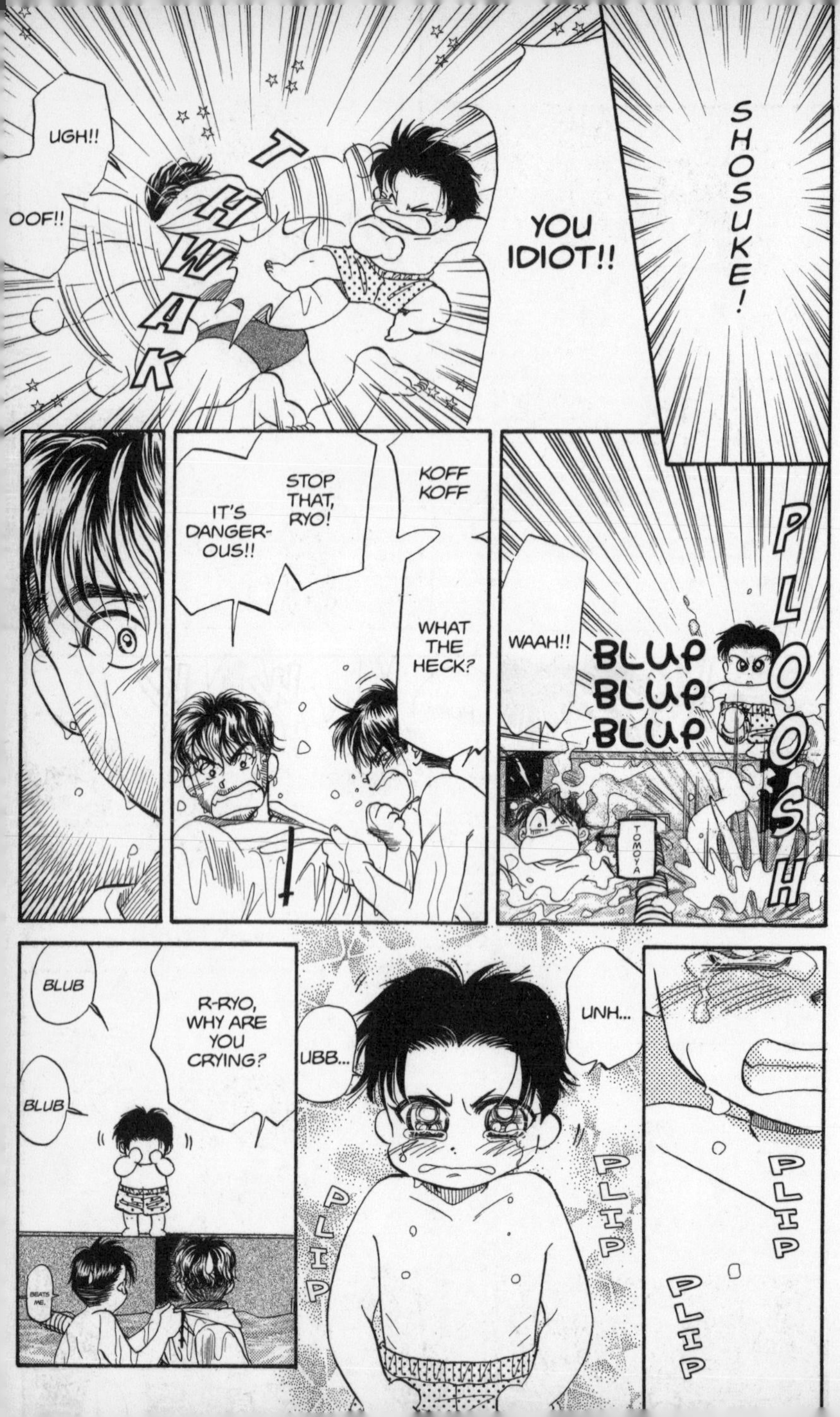
SHOSUKE!
YOU IDIOT!!
THWAK
UGH!!
OOF!!
PLOOOSH
BLUP BLUP BLUP
WAAH!!
TOMOYA
KOFF KOFF
WHAT THE HECK?
STOP THAT, RYO!
IT'S DANGER-OUS!!
PLIP
UNH...
UBB...
PLIP
PLIP
PLIP
R-RYO, WHY ARE YOU CRYING?
BLUB
BLUB
BEATS ME.

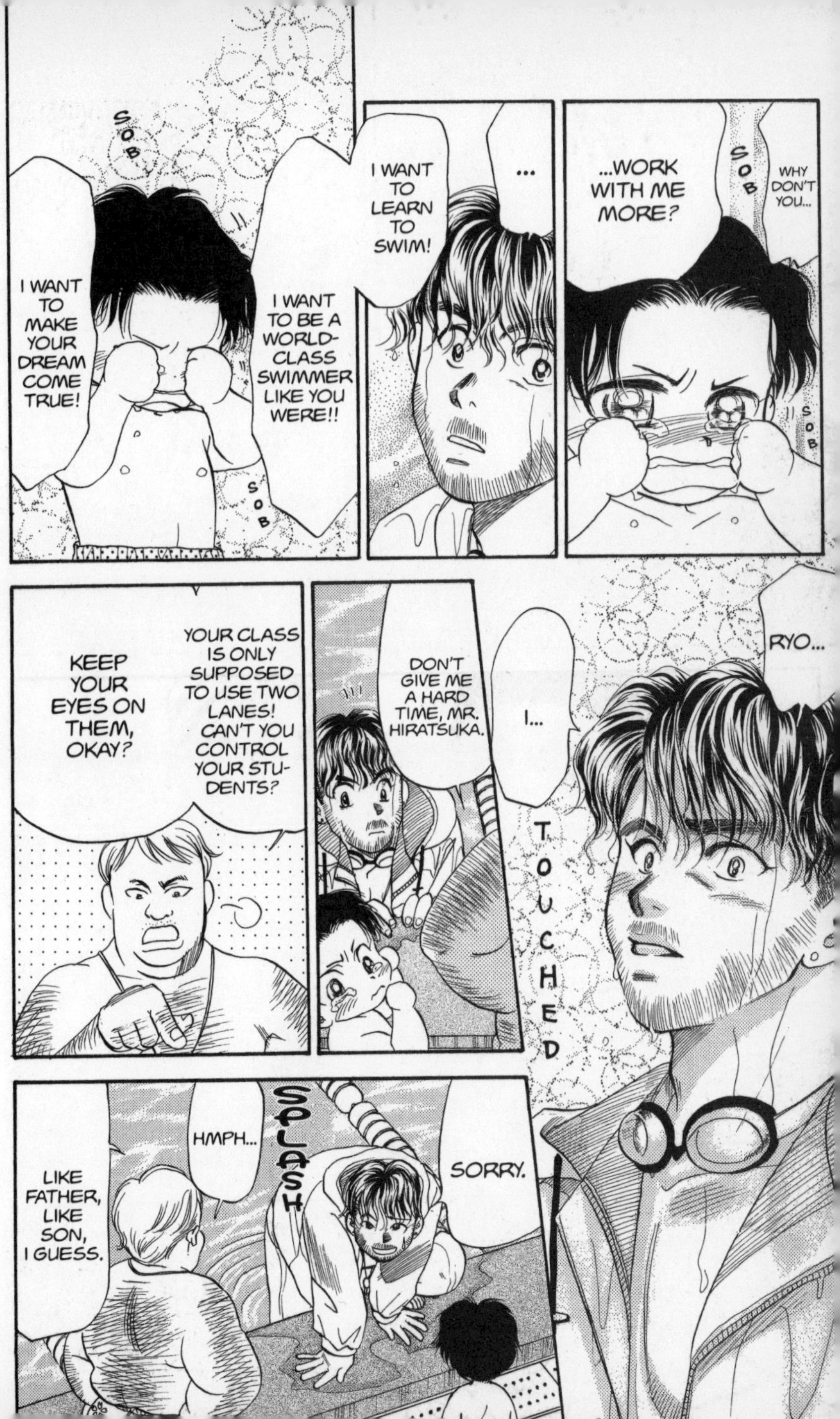
WHY DON'T YOU...
SOB
...WORK WITH ME MORE?
SOB
...
I WANT TO LEARN TO SWIM!
I WANT TO BE A WORLD-CLASS SWIMMER LIKE YOU WERE!!
SOB
I WANT TO MAKE YOUR DREAM COME TRUE!
SOB
RYO...
I...
TOUCHED
DON'T GIVE ME A HARD TIME, MR. HIRATSUKA.
YOUR CLASS IS ONLY SUPPOSED TO USE TWO LANES! CAN'T YOU CONTROL YOUR STUDENTS?
KEEP YOUR EYES ON THEM, OKAY?
SORRY.
SPLASH
HMPH...
LIKE FATHER, LIKE SON, I GUESS.

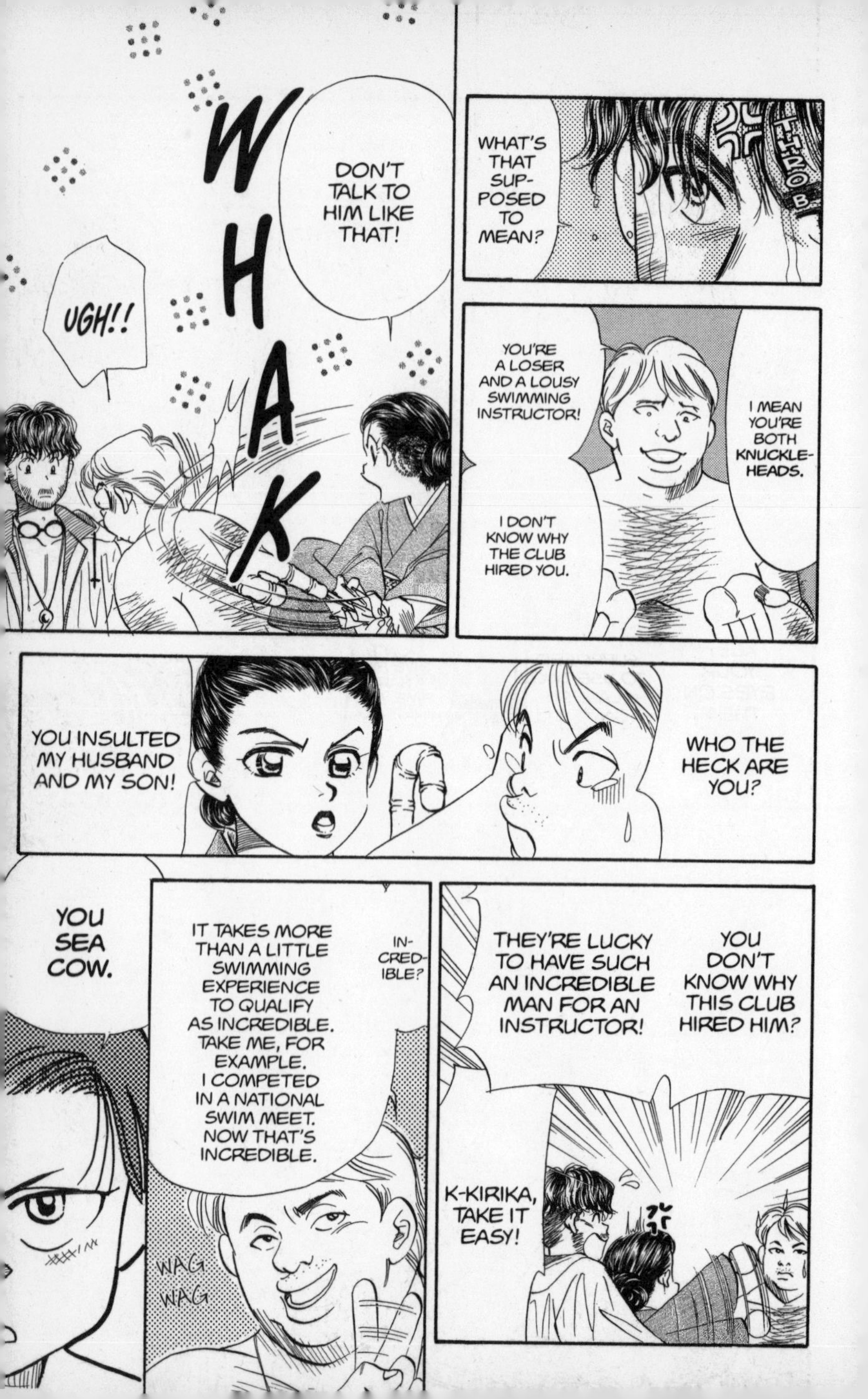
WHAT'S THAT SUP-POSED TO MEAN?
YOU'RE A LOSER AND A LOUSY SWIMMING INSTRUCTOR!
I MEAN YOU'RE BOTH KNUCKLE-HEADS.
I DON'T KNOW WHY THE CLUB HIRED YOU.
DON'T TALK TO HIM LIKE THAT!
WHAK
UGH!!
WHO THE HECK ARE YOU?
YOU INSULTED MY HUSBAND AND MY SON!
YOU DON'T KNOW WHY THIS CLUB HIRED HIM?
THEY'RE LUCKY TO HAVE SUCH AN INCREDIBLE MAN FOR AN INSTRUCTOR!
K-KIRIKA, TAKE IT EASY!
IN-CRED-IBLE?
IT TAKES MORE THAN A LITTLE SWIMMING EXPERIENCE TO QUALIFY AS INCREDIBLE. TAKE ME, FOR EXAMPLE. I COMPETED IN A NATIONAL SWIM MEET. NOW THAT'S INCREDIBLE.
WAG WAG
YOU SEA COW.

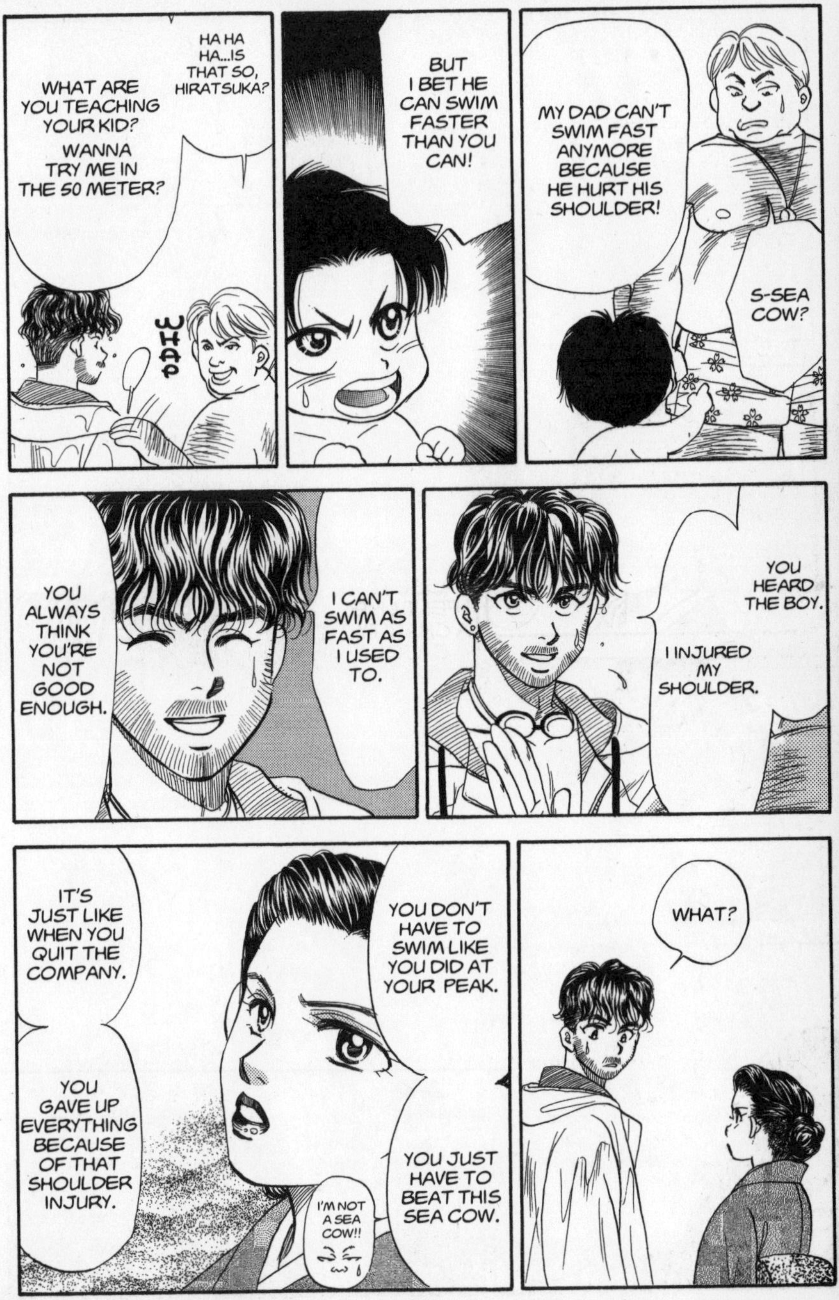
MY DAD CAN'T SWIM FAST ANYMORE BECAUSE HE HURT HIS SHOULDER!
S-SEA COW?
BUT I BET HE CAN SWIM FASTER THAN YOU CAN!
HA HA HA...IS THAT SO, HIRATSUKA?
WHAT ARE YOU TEACHING YOUR KID?
WANNA TRY ME IN THE 50 METER?
WHAP
YOU HEARD THE BOY.
I INJURED MY SHOULDER.
I CAN'T SWIM AS FAST AS I USED TO.
YOU ALWAYS THINK YOU'RE NOT GOOD ENOUGH.
WHAT?
YOU DON'T HAVE TO SWIM LIKE YOU DID AT YOUR PEAK.
IT'S JUST LIKE WHEN YOU QUIT THE COMPANY.
YOU JUST HAVE TO BEAT THIS SEA COW.
I'M NOT A SEA COW!!
YOU GAVE UP EVERYTHING BECAUSE OF THAT SHOULDER INJURY.

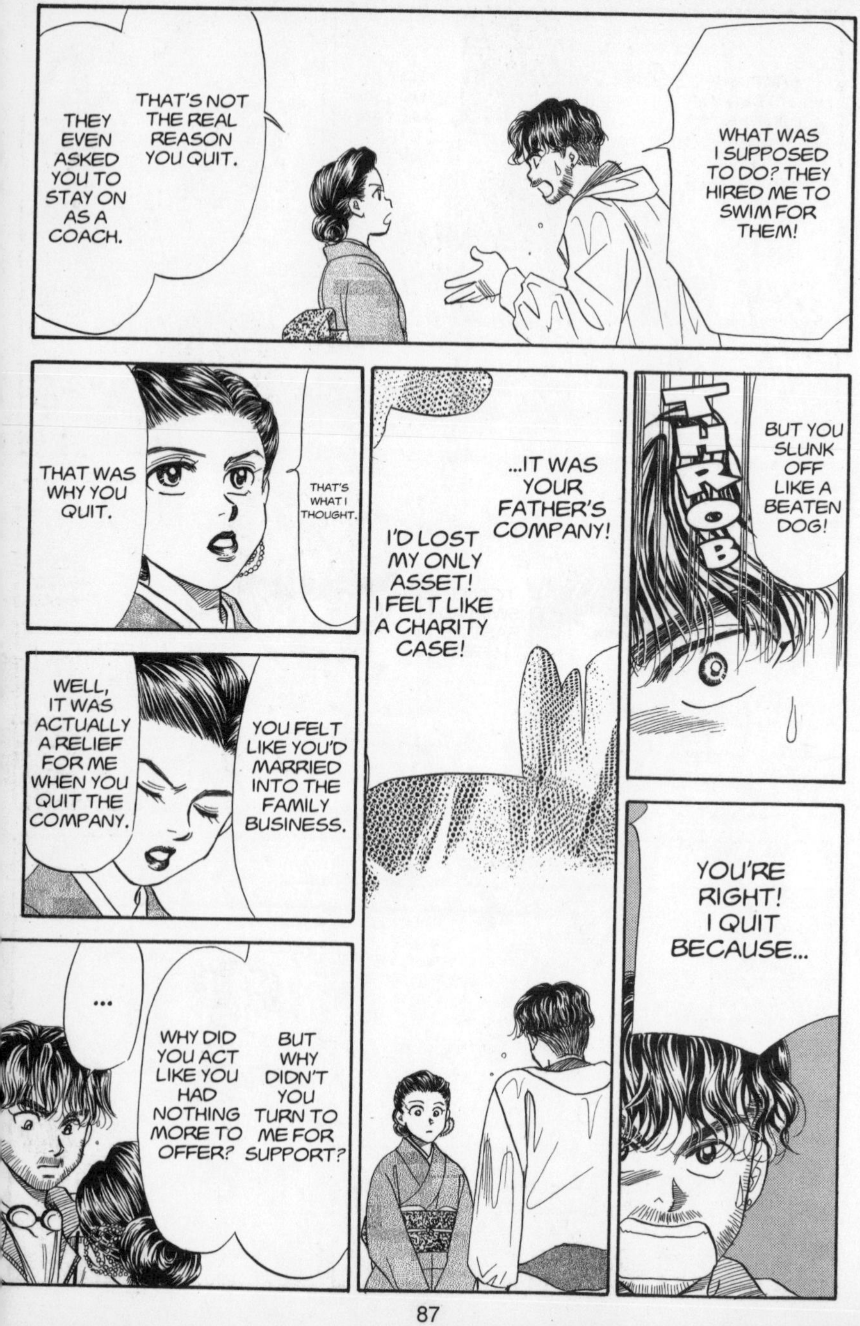
WHAT WAS I SUPPOSED TO DO? THEY HIRED ME TO SWIM FOR THEM!
THAT'S NOT THE REAL REASON YOU QUIT.
THEY EVEN ASKED YOU TO STAY ON AS A COACH.
THROB
BUT YOU SLUNK OFF LIKE A BEATEN DOG!
YOU'RE RIGHT! I QUIT BECAUSE...
...IT WAS YOUR FATHER'S COMPANY!
I'D LOST MY ONLY ASSET! I FELT LIKE A CHARITY CASE!
THAT'S WHAT I THOUGHT.
THAT WAS WHY YOU QUIT.
YOU FELT LIKE YOU'D MARRIED INTO THE FAMILY BUSINESS.
WELL, IT WAS ACTUALLY A RELIEF FOR ME WHEN YOU QUIT THE COMPANY.
BUT WHY DIDN'T YOU TURN TO ME FOR SUPPORT?
WHY DID YOU ACT LIKE YOU HAD NOTHING MORE TO OFFER?
...

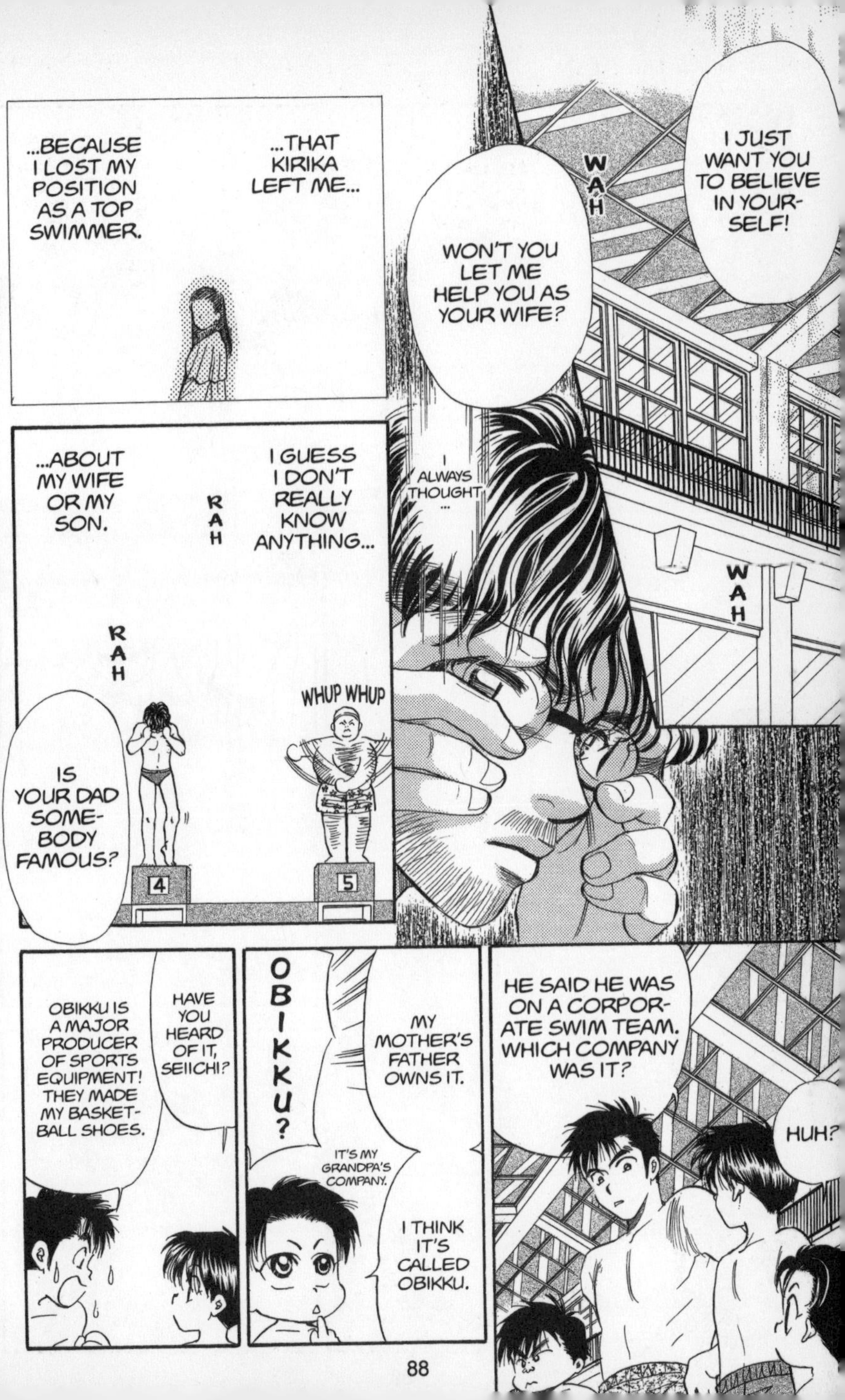
I JUST WANT YOU TO BELIEVE IN YOURSELF!
WAH
WON'T YOU LET ME HELP YOU AS YOUR WIFE?
I ALWAYS THOUGHT...
WAH
...THAT KIRIKA LEFT ME...
...BECAUSE I LOST MY POSITION AS A TOP SWIMMER.
I GUESS I DON'T REALLY KNOW ANYTHING...
RAH
...ABOUT MY WIFE OR MY SON.
WHUP WHUP
RAH
IS YOUR DAD SOMEBODY FAMOUS?
HUH?
HE SAID HE WAS ON A CORPORATE SWIM TEAM. WHICH COMPANY WAS IT?
MY MOTHER'S FATHER OWNS IT.
OBIKKU?
IT'S MY GRANDPA'S COMPANY.
I THINK IT'S CALLED OBIKKU.
HAVE YOU HEARD OF IT, SEIICHI?
OBIKKU IS A MAJOR PRODUCER OF SPORTS EQUIPMENT! THEY MADE MY BASKETBALL SHOES.

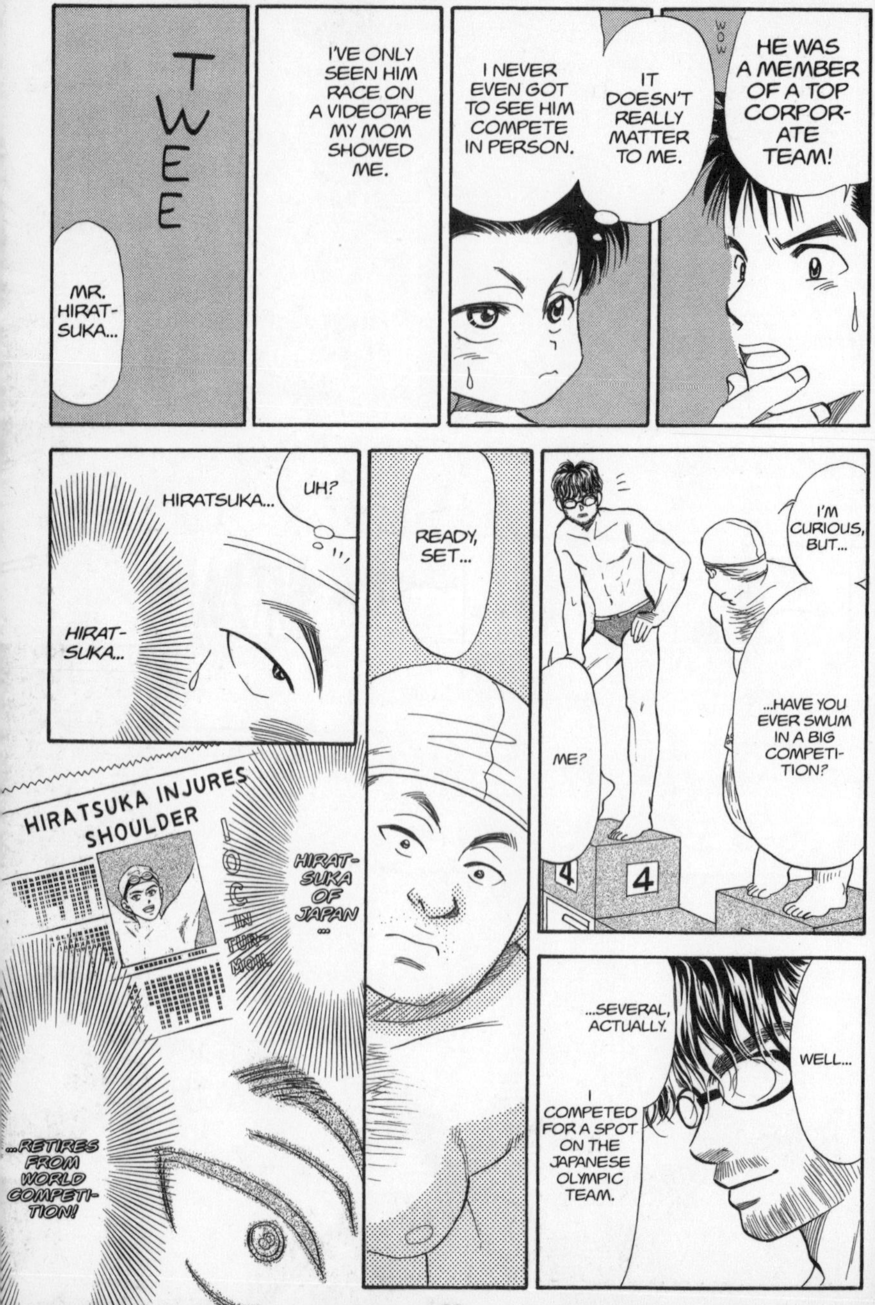
WOW
HE WAS A MEMBER OF A TOP CORPORATE TEAM!
IT DOESN'T REALLY MATTER TO ME.
I NEVER EVEN GOT TO SEE HIM COMPETE IN PERSON.
I'VE ONLY SEEN HIM RACE ON A VIDEOTAPE MY MOM SHOWED ME.
TWEE
MR. HIRATSUKA...
I'M CURIOUS, BUT...
...HAVE YOU EVER SWUM IN A BIG COMPETITION?
ME?
WELL...
...SEVERAL, ACTUALLY.
I COMPETED FOR A SPOT ON THE JAPANESE OLYMPIC TEAM.
READY, SET...
UH?
HIRATSUKA...
HIRATSUKA...
HIRATSUKA INJURES SHOULDER
HIRATSUKA OF JAPAN...
...RETIRES FROM WORLD COMPETITION!

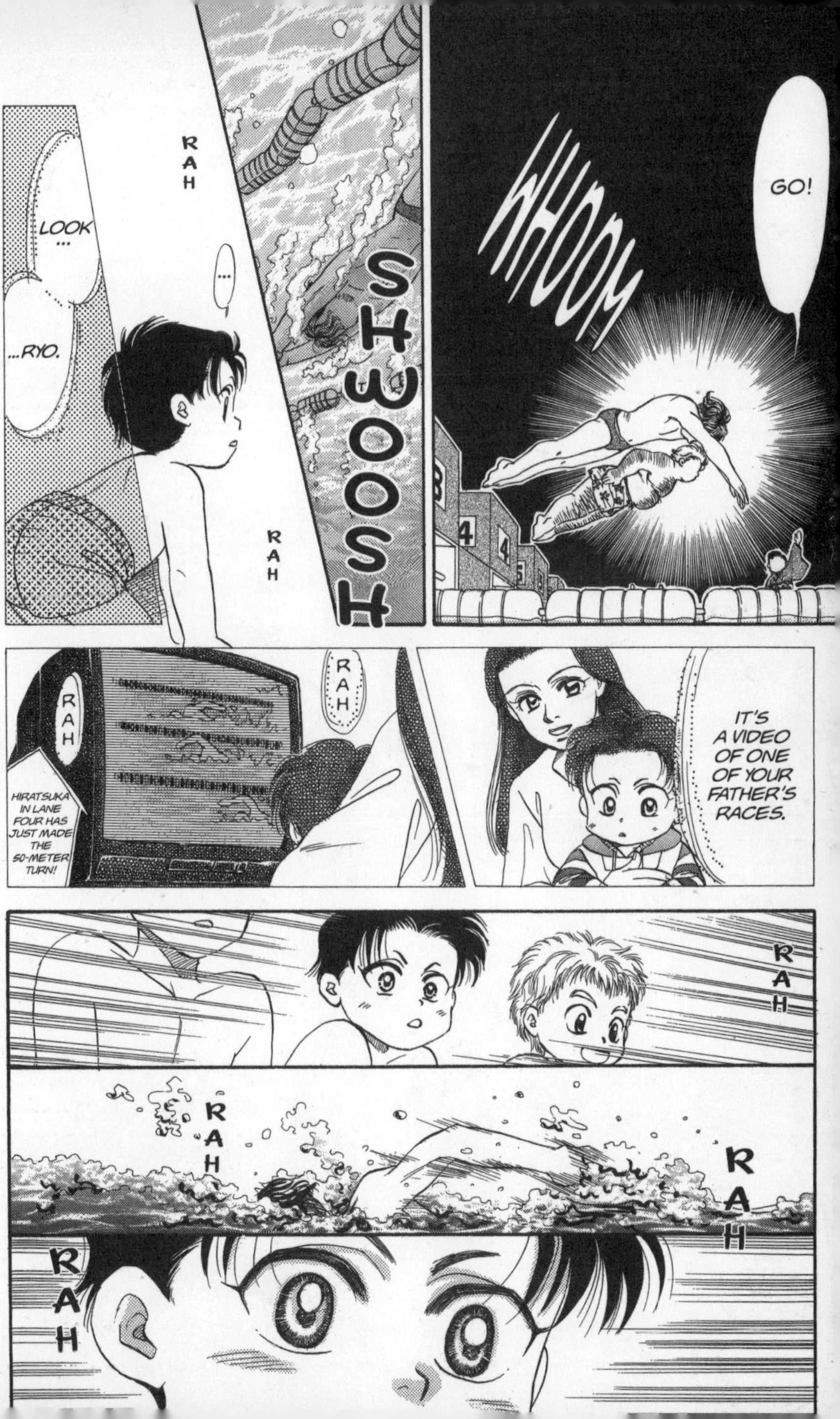
GO!
KHOOM
SHWOOSH
...
RAH
RAH
LOOK...
...RYO.
IT'S A VIDEO OF ONE OF YOUR FATHER'S RACES.
RAH
RAH
HIRATSUKA IN LANE FOUR HAS JUST MADE THE 50-METER TURN!
RAH
RAH
RAH
RAH

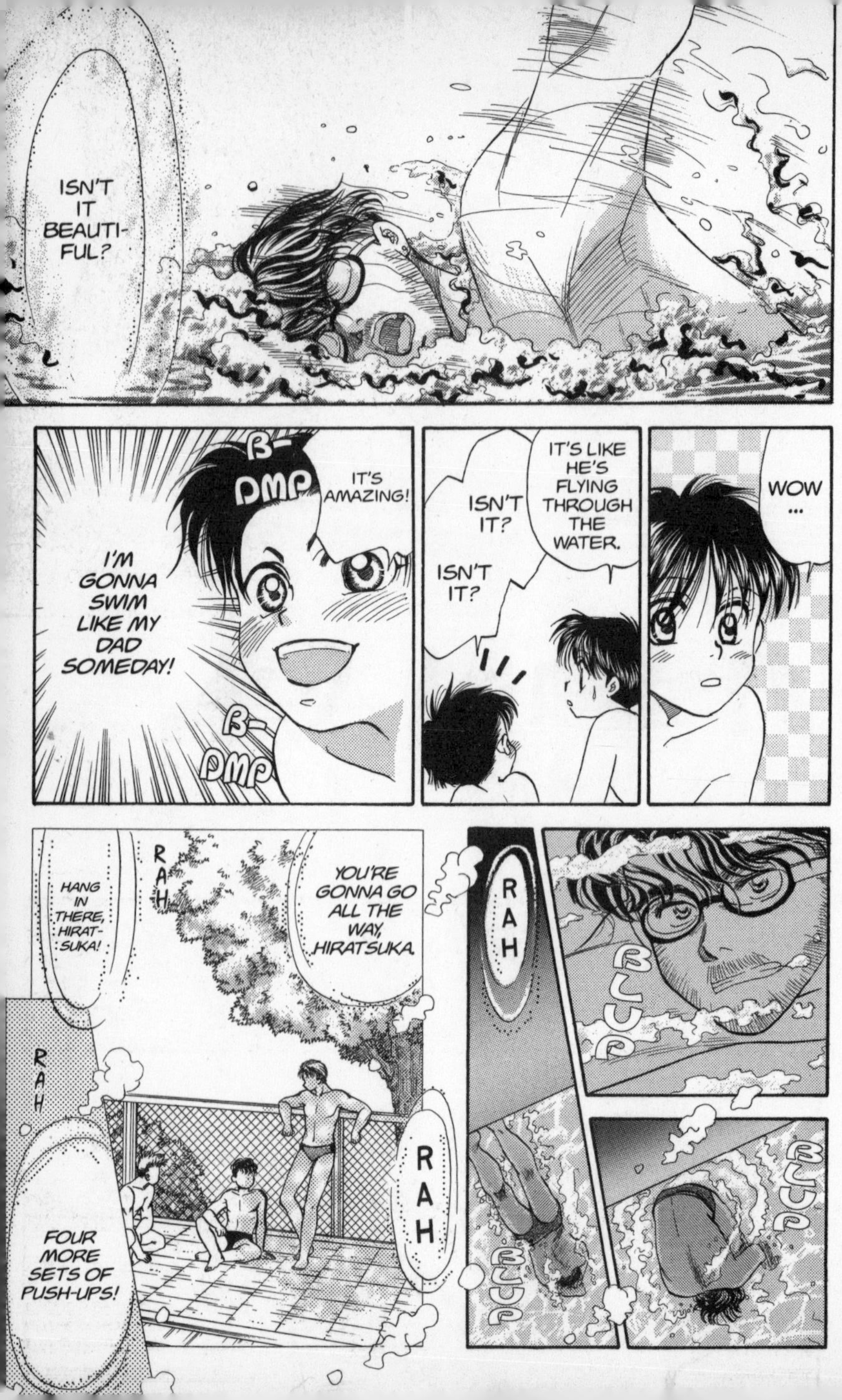
ISN'T IT BEAUTIFUL?
WOW ...
IT'S LIKE HE'S FLYING THROUGH THE WATER.
ISN'T IT?
ISN'T IT?
B-DMP
IT'S AMAZING!
I'M GONNA SWIM LIKE MY DAD SOMEDAY!
B-DMP
RAH
BLUP
BLUP
BLUP
YOU'RE GONNA GO ALL THE WAY, HIRATSUKA.
RAH
HANG IN THERE, HIRATSUKA!
RAH
RAH
FOUR MORE SETS OF PUSH-UPS!

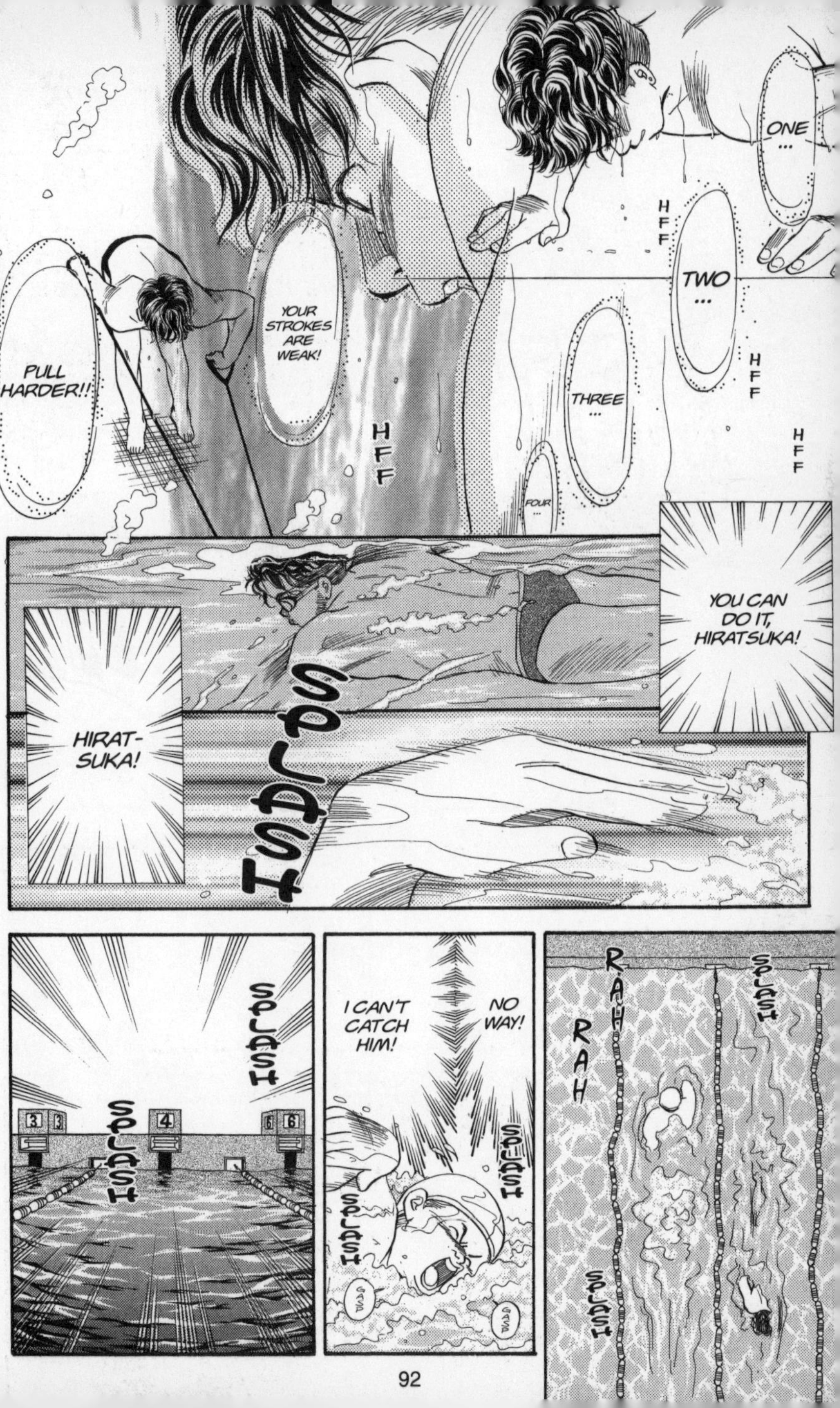
ONE ...
HFF
TWO ...
HFF
THREE ...
HFF
FOUR ...
HFF
YOUR STROKES ARE WEAK!
PULL HARDER!!
YOU CAN DO IT, HIRATSUKA!
SPLASH
HIRAT-SUKA!
SPLASH
RAH
RAH
SPLASH
NO WAY!
I CAN'T CATCH HIM!
SPLASH
SPLASH
GASP
GASP
SPLASH
SPLASH

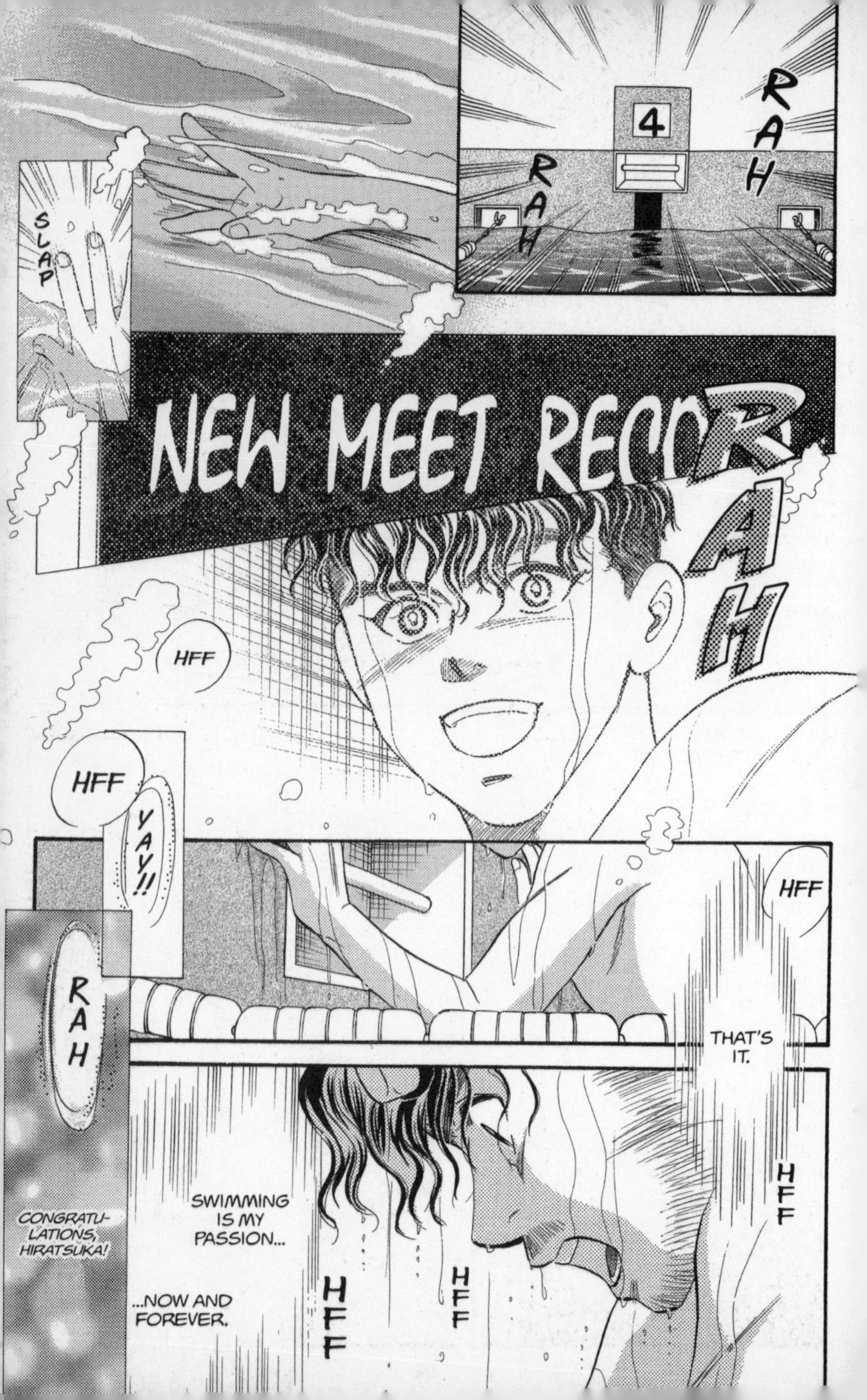
RAH
RAH
SLAP
NEW MEET RECO
RAH
HFF
HFF
YAY!!
HFF
THAT'S IT.
RAH
HFF
SWIMMING IS MY PASSION...
HFF
HFF
...NOW AND FOREVER.
CONGRATU-LATIONS, HIRATSUKA!

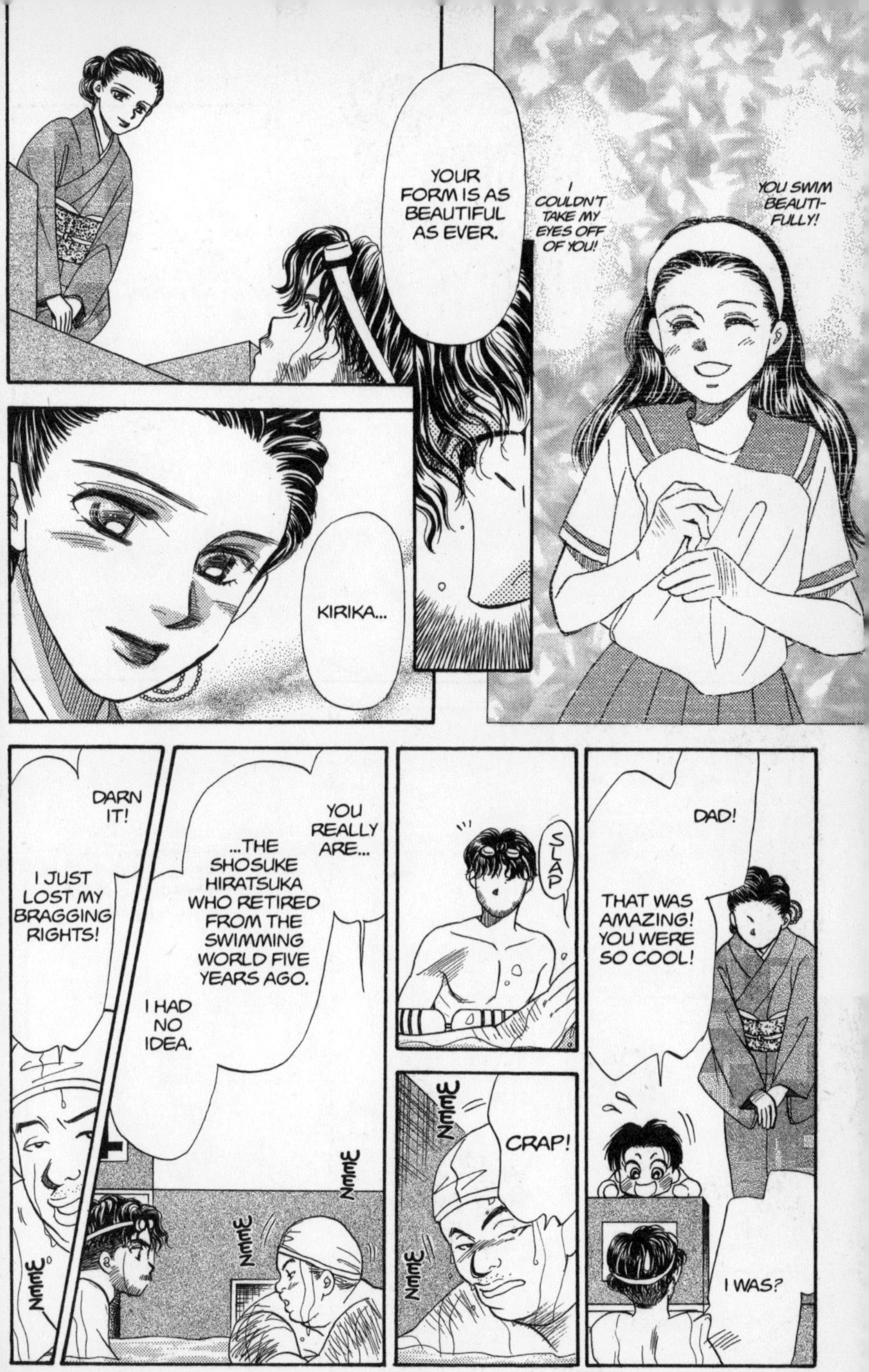
YOU SWIM BEAUTI-FULLY!
I COULDN'T TAKE MY EYES OFF OF YOU!
YOUR FORM IS AS BEAUTIFUL AS EVER.
KIRIKA...
DAD!
THAT WAS AMAZING! YOU WERE SO COOL!
I WAS?
SLAP
CRAP!
WEEN
WEEN
YOU REALLY ARE...
...THE SHOSUKE HIRATSUKA WHO RETIRED FROM THE SWIMMING WORLD FIVE YEARS AGO.
I HAD NO IDEA.
WEEEN
WEEN
DARN IT!
I JUST LOST MY BRAGGING RIGHTS!
WEEEN

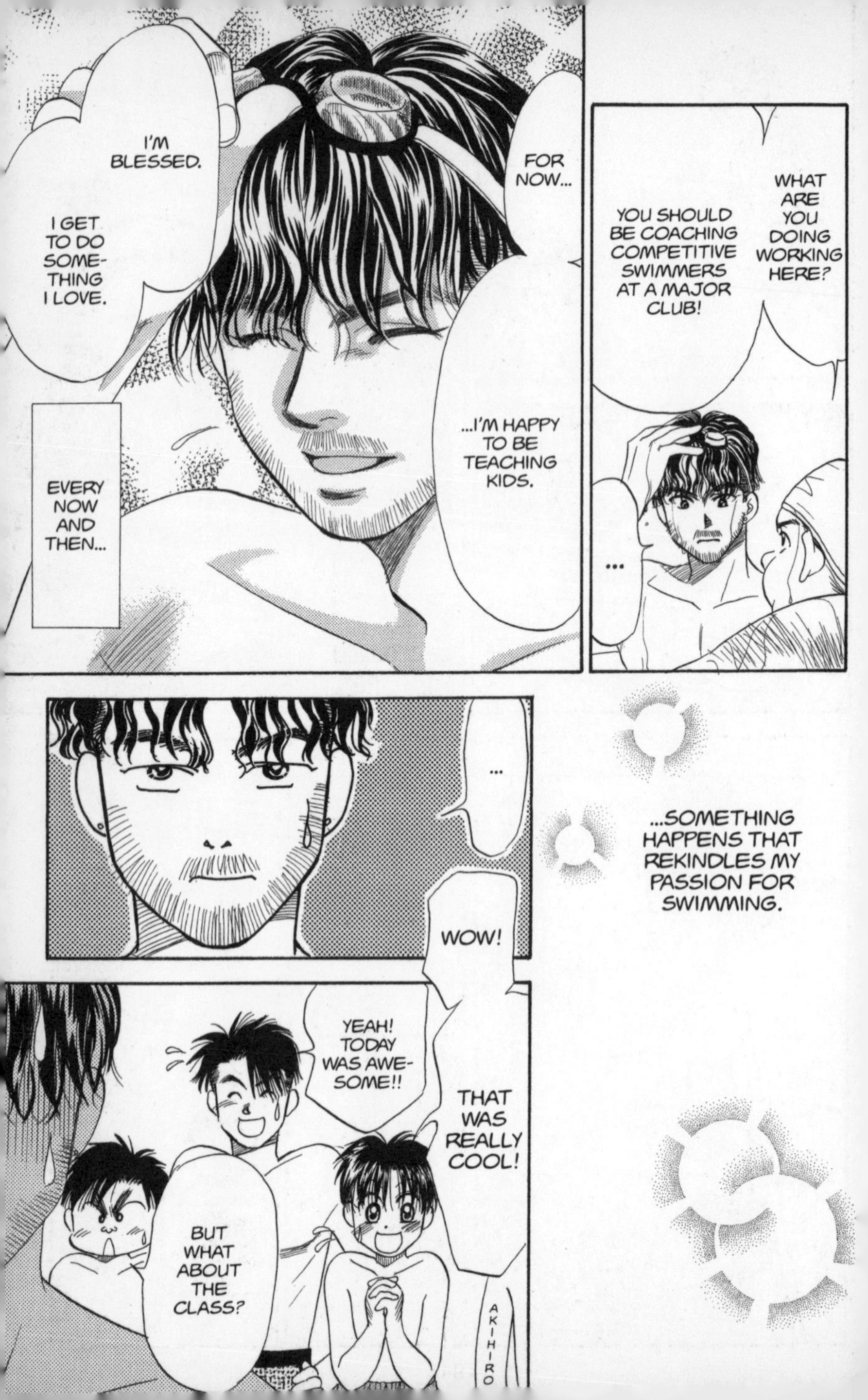
WHAT ARE YOU DOING WORKING HERE?
YOU SHOULD BE COACHING COMPETITIVE SWIMMERS AT A MAJOR CLUB!
...
FOR NOW...
...I'M HAPPY TO BE TEACHING KIDS.
I'M BLESSED.
I GET TO DO SOME-THING I LOVE.
EVERY NOW AND THEN...
...SOMETHING HAPPENS THAT REKINDLES MY PASSION FOR SWIMMING.
...
WOW!
THAT WAS REALLY COOL!
YEAH! TODAY WAS AWE-SOME!!
BUT WHAT ABOUT THE CLASS?
AKIHIRO

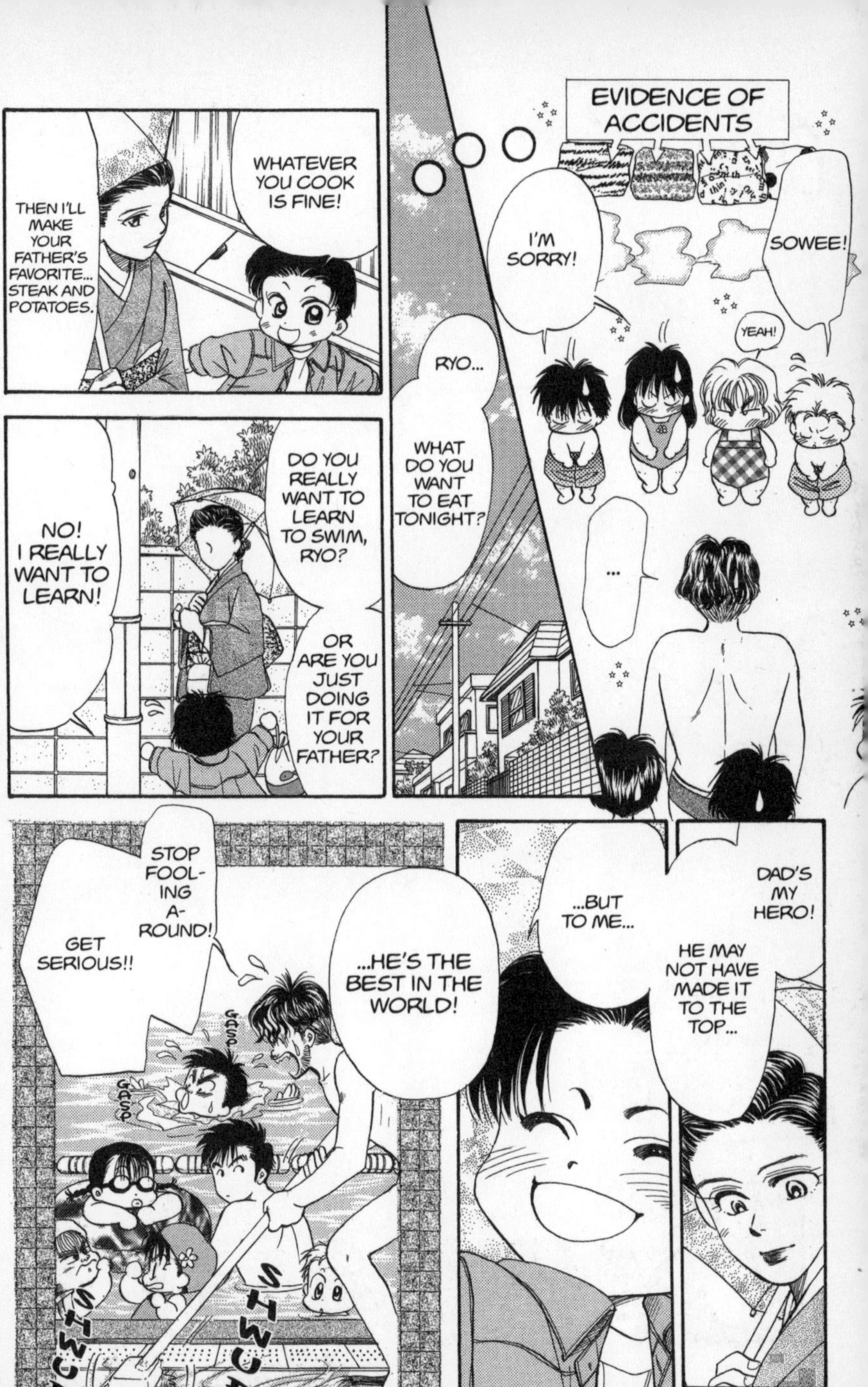
EVIDENCE OF ACCIDENTS
SOWEE!
YEAH!
I'M SORRY!
...
RYO...
WHAT DO YOU WANT TO EAT TONIGHT?
WHATEVER YOU COOK IS FINE!
THEN I'LL MAKE YOUR FATHER'S FAVORITE... STEAK AND POTATOES.
DO YOU REALLY WANT TO LEARN TO SWIM, RYO?
OR ARE YOU JUST DOING IT FOR YOUR FATHER?
NO! I REALLY WANT TO LEARN!
DAD'S MY HERO!
HE MAY NOT HAVE MADE IT TO THE TOP...
...BUT TO ME...
...HE'S THE BEST IN THE WORLD!
STOP FOOLING-AROUND!
GET SERIOUS!!
GASP
GASP
SHWUFF
SHWUFF

Chapter 83 / The End

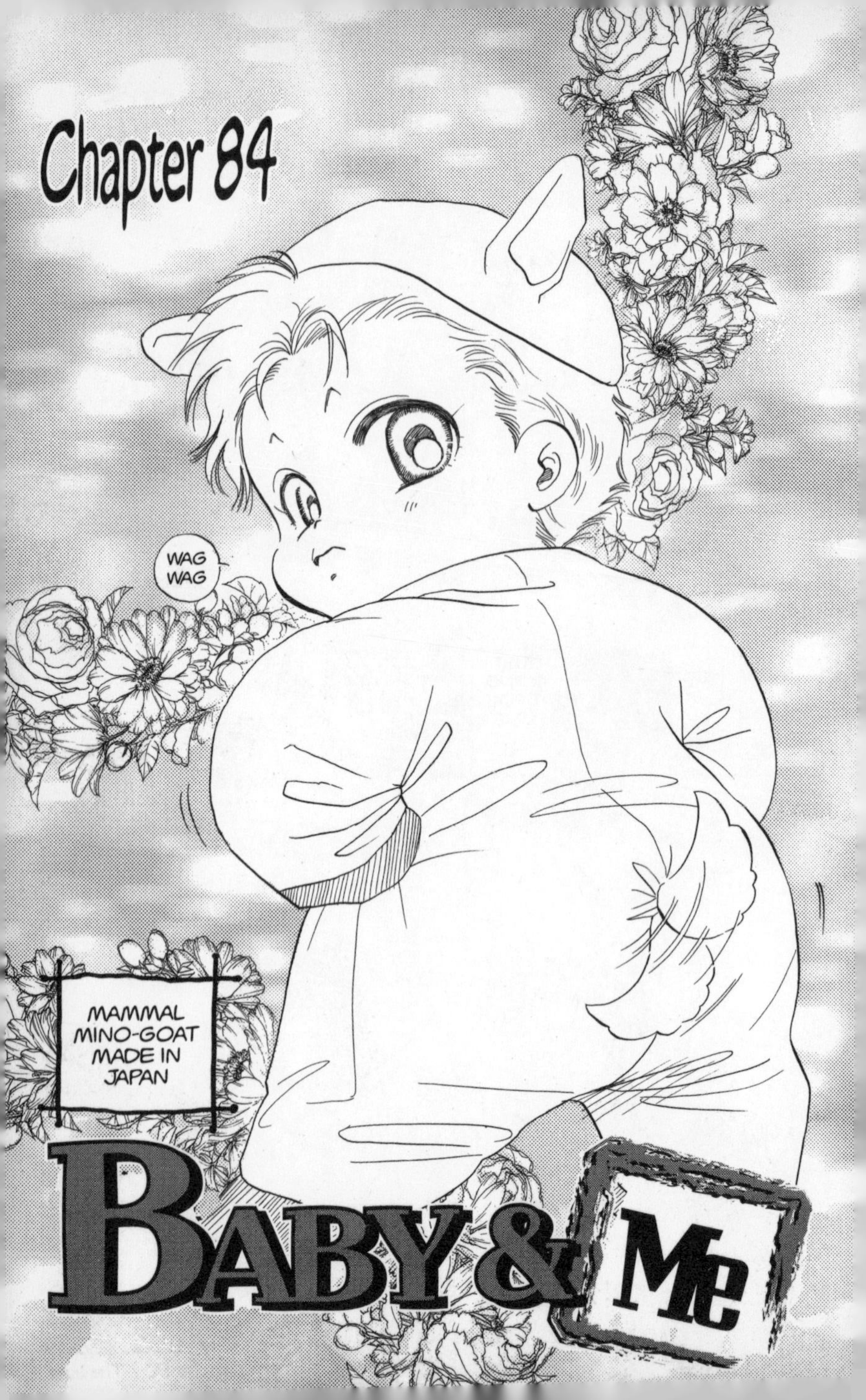
Chapter 84
WAG WAG
MAMMAL MINO-GOAT MADE IN JAPAN
BABY & Me

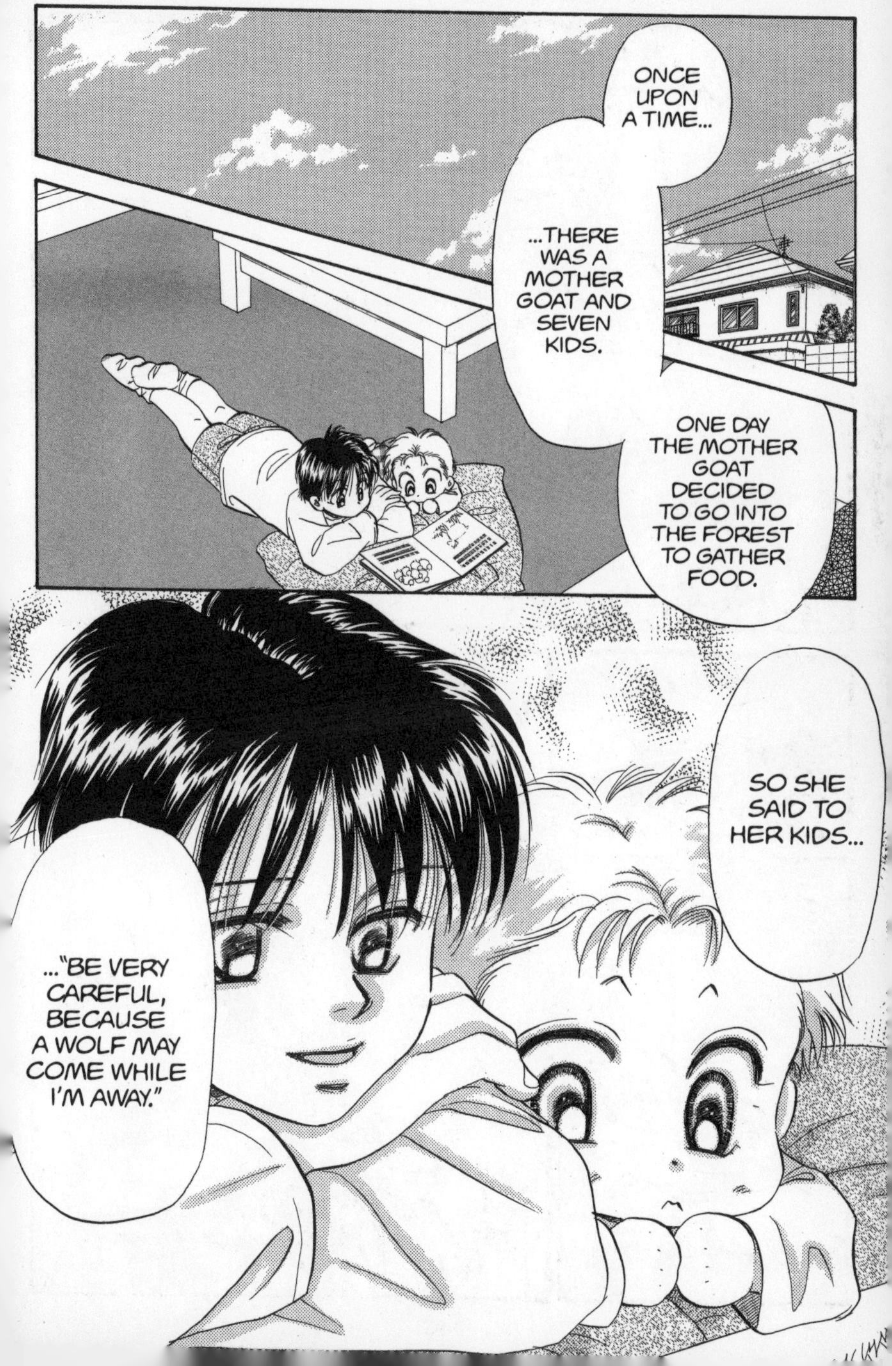
ONCE UPON A TIME...
...THERE WAS A MOTHER GOAT AND SEVEN KIDS.
ONE DAY THE MOTHER GOAT DECIDED TO GO INTO THE FOREST TO GATHER FOOD.
SO SHE SAID TO HER KIDS...
..."BE VERY CAREFUL, BECAUSE A WOLF MAY COME WHILE I'M AWAY."

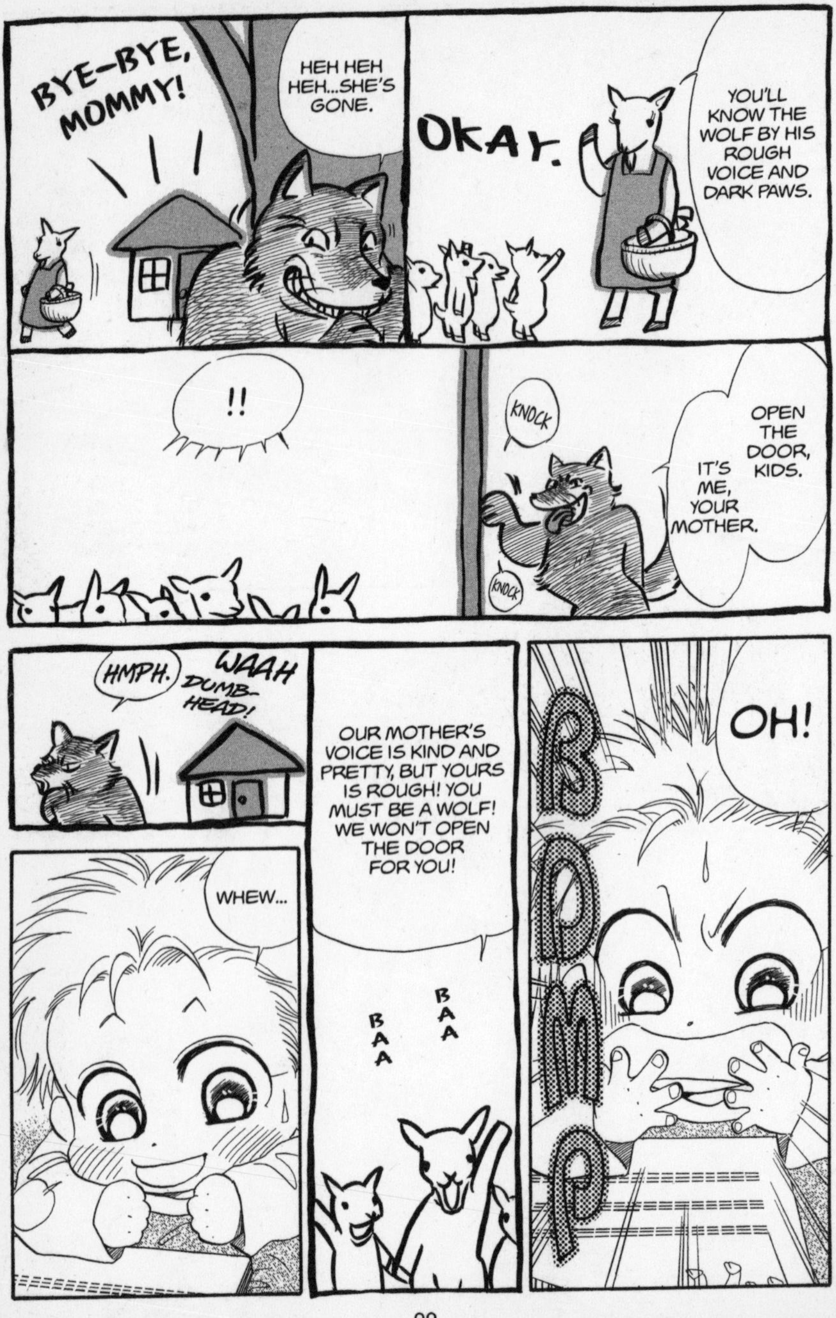

YOU'LL KNOW THE WOLF BY HIS ROUGH VOICE AND DARK PAWS.
OKAY.
HEH HEH HEH...SHE'S GONE.
BYE-BYE, MOMMY!
OPEN THE DOOR, KIDS.
IT'S ME, YOUR MOTHER.
KNOCK
KNOCK
!!
OH!
BOMP
OUR MOTHER'S VOICE IS KIND AND PRETTY, BUT YOURS IS ROUGH! YOU MUST BE A WOLF! WE WON'T OPEN THE DOOR FOR YOU!
BAA
BAA
WAAH
DUMB-HEAD!
HMPH.
WHEW...

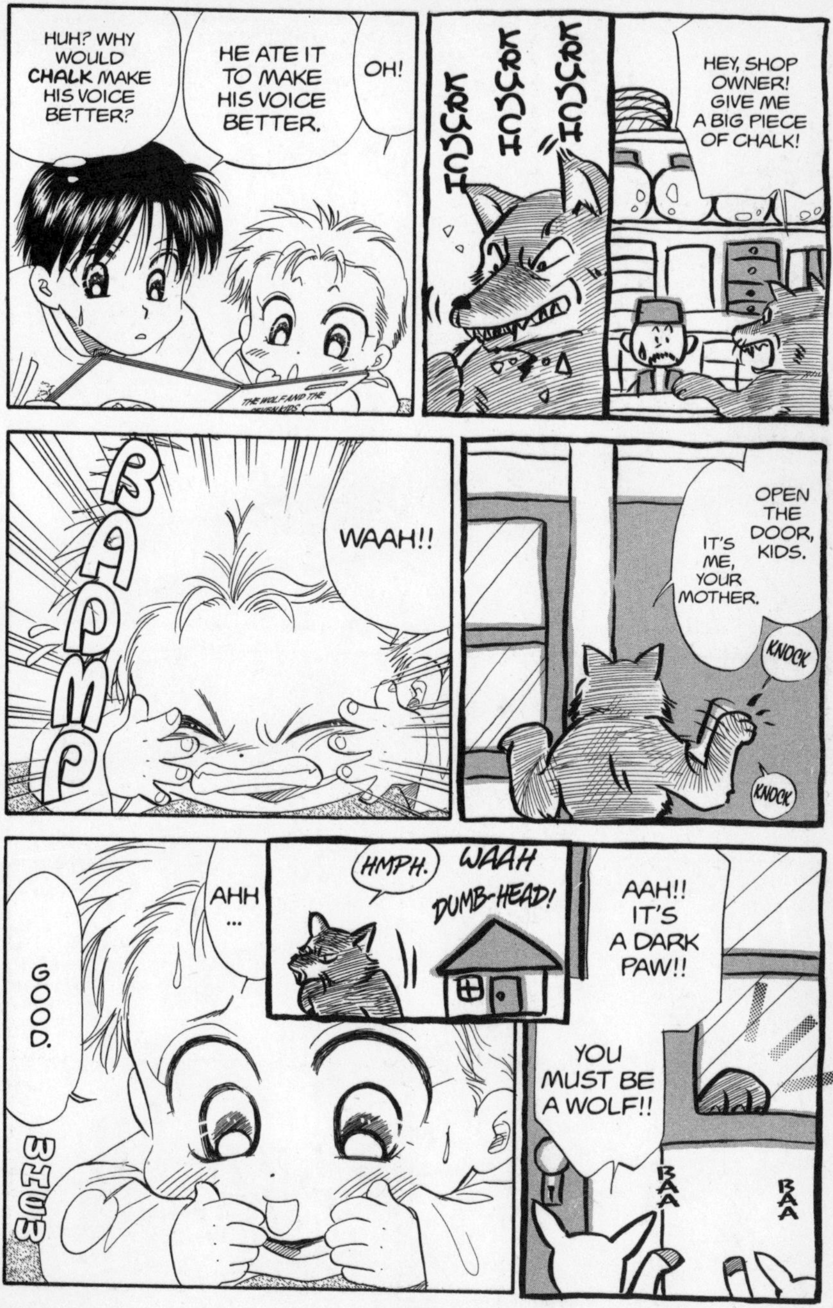
HEY, SHOP OWNER! GIVE ME A BIG PIECE OF CHALK!
KRUNCH
KRUNCH
KRUNCH
OH!
HE ATE IT TO MAKE HIS VOICE BETTER.
HUH? WHY WOULD CHALK MAKE HIS VOICE BETTER?
OPEN THE DOOR, KIDS.
IT'S ME, YOUR MOTHER.
KNOCK
KNOCK
WAAH!!
BADUMP
AAH!! IT'S A DARK PAW!!
YOU MUST BE A WOLF!!
RAA
RAA
WAAH
DUMB-HEAD!
HMPH.
AHH ...
GOOD.
WHEW

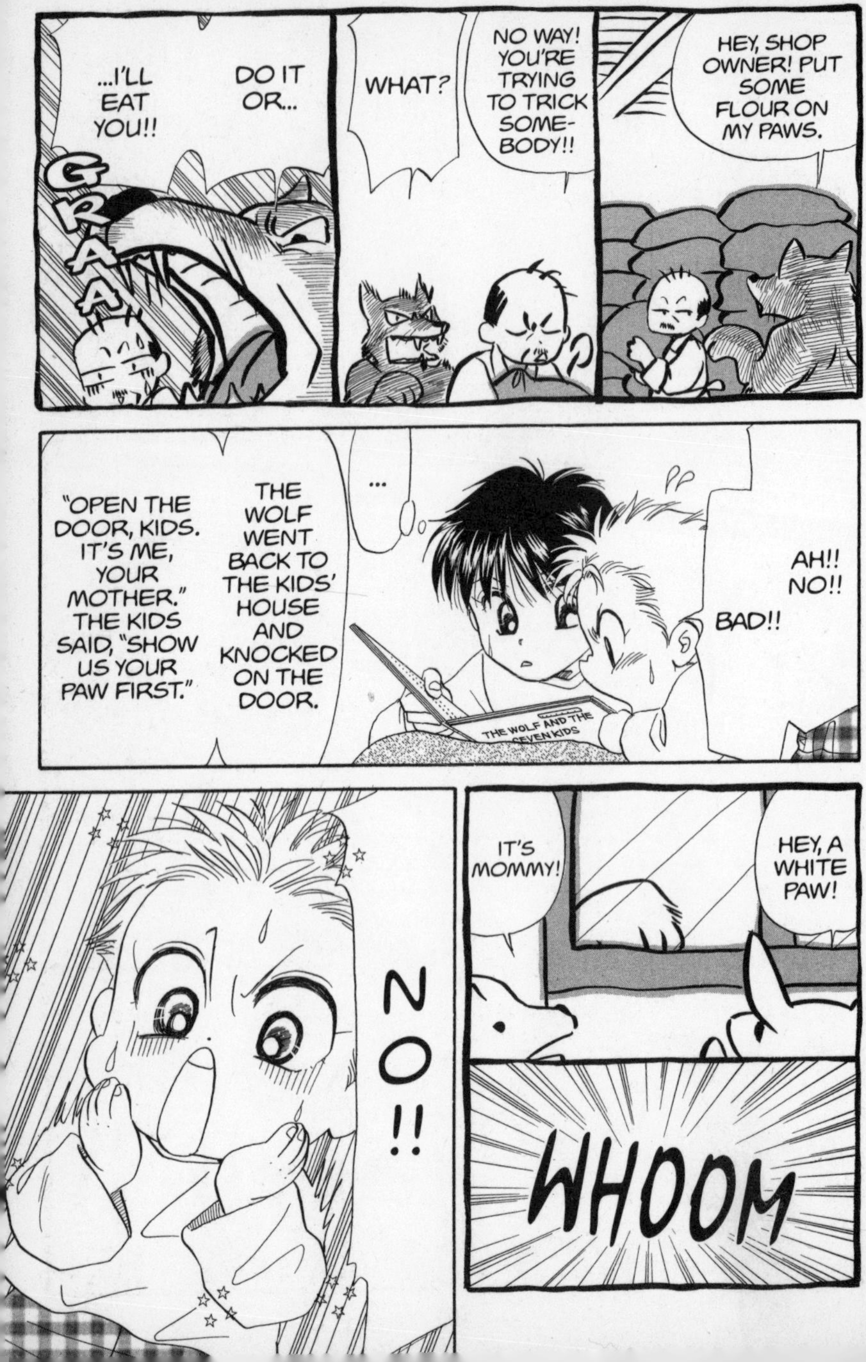
HEY, SHOP OWNER! PUT SOME FLOUR ON MY PAWS.
NO WAY! YOU'RE TRYING TO TRICK SOMEBODY!!
WHAT?
DO IT OR...
...I'LL EAT YOU!!
GRAAA
AH!! NO!!
BAD!!
...
THE WOLF WENT BACK TO THE KIDS' HOUSE AND KNOCKED ON THE DOOR.
"OPEN THE DOOR, KIDS. IT'S ME, YOUR MOTHER." THE KIDS SAID, "SHOW US YOUR PAW FIRST."
THE WOLF AND THE SEVEN KIDS
HEY, A WHITE PAW!
IT'S MOMMY!
WHOOM
NO!!

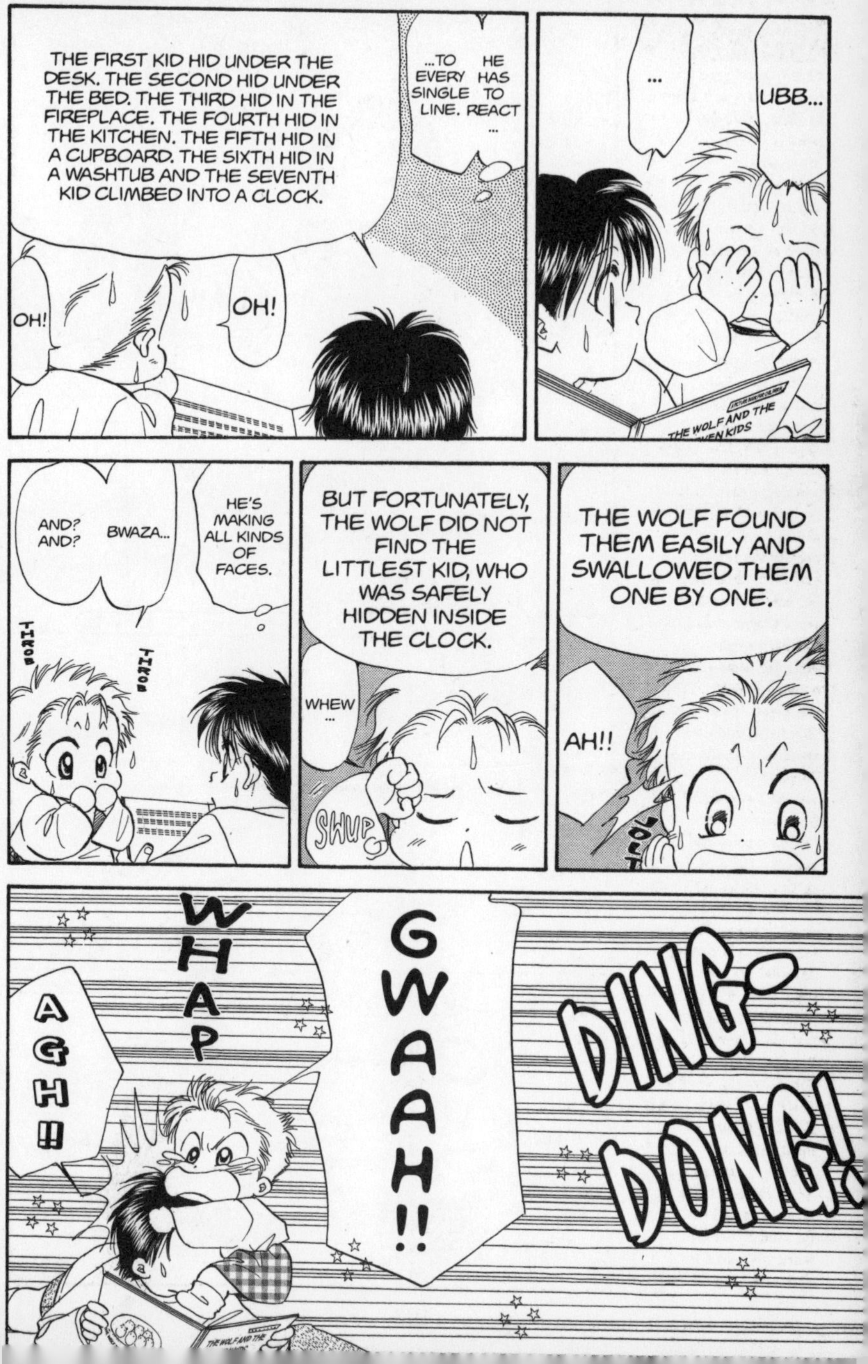
UBB...
...
HE HAS TO REACT ...
...TO EVERY SINGLE LINE.
THE FIRST KID HID UNDER THE DESK. THE SECOND HID UNDER THE BED. THE THIRD HID IN THE FIREPLACE. THE FOURTH HID IN THE KITCHEN. THE FIFTH HID IN A CUPBOARD. THE SIXTH HID IN A WASHTUB AND THE SEVENTH KID CLIMBED INTO A CLOCK.
OH!
OH!
THE WOLF FOUND THEM EASILY AND SWALLOWED THEM ONE BY ONE.
AH!!
BUT FORTUNATELY, THE WOLF DID NOT FIND THE LITTLEST KID, WHO WAS SAFELY HIDDEN INSIDE THE CLOCK.
WHEW ...
SHWP
HE'S MAKING ALL KINDS OF FACES.
BWAZA...
AND? AND?
THROB
THROB
DING-DONG!
GWAAH!!
WHAP
AGH!!

Author's Note Part 4

Devil F's Corner:
Exposing Ragawa's Secrets

Nice to meet you. I'm Marimo Ragawa's older brother. (Actually, I'm her brother-in-law.) This is my reward for helping her apply screentone when she was up against a deadline. So now I'm going to reveal some of Marimo Ragawa's secrets. But I'm no good at drawing, so it's all in words.

First of all, for some reason, Marimo is good at cutting hair. I didn't trust her in the beginning. Every time she offered to cut my hair, I politely told her no thank you. Then, one day, I decided to let her cut my hair, and she did as good a job as my regular barber. So why pay good money to get a haircut? For the last four years Marimo has been cutting my hair.

Also, for some reason, Marimo is good at giving massages. If you complain about stiff and achy shoulders, she'll creep up on you from behind when you least suspect it, deftly find the most painful pressure point and knead away the stiffness with her golden fingers, which she has strengthened by drawing manga for more than a decade. I can't even describe the feeling.

Finally, Marimo loves to sleep. If you call her up and she doesn't answer the phone, chances are she's sleeping. On the other hand, when I'm just about to go to bed late at night, she'll suddenly call and say, "I can't record on this MiniDisc! I don't know why! Do something!" That's the kind of person Marimo Ragawa is.

Ha ha ha...

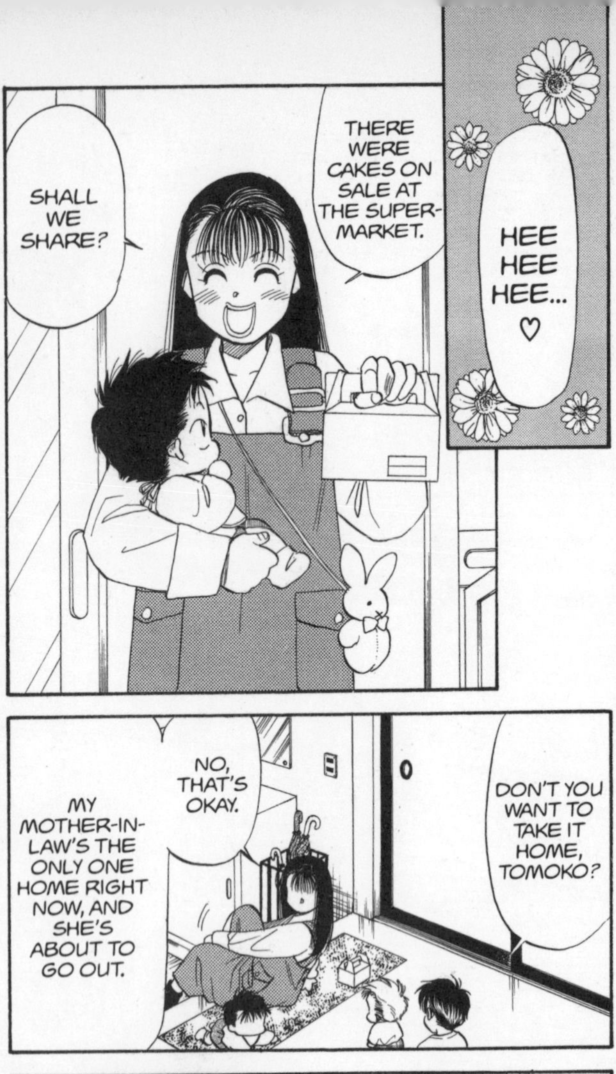
HEE HEE HEE... ♡
THERE WERE CAKES ON SALE AT THE SUPER-MARKET.
SHALL WE SHARE?
DON'T YOU WANT TO TAKE IT HOME, TOMOKO?
NO, THAT'S OKAY.
MY MOTHER-IN-LAW'S THE ONLY ONE HOME RIGHT NOW, AND SHE'S ABOUT TO GO OUT.
OH? WHERE'S YOUR DAD?
DAD?
HE HAD TO GO TO WORK.
ON A SATUR-DAY? THAT'S TOO BAD.

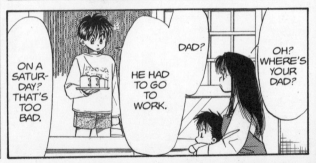

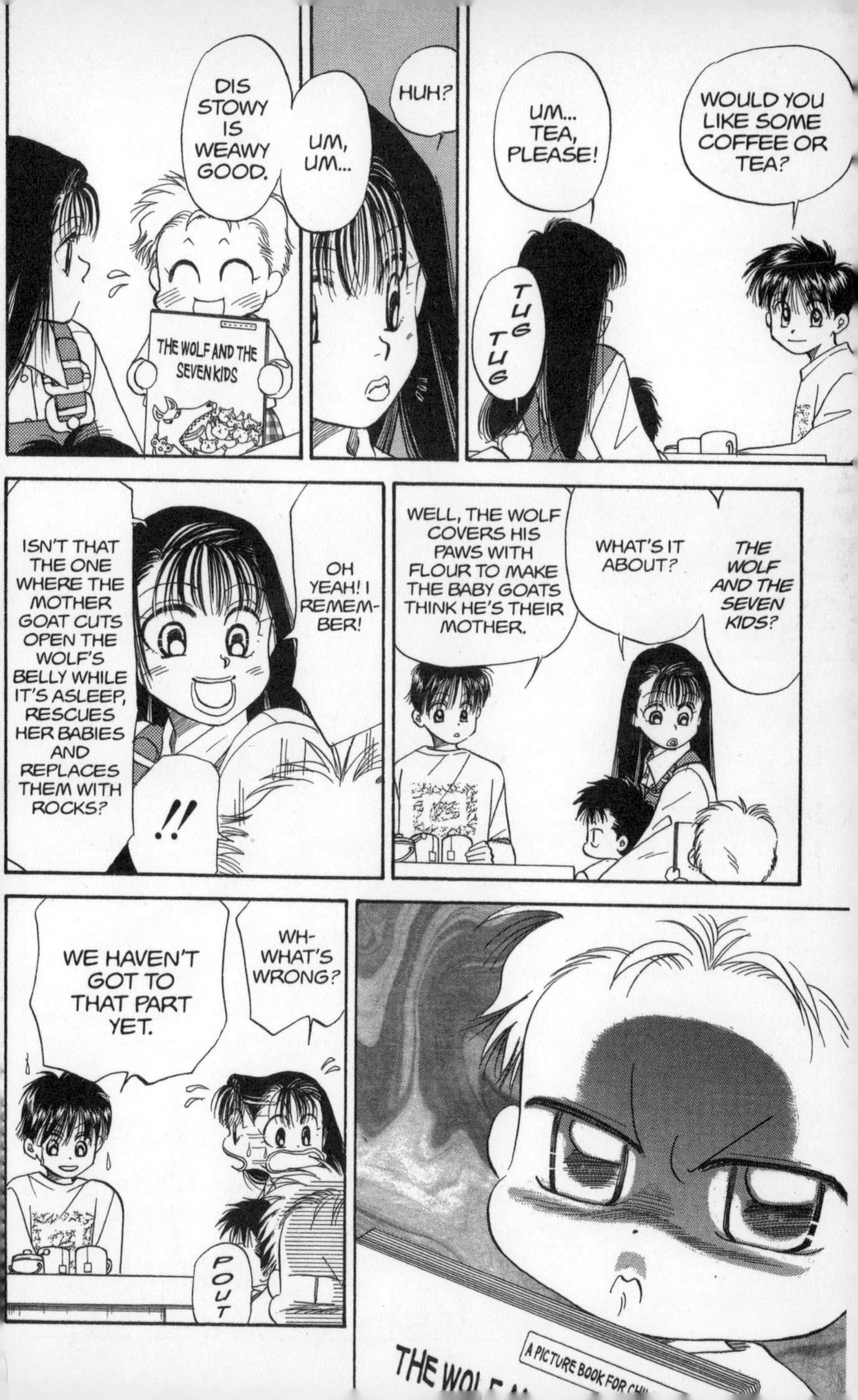
WOULD YOU LIKE SOME COFFEE OR TEA?
UM... TEA, PLEASE!
TUG TUG
HUH?
UM, UM...
DIS STOWY IS WEAWY GOOD.
THE WOLF AND THE SEVEN KIDS
THE WOLF AND THE SEVEN KIDS?
WHAT'S IT ABOUT?
WELL, THE WOLF COVERS HIS PAWS WITH FLOUR TO MAKE THE BABY GOATS THINK HE'S THEIR MOTHER.
OH YEAH! I REMEMBER!
ISN'T THAT THE ONE WHERE THE MOTHER GOAT CUTS OPEN THE WOLF'S BELLY WHILE IT'S ASLEEP, RESCUES HER BABIES AND REPLACES THEM WITH ROCKS?
!!
WH-WHAT'S WRONG?
WE HAVEN'T GOT TO THAT PART YET.
POUT

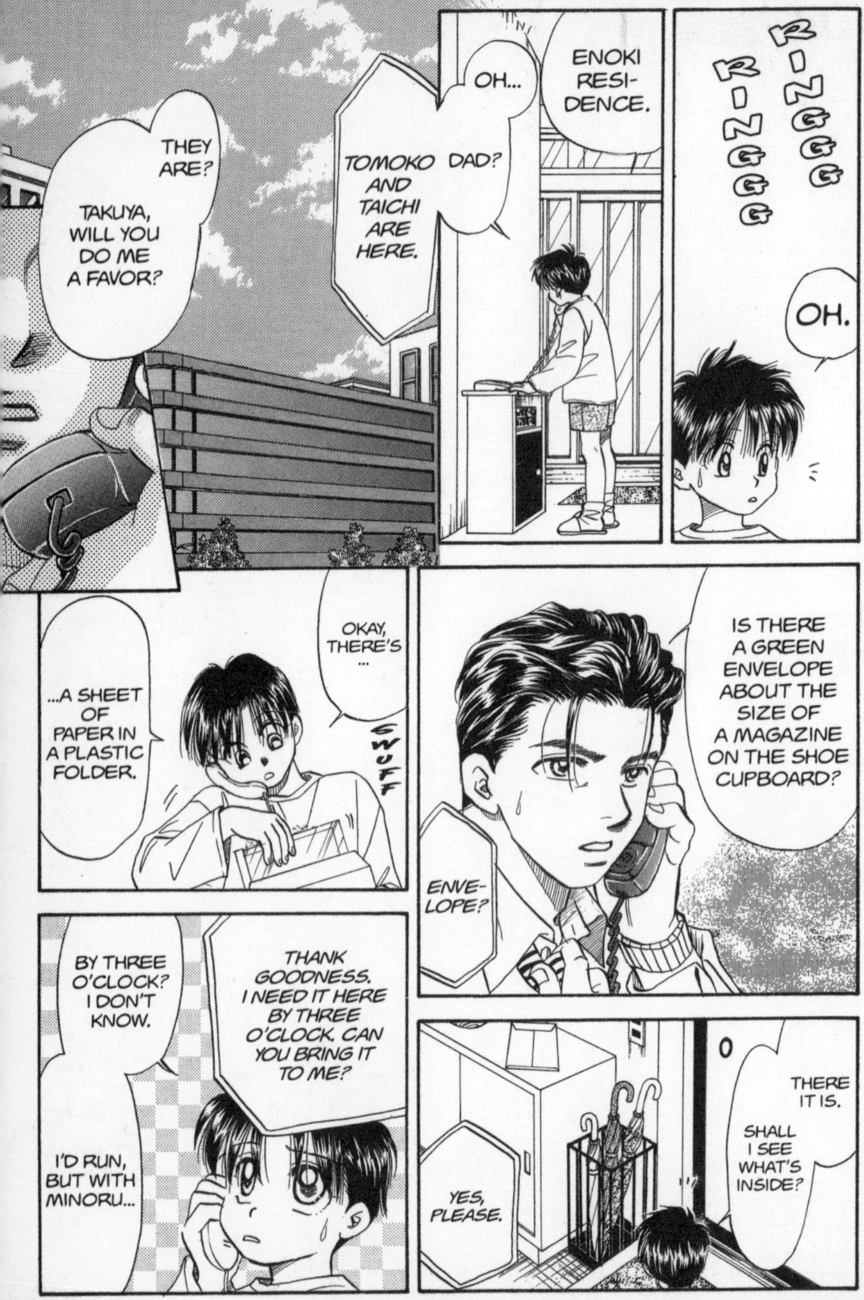
RINGGG RINGGG
OH.
ENOKI RESIDENCE.
OH... DAD?
TOMOKO AND TAICHI ARE HERE.
THEY ARE?
TAKUYA, WILL YOU DO ME A FAVOR?
IS THERE A GREEN ENVELOPE ABOUT THE SIZE OF A MAGAZINE ON THE SHOE CUPBOARD?
ENVELOPE?
THERE IT IS.
SHALL I SEE WHAT'S INSIDE?
YES, PLEASE.
OKAY, THERE'S ...
SWUFF
...A SHEET OF PAPER IN A PLASTIC FOLDER.
THANK GOODNESS. I NEED IT HERE BY THREE O'CLOCK. CAN YOU BRING IT TO ME?
BY THREE O'CLOCK? I DON'T KNOW.
I'D RUN, BUT WITH MINORU...

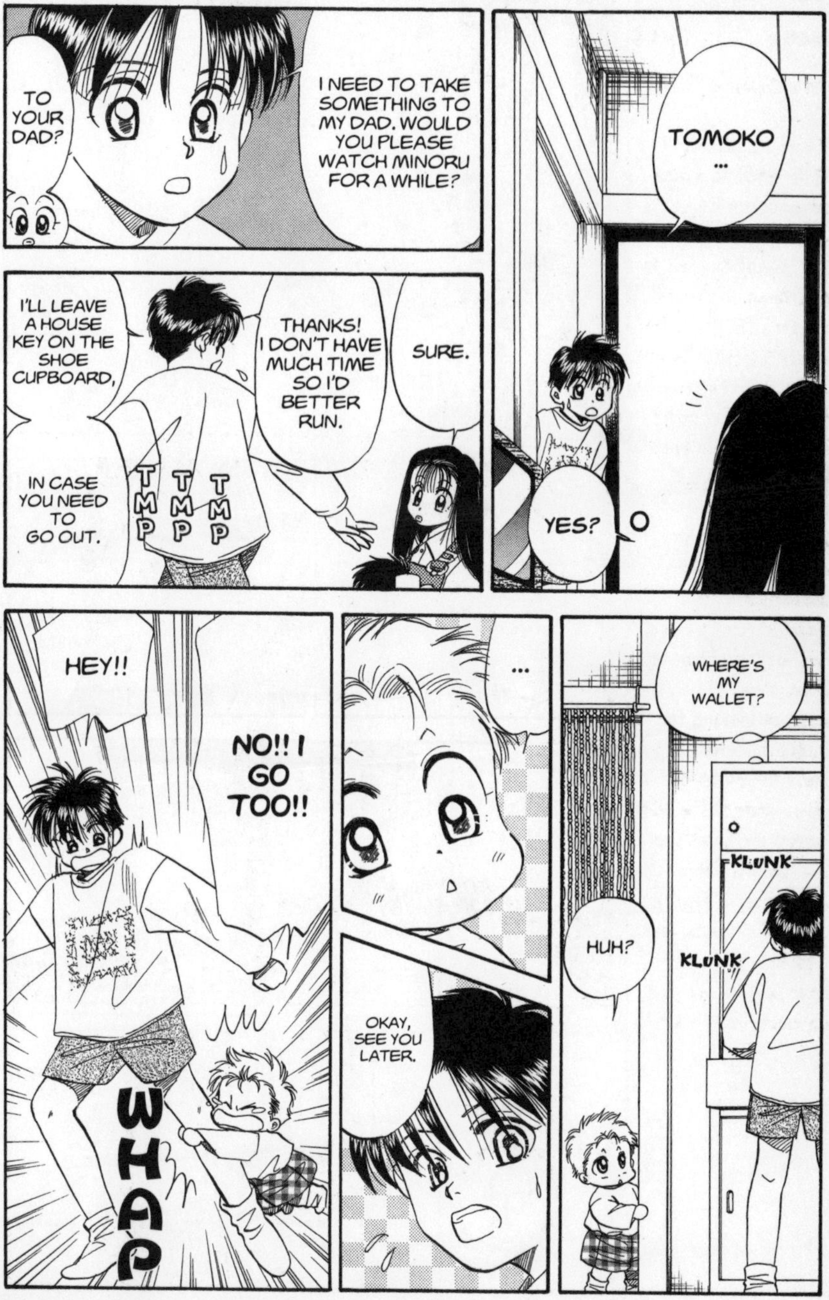
TOMOKO ...
YES?
I NEED TO TAKE SOMETHING TO MY DAD. WOULD YOU PLEASE WATCH MINORU FOR A WHILE?
TO YOUR DAD?
SURE.
THANKS! I DON'T HAVE MUCH TIME SO I'D BETTER RUN.
I'LL LEAVE A HOUSE KEY ON THE SHOE CUPBOARD,
IN CASE YOU NEED TO GO OUT.
TMP TMP TMP
WHERE'S MY WALLET?
KLUNK
KLUNK
HUH?
...
OKAY, SEE YOU LATER.
HEY!!
NO!! I GO TOO!!
WHAP

Author's Note Part 5

On a Beehive

It was August of 1996, and the weeds around our house were about three feet tall, so we decided to pull them. When we finished the job a few hours later, we found a shabby little beehive on the side of our house that had been hidden by the tall weeds. It was only about an inch in diameter and two bees seemed to be guarding it. The next day, one of them was gone. Devil F said it was out looking for building materials while the other one stood guard. The idea moved me somehow. But several more days passed, and the bee hadn't come back. I thought it must have had an accident.

Continued in Part 6

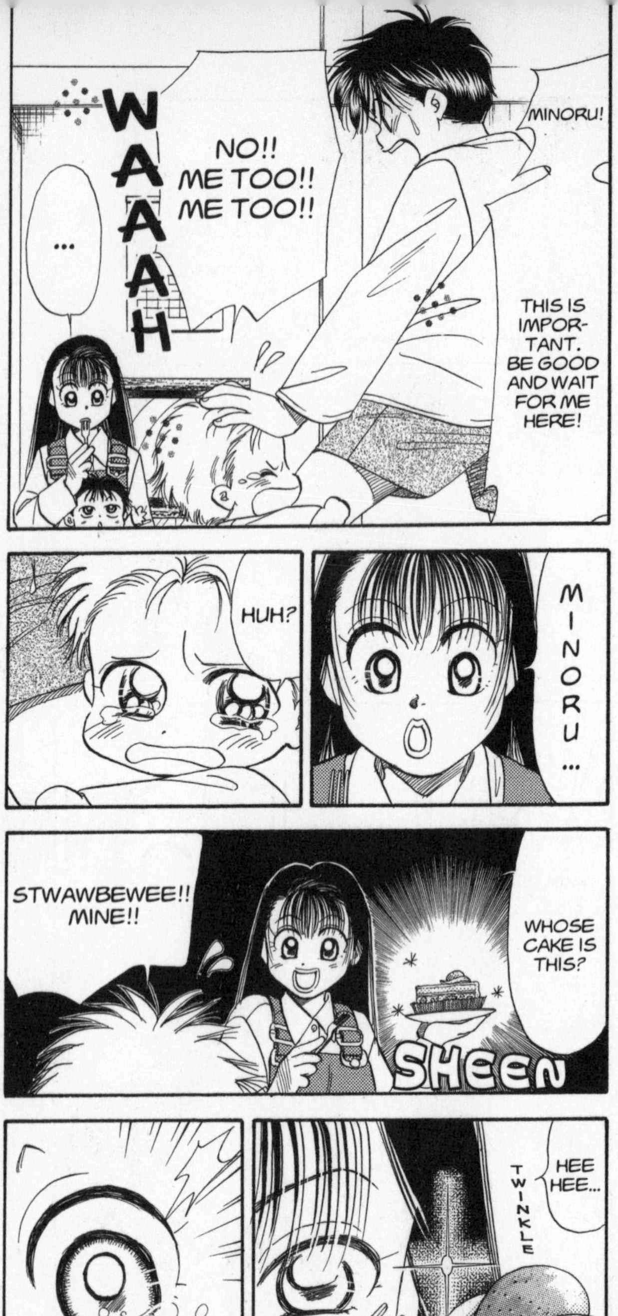
MINORU!
THIS IS IMPORTANT. BE GOOD AND WAIT FOR ME HERE!
NO!! ME TOO!! ME TOO!!
WAAAAH
...
MINORU...
HUH?
WHOSE CAKE IS THIS?
SHEEN
STWAWBEWEE!! MINE!!
HEE HEE...
TWINKLE

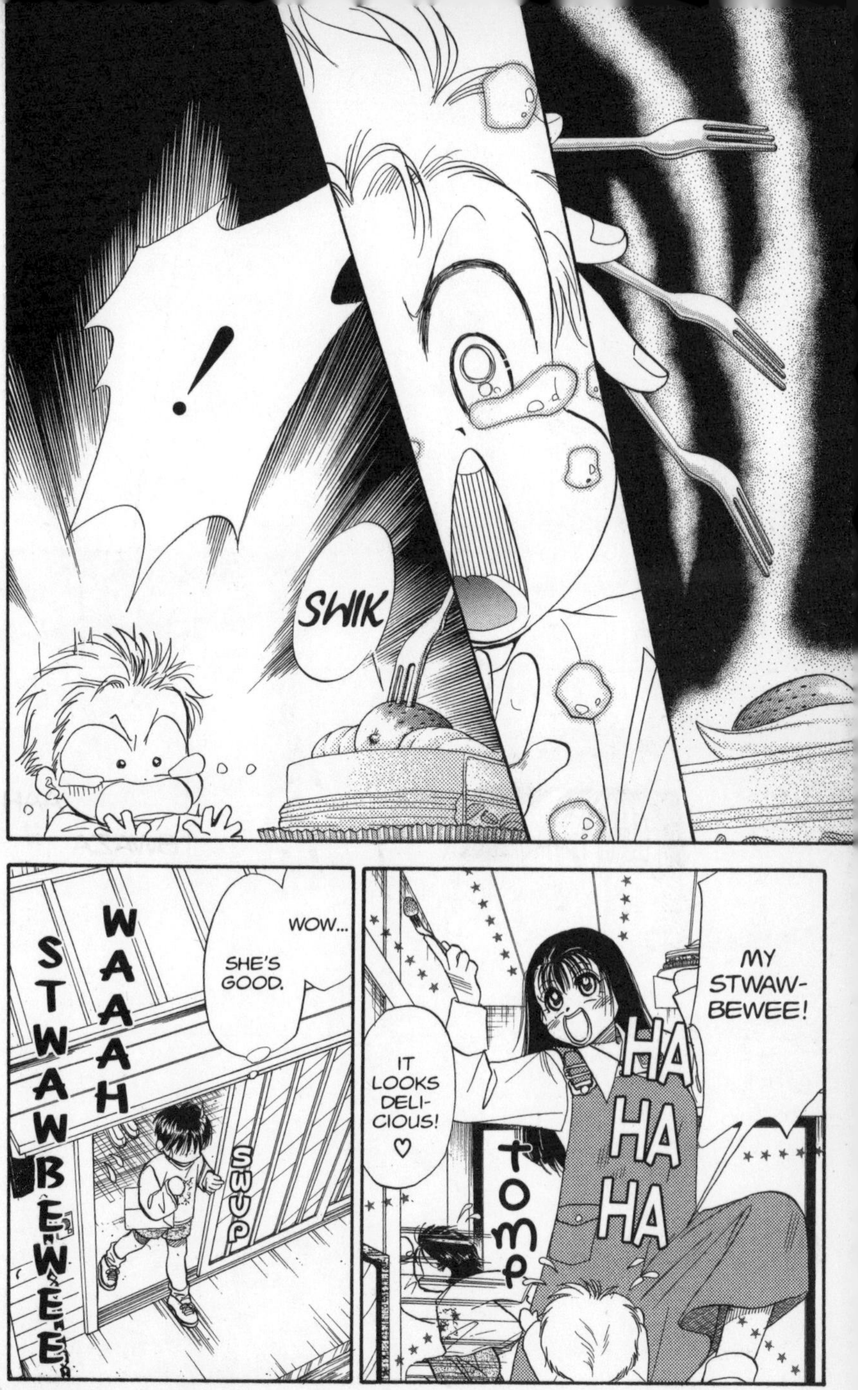
!
SWIK
MY STWAW-BEWEE!
HA HA HA
IT LOOKS DELI-CIOUS! ♥
TOMP
WOW...
SHE'S GOOD.
WAAAAH
STWAWBEWEE
SWUP

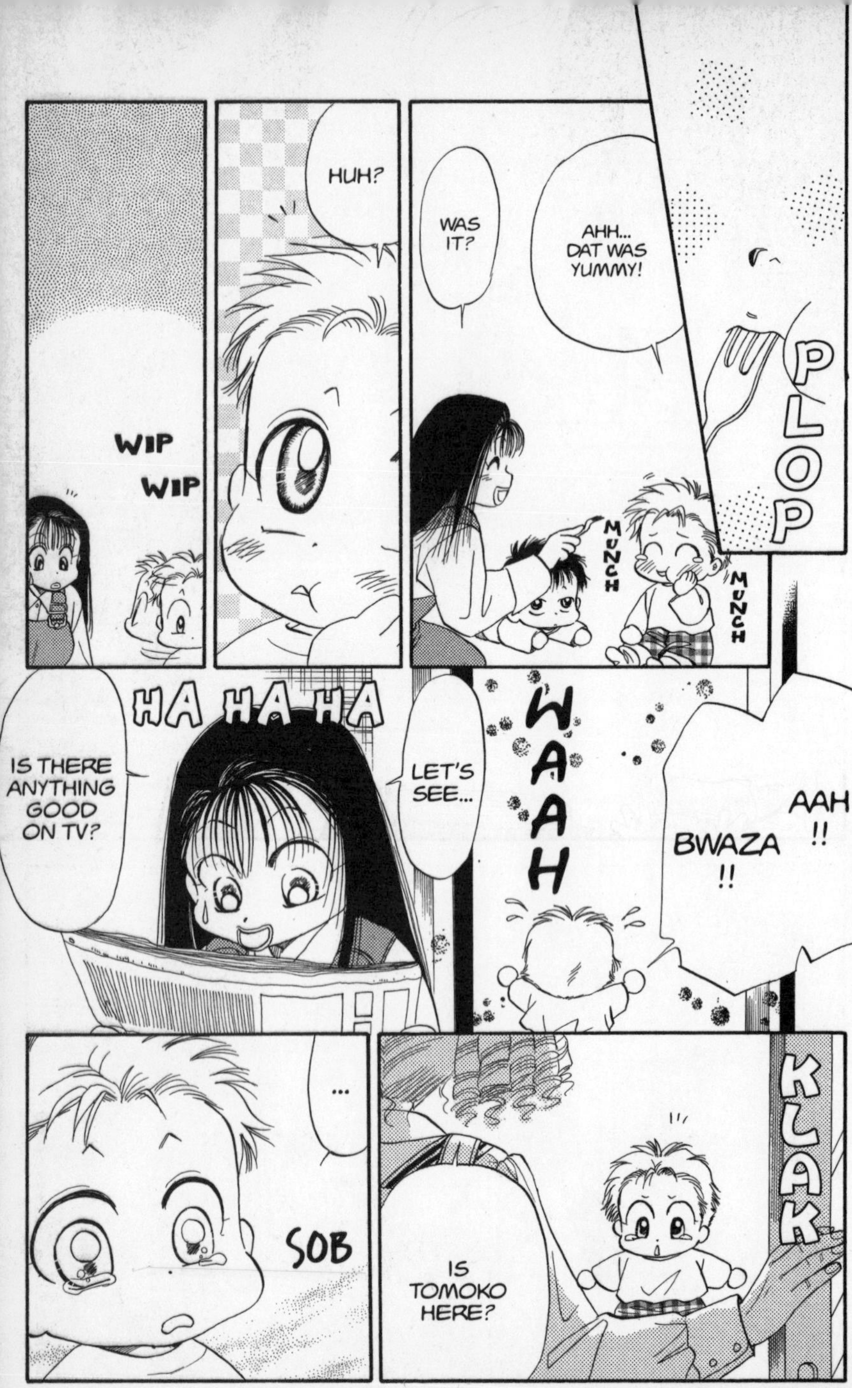
PLOP
AHH... DAT WAS YUMMY!
WAS IT?
MUNCH
MUNCH
HUH?
WIP
WIP
AAH!!
BWAZA!!
WAAH
LET'S SEE...
HA HA HA
IS THERE ANYTHING GOOD ON TV?
KLAK
IS TOMOKO HERE?
...
SOB

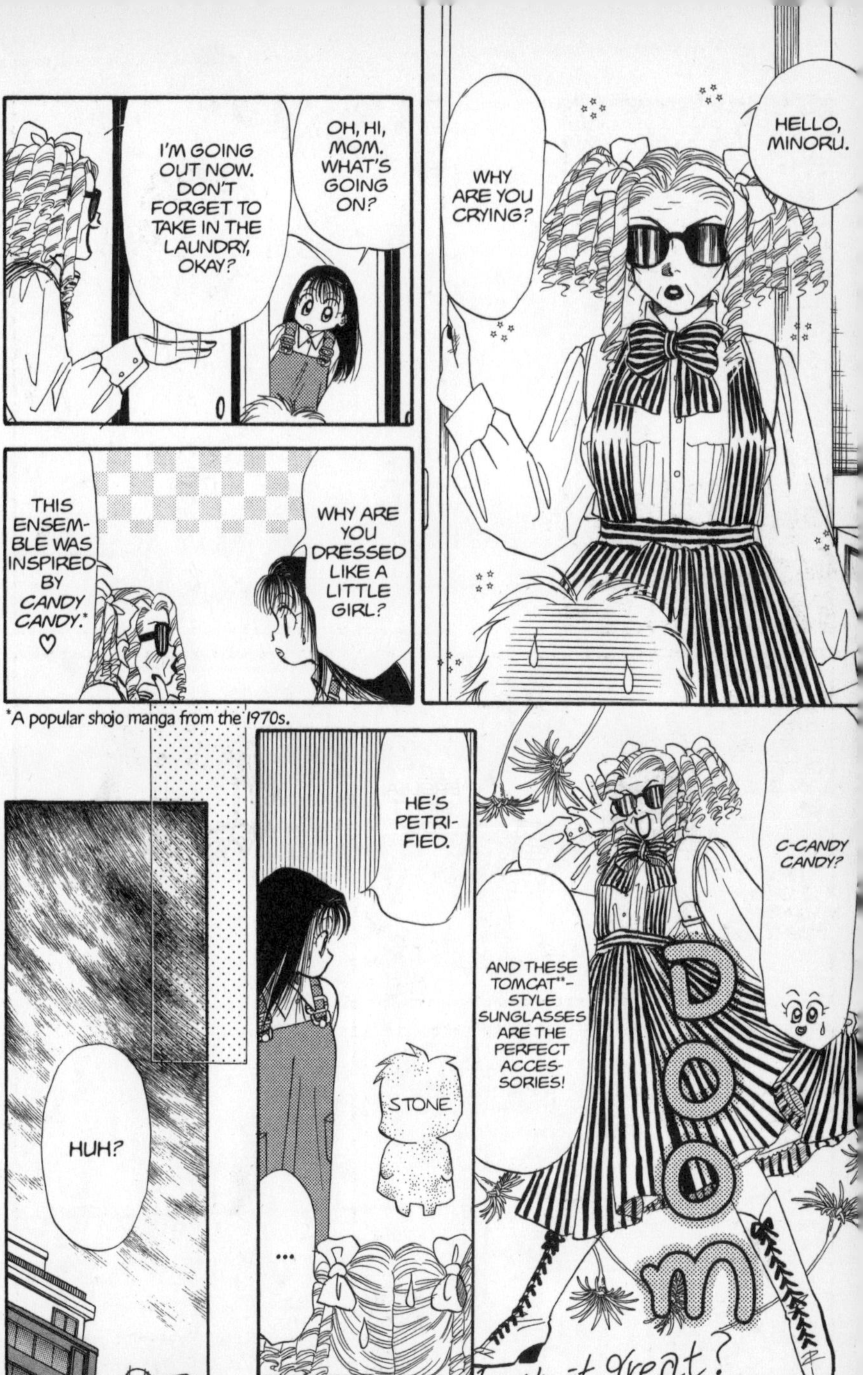
HELLO, MINORU.
WHY ARE YOU CRYING?
OH, HI, MOM. WHAT'S GOING ON?
I'M GOING OUT NOW. DON'T FORGET TO TAKE IN THE LAUNDRY, OKAY?
WHY ARE YOU DRESSED LIKE A LITTLE GIRL?
THIS ENSEMBLE WAS INSPIRED BY *CANDY CANDY*.* ♡
C-CANDY CANDY?
AND THESE TOMCAT**-STYLE SUNGLASSES ARE THE PERFECT ACCESSORIES!
DOOM
Isn't it great?
HE'S PETRIFIED.
STONE
...
HUH?

*A popular shojo manga from the 1970s.

**A Japanese singer.

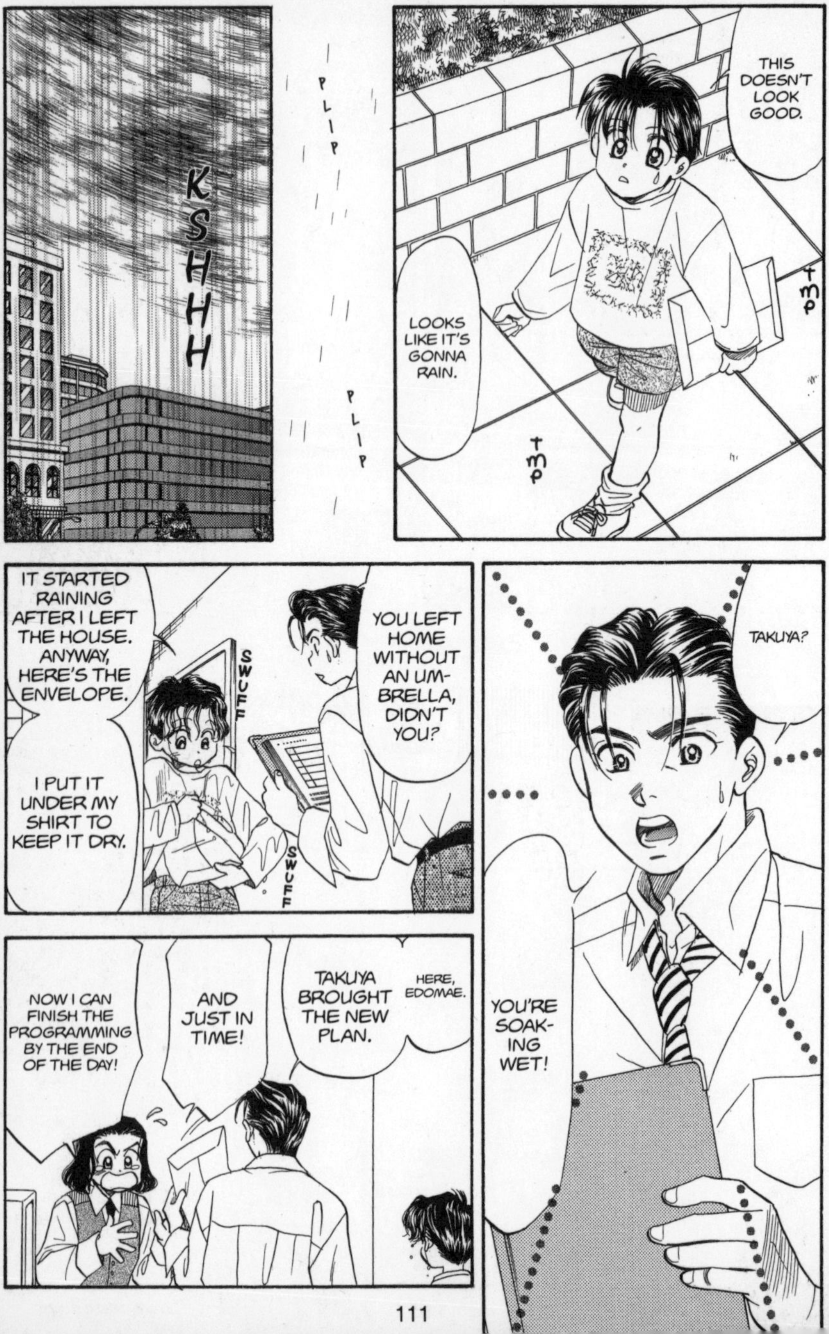
THIS DOESN'T LOOK GOOD.
TMP
LOOKS LIKE IT'S GONNA RAIN.
TMP
PLIP
PLIP
KSHHHH
TAKUYA?
YOU'RE SOAKING WET!
YOU LEFT HOME WITHOUT AN UMBRELLA, DIDN'T YOU?
SWUFF
SWUFF
IT STARTED RAINING AFTER I LEFT THE HOUSE. ANYWAY, HERE'S THE ENVELOPE.
I PUT IT UNDER MY SHIRT TO KEEP IT DRY.
HERE, EDOMAE.
TAKUYA BROUGHT THE NEW PLAN.
AND JUST IN TIME!
NOW I CAN FINISH THE PROGRAMMING BY THE END OF THE DAY!

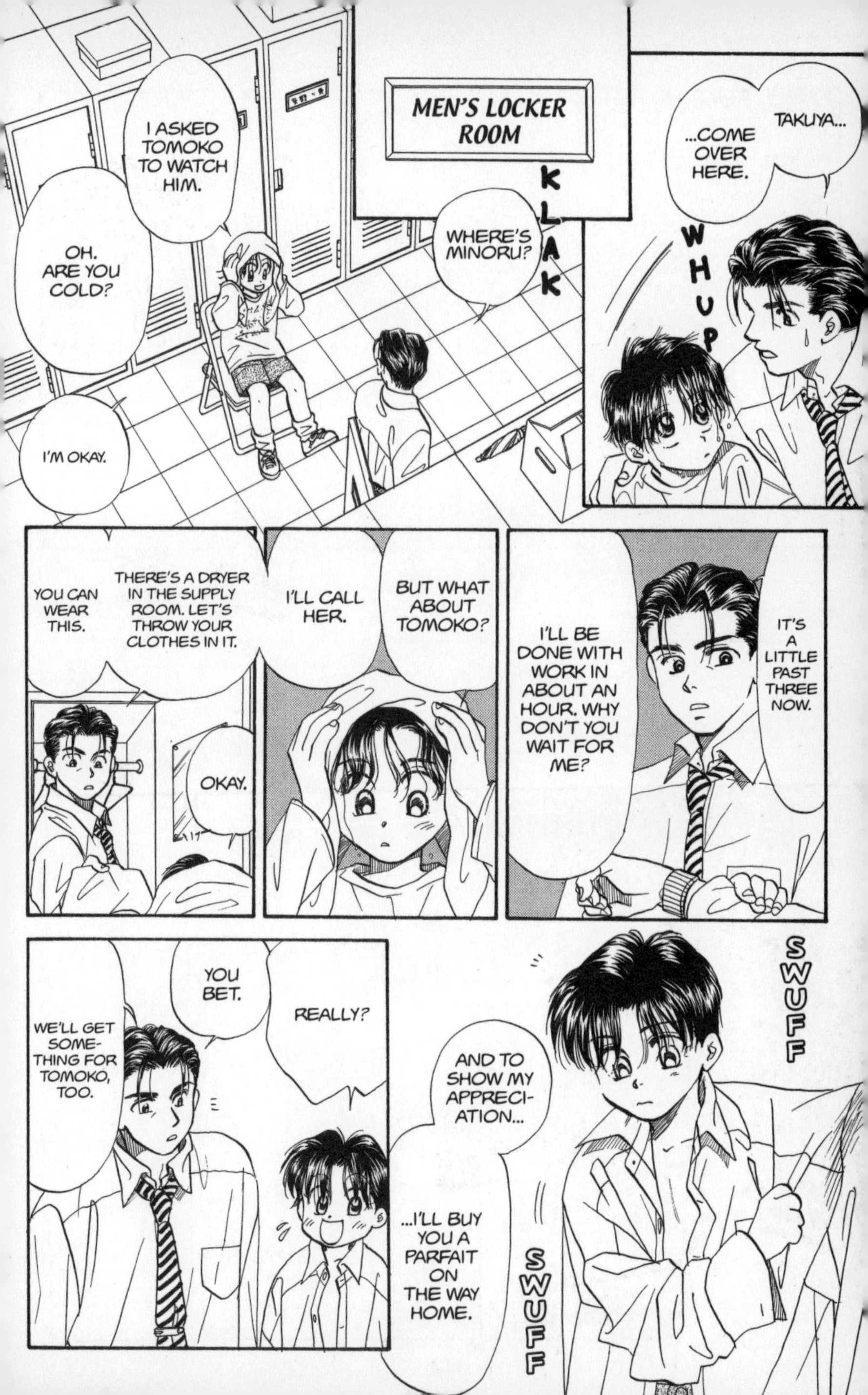
TAKUYA...
...COME OVER HERE.
WHUP
MEN'S LOCKER ROOM
KLAK
WHERE'S MINORU?
I ASKED TOMOKO TO WATCH HIM.
OH. ARE YOU COLD?
I'M OKAY.
IT'S A LITTLE PAST THREE NOW.
I'LL BE DONE WITH WORK IN ABOUT AN HOUR. WHY DON'T YOU WAIT FOR ME?
BUT WHAT ABOUT TOMOKO?
I'LL CALL HER.
THERE'S A DRYER IN THE SUPPLY ROOM. LET'S THROW YOUR CLOTHES IN IT.
YOU CAN WEAR THIS.
OKAY.
SWUFF
AND TO SHOW MY APPRECI-ATION...
...I'LL BUY YOU A PARFAIT ON THE WAY HOME.
SWUFF
REALLY?
YOU BET.
WE'LL GET SOME-THING FOR TOMOKO, TOO.

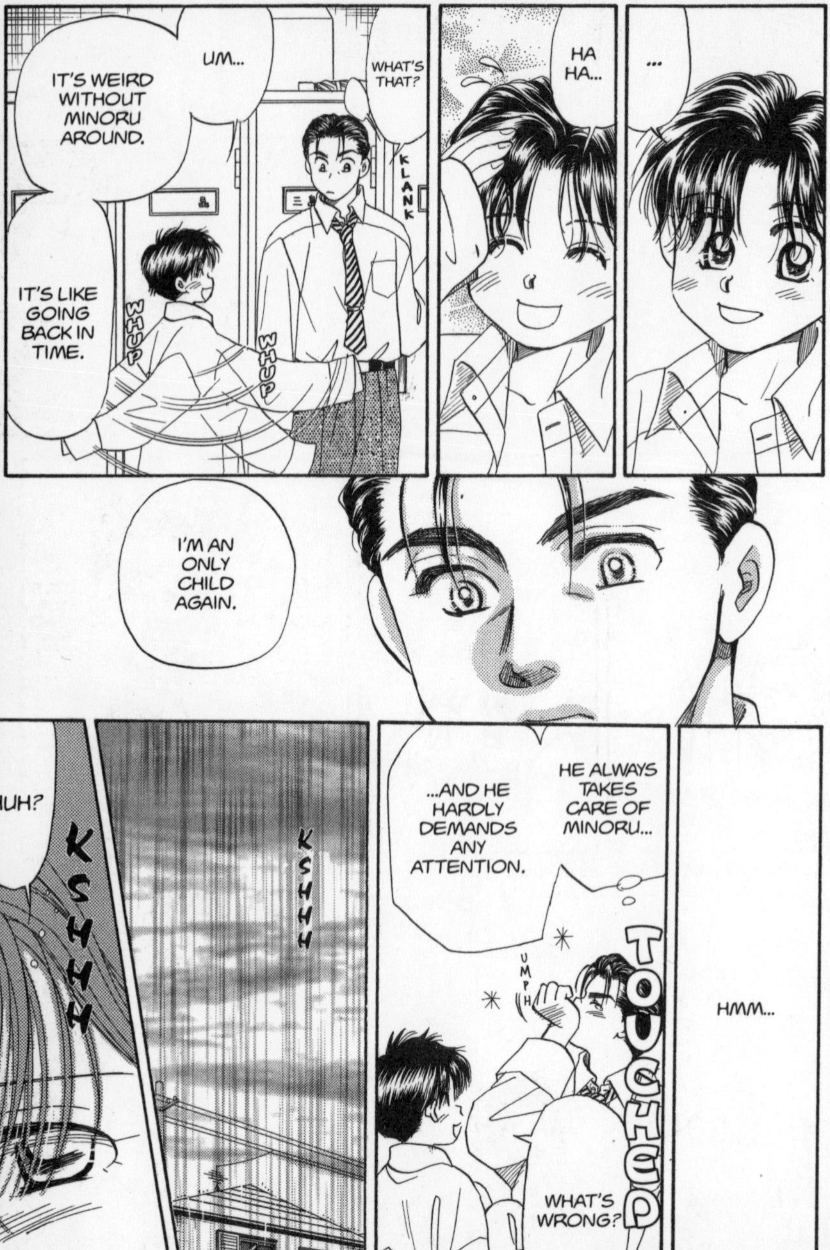
...
HA HA...
WHAT'S THAT?
KLANK
UM...
IT'S WEIRD WITHOUT MINORU AROUND.
WHUP
WHUP
IT'S LIKE GOING BACK IN TIME.
I'M AN ONLY CHILD AGAIN.
HMM...
HE ALWAYS TAKES CARE OF MINORU...
...AND HE HARDLY DEMANDS ANY ATTENTION.
TOUCHED
UMPH
WHAT'S WRONG?
KSHHH
HUH?
KSHHH

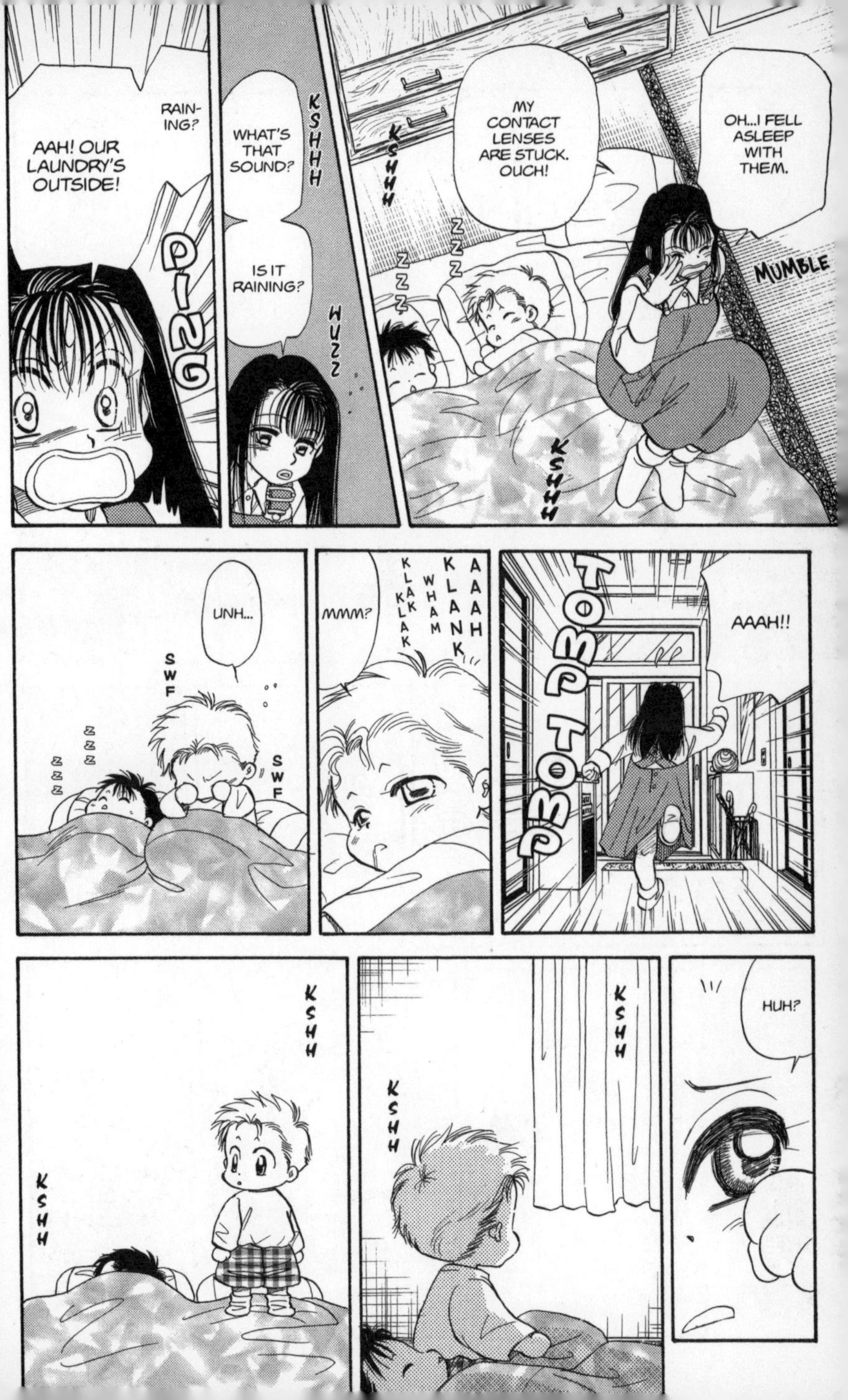
OH...I FELL ASLEEP WITH THEM.
MUMBLE
MY CONTACT LENSES ARE STUCK. OUCH!
KSHHH
ZZZ
ZZZ
KSHHH
KSHHH
WHAT'S THAT SOUND?
IS IT RAINING?
HUZZ
RAINING?
AAH! OUR LAUNDRY'S OUTSIDE!
DING
AAAH!!
TOMP TOMP TOMP
AAAH
KLANK
WHAM
KLAK KLAK
MMM?
UNH...
SWF
SWF
ZZZ
ZZZ
HUH?
KSHH
KSHH
KSHH
KSHH

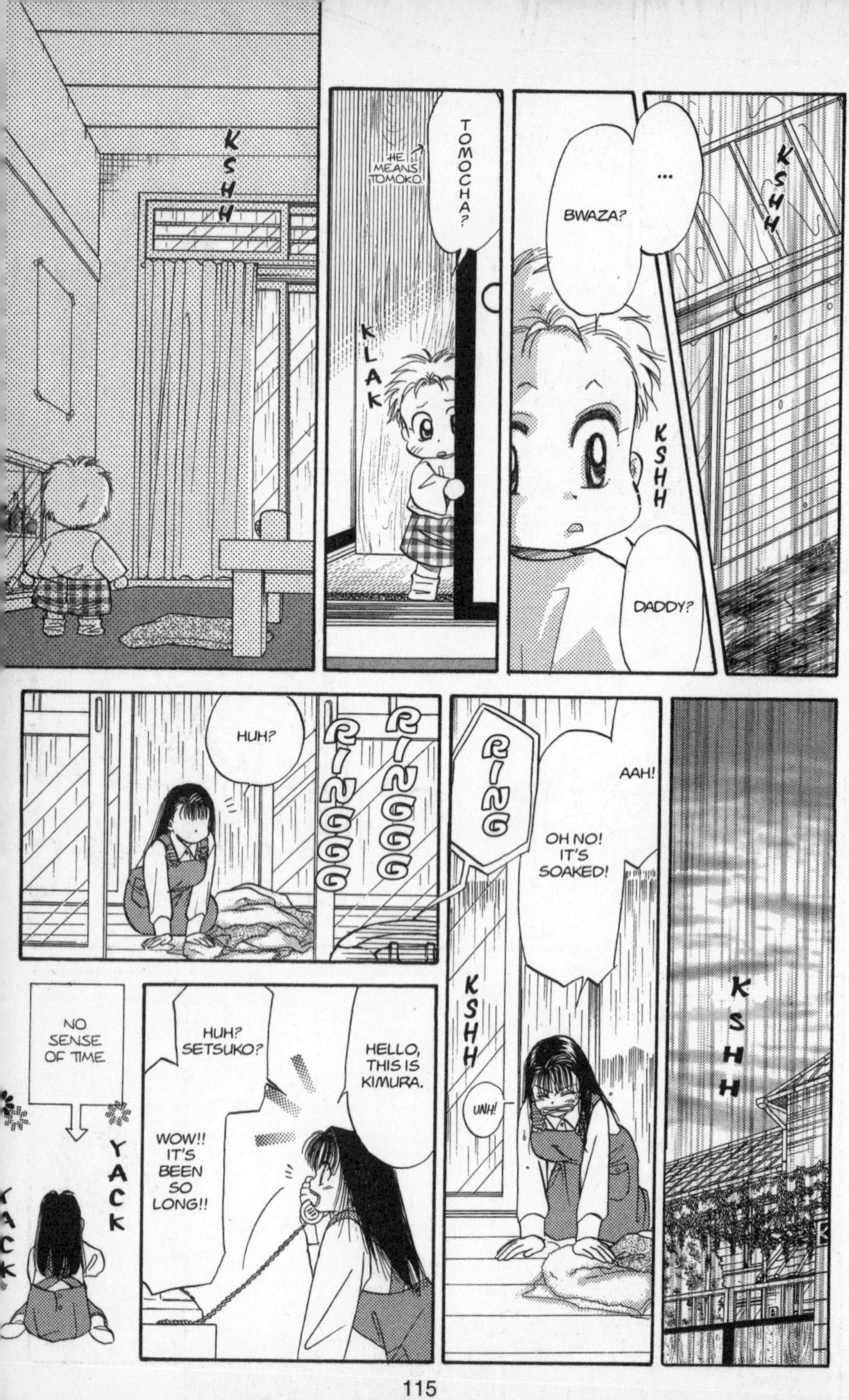
KSHH
...
BWAZA?
KSHH
DADDY?
TOMOCHA?
HE MEANS TOMOKO
KLAK
KSHH
KSHH
RING
AAH!
OH NO! IT'S SOAKED!
KSHH
UNH!
RINGGG
RINGGG
HUH?
HELLO, THIS IS KIMURA.
HUH? SETSUKO?
WOW!! IT'S BEEN SO LONG!!
NO SENSE OF TIME
YACK
YACK

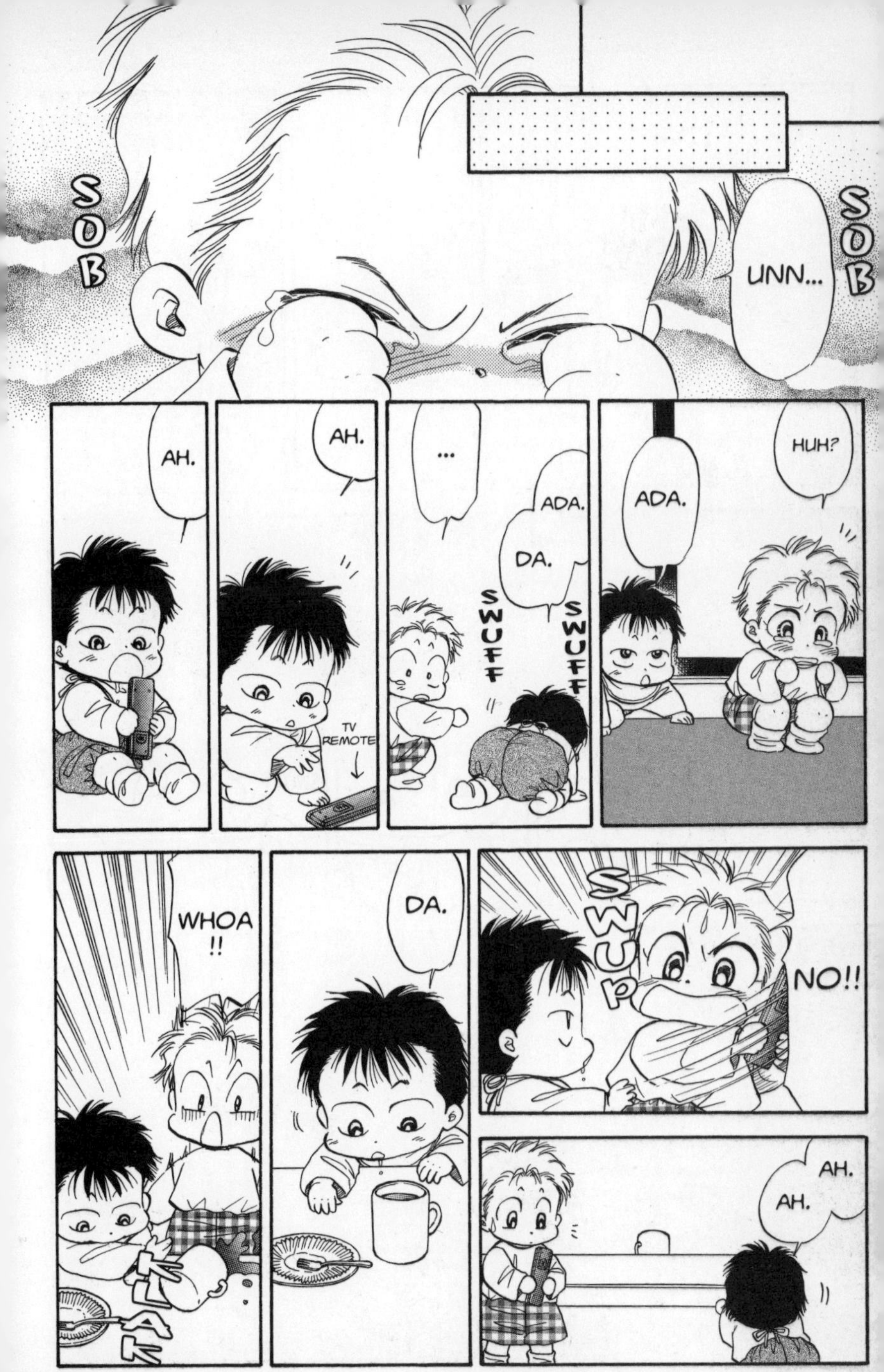
SOB
UNN...
SOB
HUH?
ADA.
...
ADA.
DA.
SWUFF
SWUFF
AH.
TV REMOTE
AH.
SWUP
NO!!
AH.
AH.
DA.
WHOA!!
KLAK

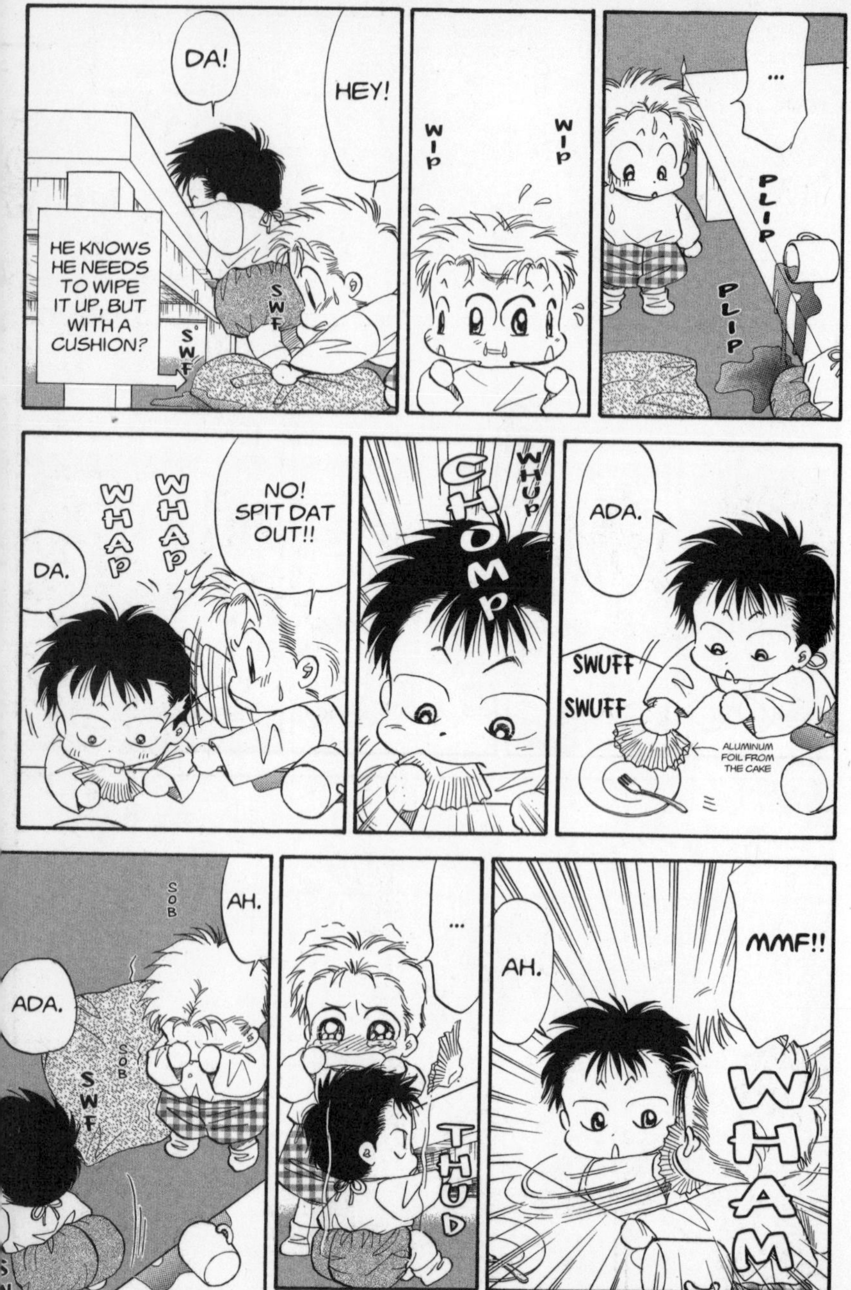
...
PLIP
PLIP
PLIP
WIP
WIP
HEY!
DA!
HE KNOWS HE NEEDS TO WIPE IT UP, BUT WITH A CUSHION?
SWF
SWF
ADA.
SWUFF
SWUFF
ALUMINUM FOIL FROM THE CAKE
WHUP
CHOMP
NO! SPIT DAT OUT!!
WHAP
WHAP
DA.
MMF!!
AH.
WHAM
...
THUD
AH.
SOB
ADA.
SOB
SWF
SWF

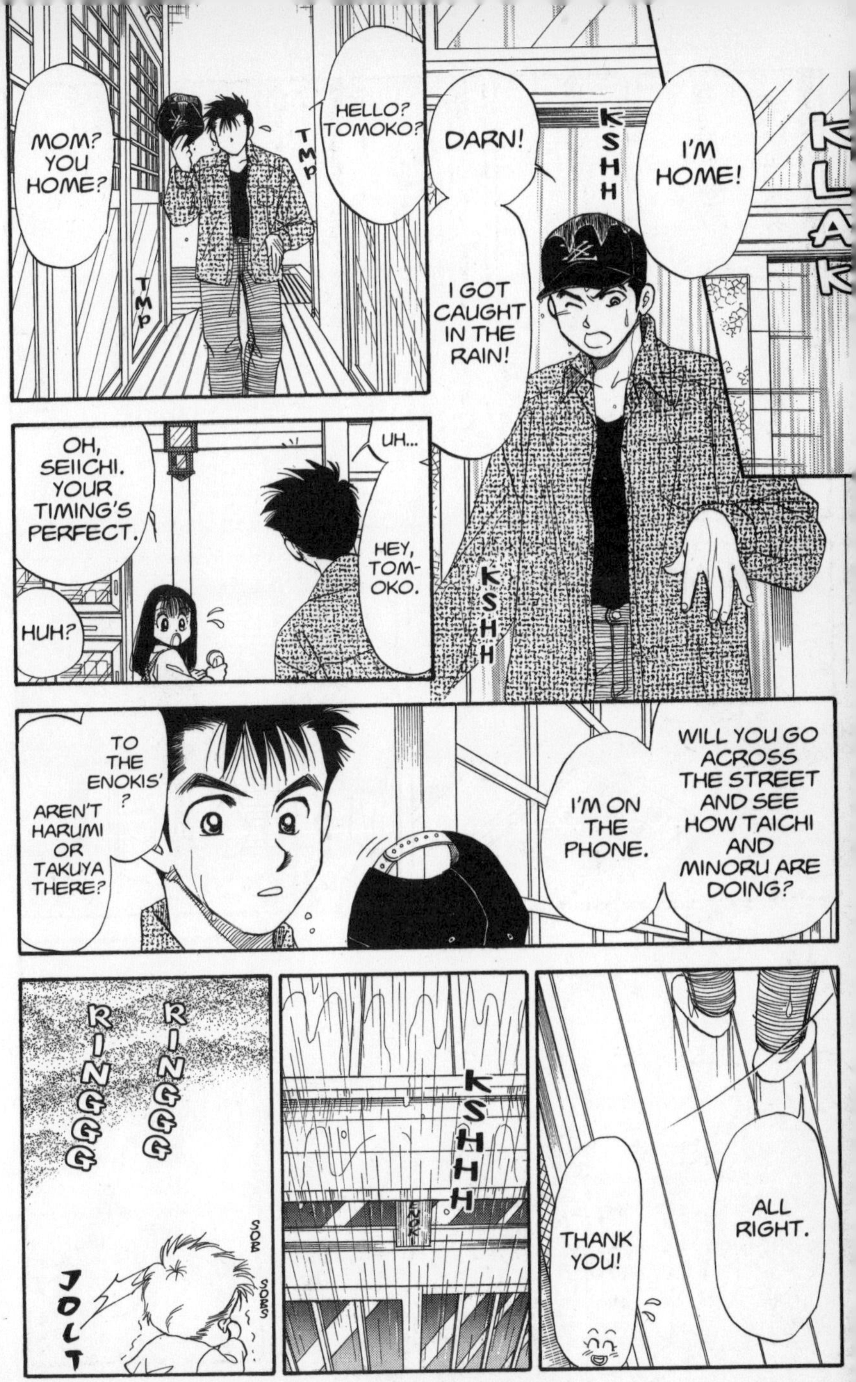
KLAK
I'M HOME!
KSHH
DARN!
I GOT CAUGHT IN THE RAIN!
KSHH
HELLO? TOMOKO?
TMP
MOM? YOU HOME?
TMP
UH...
HEY, TOMOKO.
OH, SEIICHI. YOUR TIMING'S PERFECT.
HUH?
WILL YOU GO ACROSS THE STREET AND SEE HOW TAICHI AND MINORU ARE DOING?
I'M ON THE PHONE.
TO THE ENOKIS'?
AREN'T HARUMI OR TAKUYA THERE?
ALL RIGHT.
THANK YOU!
KSHHH
ENOKI
RINGGG
RINGGG
SOB
SOBS
JOLT

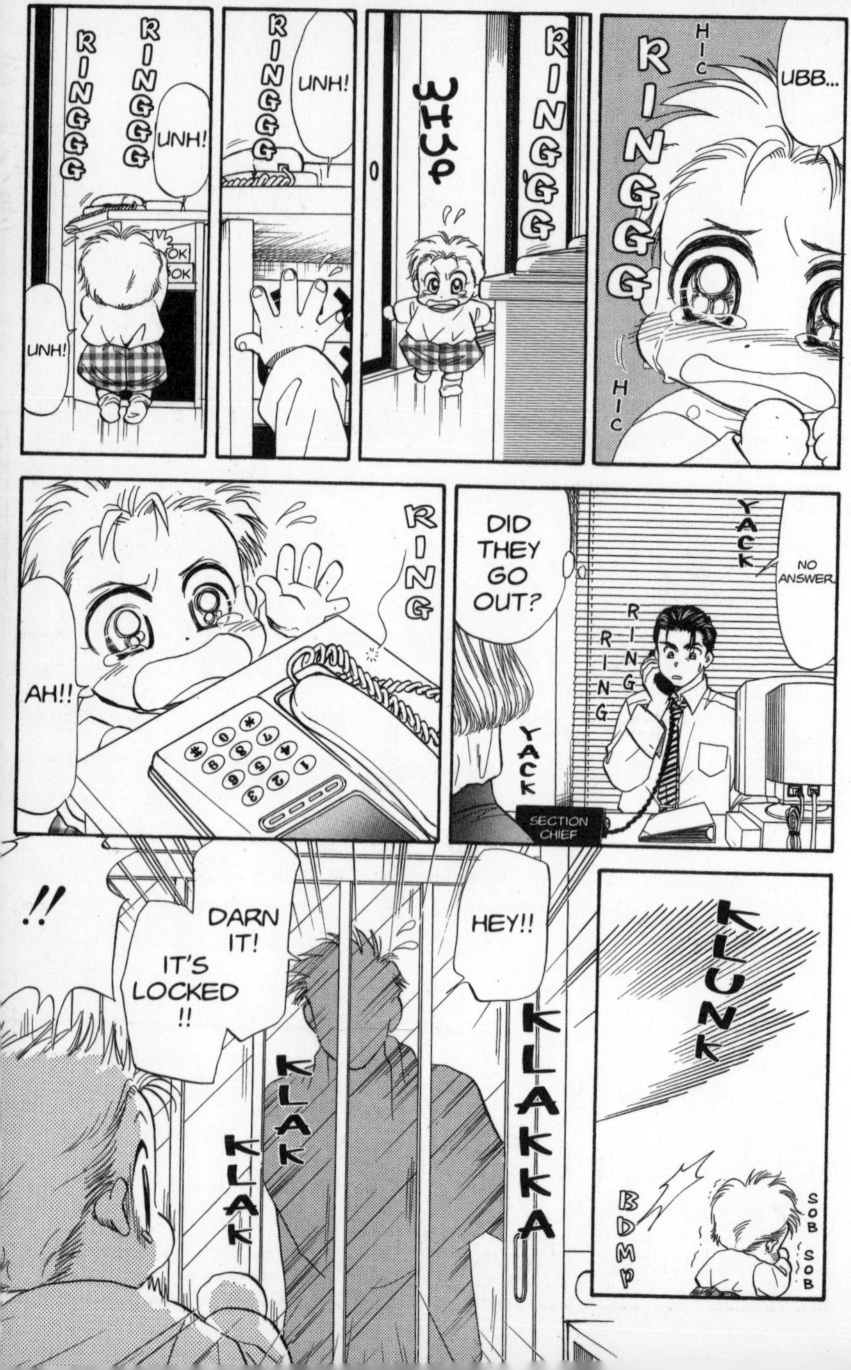
HIC
RINGGG
UBB...
HIC
RINGGG
WHUP
RINGGG
UNH!
RINGGG
RINGGG
UNH!
UNH!
YACK
NO ANSWER.
RING RING
DID THEY GO OUT?
YACK
SECTION CHIEF
RING
AH!!
KLUNK
SOB SOB
BDMP
HEY!!
KLAKKA
DARN IT! IT'S LOCKED!!
KLAK KLAK
!!

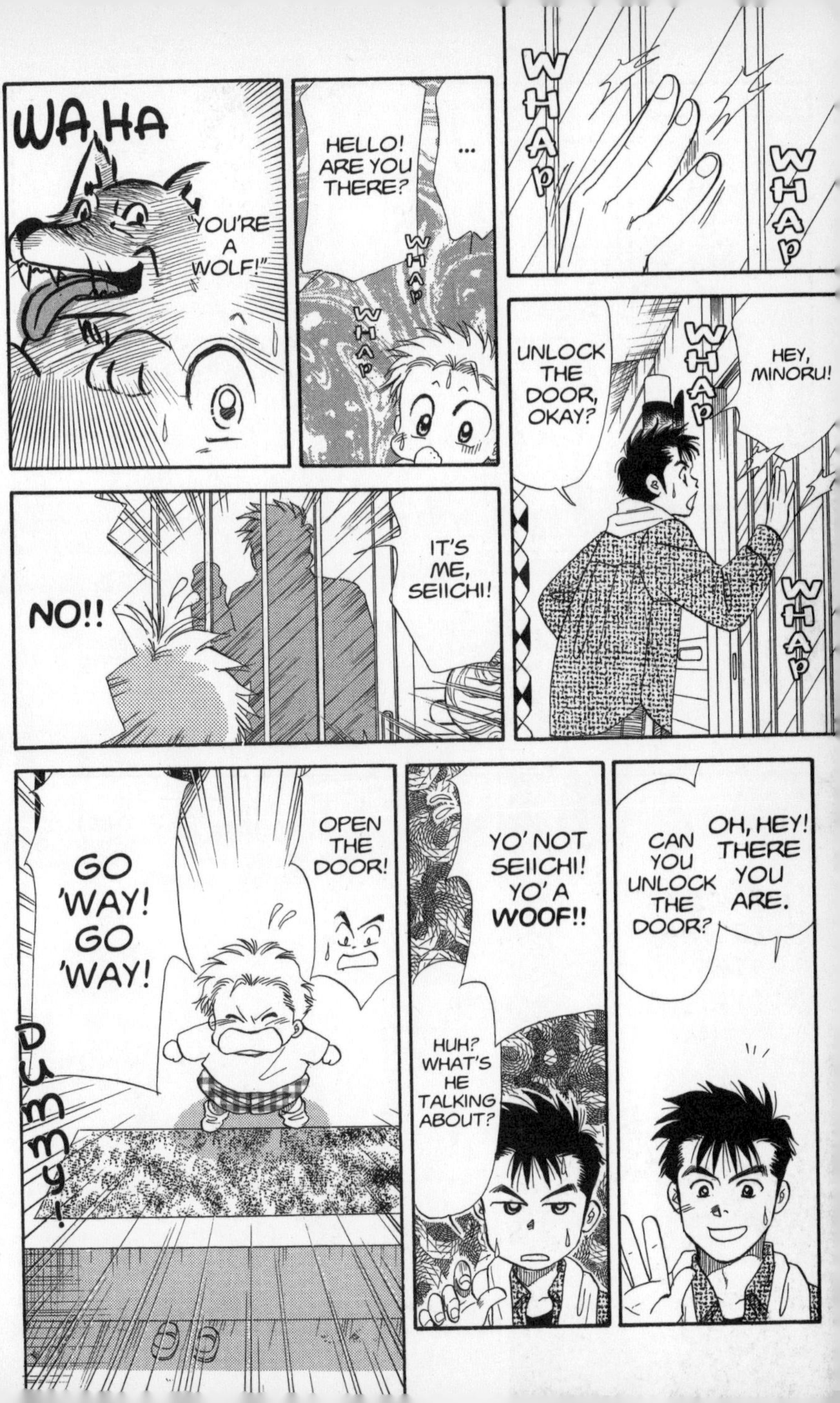
WHAP
WHAP
HEY, MINORU!
WHAP
UNLOCK THE DOOR, OKAY?
WHAP
...
HELLO! ARE YOU THERE?
WHAP
WHAP
WA HA
"YOU'RE A WOLF!"
IT'S ME, SEIICHI!
NO!!
OH, HEY! THERE YOU ARE.
CAN YOU UNLOCK THE DOOR?
YO' NOT SEIICHI! YO' A WOOF!!
HUH? WHAT'S HE TALKING ABOUT?
OPEN THE DOOR!
GO 'WAY! GO 'WAY!
DUMMY!

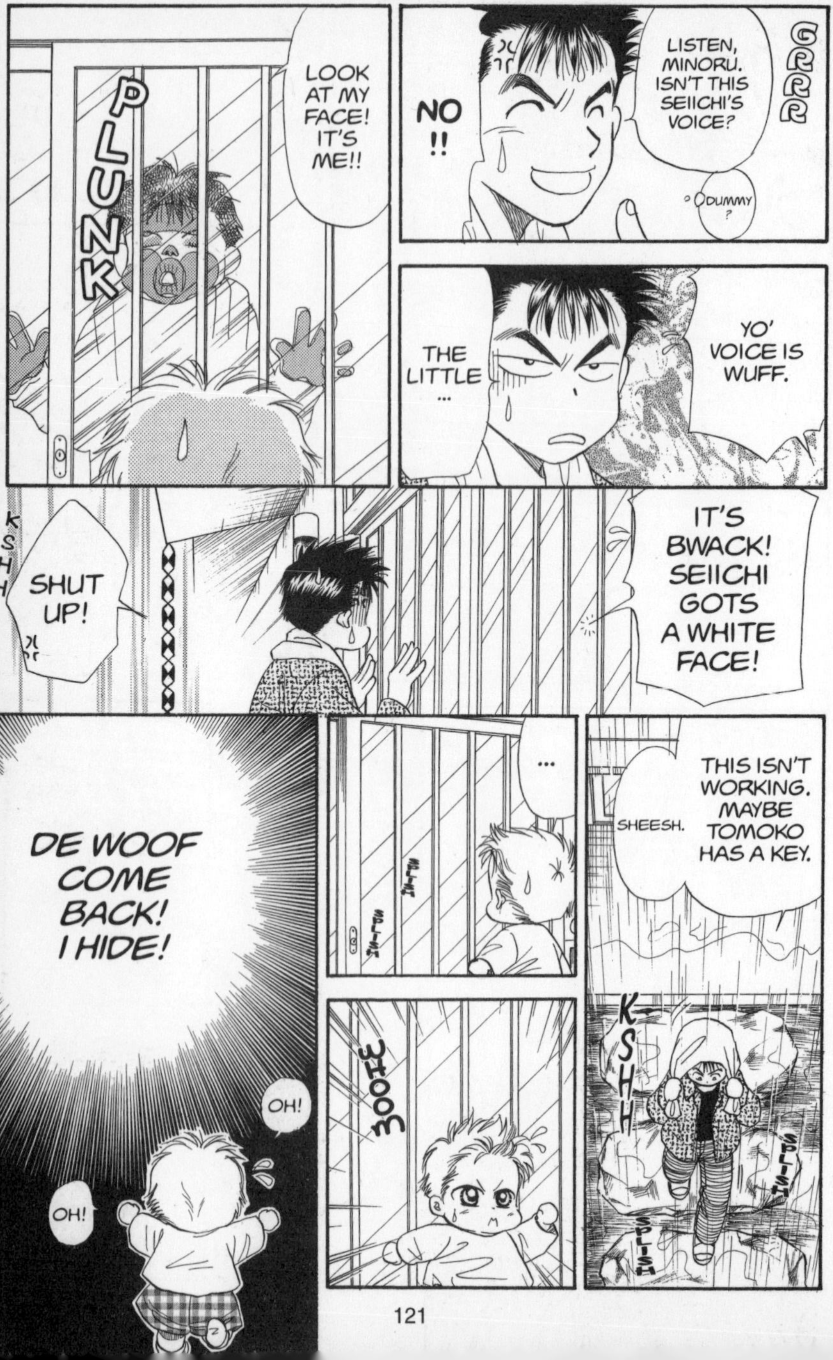
GRRR
LISTEN, MINORU. ISN'T THIS SEIICHI'S VOICE?
NO!!
DUMMY?
YO' VOICE IS WUFF.
THE LITTLE...
LOOK AT MY FACE! IT'S ME!!
PLUNK
IT'S BWACK! SEIICHI GOTS A WHITE FACE!
SHUT UP!
KSHH
THIS ISN'T WORKING. MAYBE TOMOKO HAS A KEY.
SHEESH.
KSHH
SPLISH
SPLISH
...
SPLISH
SPLISH
WHOOM
DE WOOF COME BACK! I HIDE!
OH!
OH!

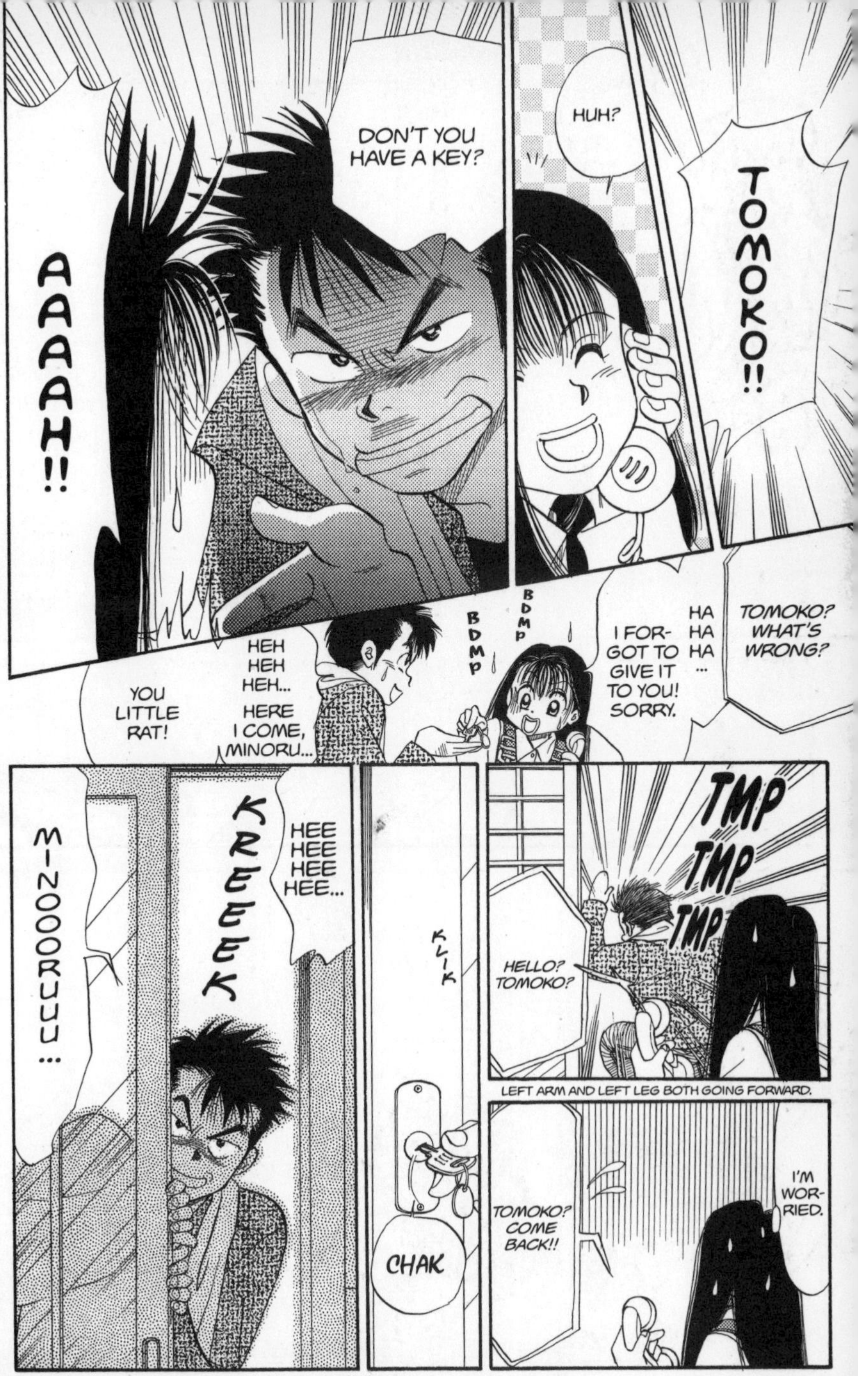
TOMOKO!!
HUH?
DON'T YOU HAVE A KEY?
AAAAAH!!
TOMOKO? WHAT'S WRONG?
HA HA HA ...
I FORGOT TO GIVE IT TO YOU! SORRY.
BDMP BDMP
HEH HEH HEH...
HERE I COME, MINORU...
YOU LITTLE RAT!
TMP TMP TMP
HELLO? TOMOKO?
LEFT ARM AND LEFT LEG BOTH GOING FORWARD.
I'M WORRIED.
TOMOKO? COME BACK!!
KLIK
CHAK
HEE HEE HEE HEE...
KREEEK
MINOOORUUU...

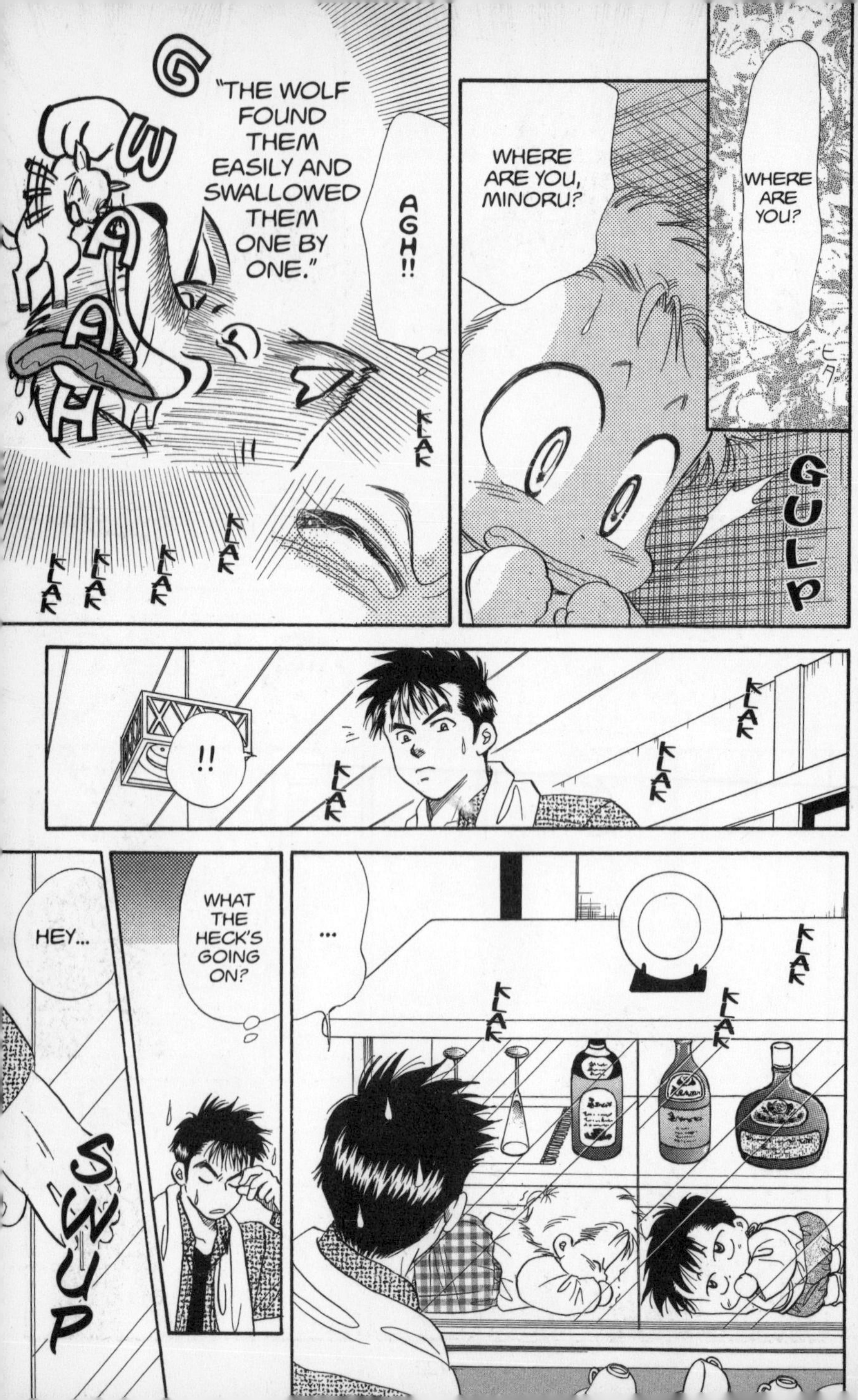
WHERE ARE YOU?
ヒタ
WHERE ARE YOU, MINORU?
GULP
AGH!!
"THE WOLF FOUND THEM EASILY AND SWALLOWED THEM ONE BY ONE."
G
WAAAH
KLAK
KLAK
KLAK
KLAK
KLAK
KLAK
KLAK
KLAK
!!
KLAK
KLAK
KLAK
KLAK
...
WHAT THE HECK'S GOING ON?
HEY...
SWUP

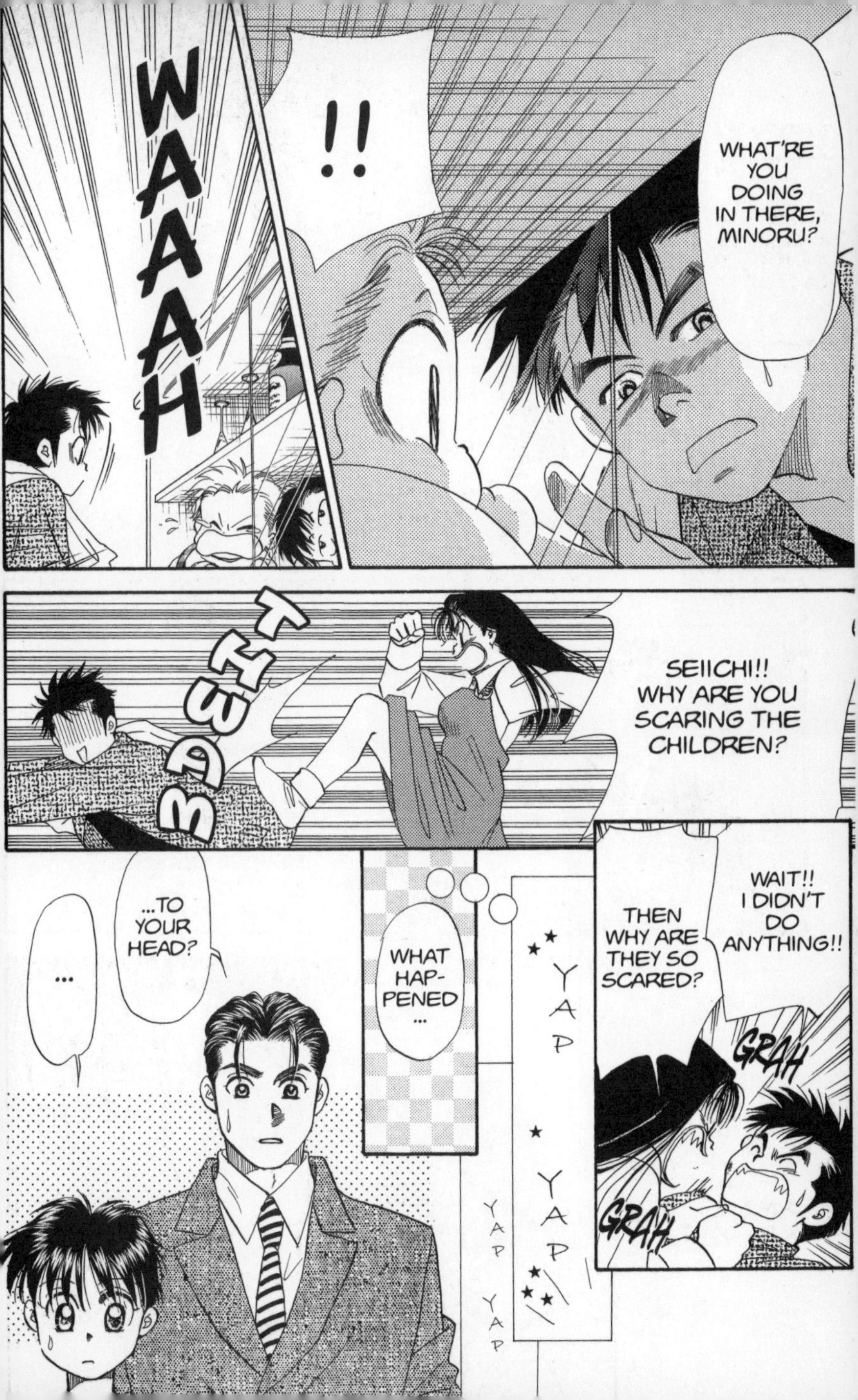
WHAT'RE YOU DOING IN THERE, MINORU?
!!
WAAAAH
SEIICHI!! WHY ARE YOU SCARING THE CHILDREN?
THWUM
WAIT!! I DIDN'T DO ANYTHING!!
THEN WHY ARE THEY SO SCARED?
GRAH
GRAH
YAP YAP
YAP YAP
WHAT HAP-PENED ...
...TO YOUR HEAD?
...

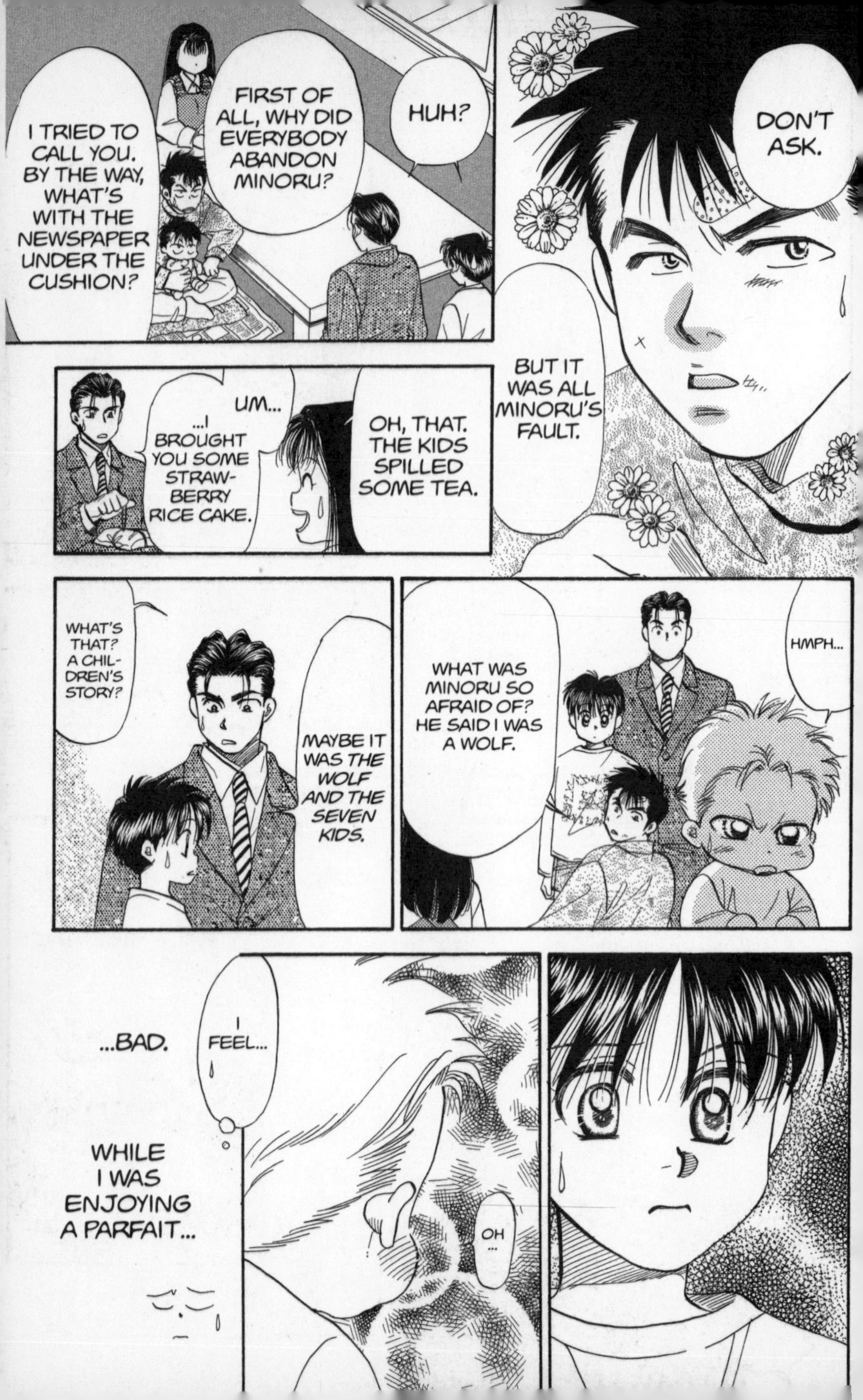
DON'T ASK.
BUT IT WAS ALL MINORU'S FAULT.
HUH?
FIRST OF ALL, WHY DID EVERYBODY ABANDON MINORU?
I TRIED TO CALL YOU. BY THE WAY, WHAT'S WITH THE NEWSPAPER UNDER THE CUSHION?
OH, THAT. THE KIDS SPILLED SOME TEA.
UM...
...I BROUGHT YOU SOME STRAW-BERRY RICE CAKE.
HMPH...
WHAT WAS MINORU SO AFRAID OF? HE SAID I WAS A WOLF.
MAYBE IT WAS THE WOLF AND THE SEVEN KIDS.
WHAT'S THAT? A CHIL-DREN'S STORY?
I FEEL...
...BAD.
OH ...
WHILE I WAS ENJOYING A PARFAIT...

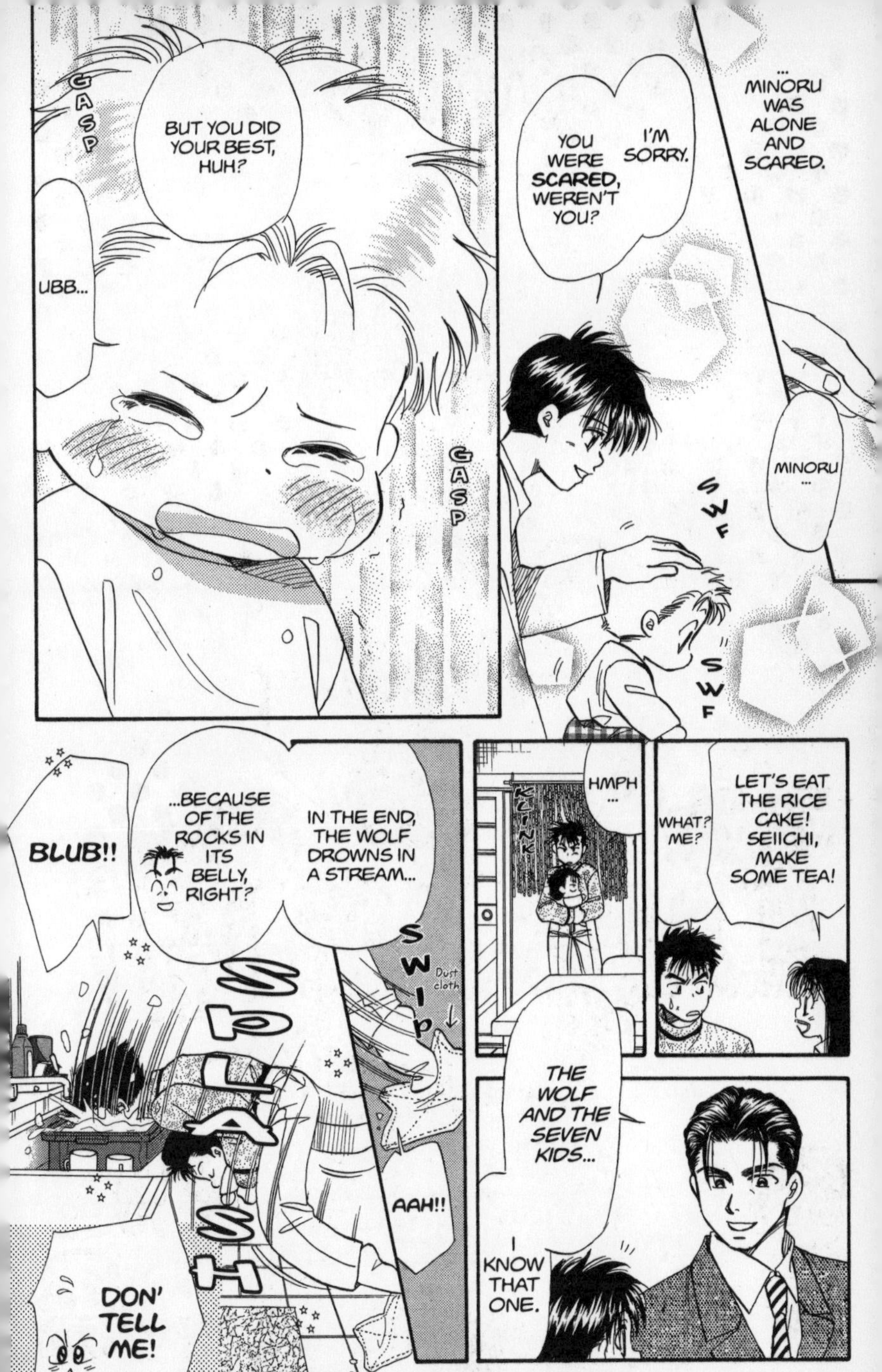
...MINORU WAS ALONE AND SCARED.
I'M SORRY.
YOU WERE SCARED, WEREN'T YOU?
MINORU ...
SWF
SWF
BUT YOU DID YOUR BEST, HUH?
GASP
UBB...
GASP
LET'S EAT THE RICE CAKE! SEIICHI, MAKE SOME TEA!
WHAT? ME?
HMPH ...
KLINK
THE WOLF AND THE SEVEN KIDS...
I KNOW THAT ONE.
IN THE END, THE WOLF DROWNS IN A STREAM...
...BECAUSE OF THE ROCKS IN ITS BELLY, RIGHT?
BLUB!!
SWIP
Dust cloth
SPLASH
AAH!!
DON'T TELL ME!

Chapter 84 / The End

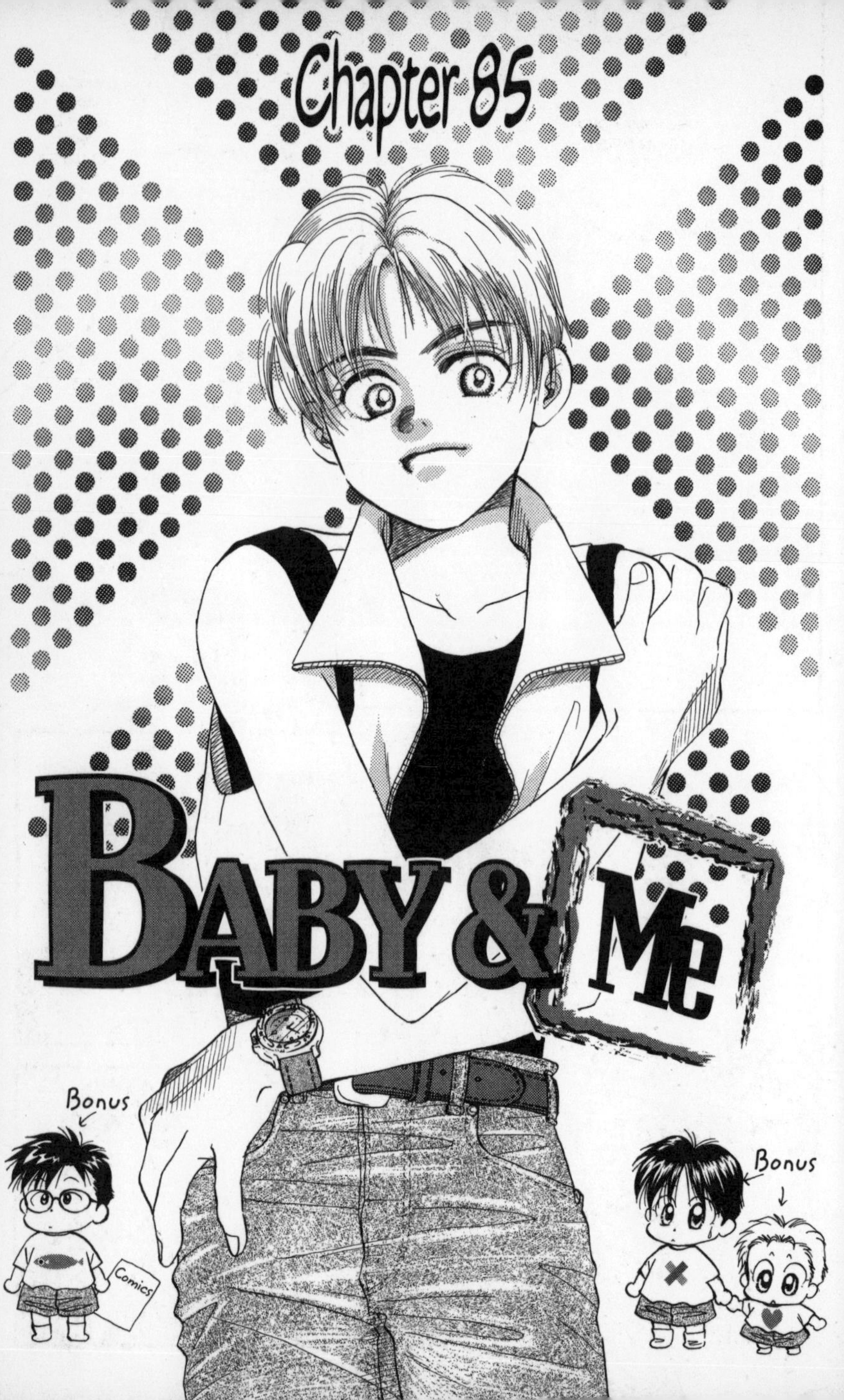

Chapter 85
BABY & Me
Bonus
Comics
Bonus

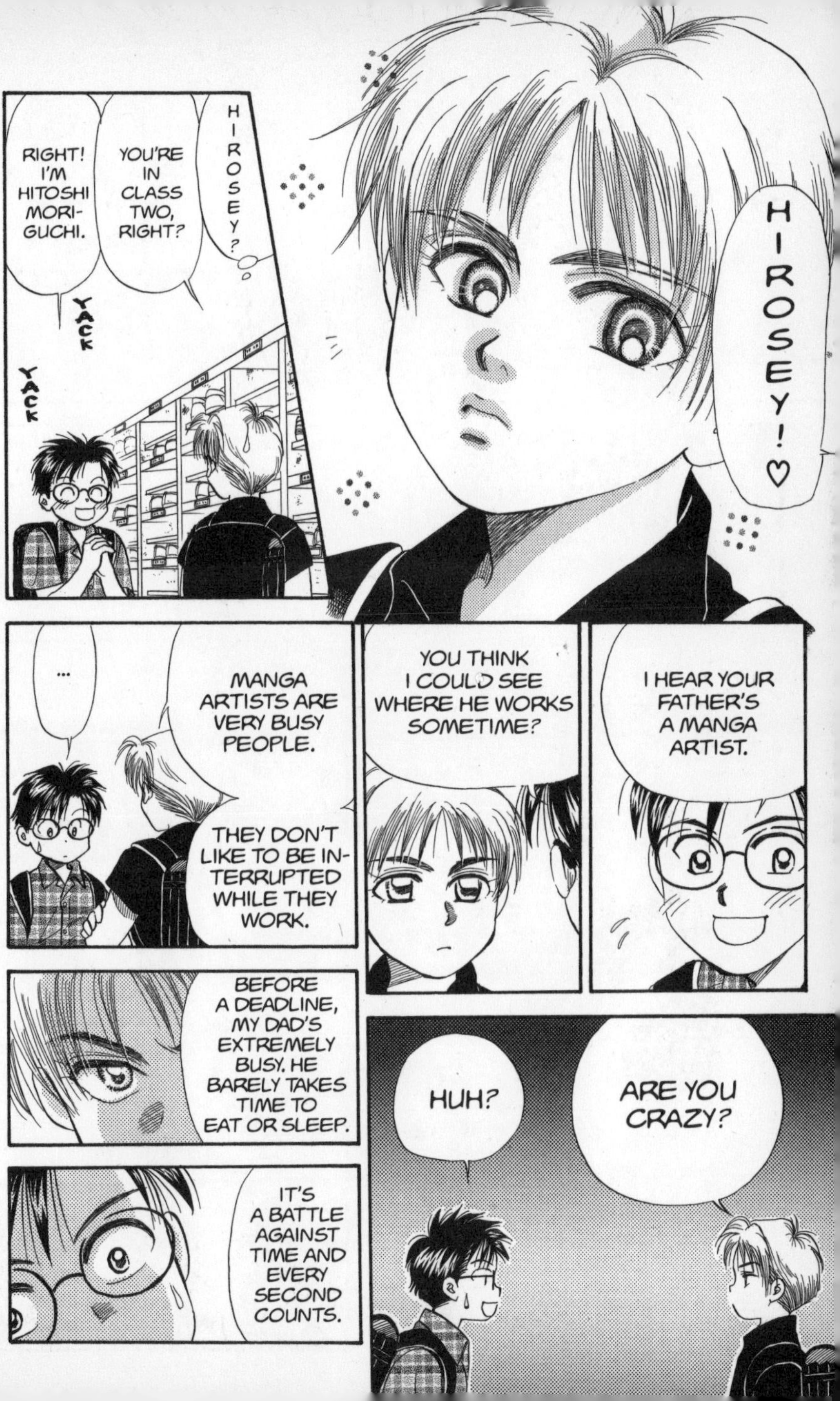
HIROSEY!♡
HIROSEY?
YOU'RE IN CLASS TWO, RIGHT?
RIGHT! I'M HITOSHI MORI-GUCHI.
YACK
YACK
I HEAR YOUR FATHER'S A MANGA ARTIST.
YOU THINK I COULD SEE WHERE HE WORKS SOMETIME?
MANGA ARTISTS ARE VERY BUSY PEOPLE.
THEY DON'T LIKE TO BE IN-TERRUPTED WHILE THEY WORK.
...
ARE YOU CRAZY?
HUH?
BEFORE A DEADLINE, MY DAD'S EXTREMELY BUSY. HE BARELY TAKES TIME TO EAT OR SLEEP.
IT'S A BATTLE AGAINST TIME AND EVERY SECOND COUNTS.

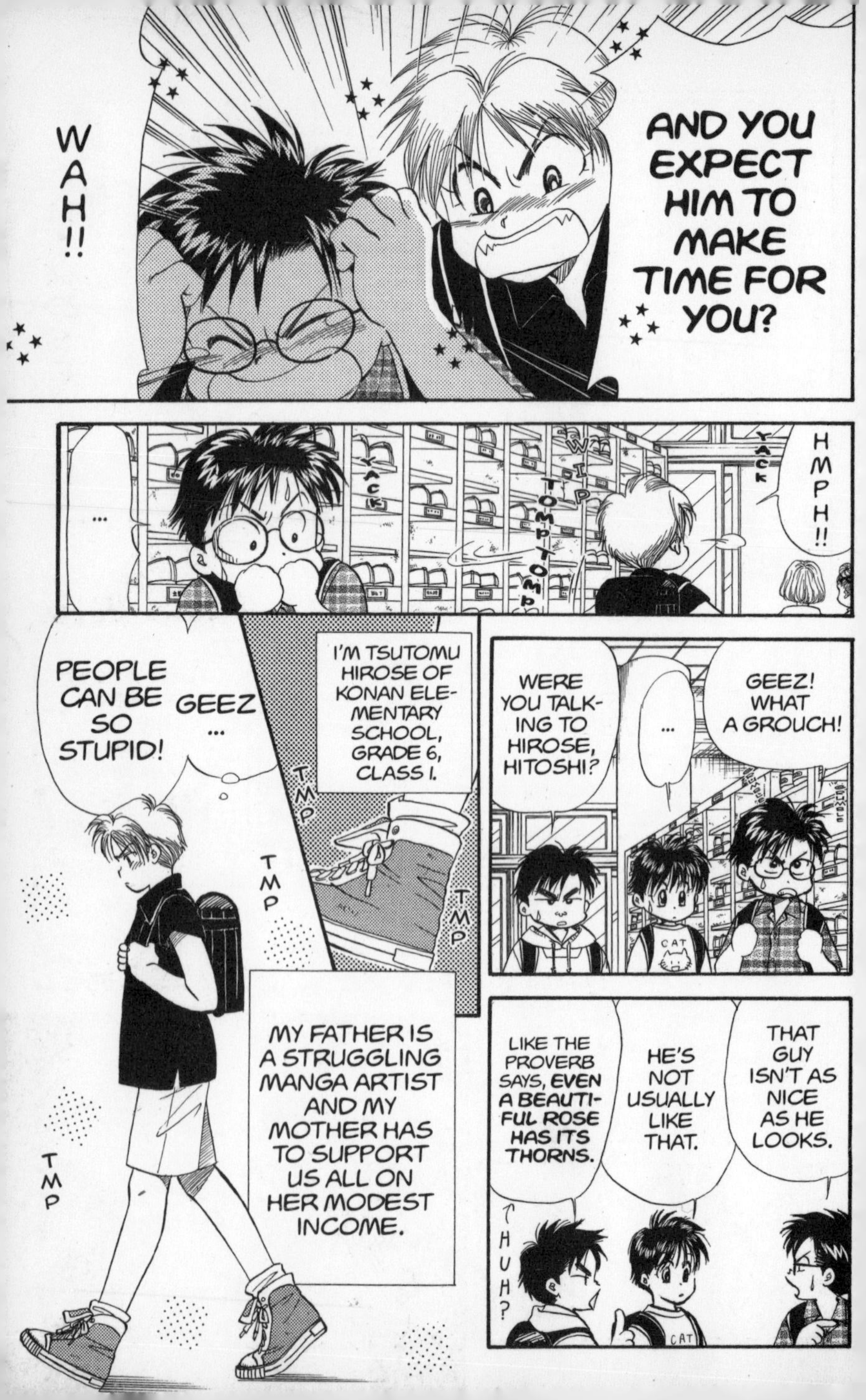
AND YOU EXPECT HIM TO MAKE TIME FOR YOU?
WAH!!
HMPH!!
YACK
WIP
TOMP TOMP TOMP
YACK
...
GEEZ! WHAT A GROUCH!
...
WERE YOU TALKING TO HIROSE, HITOSHI?
THAT GUY ISN'T AS NICE AS HE LOOKS.
HE'S NOT USUALLY LIKE THAT.
LIKE THE PROVERB SAYS, EVEN A BEAUTIFUL ROSE HAS ITS THORNS.
HUH?
I'M TSUTOMU HIROSE OF KONAN ELEMENTARY SCHOOL, GRADE 6, CLASS 1.
TMP
TMP
PEOPLE CAN BE SO STUPID!
GEEZ...
TMP
MY FATHER IS A STRUGGLING MANGA ARTIST AND MY MOTHER HAS TO SUPPORT US ALL ON HER MODEST INCOME.
TMP

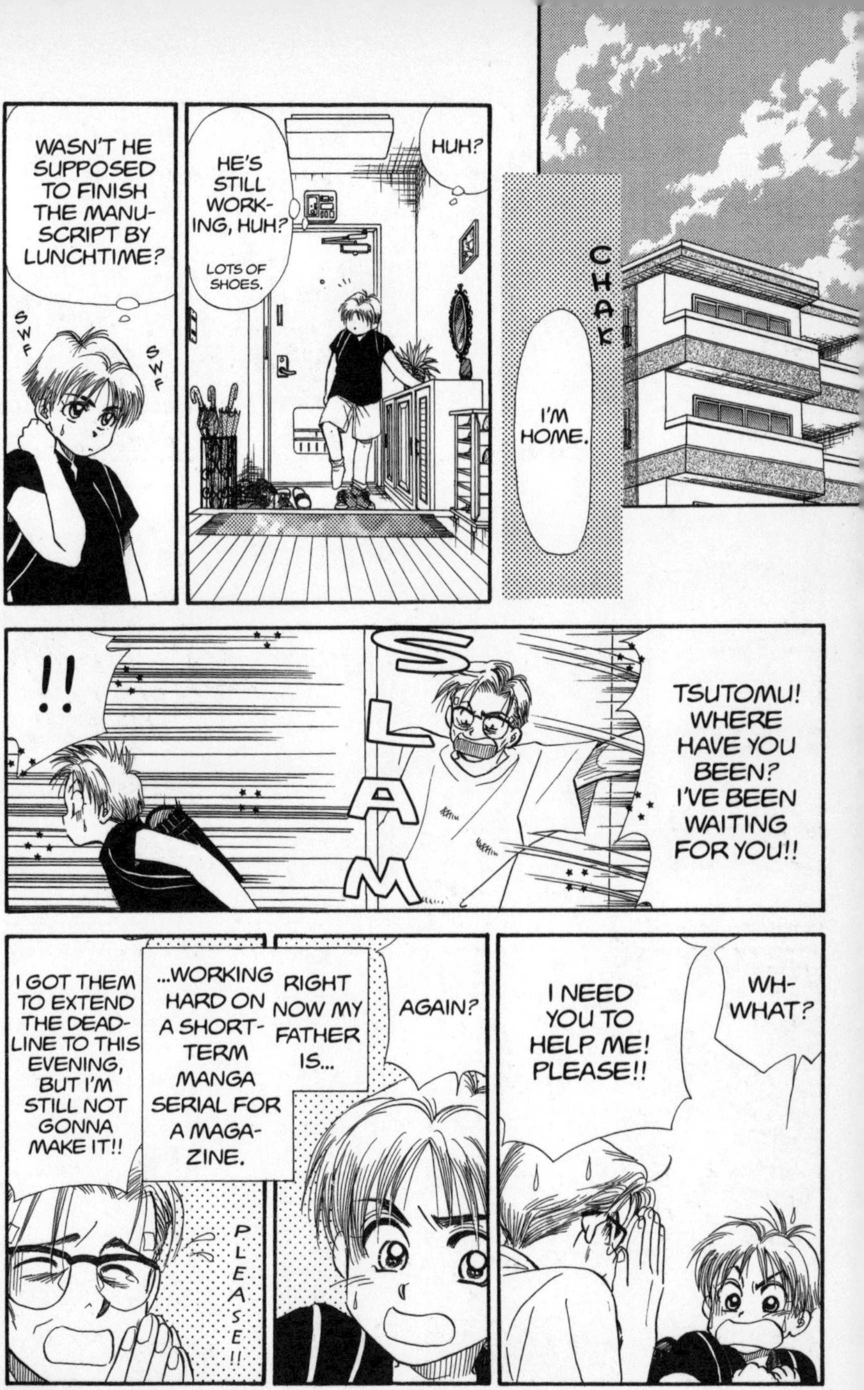
CHAK
I'M HOME.
HUH?
HE'S STILL WORKING, HUH?
LOTS OF SHOES.
WASN'T HE SUPPOSED TO FINISH THE MANUSCRIPT BY LUNCHTIME?
SWF
SWF
SLAM
TSUTOMU! WHERE HAVE YOU BEEN? I'VE BEEN WAITING FOR YOU!!
!!
WH-WHAT?
I NEED YOU TO HELP ME! PLEASE!!
AGAIN?
RIGHT NOW MY FATHER IS...
...WORKING HARD ON A SHORT-TERM MANGA SERIAL FOR A MAGAZINE.
I GOT THEM TO EXTEND THE DEADLINE TO THIS EVENING, BUT I'M STILL NOT GONNA MAKE IT!!
PLEASE!!

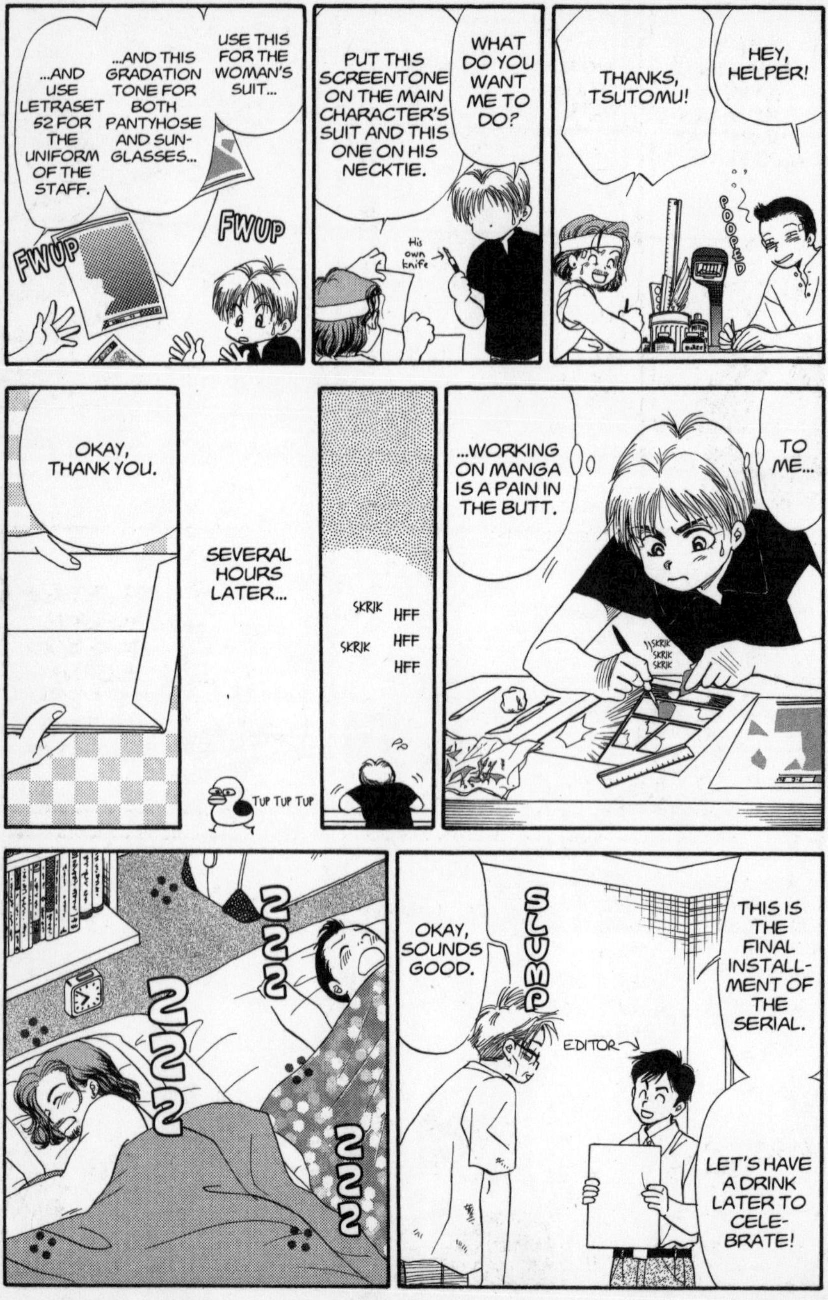
HEY, HELPER!
THANKS, TSUTOMU!
POOPED
WHAT DO YOU WANT ME TO DO?
PUT THIS SCREENTONE ON THE MAIN CHARACTER'S SUIT AND THIS ONE ON HIS NECKTIE.
His own knife
USE THIS FOR THE WOMAN'S SUIT...
...AND THIS GRADATION TONE FOR BOTH PANTYHOSE AND SUN-GLASSES...
...AND USE LETRASET 52 FOR THE UNIFORM OF THE STAFF.
FWUP
FWUP
TO ME...
...WORKING ON MANGA IS A PAIN IN THE BUTT.
SKRIK SKRIK SKRIK
HFF HFF HFF
SKRIK SKRIK
SEVERAL HOURS LATER...
TUP TUP TUP
OKAY, THANK YOU.
THIS IS THE FINAL INSTALL-MENT OF THE SERIAL.
SLUMP
OKAY, SOUNDS GOOD.
EDITOR
LET'S HAVE A DRINK LATER TO CELE-BRATE!
ZZZ
ZZZ
ZZZ

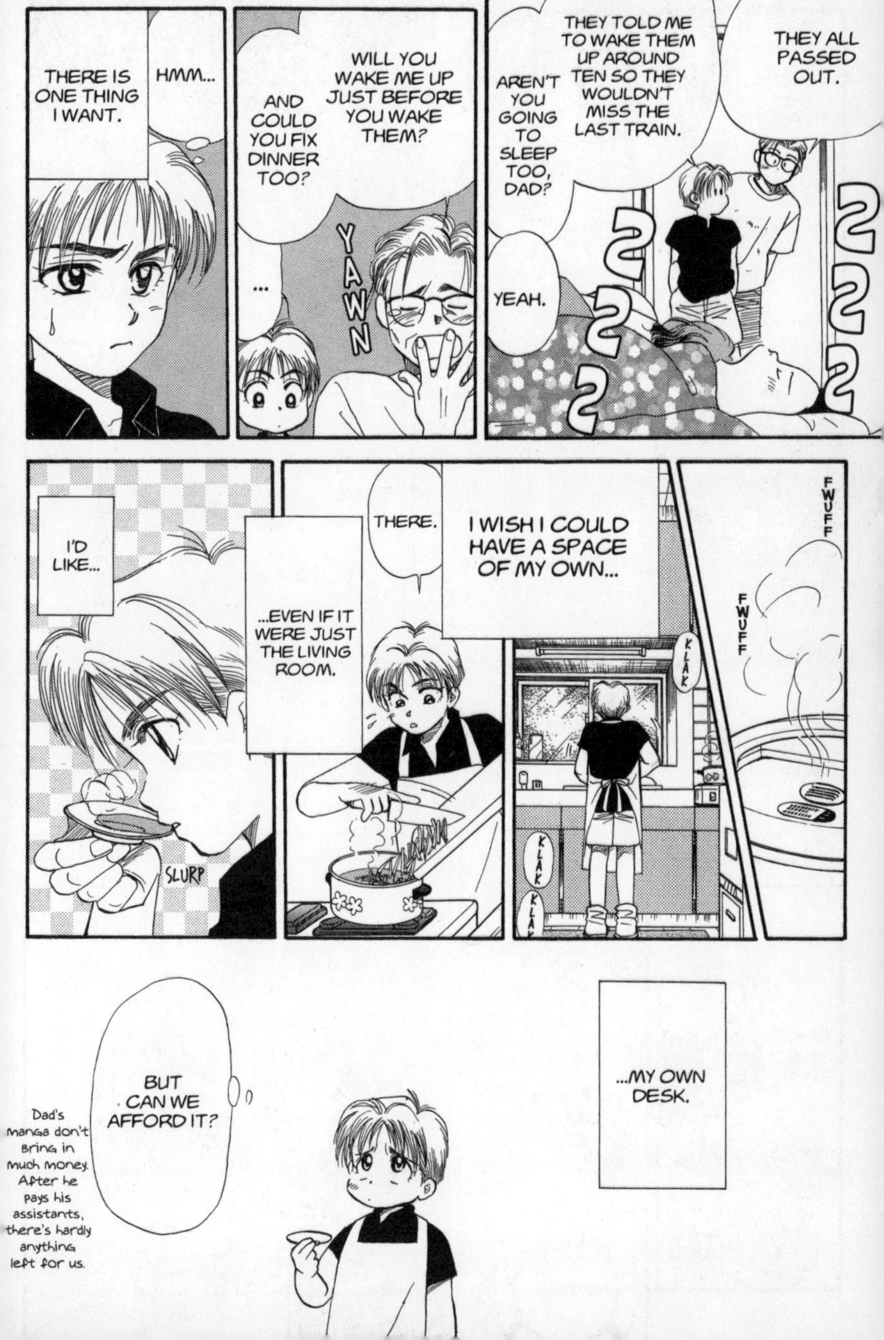
THEY ALL PASSED OUT.
THEY TOLD ME TO WAKE THEM UP AROUND TEN SO THEY WOULDN'T MISS THE LAST TRAIN.
AREN'T YOU GOING TO SLEEP TOO, DAD?
YEAH.
ZZZ
ZZZ
WILL YOU WAKE ME UP JUST BEFORE YOU WAKE THEM?
AND COULD YOU FIX DINNER TOO?
YAWN
...
HMM...
THERE IS ONE THING I WANT.
FWUFF
FWUFF
I WISH I COULD HAVE A SPACE OF MY OWN...
KLAK
KLAK
KLAK
THERE.
...EVEN IF IT WERE JUST THE LIVING ROOM.
I'D LIKE...
SLURP
...MY OWN DESK.
BUT CAN WE AFFORD IT?
Dad's manga don't bring in much money. After he pays his assistants, there's hardly anything left for us.

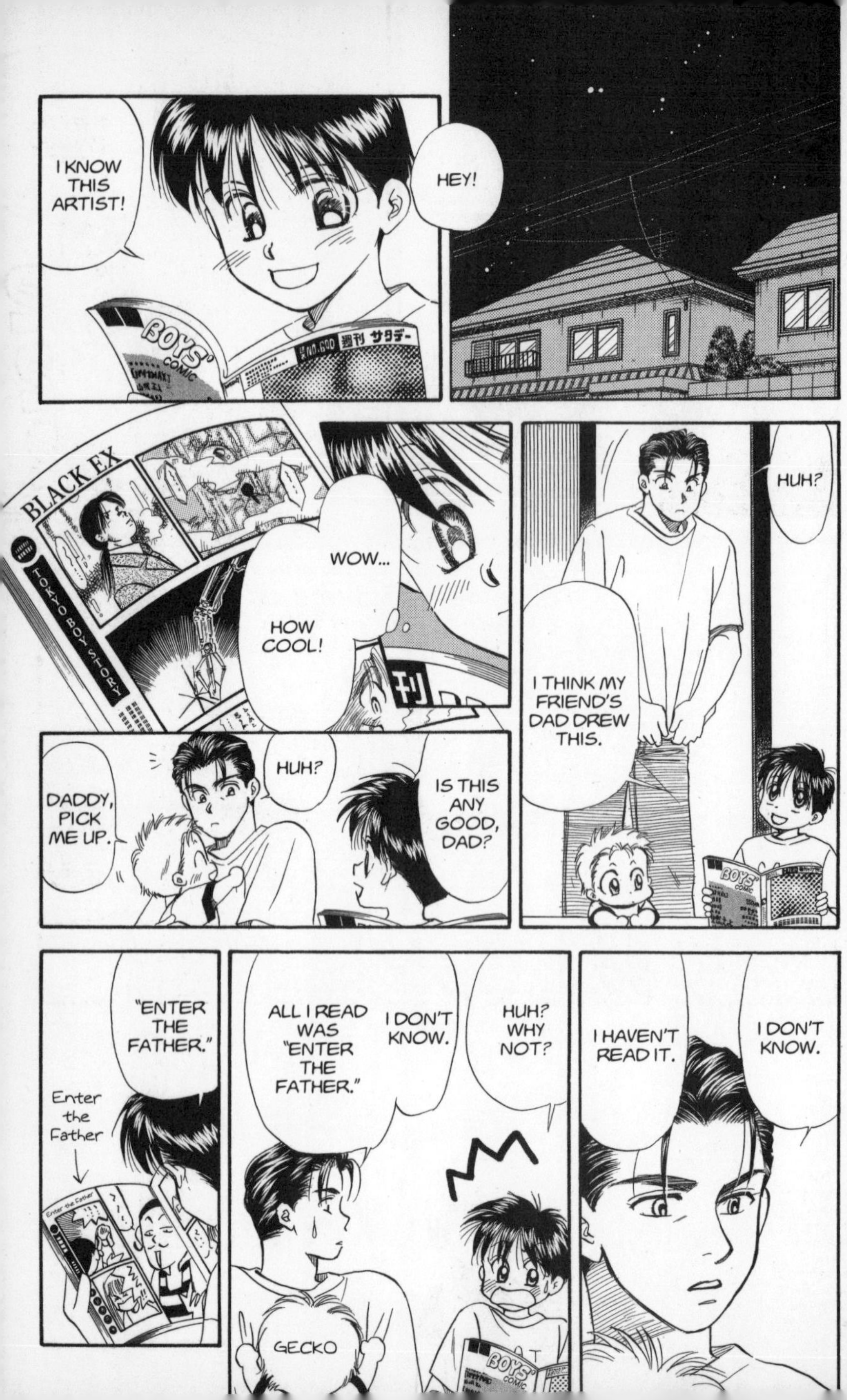
HEY!
I KNOW THIS ARTIST!
BOYS' COMIC
HUH?
I THINK MY FRIEND'S DAD DREW THIS.
BLACK EX
TOKYO BOY STORY
WOW...
HOW COOL!
IS THIS ANY GOOD, DAD?
HUH?
DADDY, PICK ME UP.
I DON'T KNOW.
I HAVEN'T READ IT.
HUH? WHY NOT?
I DON'T KNOW.
ALL I READ WAS "ENTER THE FATHER."
GECKO
"ENTER THE FATHER."
Enter the Father
Enter the Father

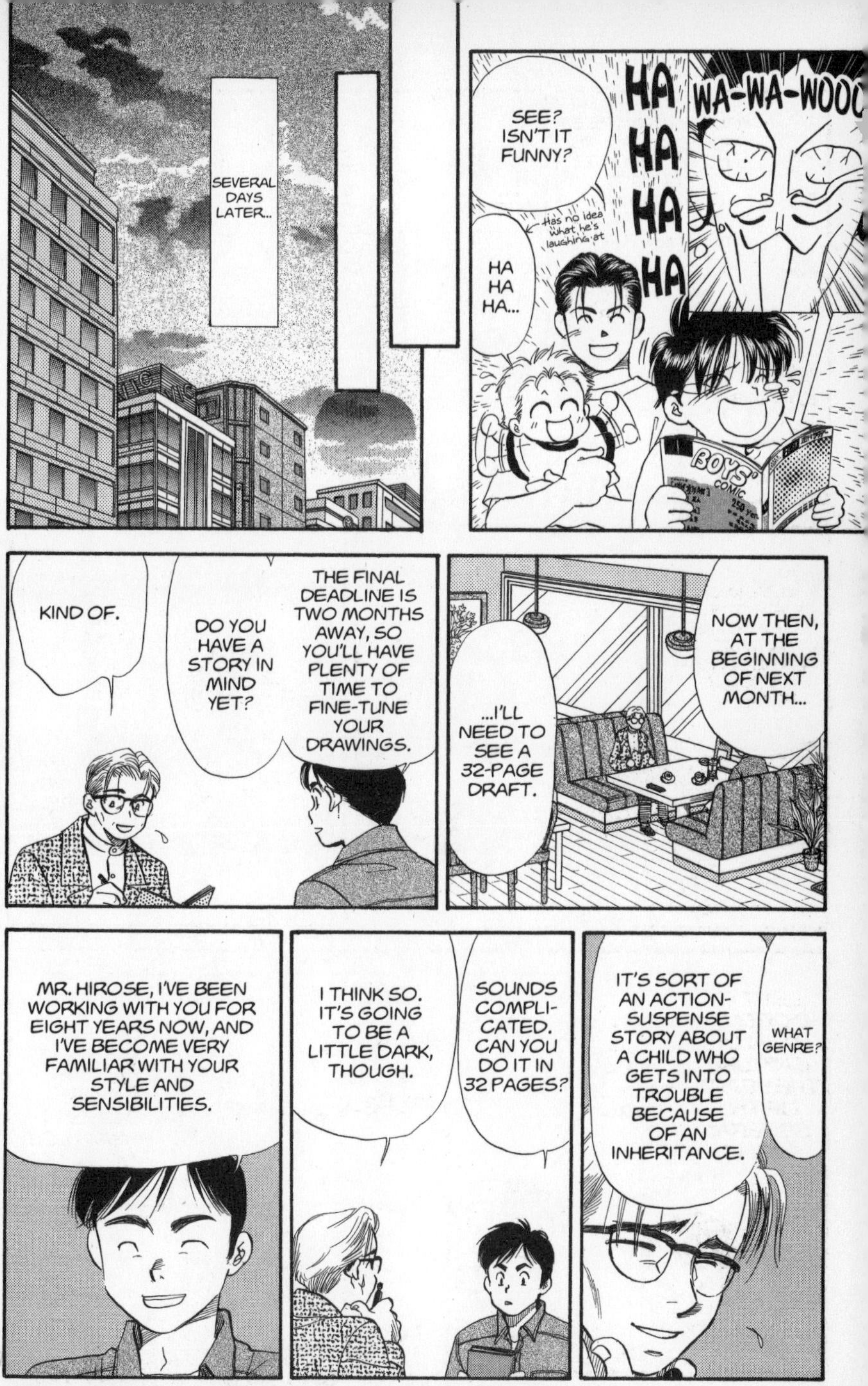
WA-WA-WOO
HA HA HA HA
SEE? ISN'T IT FUNNY?
Has no idea what he's laughing at
HA HA HA...
BOYS' COMIC 250 yen
SEVERAL DAYS LATER..
NOW THEN, AT THE BEGINNING OF NEXT MONTH...
...I'LL NEED TO SEE A 32-PAGE DRAFT.
THE FINAL DEADLINE IS TWO MONTHS AWAY, SO YOU'LL HAVE PLENTY OF TIME TO FINE-TUNE YOUR DRAWINGS.
DO YOU HAVE A STORY IN MIND YET?
KIND OF.
WHAT GENRE?
IT'S SORT OF AN ACTION-SUSPENSE STORY ABOUT A CHILD WHO GETS INTO TROUBLE BECAUSE OF AN INHERITANCE.
SOUNDS COMPLI-CATED. CAN YOU DO IT IN 32 PAGES?
I THINK SO. IT'S GOING TO BE A LITTLE DARK, THOUGH.
MR. HIROSE, I'VE BEEN WORKING WITH YOU FOR EIGHT YEARS NOW, AND I'VE BECOME VERY FAMILIAR WITH YOUR STYLE AND SENSIBILITIES.

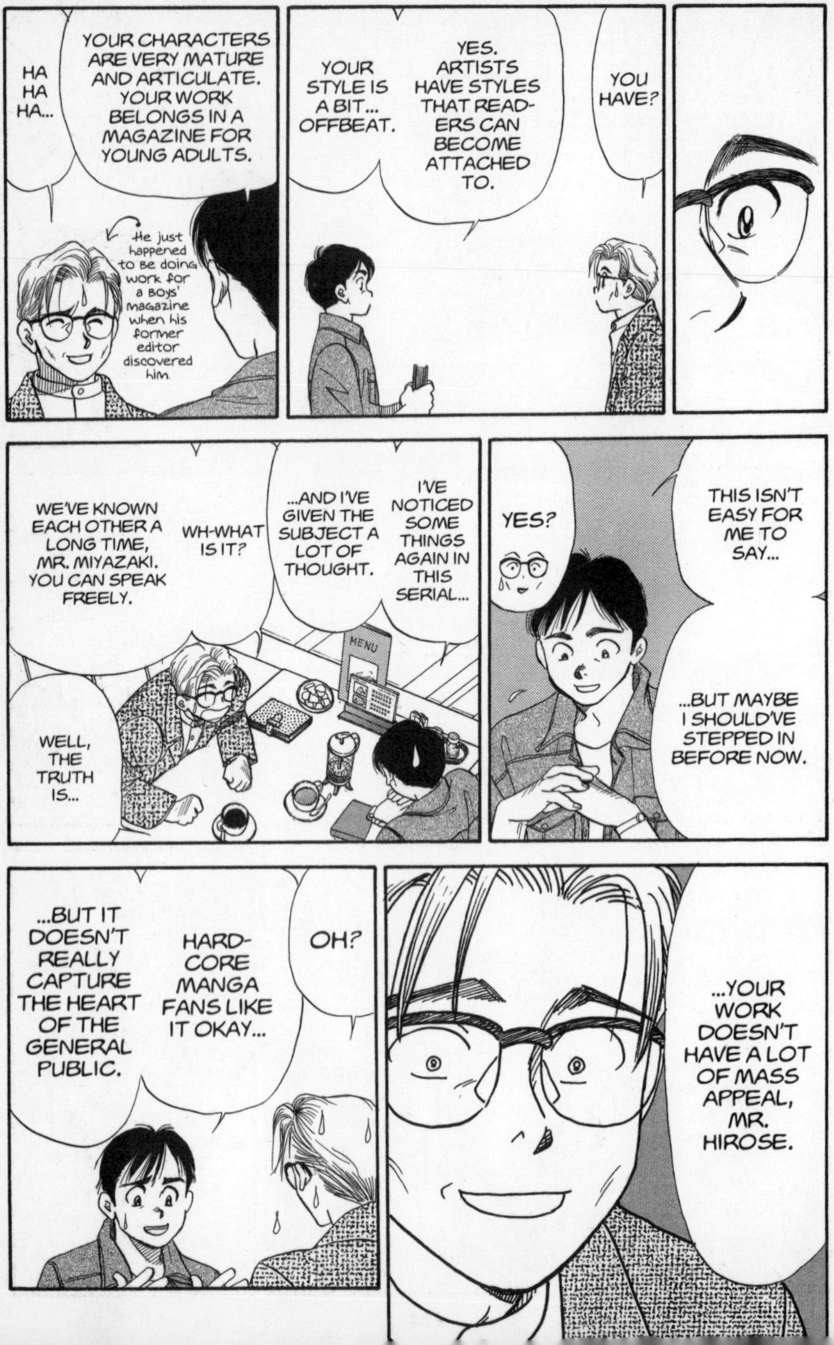
YOU HAVE?
YES. ARTISTS HAVE STYLES THAT READERS CAN BECOME ATTACHED TO.
YOUR STYLE IS A BIT... OFFBEAT.
YOUR CHARACTERS ARE VERY MATURE AND ARTICULATE. YOUR WORK BELONGS IN A MAGAZINE FOR YOUNG ADULTS.
HA HA HA...
He just happened to be doing work for a boys' magazine when his former editor discovered him.
THIS ISN'T EASY FOR ME TO SAY...
YES?
...BUT MAYBE I SHOULD'VE STEPPED IN BEFORE NOW.
I'VE NOTICED SOME THINGS AGAIN IN THIS SERIAL...
...AND I'VE GIVEN THE SUBJECT A LOT OF THOUGHT.
WH-WHAT IS IT?
WE'VE KNOWN EACH OTHER A LONG TIME, MR. MIYAZAKI. YOU CAN SPEAK FREELY.
MENU
WELL, THE TRUTH IS...
...YOUR WORK DOESN'T HAVE A LOT OF MASS APPEAL, MR. HIROSE.
OH?
HARD-CORE MANGA FANS LIKE IT OKAY...
...BUT IT DOESN'T REALLY CAPTURE THE HEART OF THE GENERAL PUBLIC.

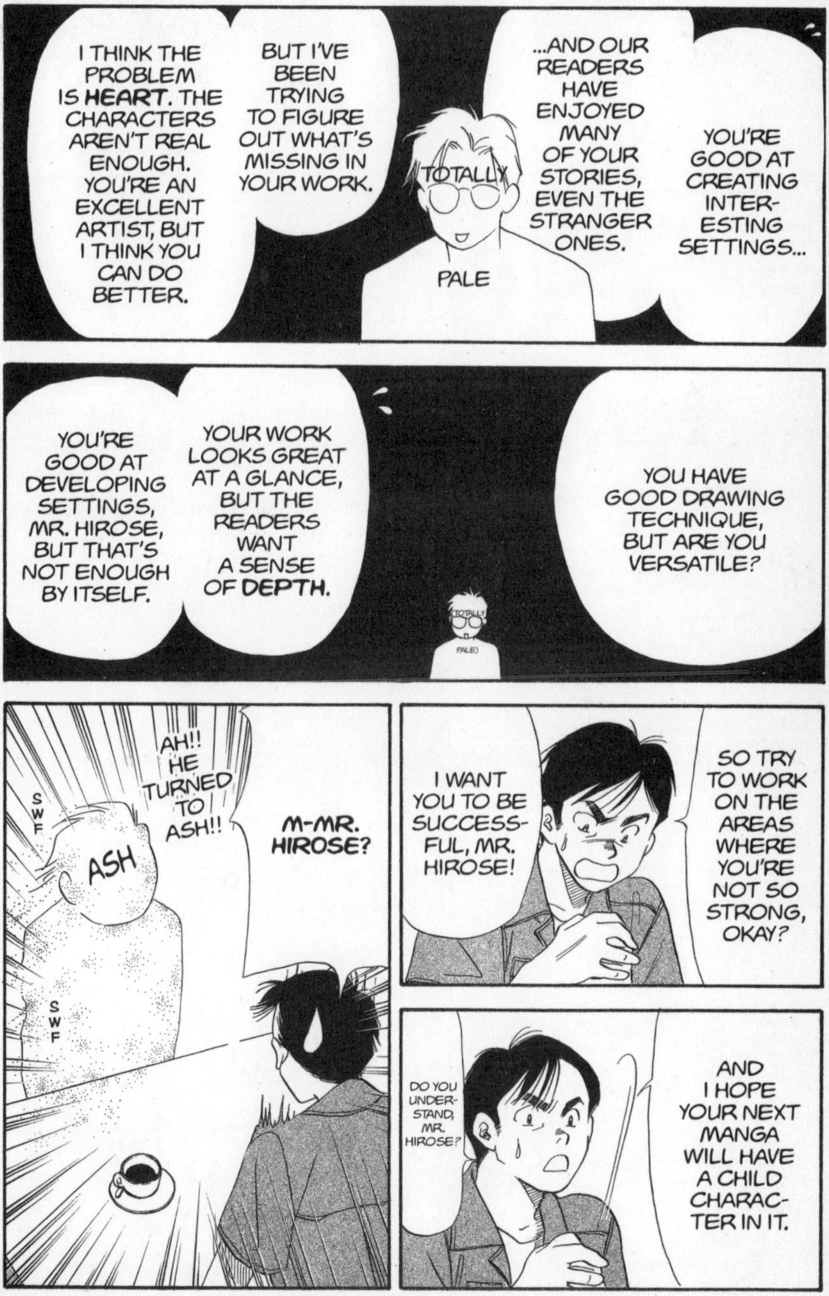
YOU'RE GOOD AT CREATING INTER-ESTING SETTINGS...
...AND OUR READERS HAVE ENJOYED MANY OF YOUR STORIES, EVEN THE STRANGER ONES.
TOTALLY
PALE
BUT I'VE BEEN TRYING TO FIGURE OUT WHAT'S MISSING IN YOUR WORK.
I THINK THE PROBLEM IS **HEART**. THE CHARACTERS AREN'T REAL ENOUGH. YOU'RE AN EXCELLENT ARTIST, BUT I THINK YOU CAN DO BETTER.
YOU HAVE GOOD DRAWING TECHNIQUE, BUT ARE YOU VERSATILE?
(TOTALLY PALE)
YOUR WORK LOOKS GREAT AT A GLANCE, BUT THE READERS WANT A SENSE OF **DEPTH**.
YOU'RE GOOD AT DEVELOPING SETTINGS, MR. HIROSE, BUT THAT'S NOT ENOUGH BY ITSELF.
SO TRY TO WORK ON THE AREAS WHERE YOU'RE NOT SO STRONG, OKAY?
I WANT YOU TO BE SUCCESS-FUL, MR. HIROSE!
AND I HOPE YOUR NEXT MANGA WILL HAVE A CHILD CHARAC-TER IN IT.
DO YOU UNDER-STAND, MR. HIROSE?
M-MR. HIROSE?
AH!! HE TURNED TO ASH!!
ASH
SWF
SWF

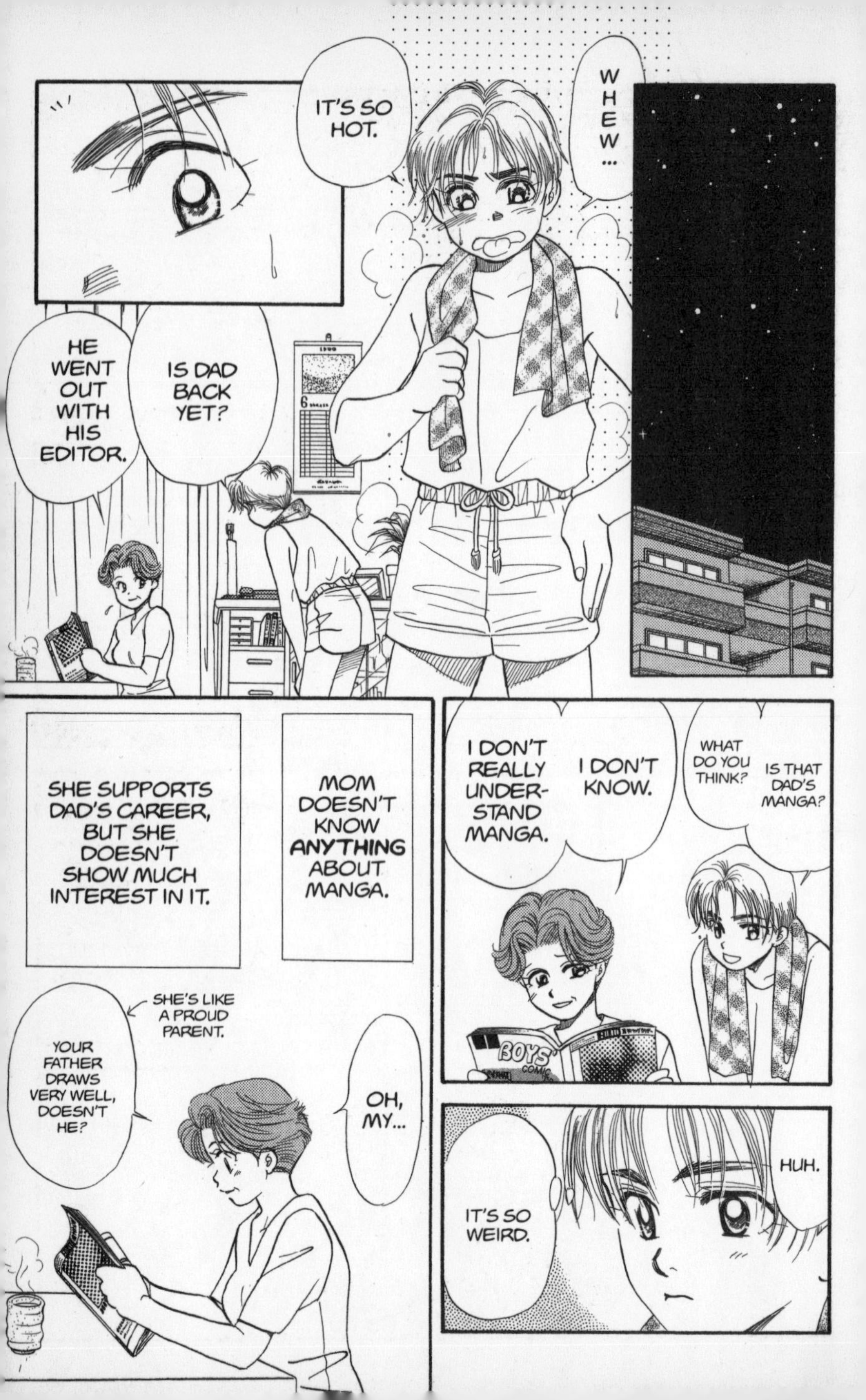
WHEW...
IT'S SO HOT.
IS DAD BACK YET?
HE WENT OUT WITH HIS EDITOR.
IS THAT DAD'S MANGA?
WHAT DO YOU THINK?
I DON'T KNOW.
I DON'T REALLY UNDERSTAND MANGA.
MOM DOESN'T KNOW **ANYTHING** ABOUT MANGA.
SHE SUPPORTS DAD'S CAREER, BUT SHE DOESN'T SHOW MUCH INTEREST IN IT.
OH, MY...
YOUR FATHER DRAWS VERY WELL, DOESN'T HE?
SHE'S LIKE A PROUD PARENT.
HUH.
IT'S SO WEIRD.

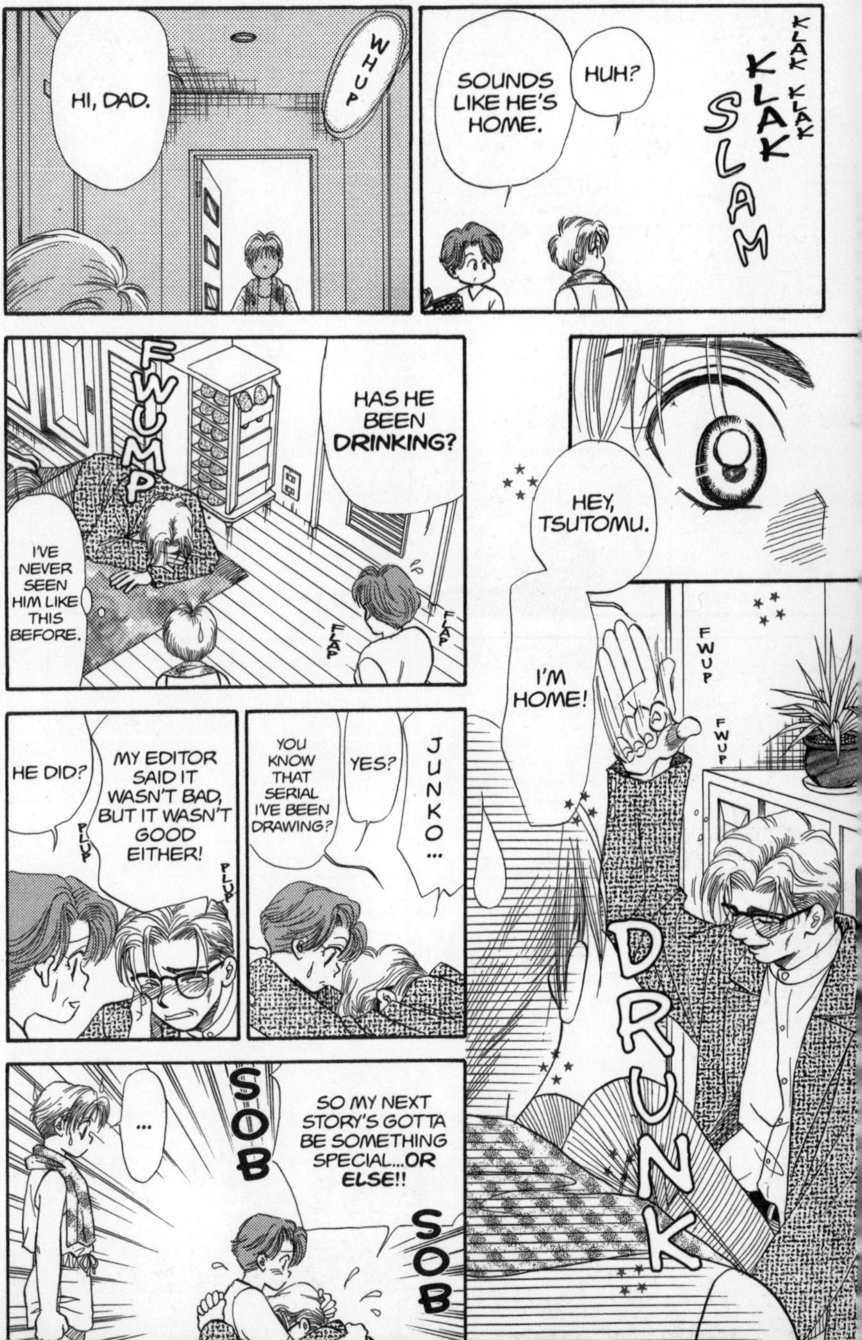
SLAM
KLAK KLAK KLAK
HUH?
SOUNDS LIKE HE'S HOME.
WHUP
HI, DAD.
HEY, TSUTOMU.
I'M HOME!
FWUP FWUP
DRUNK
HAS HE BEEN DRINKING?
FWUMP
I'VE NEVER SEEN HIM LIKE THIS BEFORE.
FLAP FLAP
JUNKO...
YES?
YOU KNOW THAT SERIAL I'VE BEEN DRAWING?
MY EDITOR SAID IT WASN'T BAD, BUT IT WASN'T GOOD EITHER!
PLUP
HE DID?
PLUP
SO MY NEXT STORY'S GOTTA BE SOMETHING SPECIAL...OR ELSE!!
SOB SOB
...

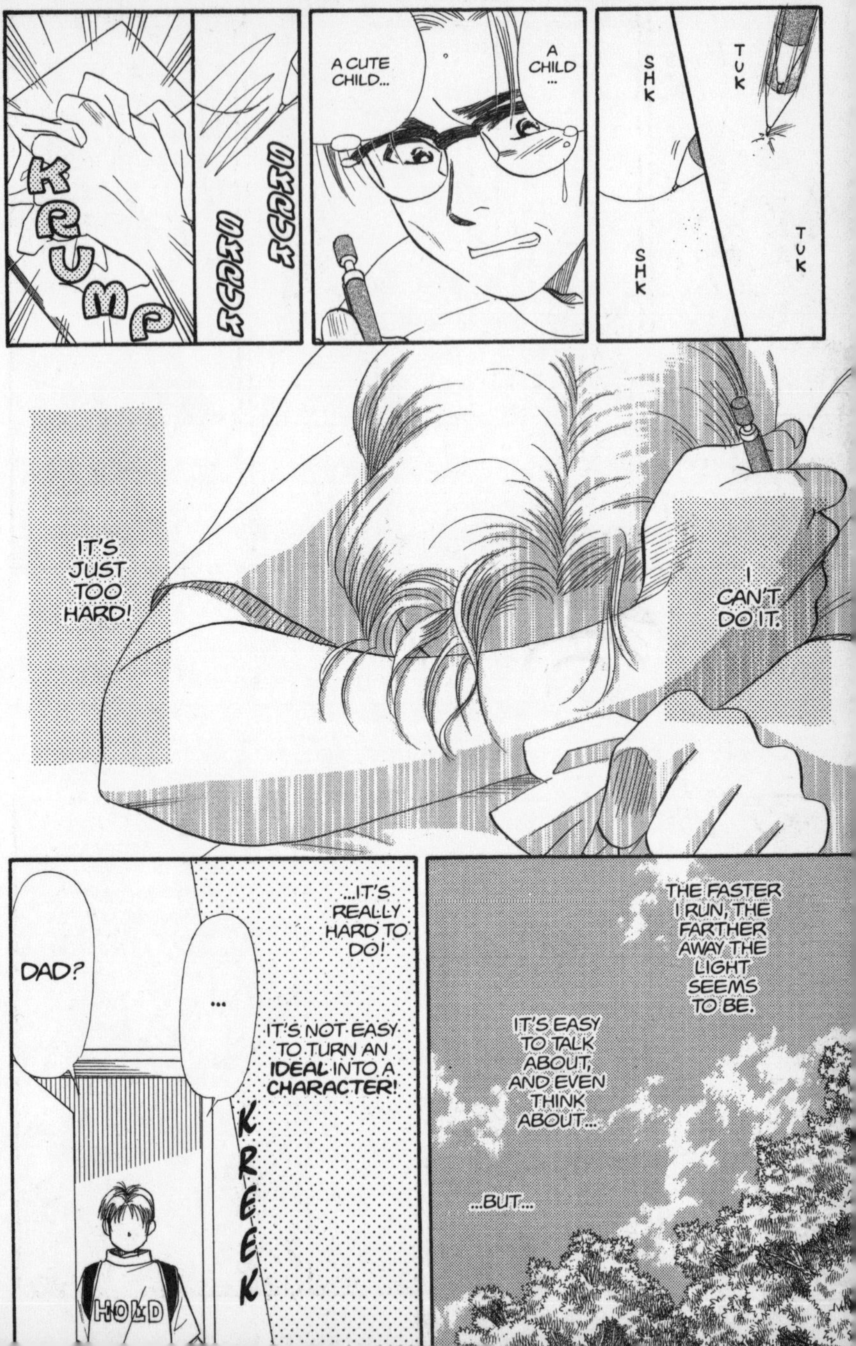
TUK
SHK
TUK
SHK
A CHILD...
A CUTE CHILD...
SCRCH
SCRCH
KRUMP
I CAN'T DO IT.
IT'S JUST TOO HARD!
THE FASTER I RUN, THE FARTHER AWAY THE LIGHT SEEMS TO BE.
IT'S EASY TO TALK ABOUT, AND EVEN THINK ABOUT...
...BUT...
...IT'S REALLY HARD TO DO!
IT'S NOT EASY TO TURN AN **IDEAL** INTO A **CHARACTER**!
KREEK
...
DAD?
HOLD

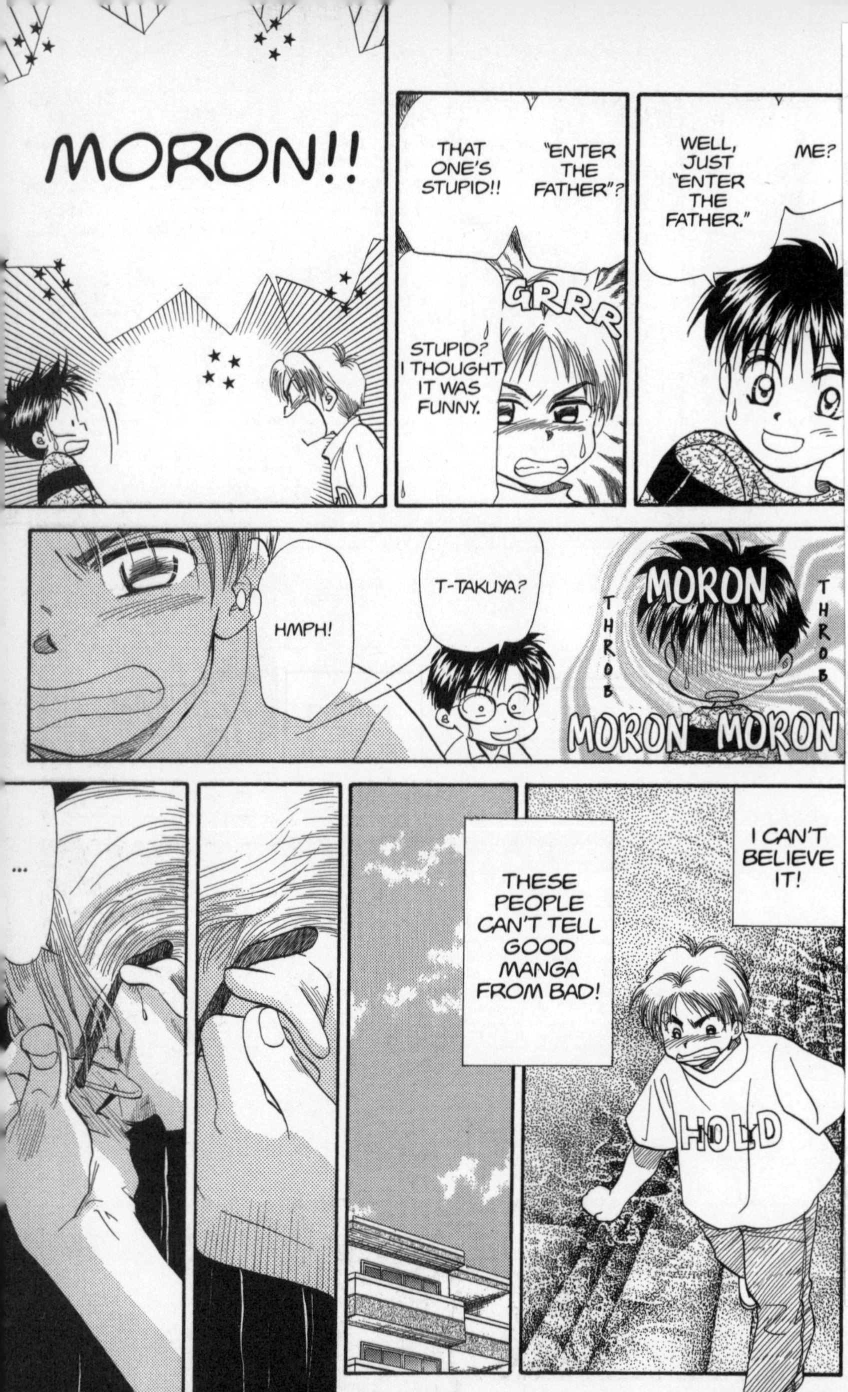
ME?
WELL, JUST "ENTER THE FATHER."
"ENTER THE FATHER"?
THAT ONE'S STUPID!!
GRRR
STUPID? I THOUGHT IT WAS FUNNY.
MORON!!
MORON
THROB
THROB
MORON MORON
T-TAKUYA?
HMPH!
I CAN'T BELIEVE IT!
THESE PEOPLE CAN'T TELL GOOD MANGA FROM BAD!
...

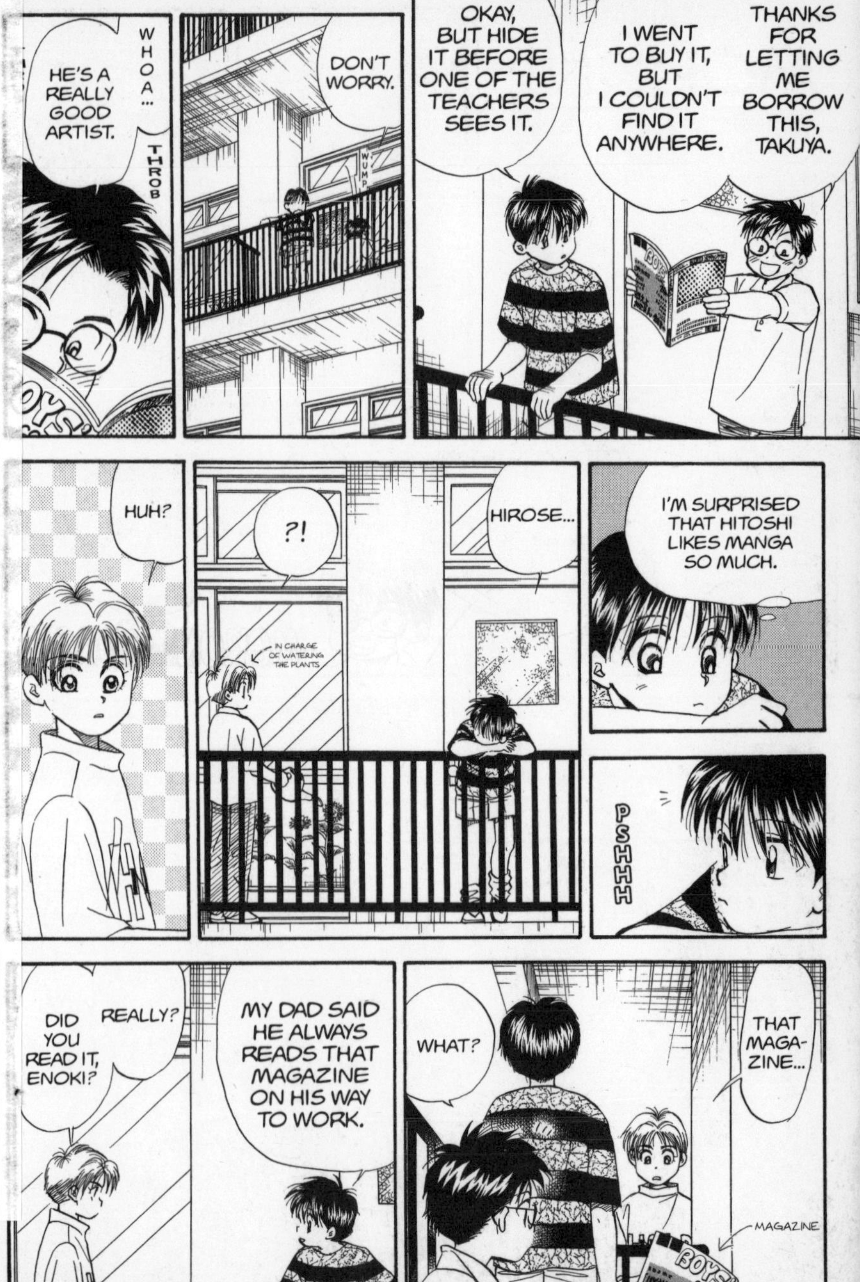
THANKS FOR LETTING ME BORROW THIS, TAKUYA.
I WENT TO BUY IT, BUT I COULDN'T FIND IT ANYWHERE.
OKAY, BUT HIDE IT BEFORE ONE OF THE TEACHERS SEES IT.
DON'T WORRY.
WUMP
WHOA...
THROB
HE'S A REALLY GOOD ARTIST.
I'M SURPRISED THAT HITOSHI LIKES MANGA SO MUCH.
PSHHH
HIROSE...
?!
IN CHARGE OF WATERING THE PLANTS
HUH?
THAT MAGA-ZINE...
WHAT?
MAGAZINE
BOYS' COMIC
MY DAD SAID HE ALWAYS READS THAT MAGAZINE ON HIS WAY TO WORK.
REALLY?
DID YOU READ IT, ENOKI?

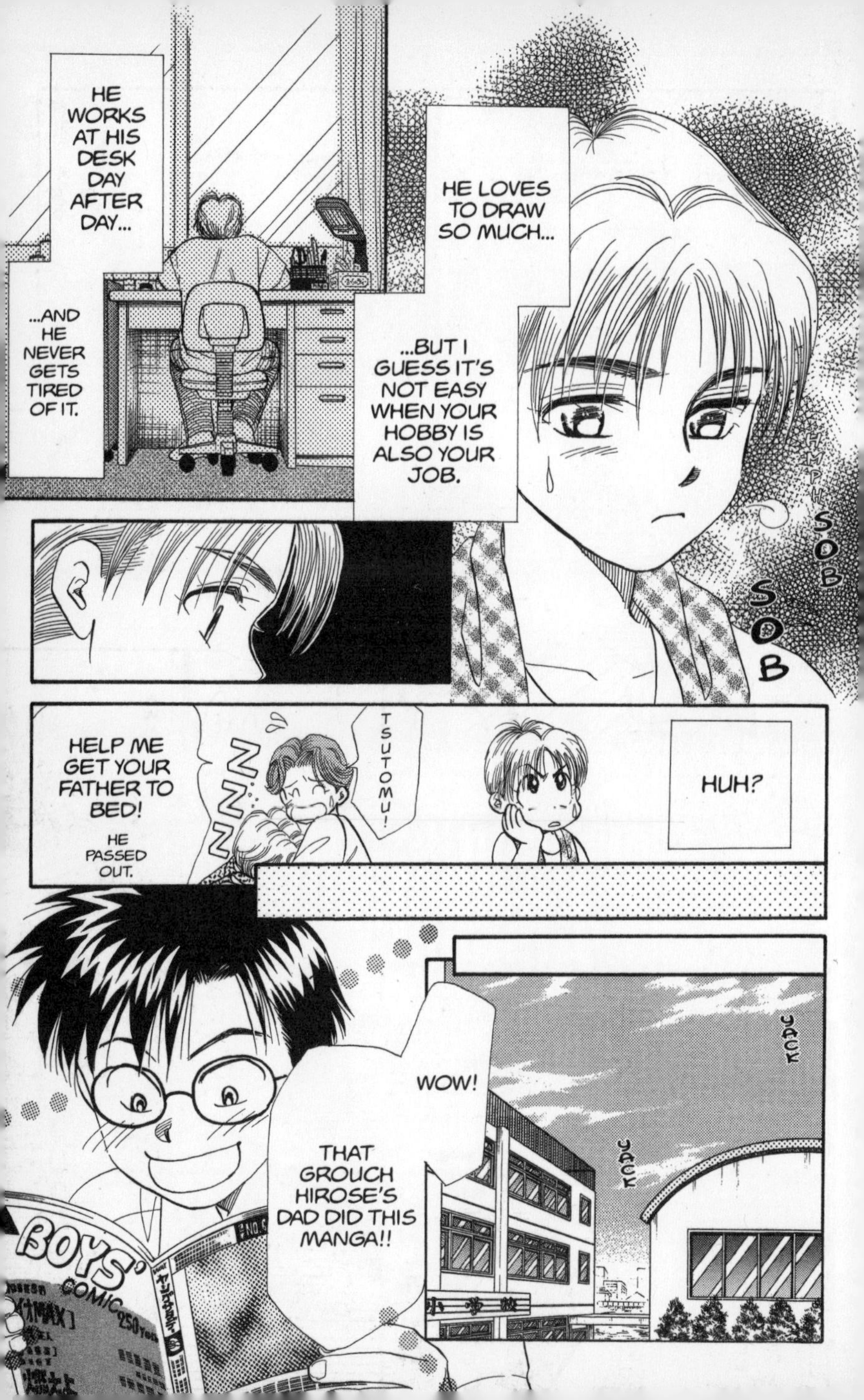
HE LOVES TO DRAW SO MUCH...
...BUT I GUESS IT'S NOT EASY WHEN YOUR HOBBY IS ALSO YOUR JOB.
HMPH
SOB
SOB
HE WORKS AT HIS DESK DAY AFTER DAY...
...AND HE NEVER GETS TIRED OF IT.
HUH?
TSUTOMU!
HELP ME GET YOUR FATHER TO BED!
HE PASSED OUT.
ZZZ
JACK
JACK
WOW!
THAT GROUCH HIROSE'S DAD DID THIS MANGA!!
BOYS' COMIC
250 Yen

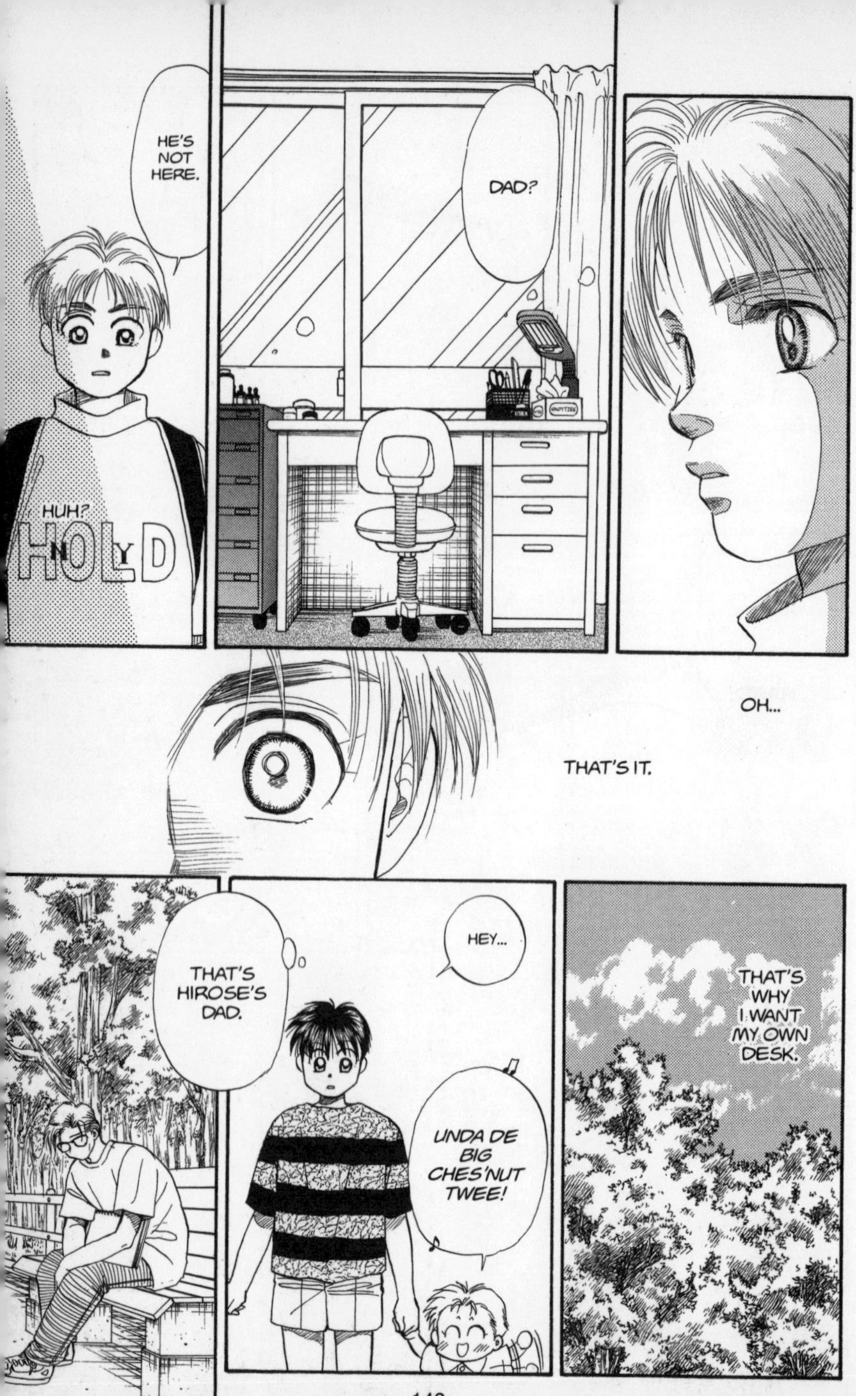
DAD?
HE'S NOT HERE.
HUH?
HOLD
OH...
THAT'S IT.
THAT'S WHY I WANT MY OWN DESK.
HEY...
UNDA DE BIG CHES'NUT TWEE!
THAT'S HIROSE'S DAD.

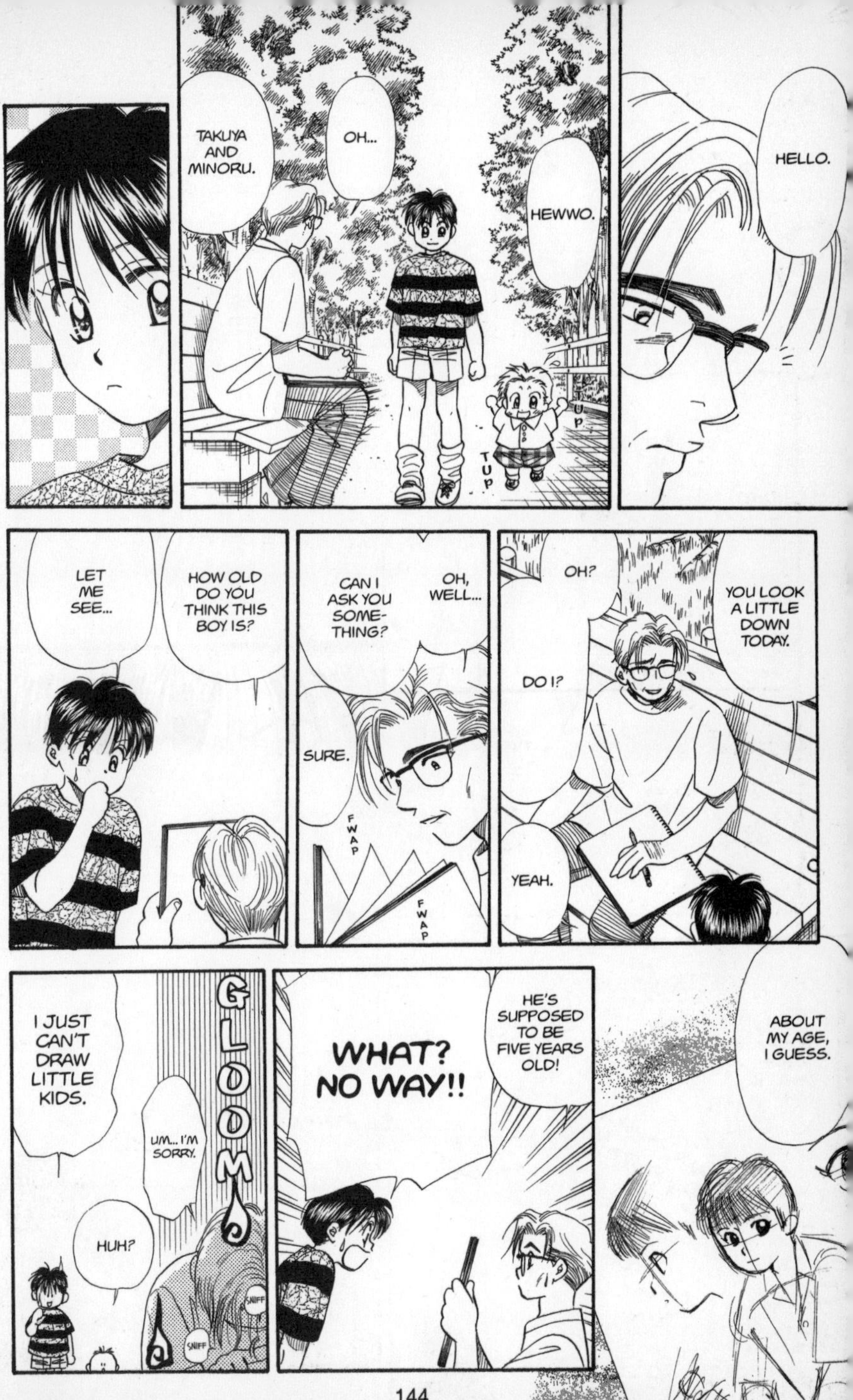

HELLO.
HEWWO.
OH...
TAKUYA AND MINORU.
TUP
TUP
YOU LOOK A LITTLE DOWN TODAY.
OH?
DO I?
YEAH.
OH, WELL...
CAN I ASK YOU SOME-THING?
SURE.
FWAP
FWAP
HOW OLD DO YOU THINK THIS BOY IS?
LET ME SEE...
ABOUT MY AGE, I GUESS.
HE'S SUPPOSED TO BE FIVE YEARS OLD!
WHAT? NO WAY!!
GLOOM
I JUST CAN'T DRAW LITTLE KIDS.
UM... I'M SORRY.
HUH?
SNIFF
SNIFF

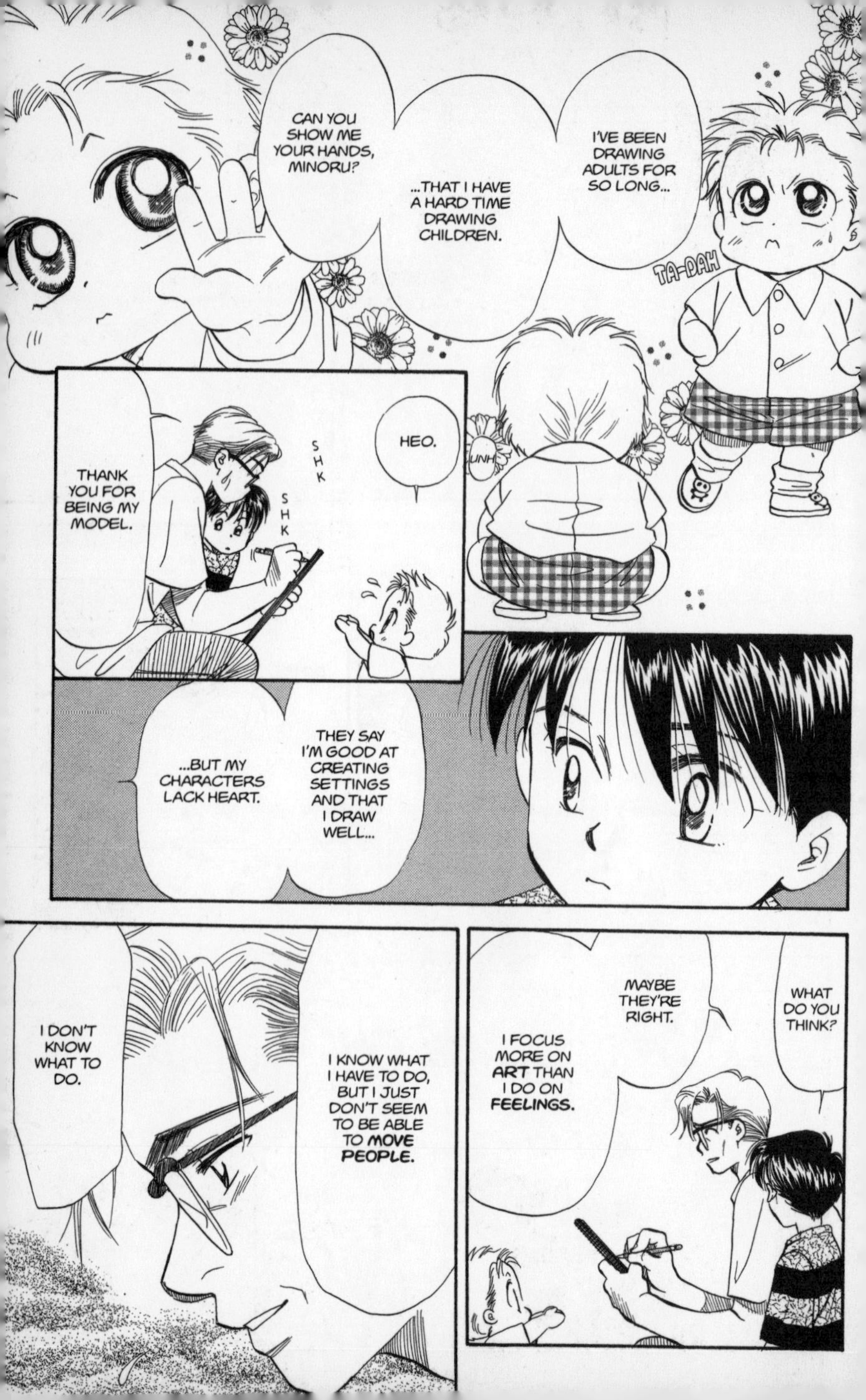
I'VE BEEN DRAWING ADULTS FOR SO LONG...
...THAT I HAVE A HARD TIME DRAWING CHILDREN.
CAN YOU SHOW ME YOUR HANDS, MINORU?
TA-DAH
UNH
HEO.
SHK
SHK
THANK YOU FOR BEING MY MODEL.
THEY SAY I'M GOOD AT CREATING SETTINGS AND THAT I DRAW WELL...
...BUT MY CHARACTERS LACK HEART.
WHAT DO YOU THINK?
MAYBE THEY'RE RIGHT.
I FOCUS MORE ON ART THAN I DO ON FEELINGS.
I KNOW WHAT I HAVE TO DO, BUT I JUST DON'T SEEM TO BE ABLE TO MOVE PEOPLE.
I DON'T KNOW WHAT TO DO.

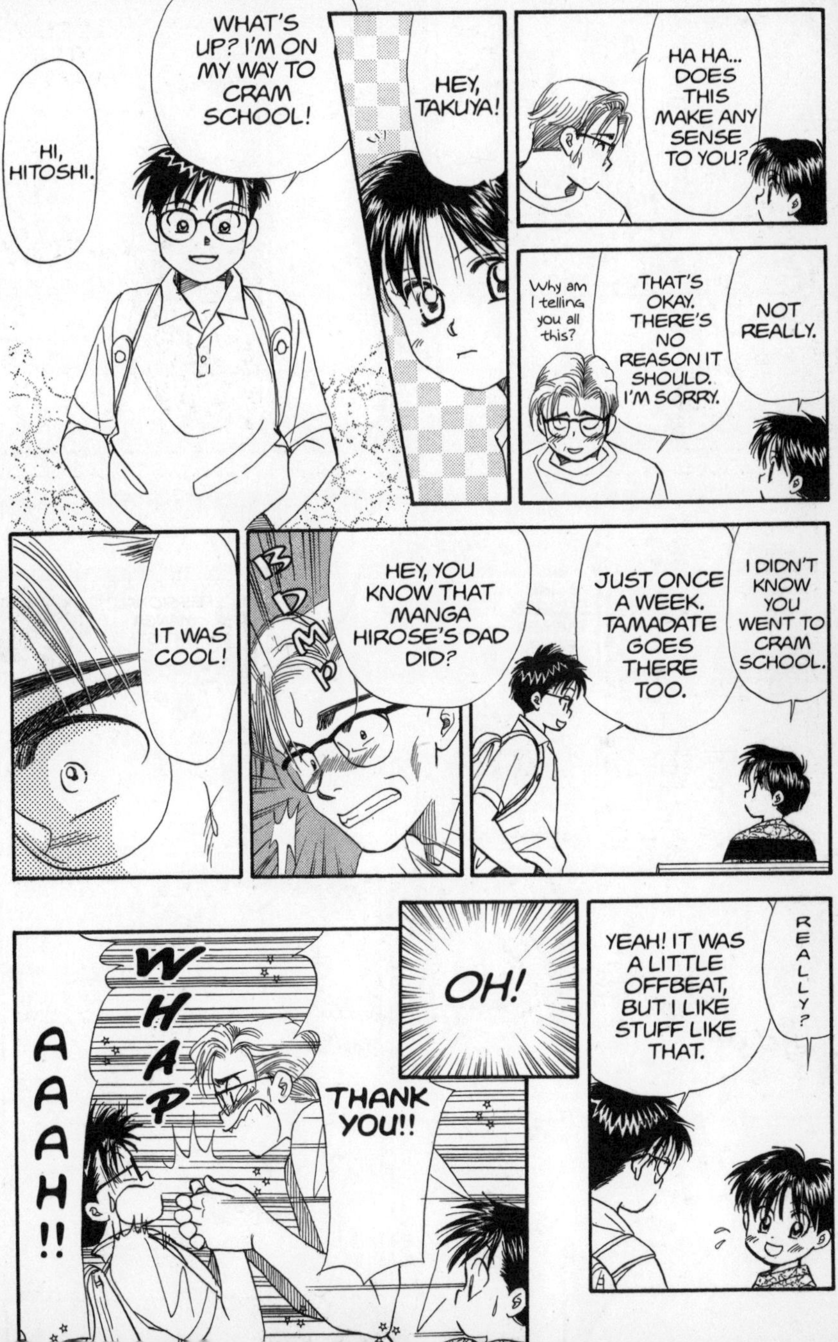
HA HA... DOES THIS MAKE ANY SENSE TO YOU?
NOT REALLY.
THAT'S OKAY. THERE'S NO REASON IT SHOULD. I'M SORRY.
Why am I telling you all this?
HEY, TAKUYA!
WHAT'S UP? I'M ON MY WAY TO CRAM SCHOOL!
HI, HITOSHI.
I DIDN'T KNOW YOU WENT TO CRAM SCHOOL.
JUST ONCE A WEEK. TAMADATE GOES THERE TOO.
HEY, YOU KNOW THAT MANGA HIROSE'S DAD DID?
BUMP
IT WAS COOL!
REALLY?
YEAH! IT WAS A LITTLE OFFBEAT, BUT I LIKE STUFF LIKE THAT.
OH!
THANK YOU!!
WHAP
AAAAH!!

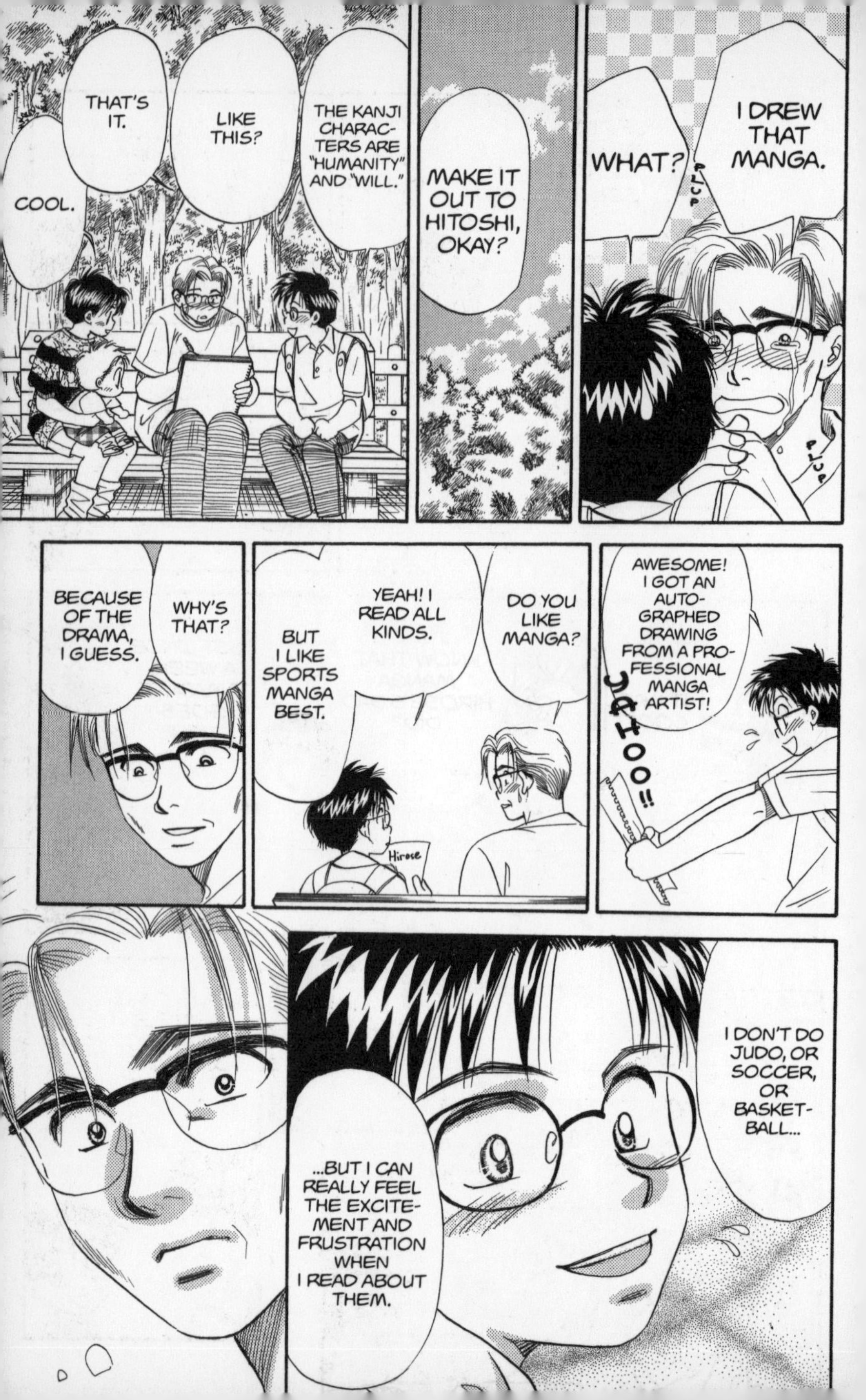
I DREW THAT MANGA.
WHAT?
PLUP
PLUP
MAKE IT OUT TO HITOSHI, OKAY?
THE KANJI CHARACTERS ARE "HUMANITY" AND "WILL."
LIKE THIS?
THAT'S IT.
COOL.
AWESOME! I GOT AN AUTOGRAPHED DRAWING FROM A PROFESSIONAL MANGA ARTIST!
YAHOO!!
DO YOU LIKE MANGA?
YEAH! I READ ALL KINDS.
BUT I LIKE SPORTS MANGA BEST.
Hirose
WHY'S THAT?
BECAUSE OF THE DRAMA, I GUESS.
I DON'T DO JUDO, OR SOCCER, OR BASKETBALL...
...BUT I CAN REALLY FEEL THE EXCITEMENT AND FRUSTRATION WHEN I READ ABOUT THEM.

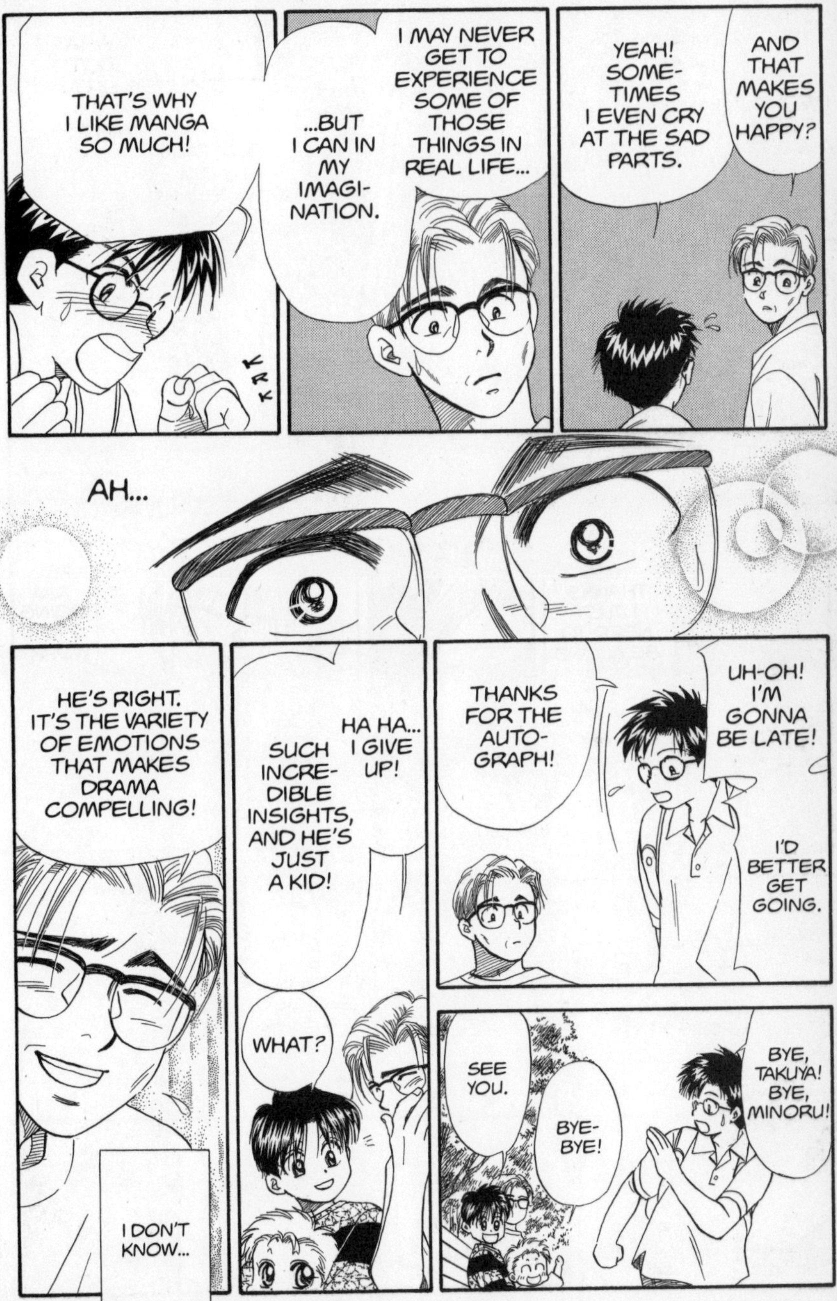
AND THAT MAKES YOU HAPPY?
YEAH! SOME-TIMES I EVEN CRY AT THE SAD PARTS.
I MAY NEVER GET TO EXPERIENCE SOME OF THOSE THINGS IN REAL LIFE...
...BUT I CAN IN MY IMAGI-NATION.
THAT'S WHY I LIKE MANGA SO MUCH!
KRK
AH...
UH-OH! I'M GONNA BE LATE!
THANKS FOR THE AUTO-GRAPH!
I'D BETTER GET GOING.
BYE, TAKUYA! BYE, MINORU!
BYE-BYE!
SEE YOU.
HA HA... I GIVE UP!
SUCH INCRE-DIBLE INSIGHTS, AND HE'S JUST A KID!
WHAT?
HE'S RIGHT. IT'S THE VARIETY OF EMOTIONS THAT MAKES DRAMA COMPELLING!
I DON'T KNOW...

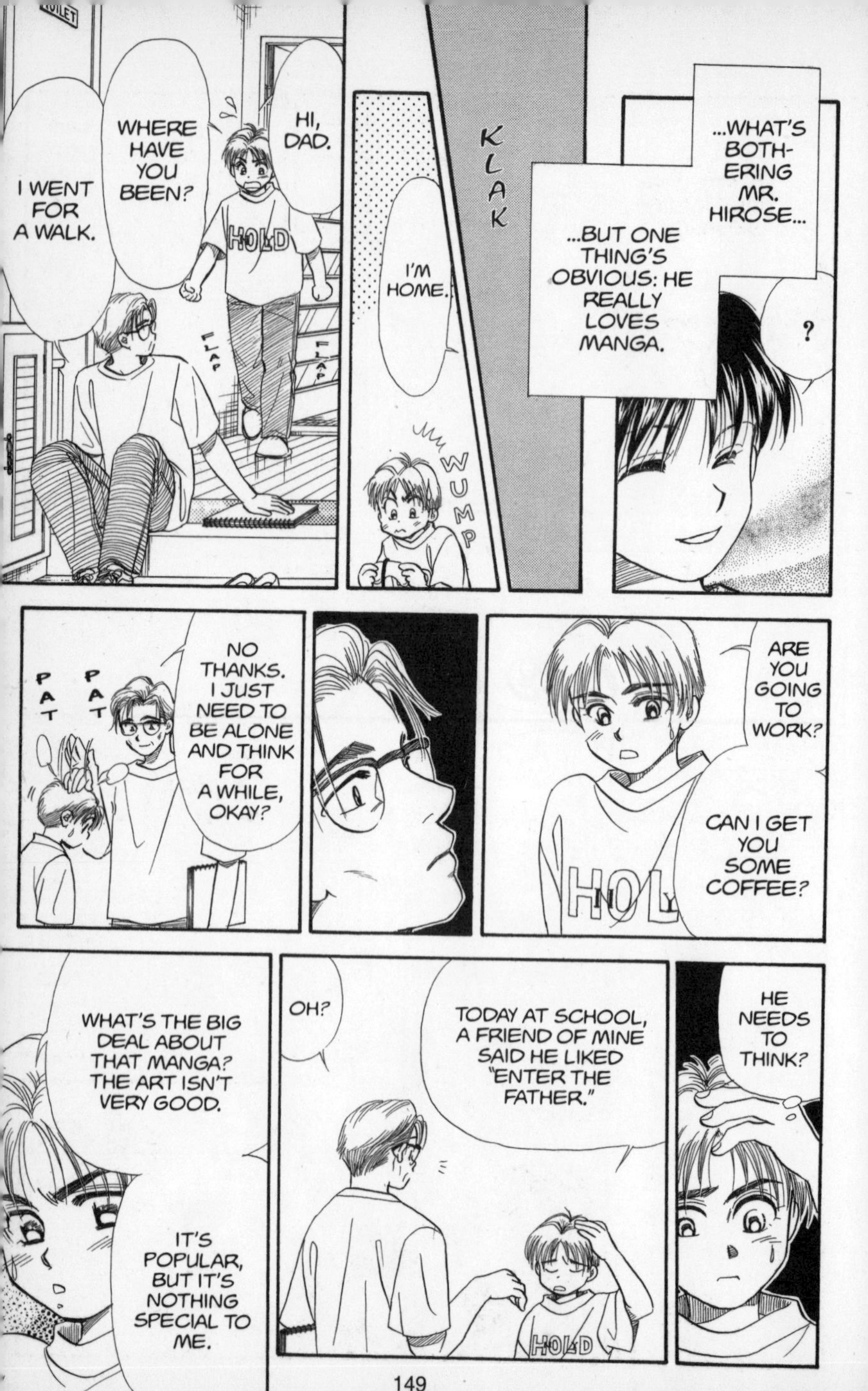
...WHAT'S BOTHERING MR. HIROSE...
...BUT ONE THING'S OBVIOUS: HE REALLY LOVES MANGA.
?
KLAK
I'M HOME.
WUMP
HI, DAD.
WHERE HAVE YOU BEEN?
I WENT FOR A WALK.
FLAP
FLAP
ARE YOU GOING TO WORK?
CAN I GET YOU SOME COFFEE?
NO THANKS. I JUST NEED TO BE ALONE AND THINK FOR A WHILE, OKAY?
PAT
PAT
HE NEEDS TO THINK?
TODAY AT SCHOOL, A FRIEND OF MINE SAID HE LIKED "ENTER THE FATHER."
OH?
WHAT'S THE BIG DEAL ABOUT THAT MANGA? THE ART ISN'T VERY GOOD.
IT'S POPULAR, BUT IT'S NOTHING SPECIAL TO ME.

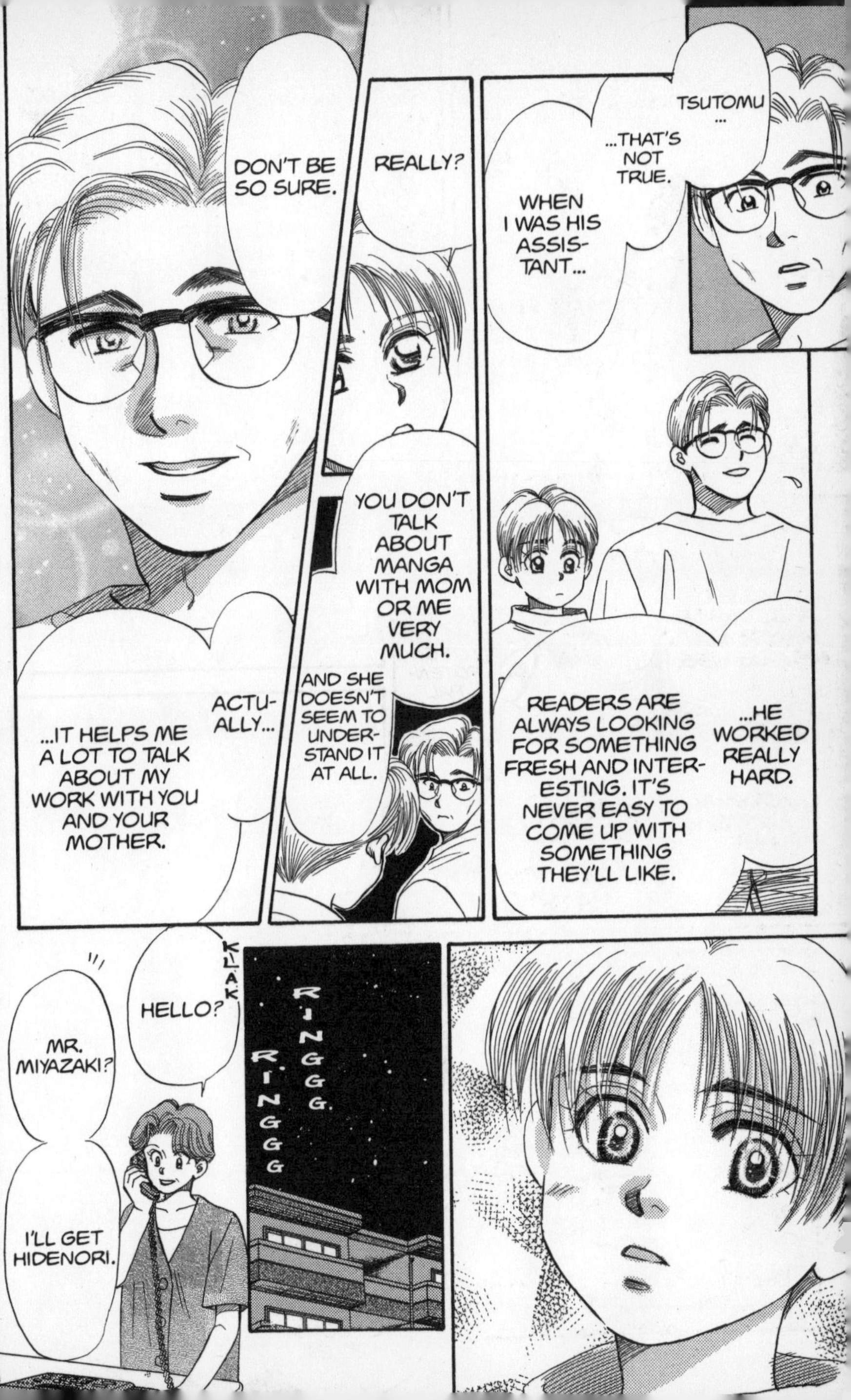
TSUTOMU...
...THAT'S NOT TRUE.
WHEN I WAS HIS ASSISTANT...
...HE WORKED REALLY HARD.
READERS ARE ALWAYS LOOKING FOR SOMETHING FRESH AND INTERESTING. IT'S NEVER EASY TO COME UP WITH SOMETHING THEY'LL LIKE.
REALLY?
YOU DON'T TALK ABOUT MANGA WITH MOM OR ME VERY MUCH.
AND SHE DOESN'T SEEM TO UNDERSTAND IT AT ALL.
DON'T BE SO SURE.
ACTUALLY...
...IT HELPS ME A LOT TO TALK ABOUT MY WORK WITH YOU AND YOUR MOTHER.
RINGGG.
RINGGG
KLAK
HELLO?
MR. MIYAZAKI?
I'LL GET HIDENORI.

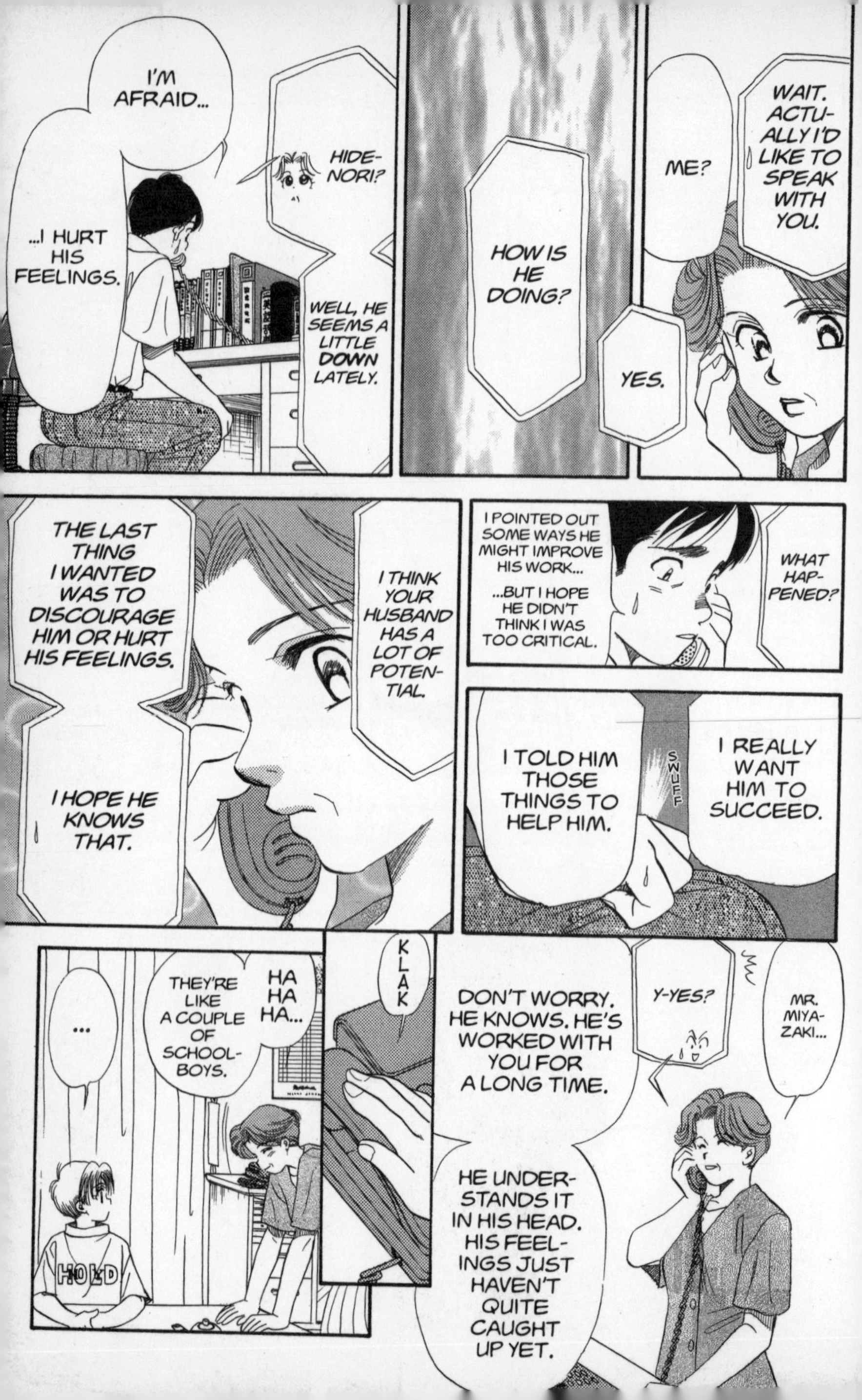

WAIT. ACTUALLY I'D LIKE TO SPEAK WITH YOU.
ME?
YES.
HOW IS HE DOING?
HIDE-NORI?
WELL, HE SEEMS A LITTLE DOWN LATELY.
I'M AFRAID...
...I HURT HIS FEELINGS.
WHAT HAPPENED?
I POINTED OUT SOME WAYS HE MIGHT IMPROVE HIS WORK...
...BUT I HOPE HE DIDN'T THINK I WAS TOO CRITICAL.
I REALLY WANT HIM TO SUCCEED.
SWUFF
I TOLD HIM THOSE THINGS TO HELP HIM.
I THINK YOUR HUSBAND HAS A LOT OF POTENTIAL.
THE LAST THING I WANTED WAS TO DISCOURAGE HIM OR HURT HIS FEELINGS.
I HOPE HE KNOWS THAT.
MR. MIYAZAKI...
Y-YES?
DON'T WORRY. HE KNOWS. HE'S WORKED WITH YOU FOR A LONG TIME.
HE UNDERSTANDS IT IN HIS HEAD. HIS FEELINGS JUST HAVEN'T QUITE CAUGHT UP YET.
KLAK
HA HA HA...
THEY'RE LIKE A COUPLE OF SCHOOLBOYS.
...
HOLD

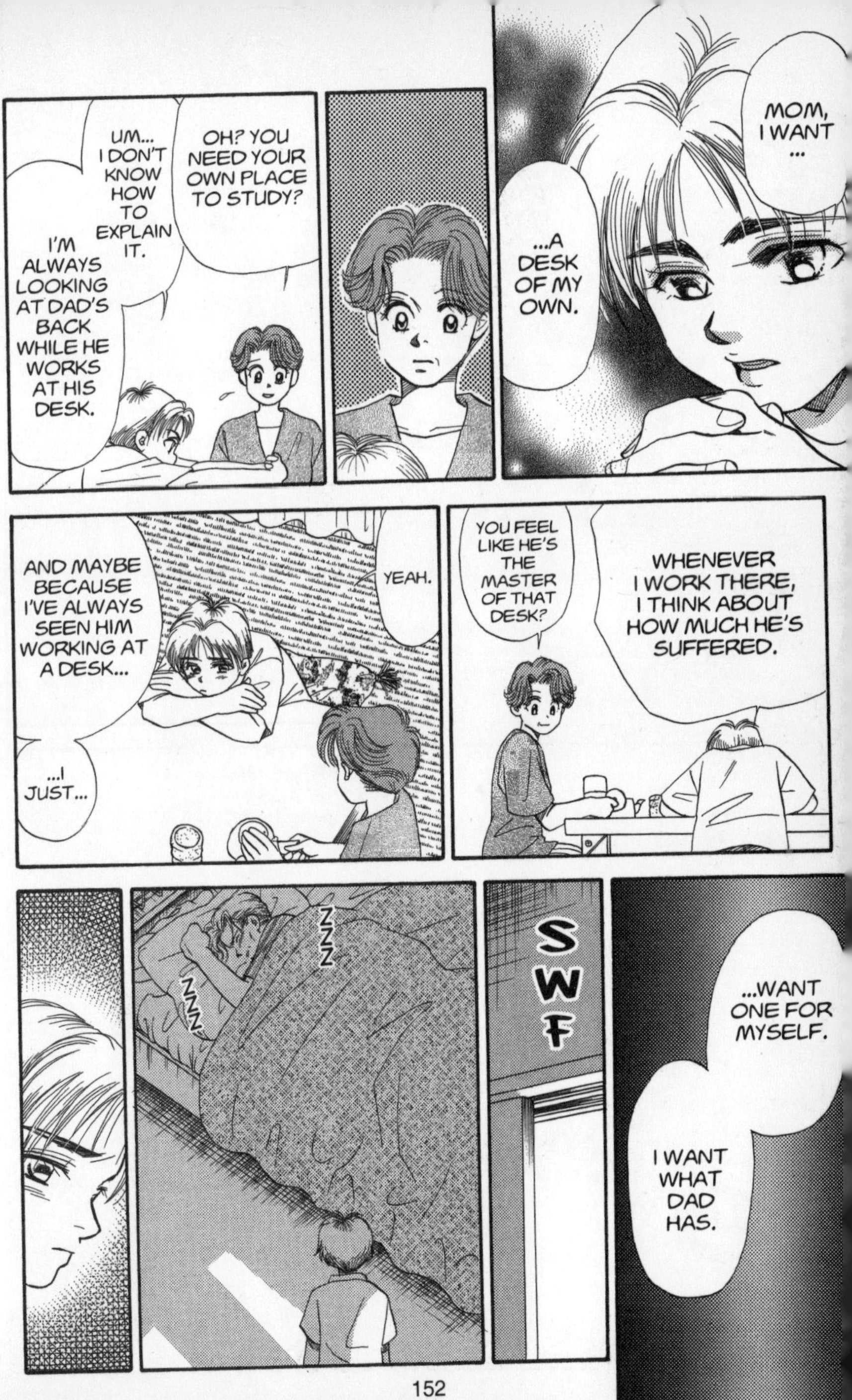
MOM, I WANT ...
...A DESK OF MY OWN.
OH? YOU NEED YOUR OWN PLACE TO STUDY?
UM... I DON'T KNOW HOW TO EXPLAIN IT.
I'M ALWAYS LOOKING AT DAD'S BACK WHILE HE WORKS AT HIS DESK.
WHENEVER I WORK THERE, I THINK ABOUT HOW MUCH HE'S SUFFERED.
YOU FEEL LIKE HE'S THE MASTER OF THAT DESK?
YEAH.
AND MAYBE BECAUSE I'VE ALWAYS SEEN HIM WORKING AT A DESK...
...I JUST...
...WANT ONE FOR MYSELF.
I WANT WHAT DAD HAS.
SWF
ZZZ
ZZZ

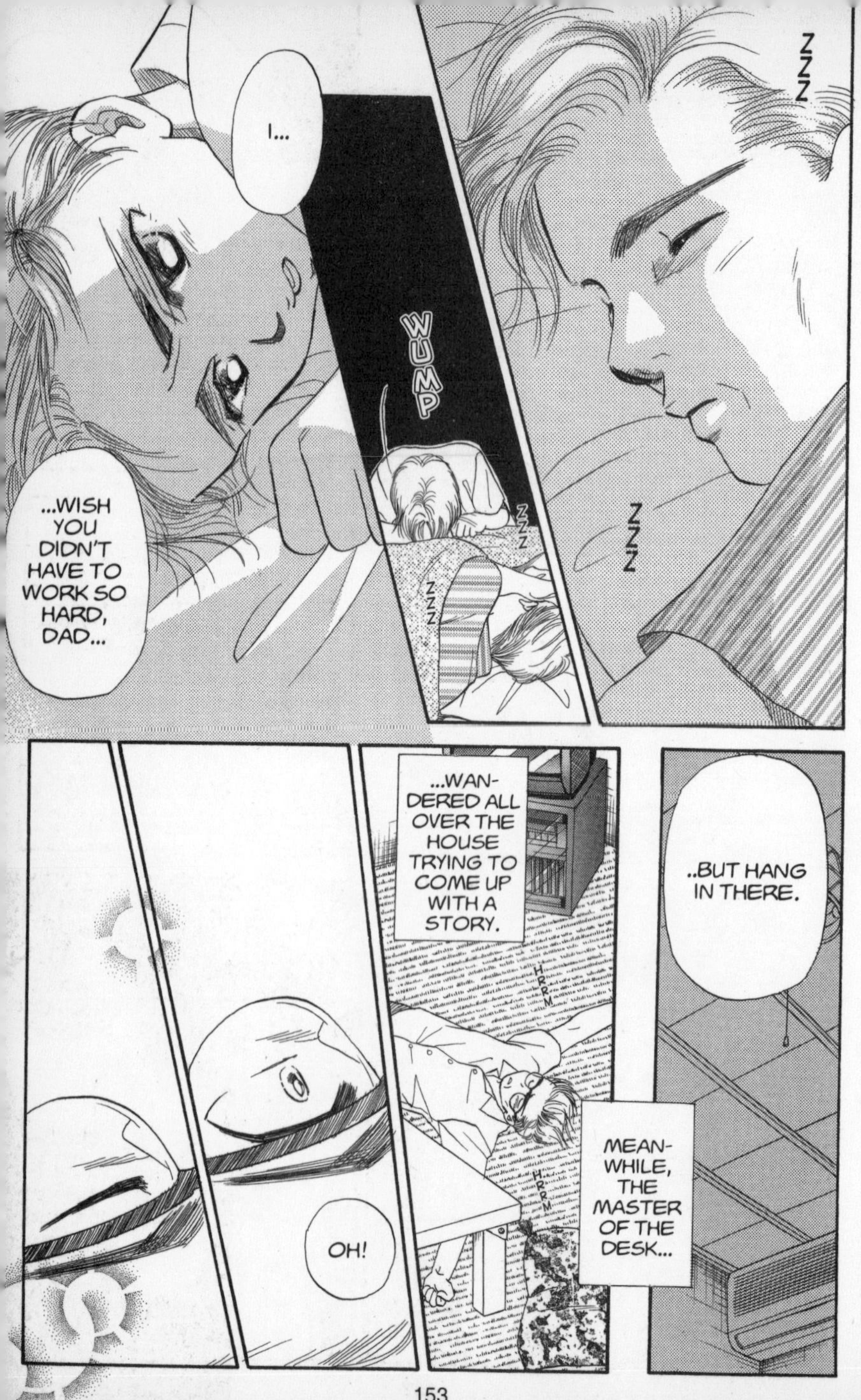
ZZZ
ZZZ
WUMP
ZZZ
ZZZ
I...
...WISH YOU DIDN'T HAVE TO WORK SO HARD, DAD...
..BUT HANG IN THERE.
MEAN-WHILE, THE MASTER OF THE DESK...
...WAN-DERED ALL OVER THE HOUSE TRYING TO COME UP WITH A STORY.
HRRM
HRRM
OH!

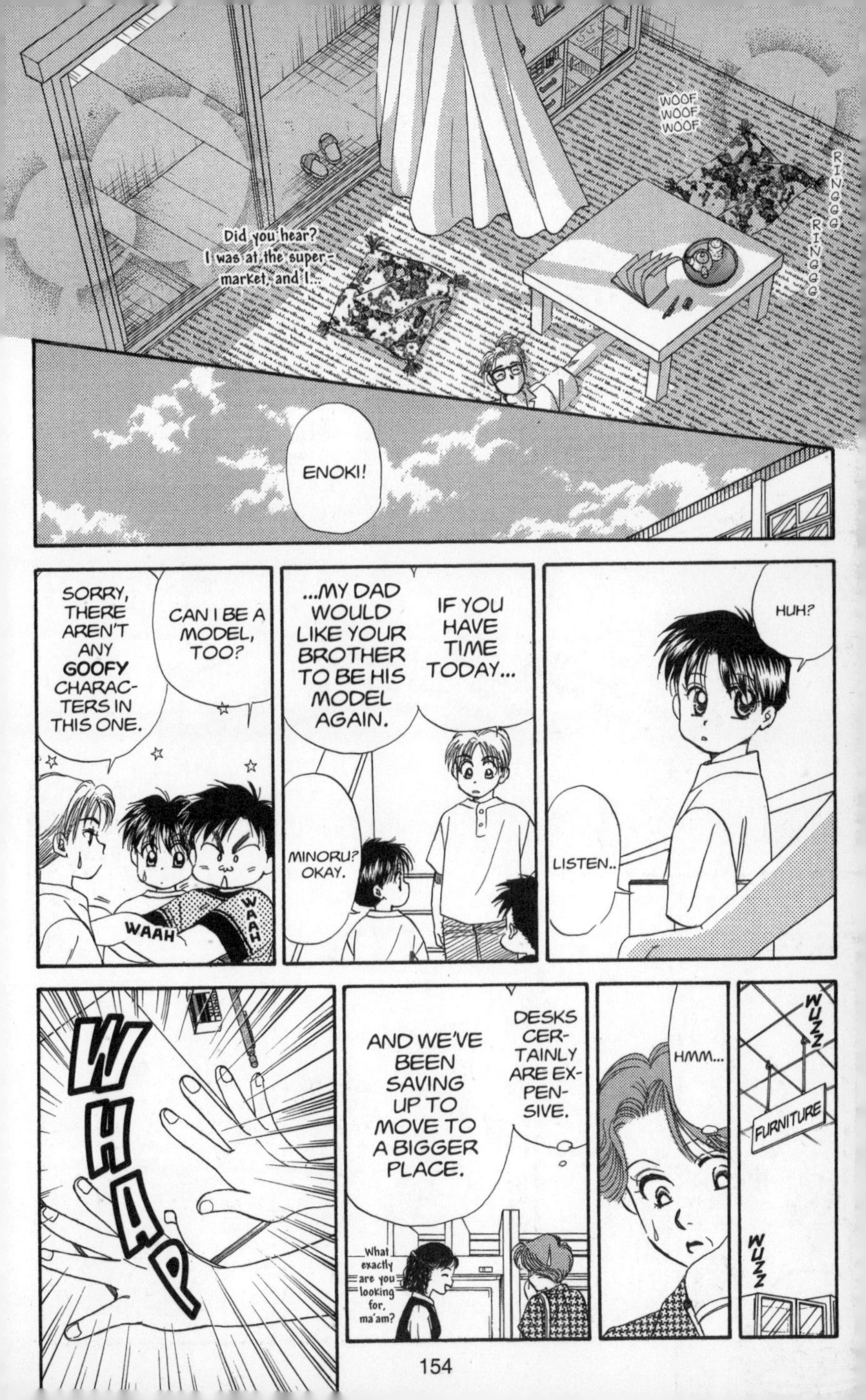
WOOF WOOF WOOF
RINGGG RINGGG
Did you hear? I was at the super-market, and I...
ENOKI!
HUH?
LISTEN...
IF YOU HAVE TIME TODAY...
...MY DAD WOULD LIKE YOUR BROTHER TO BE HIS MODEL AGAIN.
MINORU? OKAY.
CAN I BE A MODEL, TOO?
SORRY, THERE AREN'T ANY **GOOFY** CHARACTERS IN THIS ONE.
WAAH
WAAH
WUZZ
FURNITURE
WUZZ
HMM...
DESKS CERTAINLY ARE EXPENSIVE.
AND WE'VE BEEN SAVING UP TO MOVE TO A BIGGER PLACE.
What exactly are you looking for, ma'am?
WHAP

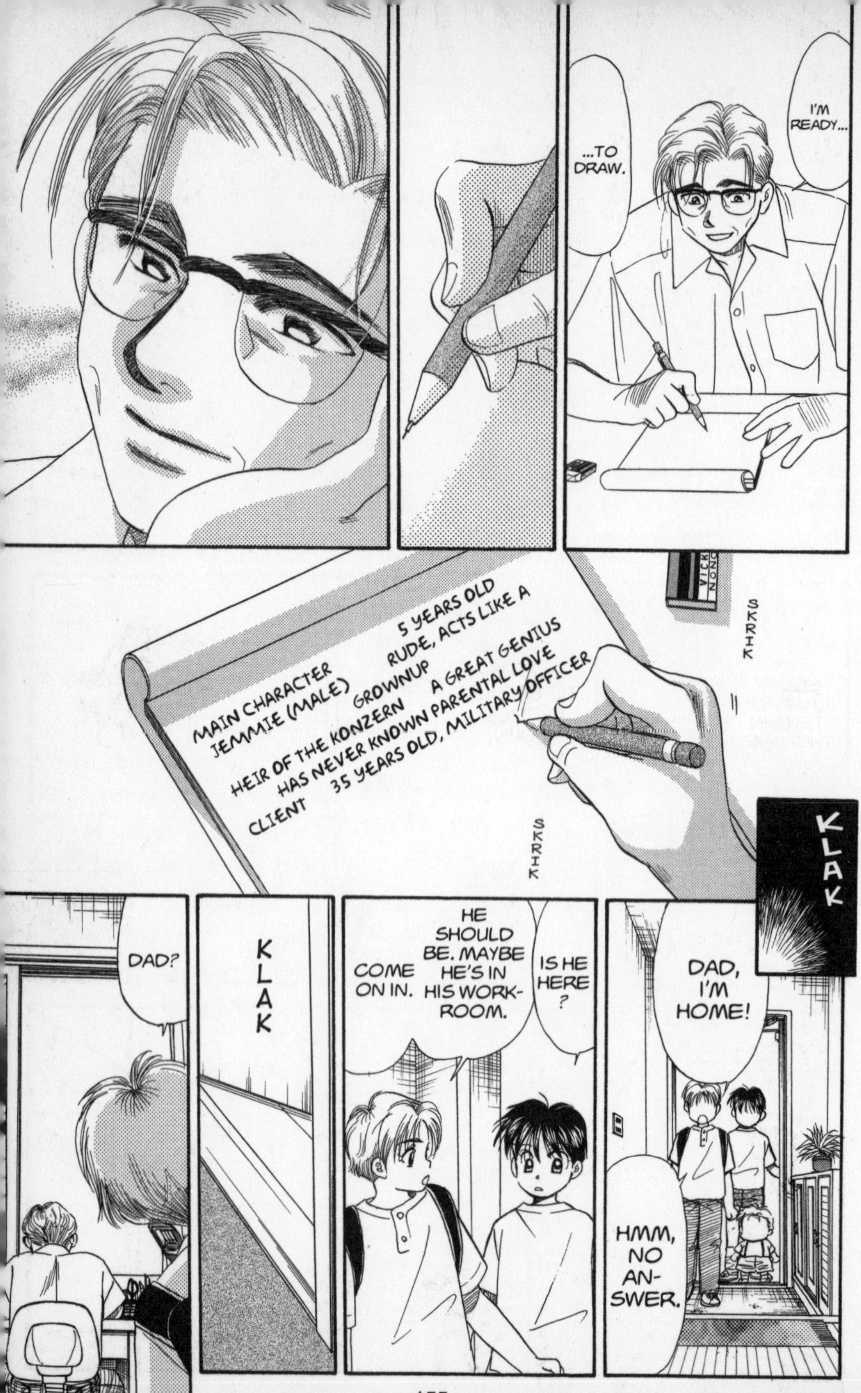
I'M READY...
...TO DRAW.
MAIN CHARACTER
5 YEARS OLD
JEMMIE (MALE)
RUDE, ACTS LIKE A GROWNUP
HEIR OF THE KONZERN
A GREAT GENIUS
HAS NEVER KNOWN PARENTAL LOVE
CLIENT
35 YEARS OLD, MILITARY OFFICER
SKRIK
SKRIK
KLAK
DAD, I'M HOME!
HMM, NO AN-SWER.
IS HE HERE?
HE SHOULD BE. MAYBE HE'S IN HIS WORK-ROOM.
COME ON IN.
KLAK
DAD?

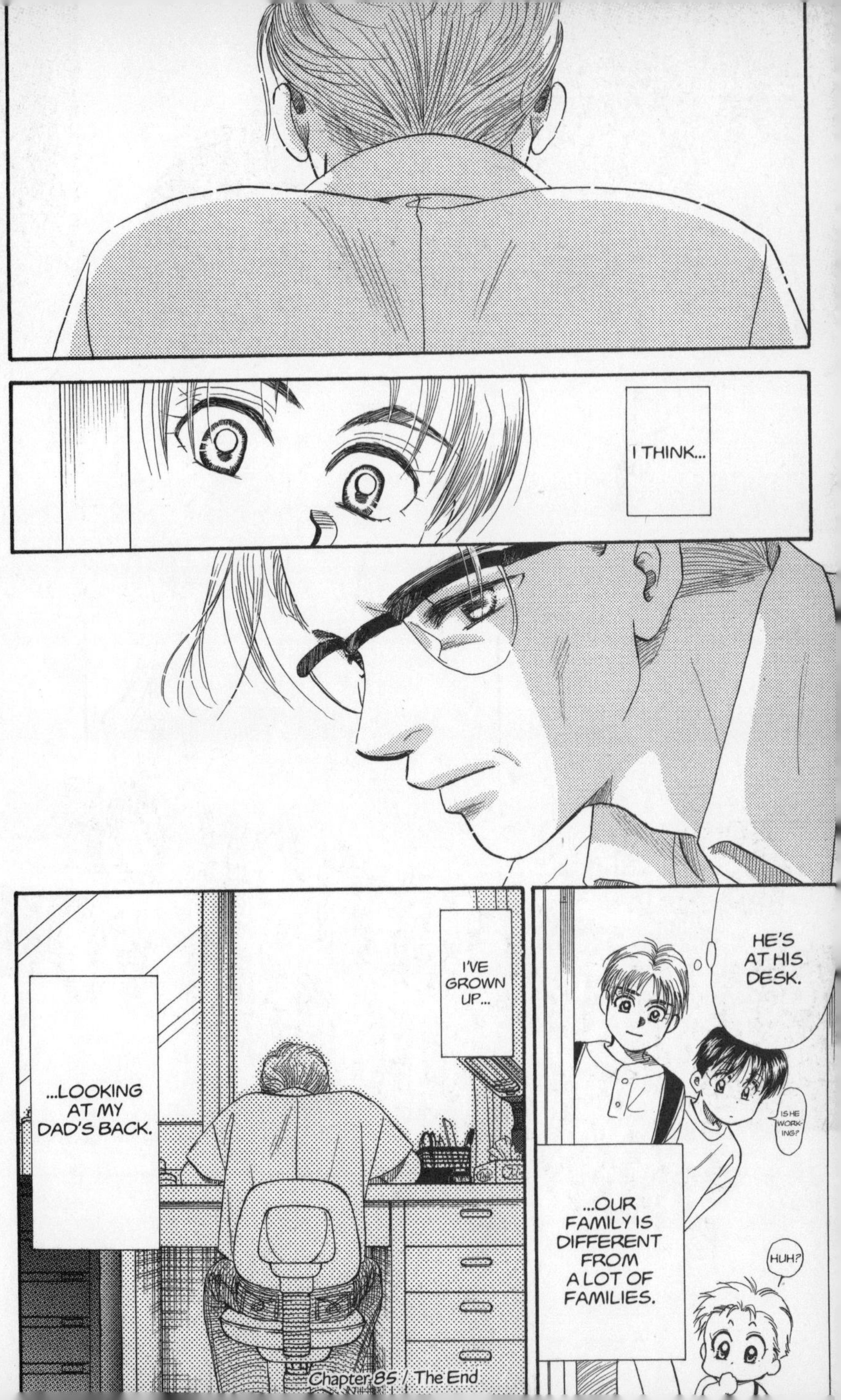
I THINK...
HE'S AT HIS DESK.
IS HE WORKING?
...OUR FAMILY IS DIFFERENT FROM A LOT OF FAMILIES.
HUH?
I'VE GROWN UP...
...LOOKING AT MY DAD'S BACK.
Chapter 85 / The End

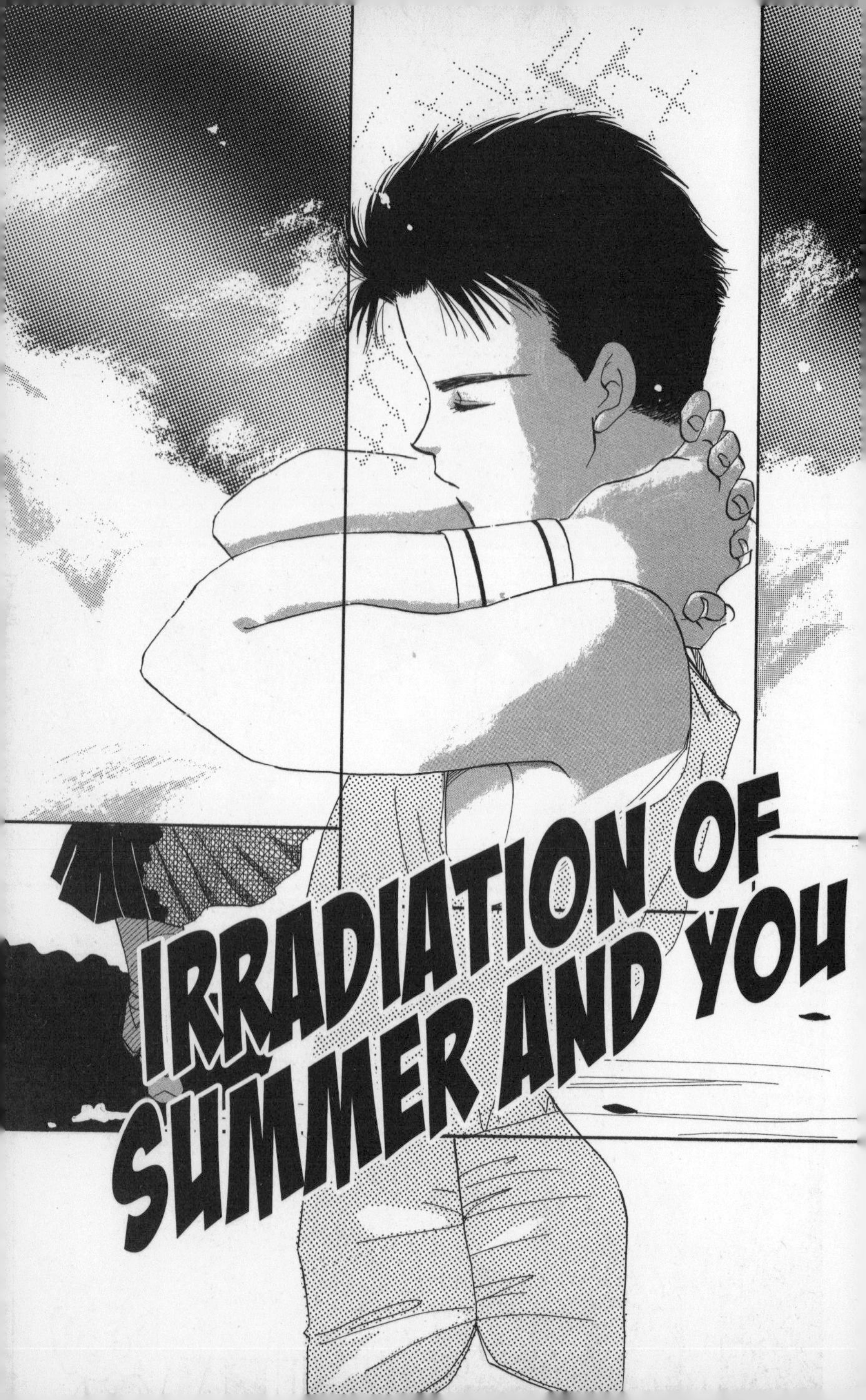
IRRADIATION OF
SUMMER AND YOU

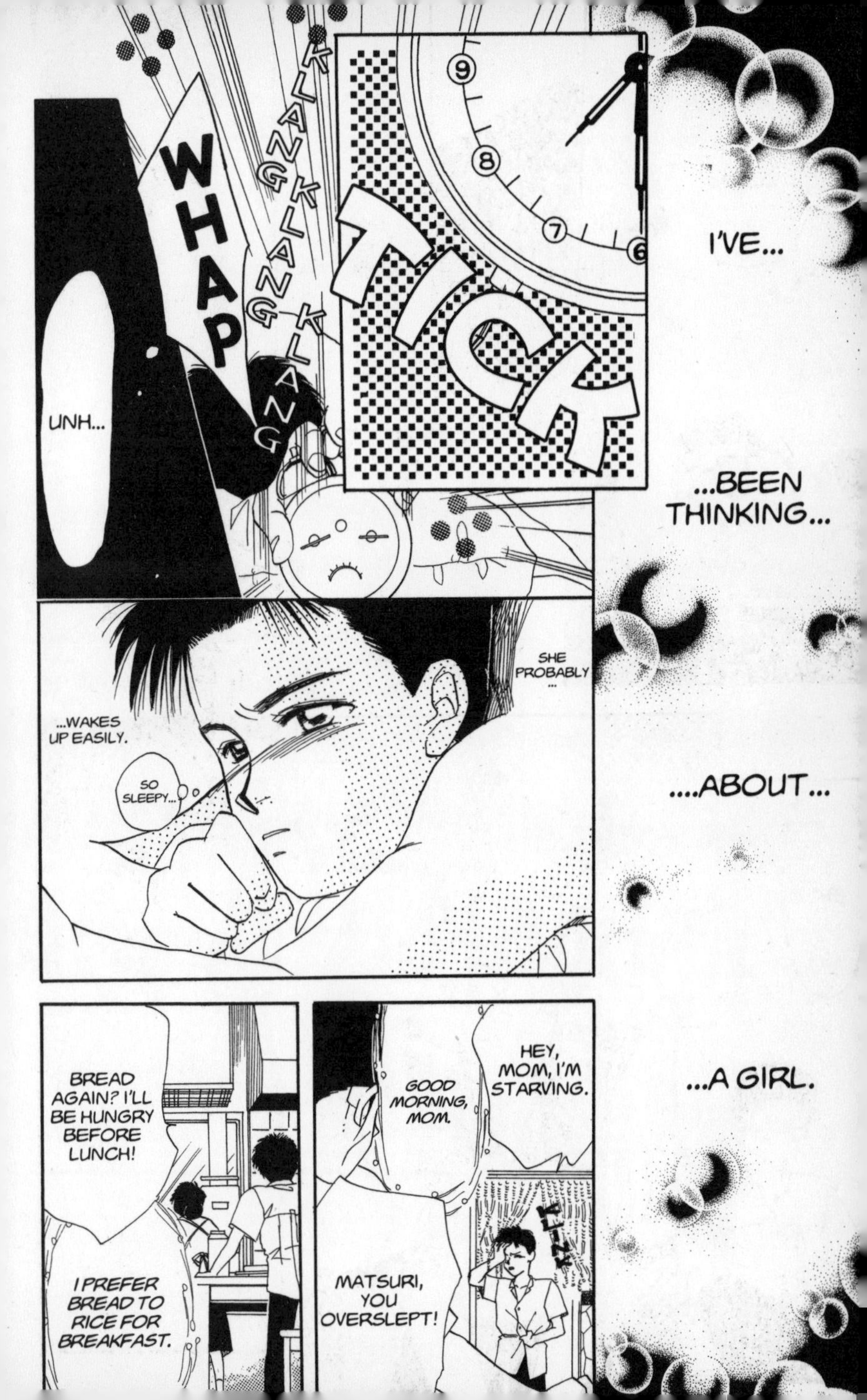
I'VE...
...BEEN THINKING...
....ABOUT...
...A GIRL.
TICK
KLANG KLANG
WHAP
UNH...
SHE PROBABLY ...
...WAKES UP EASILY.
SO SLEEPY...
HEY, MOM, I'M STARVING.
GOOD MORNING, MOM.
MATSURI, YOU OVERSLEPT!
BREAD AGAIN? I'LL BE HUNGRY BEFORE LUNCH!
I PREFER BREAD TO RICE FOR BREAKFAST.

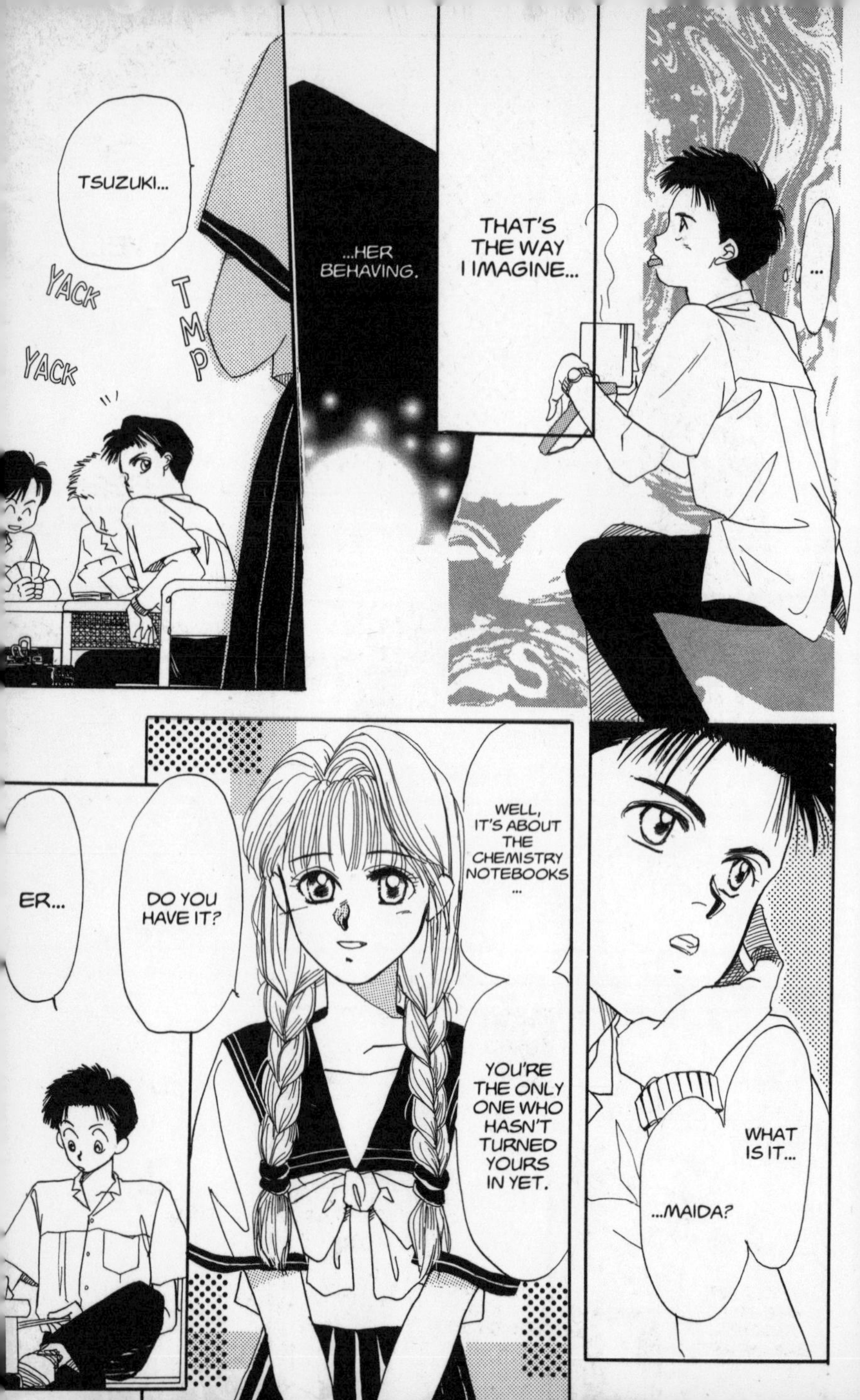
...
THAT'S THE WAY I IMAGINE...
...HER BEHAVING.
TSUZUKI...
TMP
YACK
YACK
WHAT IS IT...
...MAIDA?
WELL, IT'S ABOUT THE CHEMISTRY NOTEBOOKS...
YOU'RE THE ONLY ONE WHO HASN'T TURNED YOURS IN YET.
DO YOU HAVE IT?
ER...

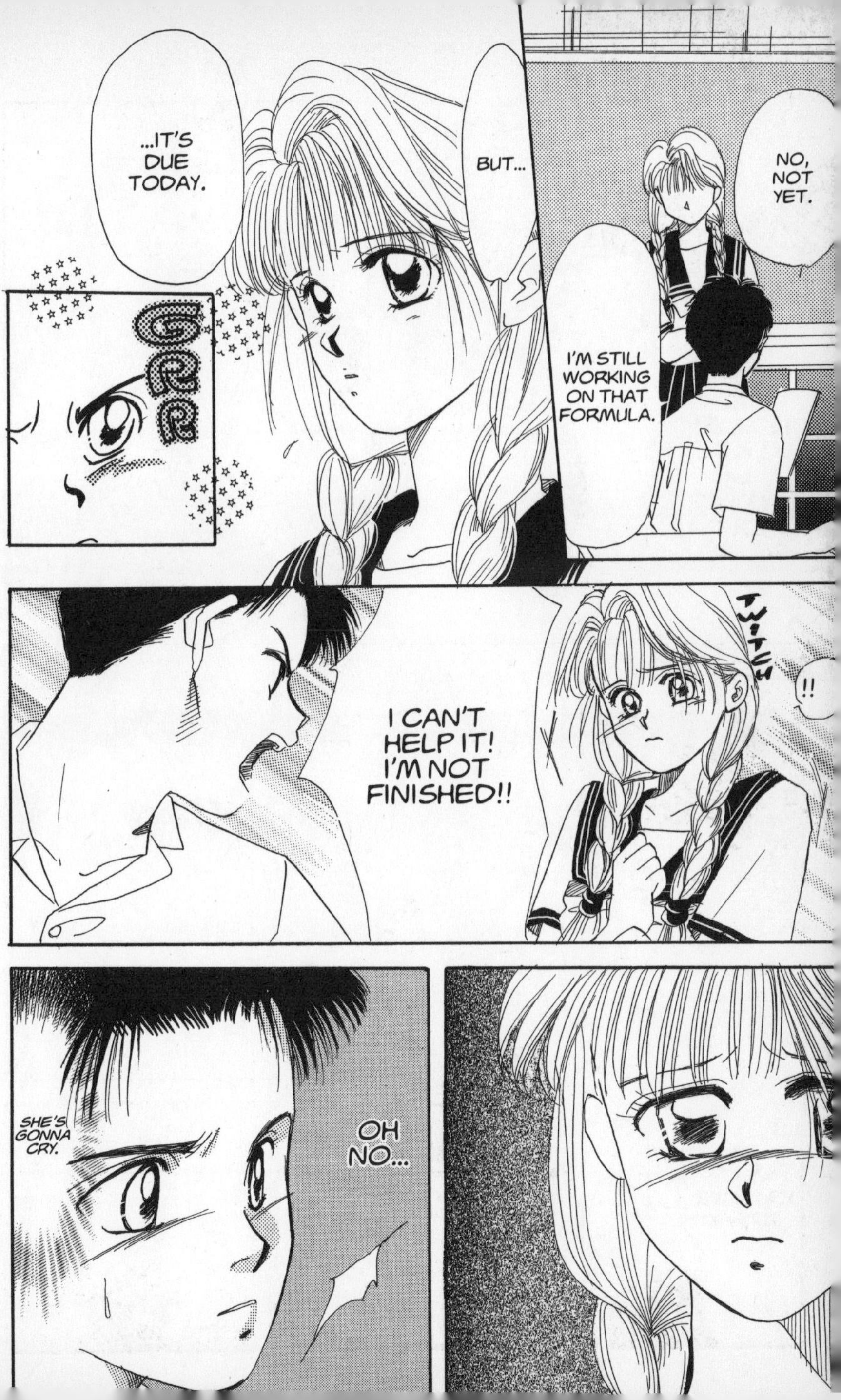
NO, NOT YET.
I'M STILL WORKING ON THAT FORMULA.
BUT...
...IT'S DUE TODAY.
GRR
TWITCH
!!
I CAN'T HELP IT! I'M NOT FINISHED!!
OH NO...
SHE'S GONNA CRY.

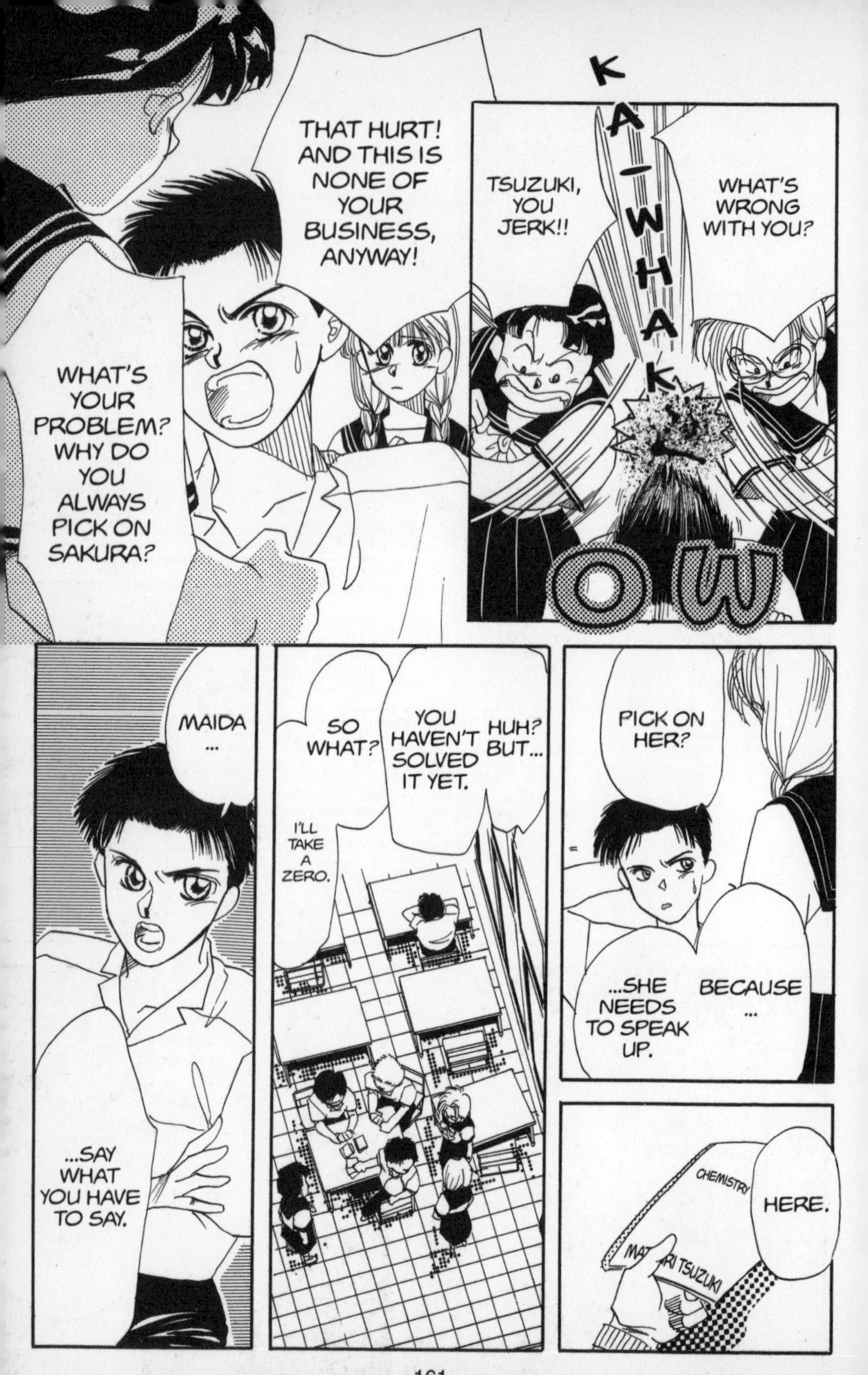
WHAT'S WRONG WITH YOU?
KA-WHAK
TSUZUKI, YOU JERK!!
OW
THAT HURT! AND THIS IS NONE OF YOUR BUSINESS, ANYWAY!
WHAT'S YOUR PROBLEM? WHY DO YOU ALWAYS PICK ON SAKURA?
PICK ON HER?
BECAUSE ...
...SHE NEEDS TO SPEAK UP.
CHEMISTRY
HERE.
HUH? BUT...
YOU HAVEN'T SOLVED IT YET.
SO WHAT?
I'LL TAKE A ZERO.
MAIDA ...
...SAY WHAT YOU HAVE TO SAY.

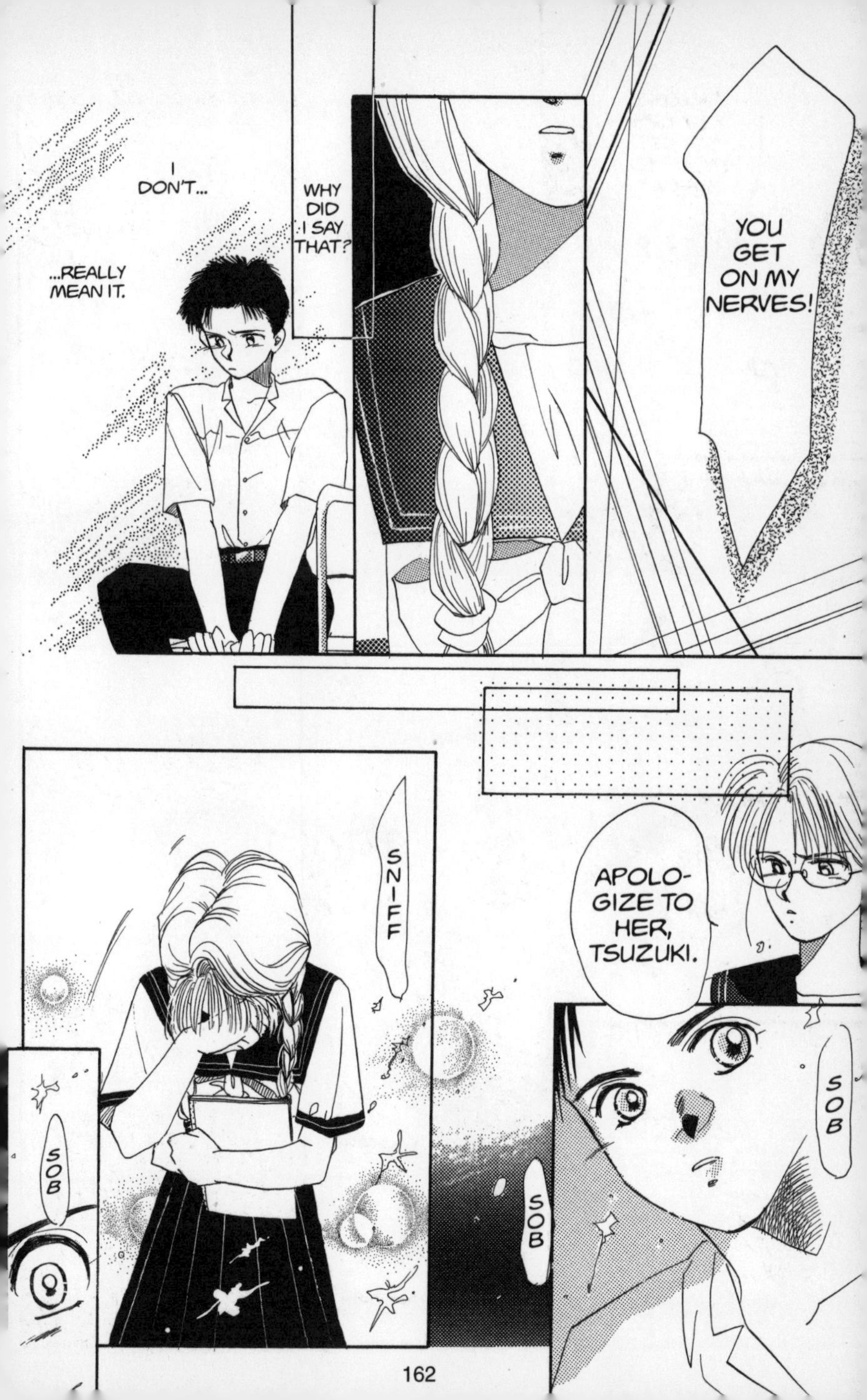
YOU GET ON MY NERVES!
WHY DID I SAY THAT?
I DON'T...
...REALLY MEAN IT.
APOLOGIZE TO HER, TSUZUKI.
SOB
SOB
SNIFF
SOB

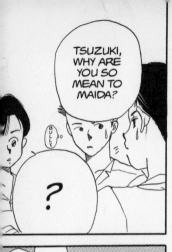

ZING
I DID IT AGAIN.
I MADE HER CRY AGAIN.
GEEZ...
SHWUFF
TSUZUKI, WHY ARE YOU SO MEAN TO MAIDA?
BULLY.
?
...
WHY?
I THOUGHT...
...AND SAW...

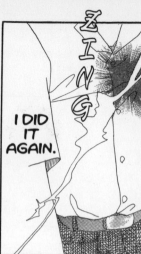

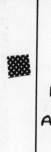

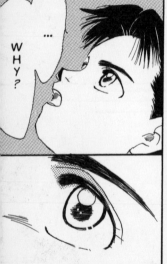

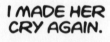

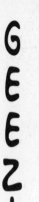

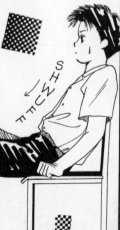

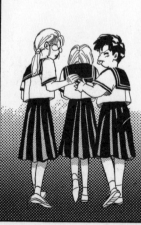

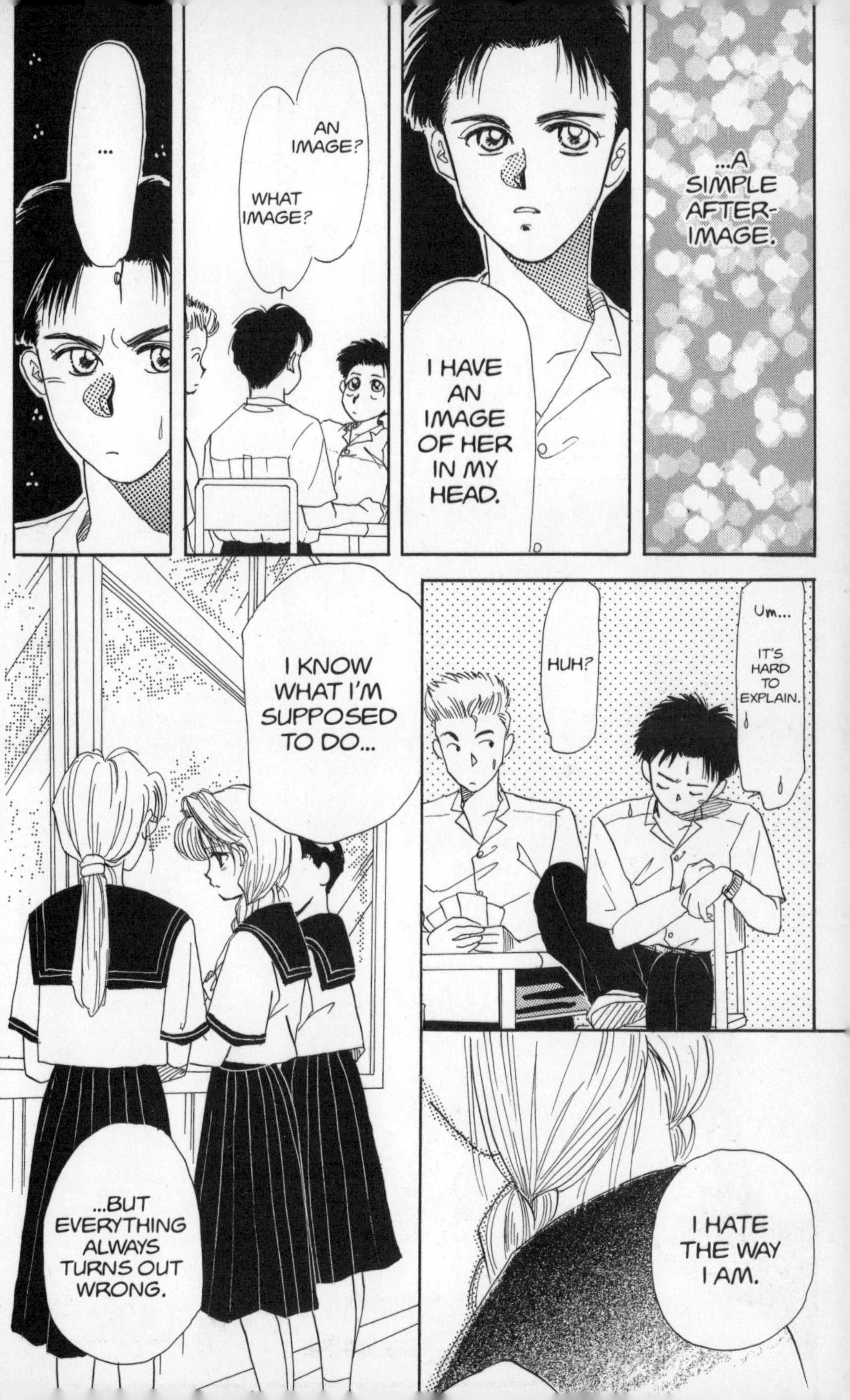
...A SIMPLE AFTER-IMAGE.
I HAVE AN IMAGE OF HER IN MY HEAD.
AN IMAGE?
WHAT IMAGE?
...
Um...
IT'S HARD TO EXPLAIN.
HUH?
I HATE THE WAY I AM.
I KNOW WHAT I'M SUPPOSED TO DO...
...BUT EVERYTHING ALWAYS TURNS OUT WRONG.

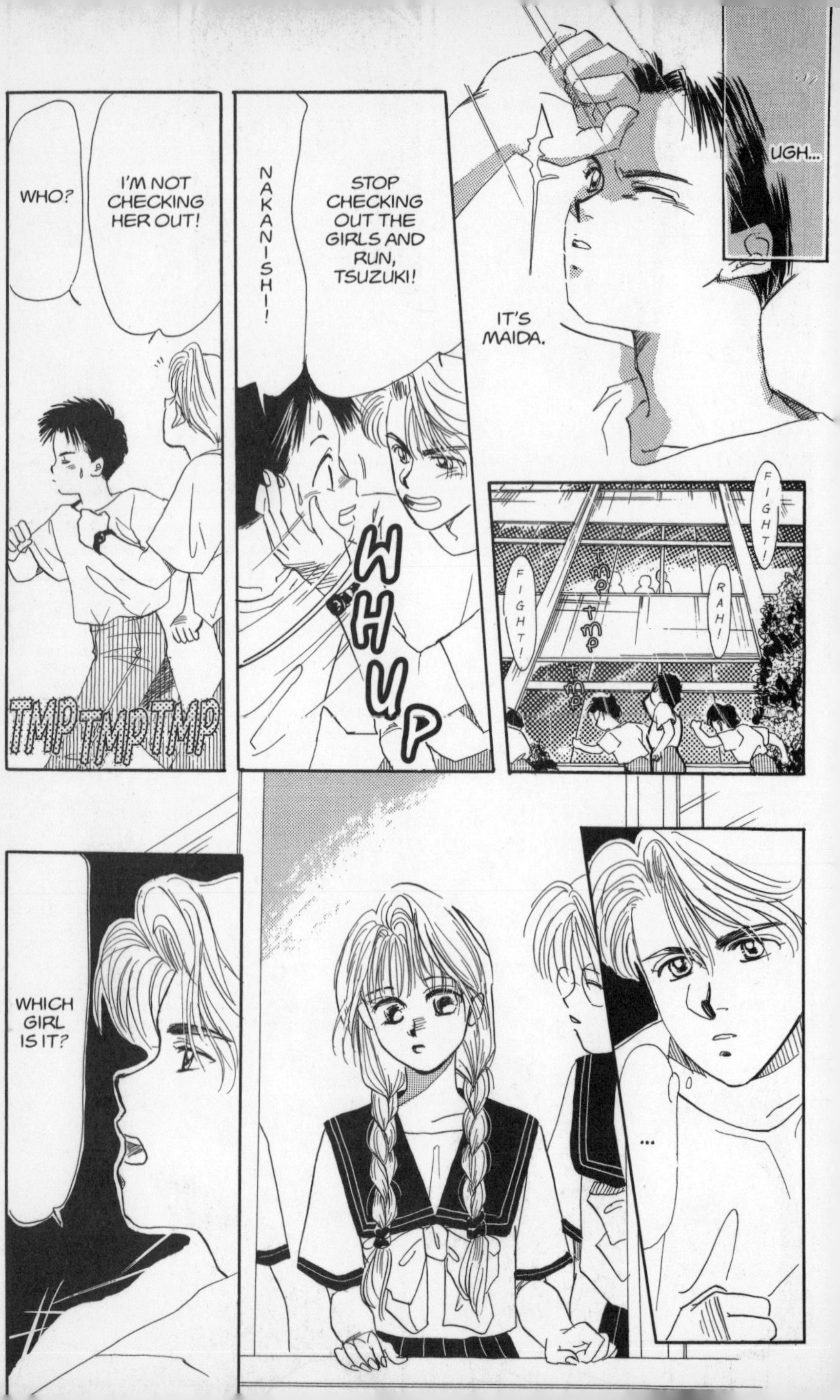
UGH...
IT'S MAIDA.
FIGHT!
RAH!
TMP TMP TMP
FIGHT!
STOP CHECKING OUT THE GIRLS AND RUN, TSUZUKI!
NAKANISHI!
WHUP
I'M NOT CHECKING HER OUT!
WHO?
TMP TMP TMP
...
WHICH GIRL IS IT?

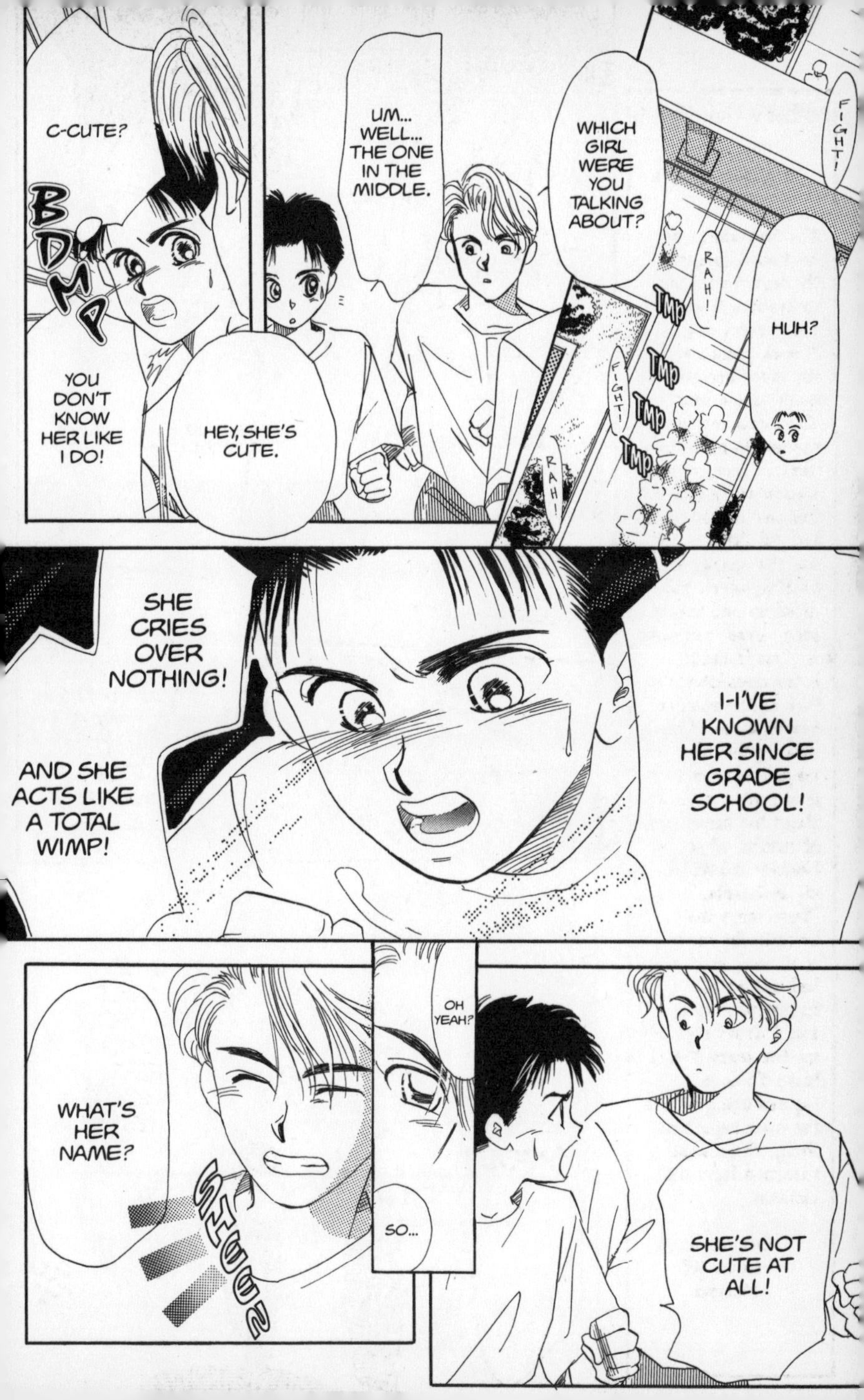
FIGHT!
RAH!
HUH?
FIGHT!
TMP TMP TMP TMP
RAH!
WHICH GIRL WERE YOU TALKING ABOUT?
UM... WELL... THE ONE IN THE MIDDLE.
HEY, SHE'S CUTE.
C-CUTE?
BDMP
YOU DON'T KNOW HER LIKE I DO!
I-I'VE KNOWN HER SINCE GRADE SCHOOL!
SHE CRIES OVER NOTHING!
AND SHE ACTS LIKE A TOTAL WIMP!
SHE'S NOT CUTE AT ALL!
SO...
OH YEAH?
WHAT'S HER NAME?
SHOON

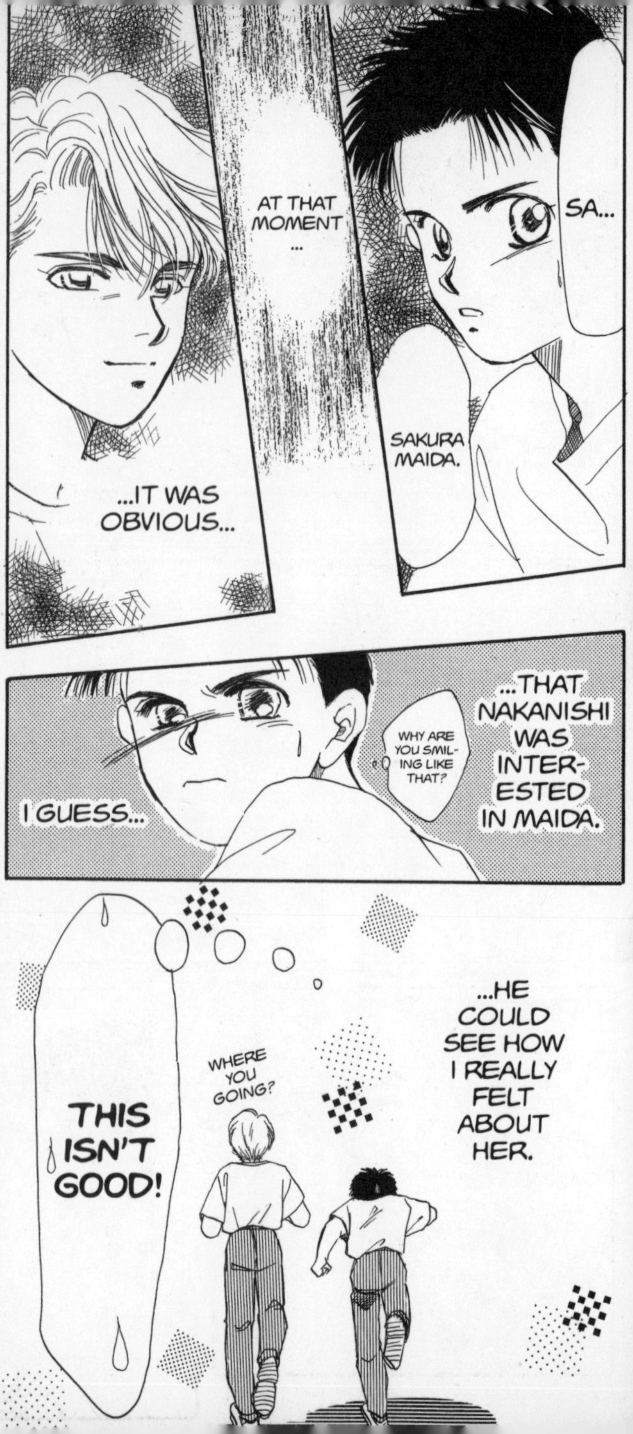
SA...
SAKURA MAIDA.
AT THAT MOMENT ...
...IT WAS OBVIOUS...
...THAT NAKANISHI WAS INTERESTED IN MAIDA.
WHY ARE YOU SMILING LIKE THAT?
I GUESS...
...HE COULD SEE HOW I REALLY FELT ABOUT HER.
WHERE YOU GOING?
THIS ISN'T GOOD!

Author's Note Part 6

On a Beehive (2)

The remaining bee continued to guard the hive. I went back to see how it was doing every day.
A week passed and the other bee still hadn't come back. The remaining bee seemed to be getting weaker. Then, after a week and a half, that bee disappeared too. All that was left was the shabby little beehive, which had dried up and looked even worse than when we first found it.
A few days later, the hive itself was gone. Maybe it was blown away by the wind, or maybe someone took it. It made me think about the harshness of nature. When I mentioned that to my assistants, S said, "Bees make their hives in the same spot every year. We had one on our house for a while, and it drove my mother crazy. You're lucky it's gone."
I guess being safe is the most important thing. That's what I learned from the incident.

See you in volume 16!
Marimo

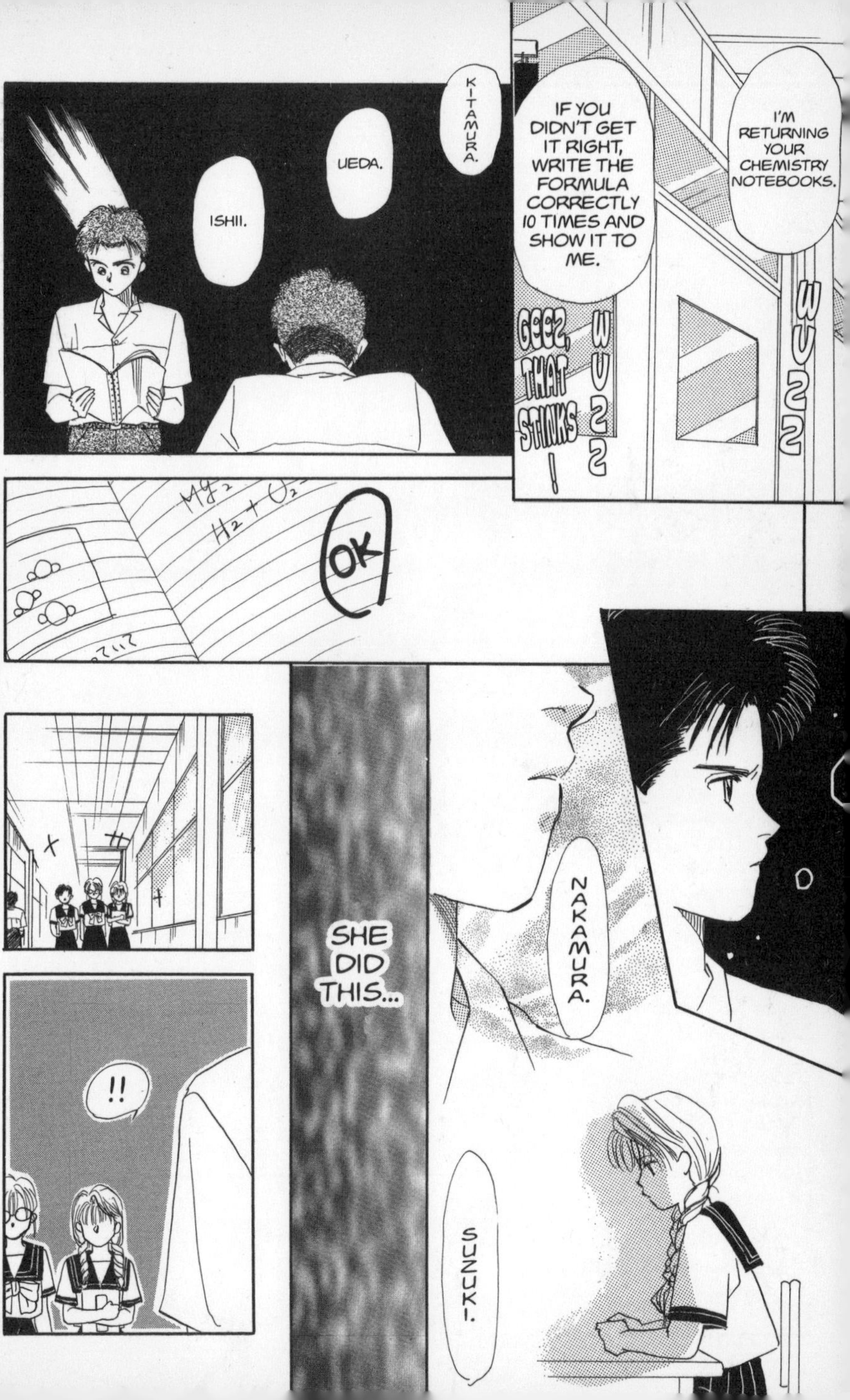
I'M RETURNING YOUR CHEMISTRY NOTEBOOKS.
IF YOU DIDN'T GET IT RIGHT, WRITE THE FORMULA CORRECTLY 10 TIMES AND SHOW IT TO ME.
WUZZ
GEEZ, THAT STINKS!
WUZZ
KITAMURA.
UEDA.
ISHII.
OK
NAKAMURA.
SUZUKI.
SHE DID THIS...
!!

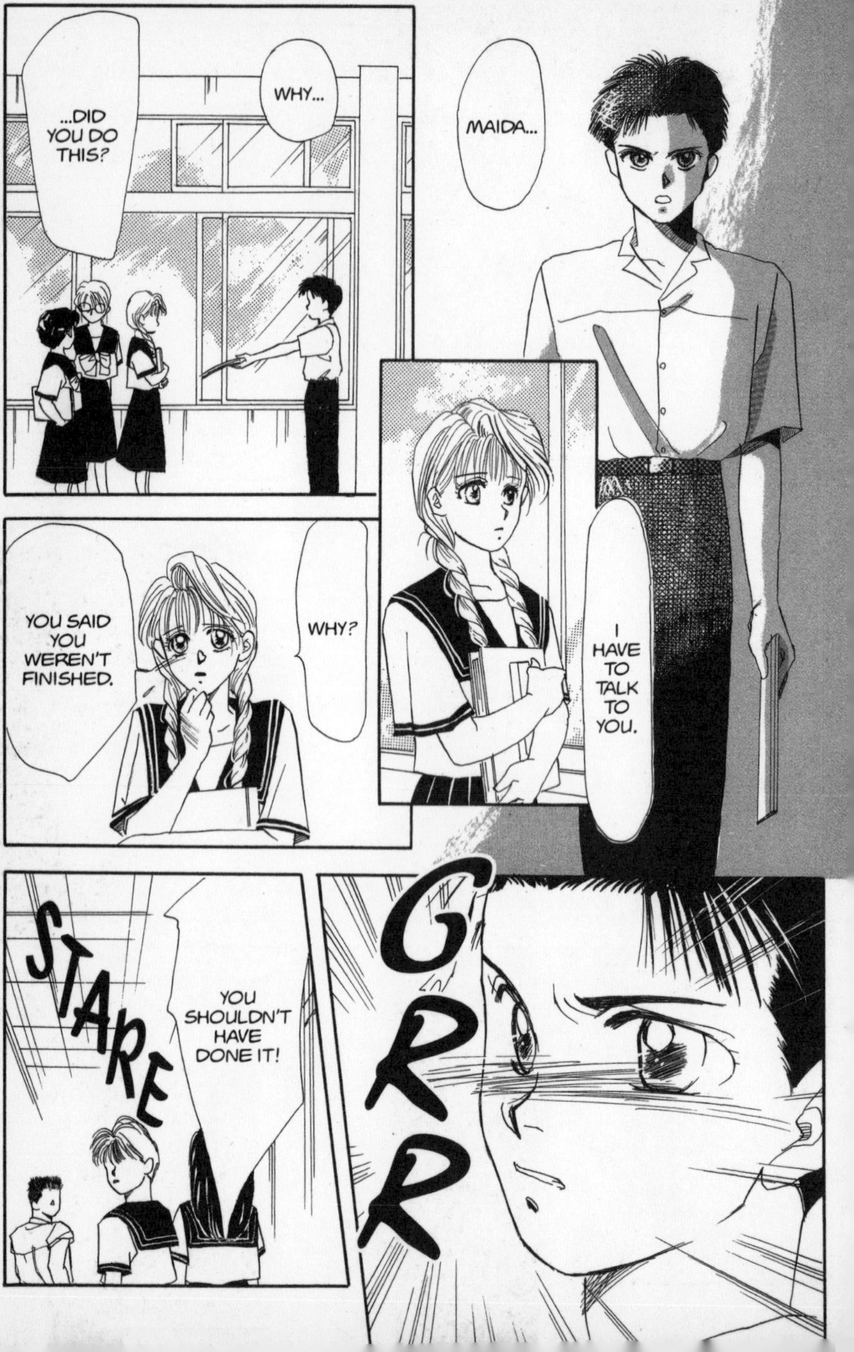

MAIDA...
I HAVE TO TALK TO YOU.
WHY...
...DID YOU DO THIS?
WHY?
YOU SAID YOU WEREN'T FINISHED.
GRRR
YOU SHOULDN'T HAVE DONE IT!
STARE

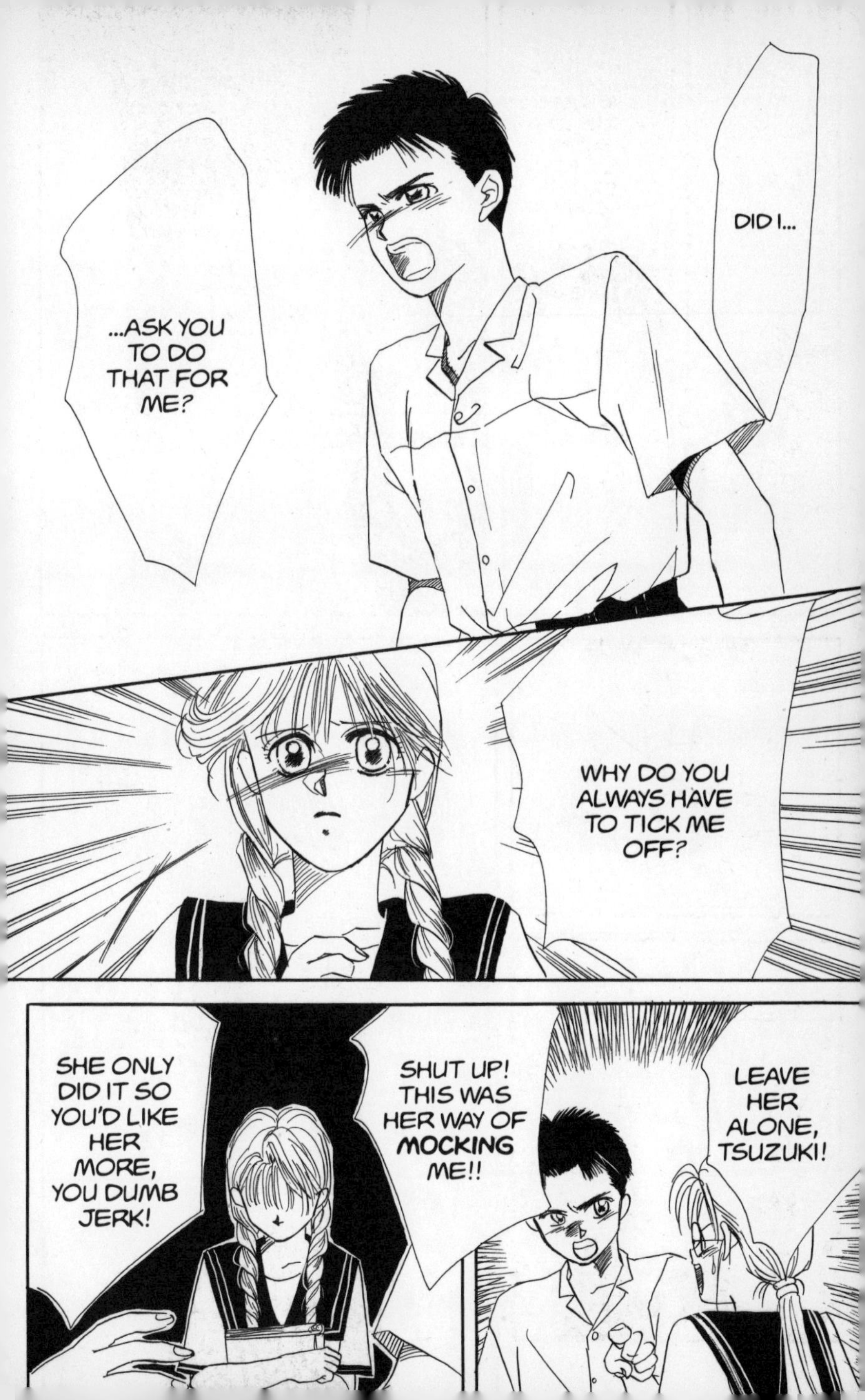
DID I...
...ASK YOU TO DO THAT FOR ME?
WHY DO YOU ALWAYS HAVE TO TICK ME OFF?
LEAVE HER ALONE, TSUZUKI!
SHUT UP! THIS WAS HER WAY OF **MOCKING** ME!!
SHE ONLY DID IT SO YOU'D LIKE HER MORE, YOU DUMB JERK!

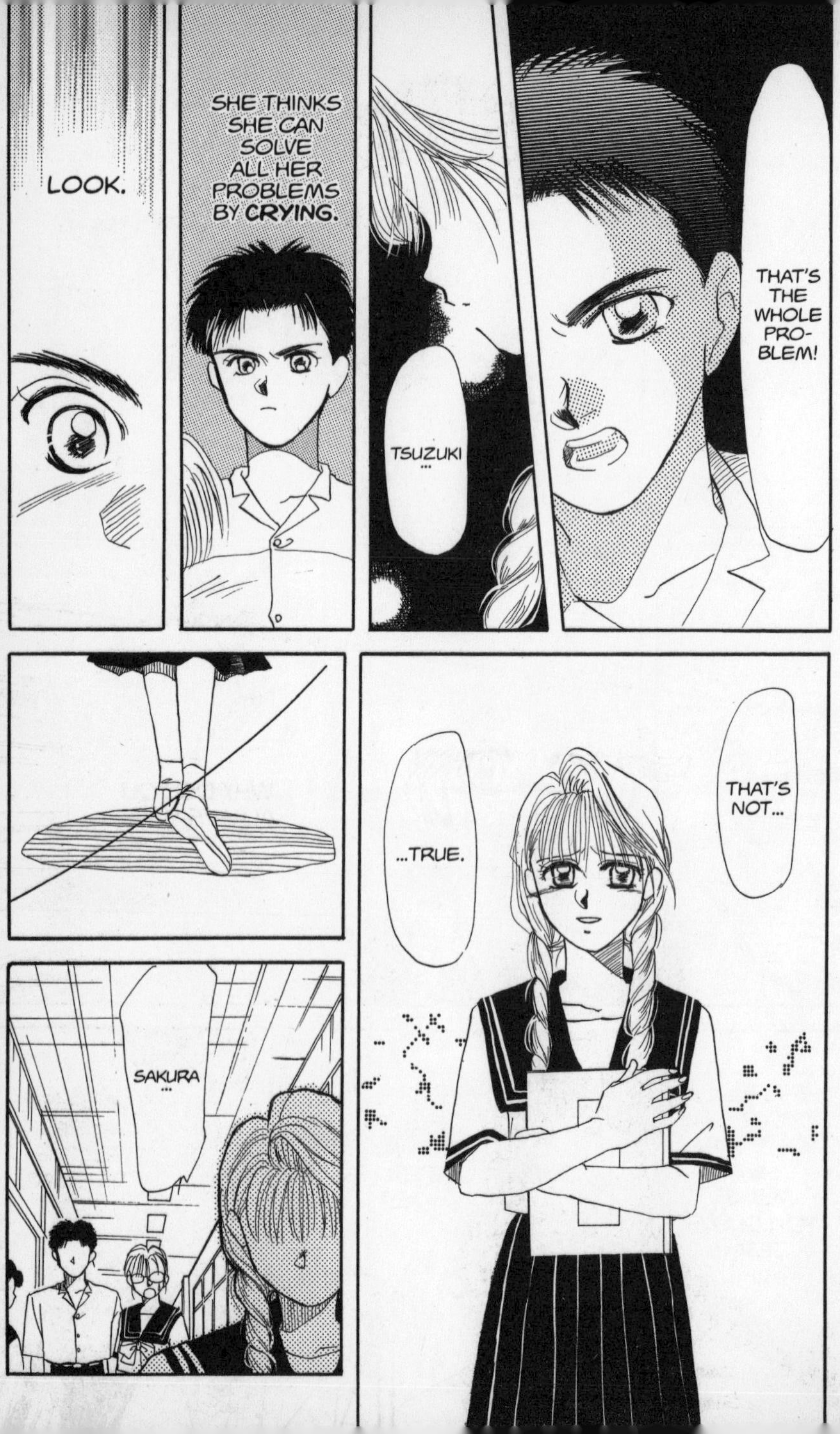
THAT'S THE WHOLE PROBLEM!
TSUZUKI ...
SHE THINKS SHE CAN SOLVE ALL HER PROBLEMS BY CRYING.
LOOK.
THAT'S NOT...
...TRUE.
SAKURA ...

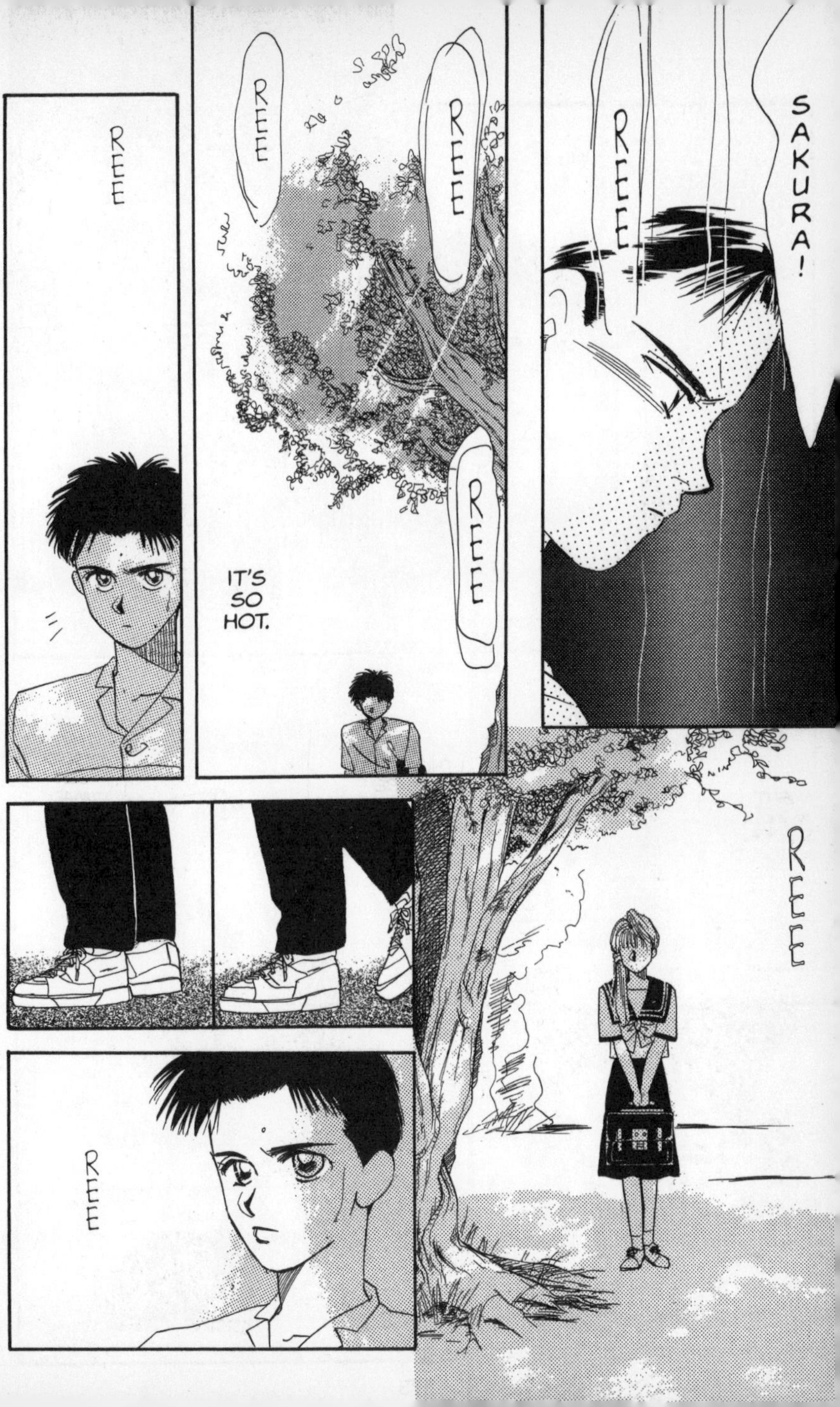
SAKURA!
REEE
REEE
REE
REEE
IT'S SO HOT.
REE
REEE
REE

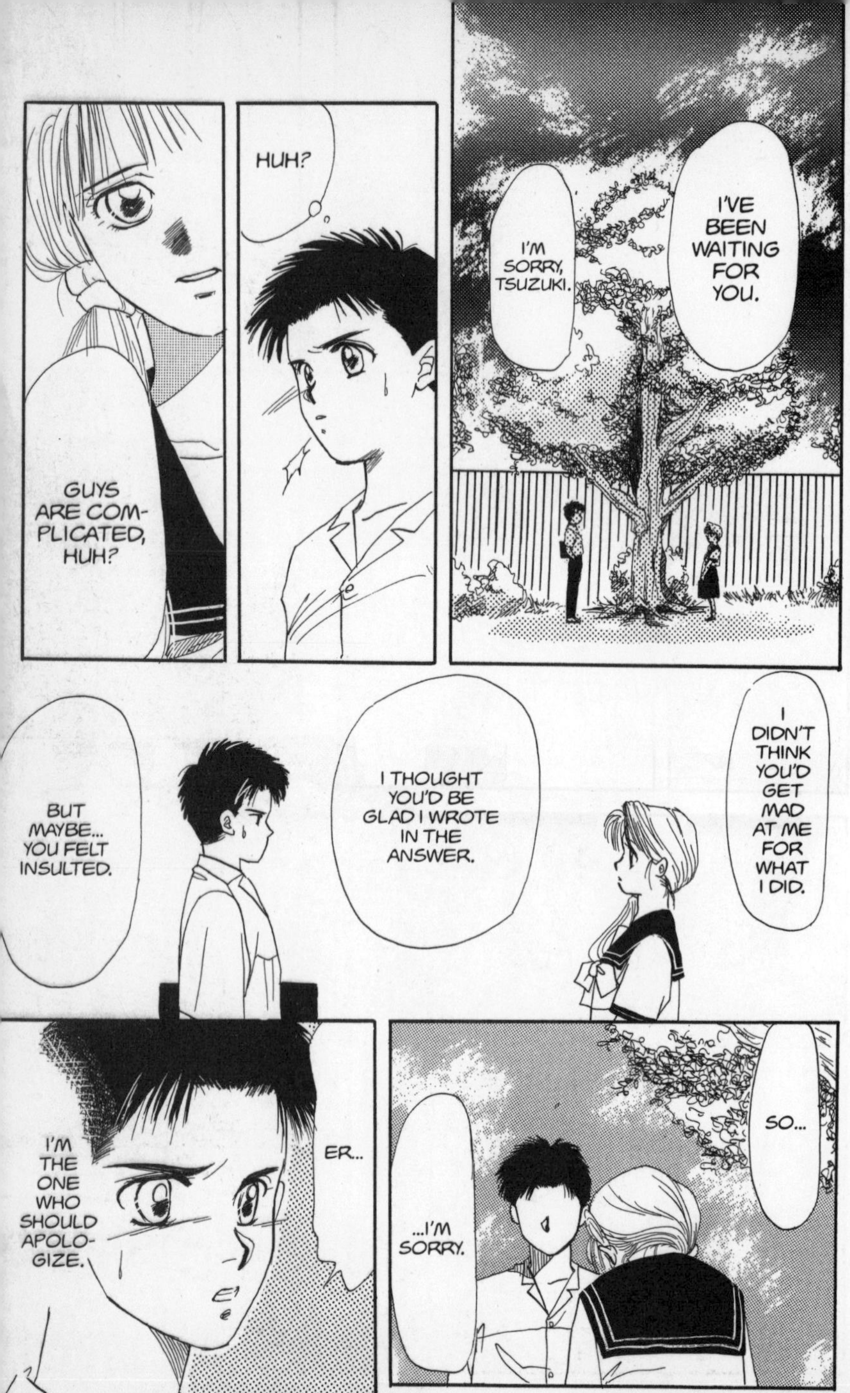
I'VE BEEN WAITING FOR YOU.
I'M SORRY, TSUZUKI.
HUH?
GUYS ARE COMPLICATED, HUH?
I DIDN'T THINK YOU'D GET MAD AT ME FOR WHAT I DID.
I THOUGHT YOU'D BE GLAD I WROTE IN THE ANSWER.
BUT MAYBE... YOU FELT INSULTED.
SO...
...I'M SORRY.
ER...
I'M THE ONE WHO SHOULD APOLOGIZE.

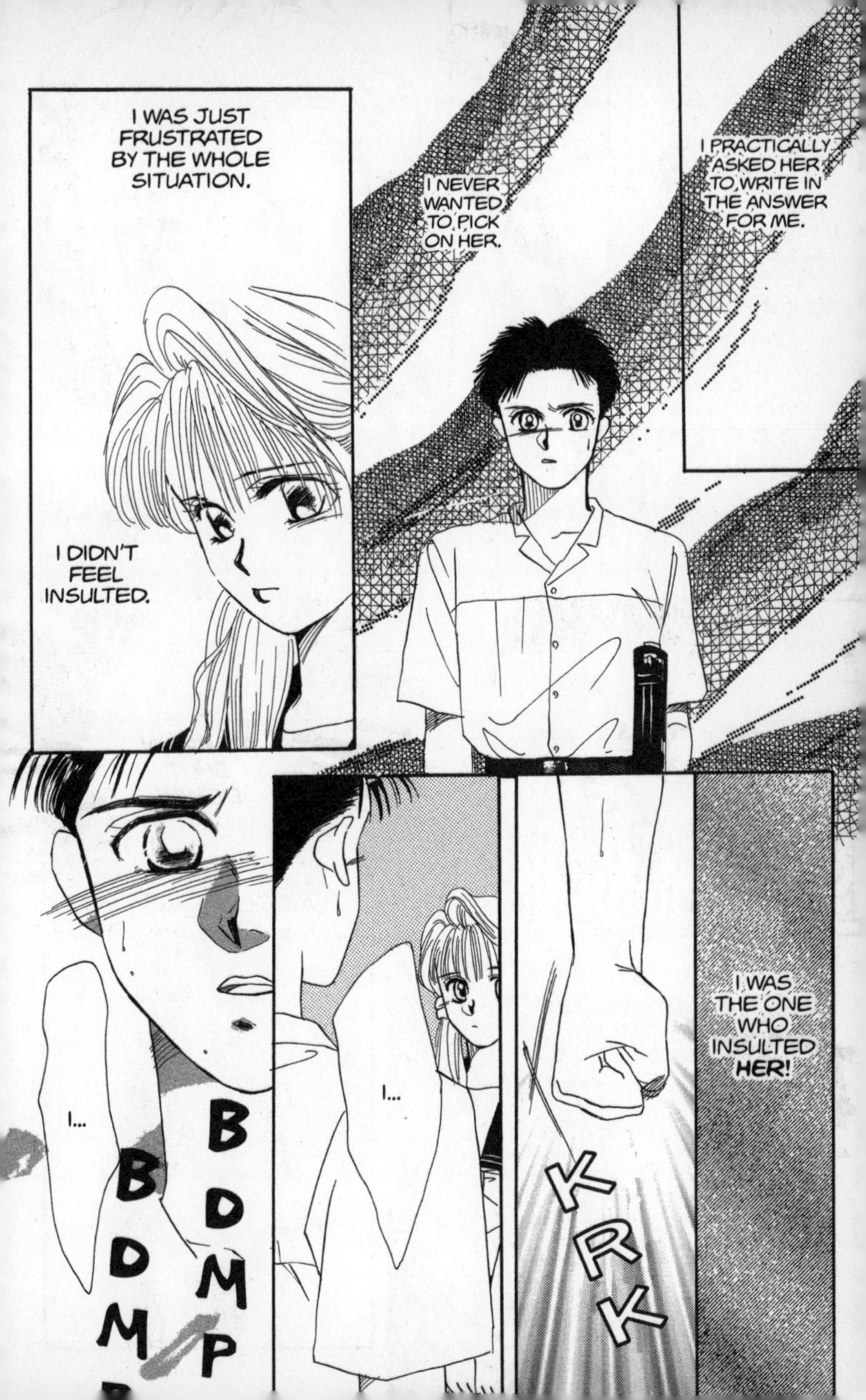
I PRACTICALLY ASKED HER TO WRITE IN THE ANSWER FOR ME.
I NEVER WANTED TO PICK ON HER.
I WAS JUST FRUSTRATED BY THE WHOLE SITUATION.
I DIDN'T FEEL INSULTED.
I WAS THE ONE WHO INSULTED HER!
KRK
I...
I...
BDMP
BDMP

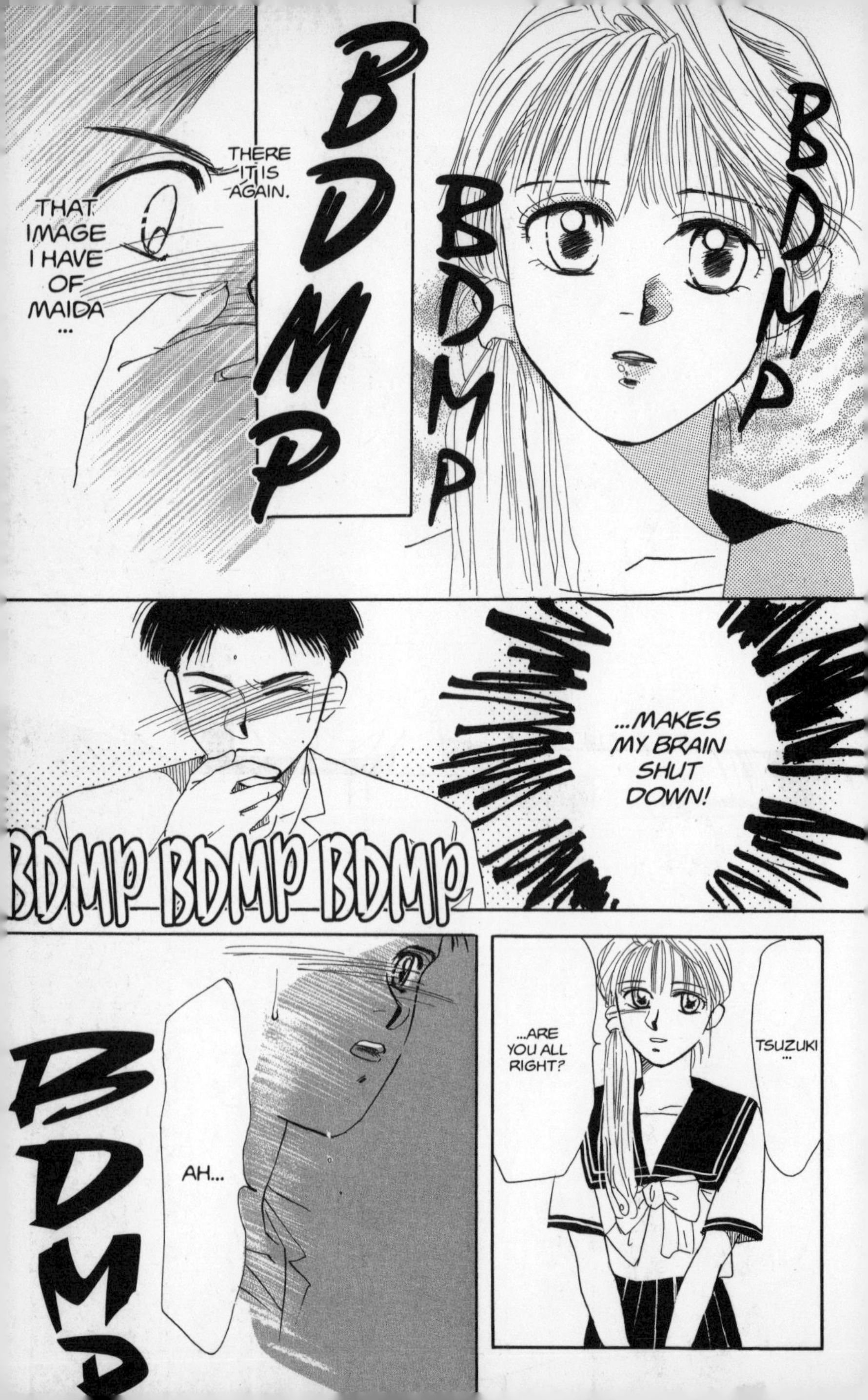
BDMP
BDMP
BDMP
THERE IT IS AGAIN.
THAT IMAGE I HAVE OF MAIDA ...
...MAKES MY BRAIN SHUT DOWN!
BDMP BDMP BDMP
TSUZUKI ...
...ARE YOU ALL RIGHT?
AH...
BDMP

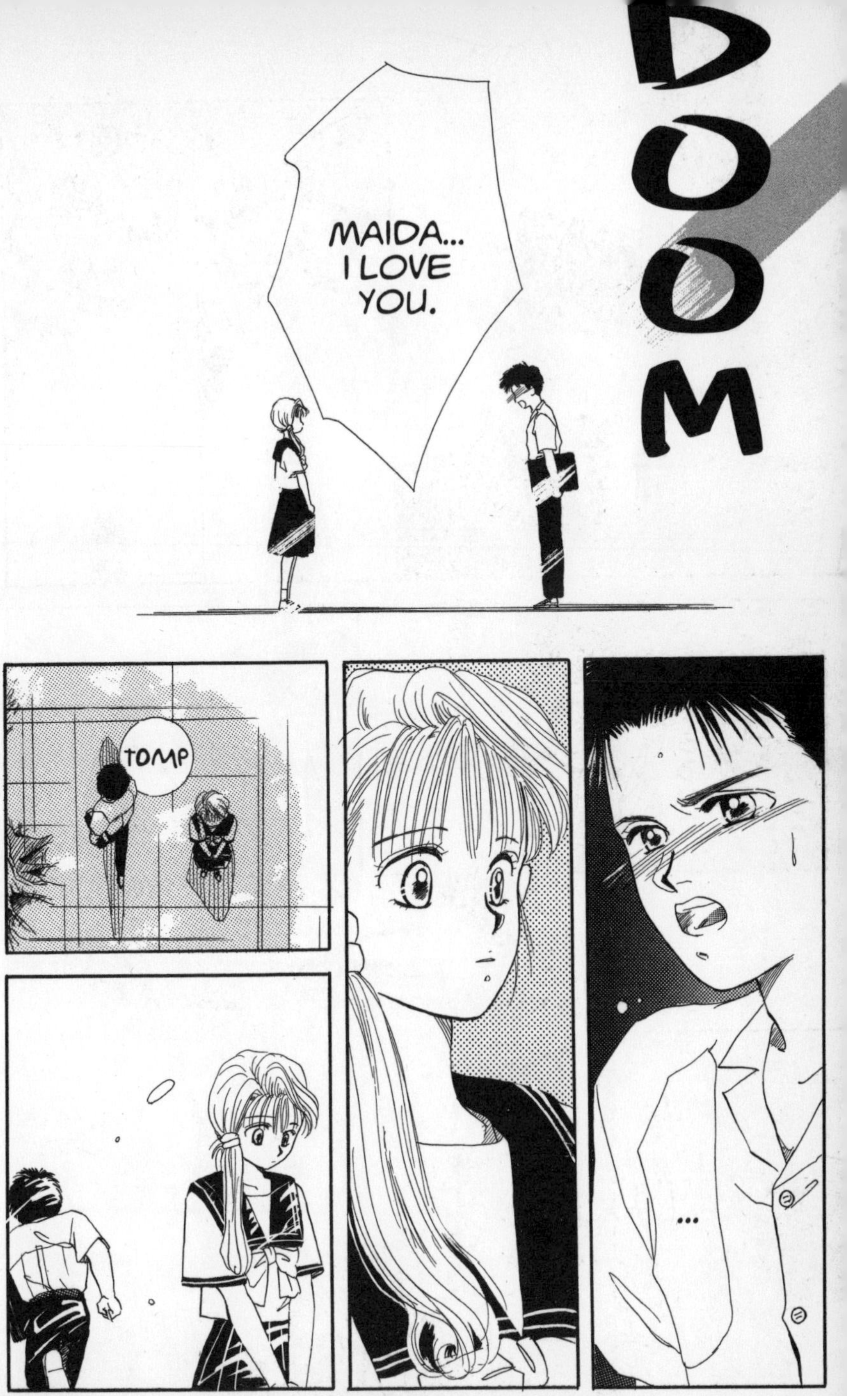
DOOM
MAIDA... I LOVE YOU.
...
TOMP

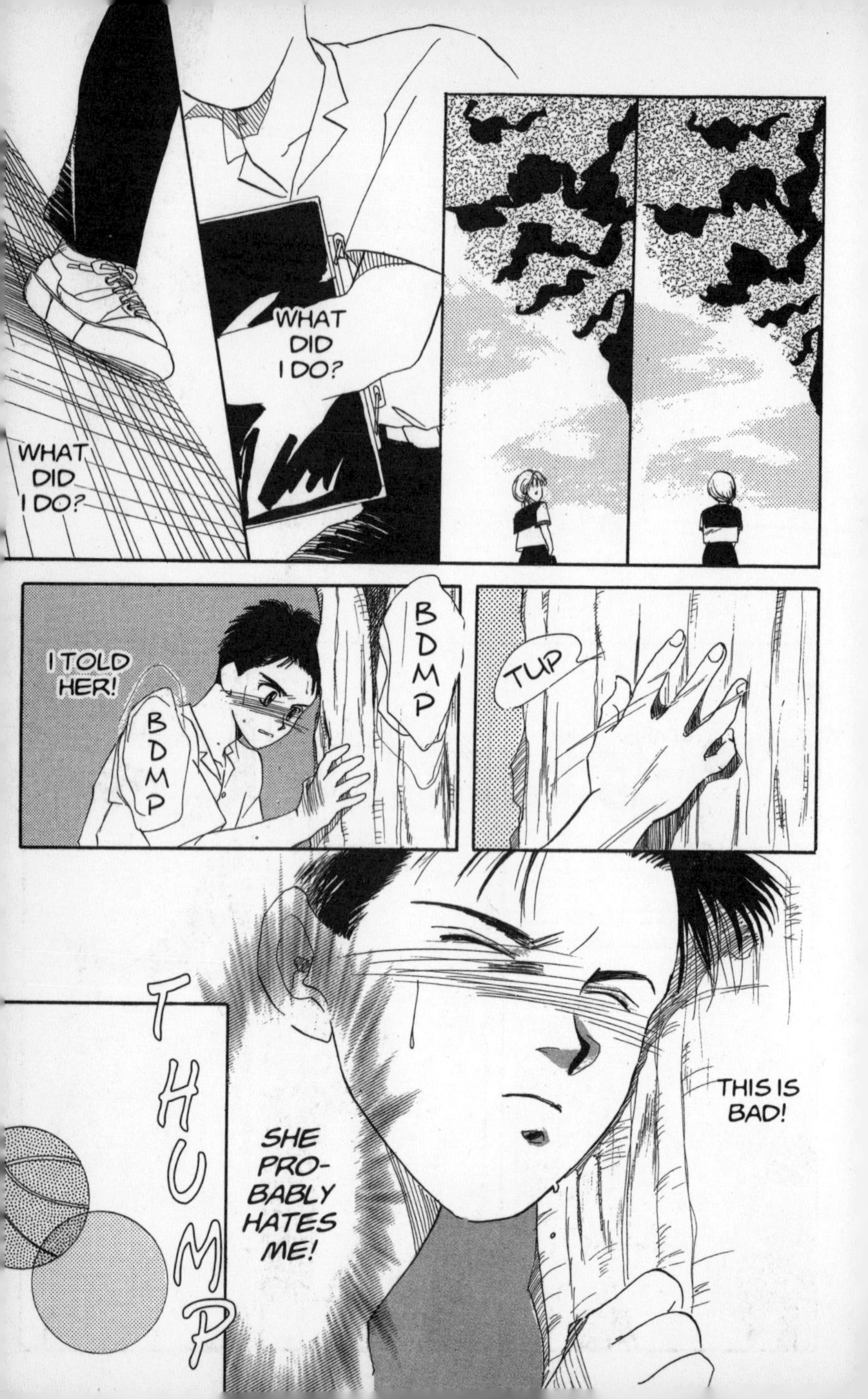
WHAT DID I DO?
WHAT DID I DO?
TUP
BDMP
I TOLD HER!
BDMP
THIS IS BAD!
SHE PRO-BABLY HATES ME!
THUMP

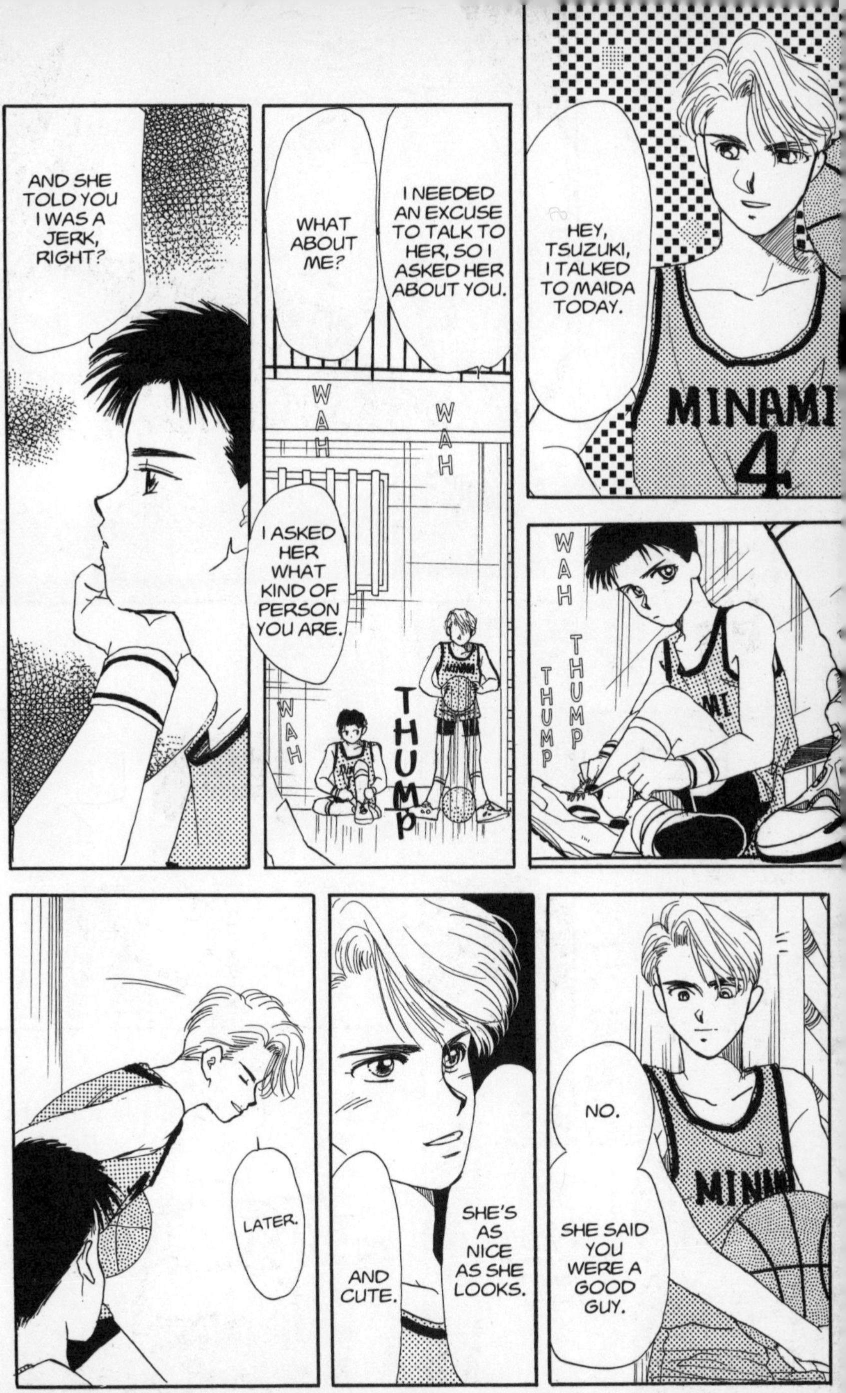
HEY, TSUZUKI, I TALKED TO MAIDA TODAY.
MINAMI 4
WAH
THUMP THUMP
I NEEDED AN EXCUSE TO TALK TO HER, SO I ASKED HER ABOUT YOU.
WHAT ABOUT ME?
WAH
WAH
I ASKED HER WHAT KIND OF PERSON YOU ARE.
WAH
THUMP
AND SHE TOLD YOU I WAS A JERK, RIGHT?
NO.
SHE SAID YOU WERE A GOOD GUY.
SHE'S AS NICE AS SHE LOOKS.
AND CUTE.
LATER.

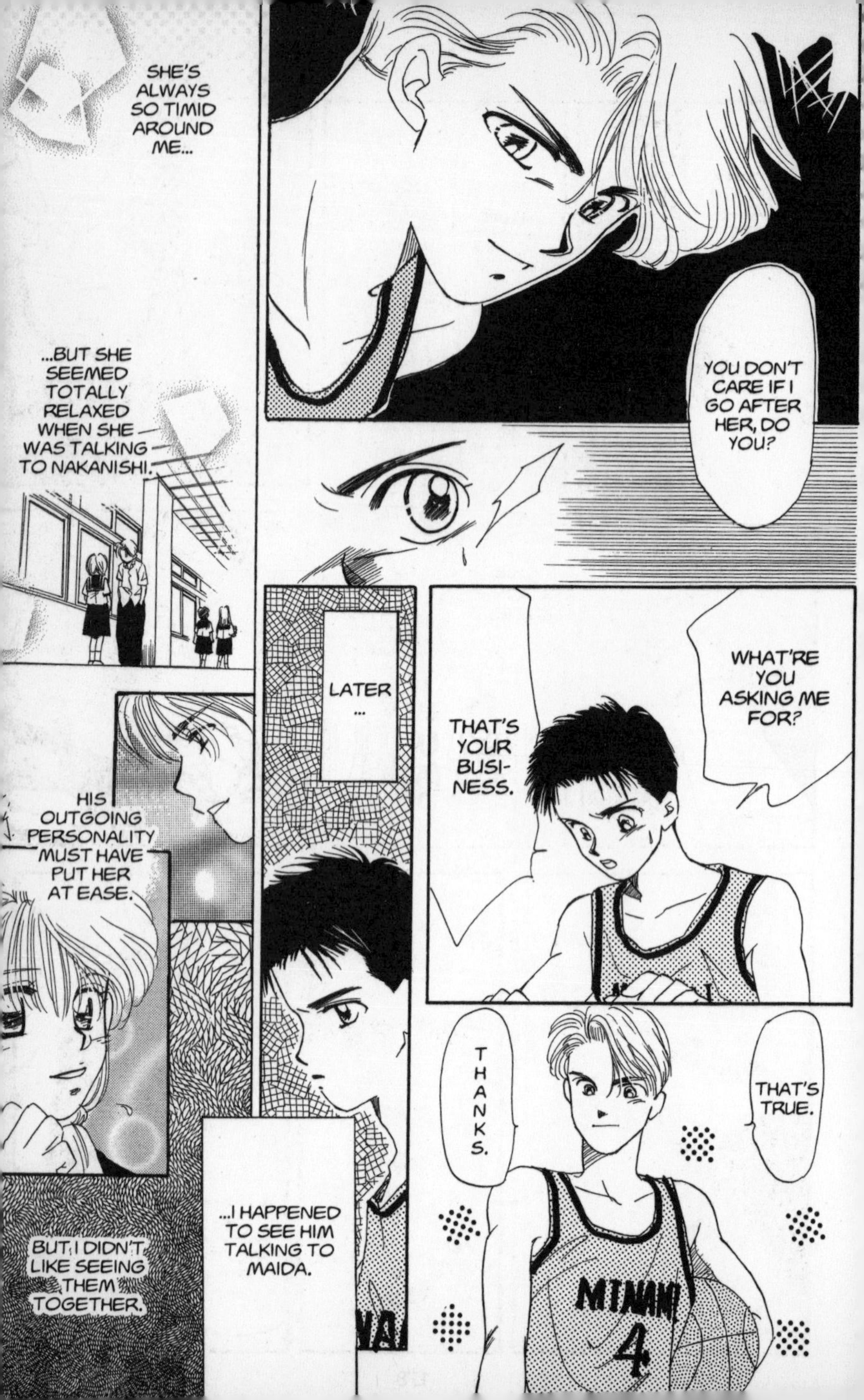
YOU DON'T CARE IF I GO AFTER HER, DO YOU?
WHAT'RE YOU ASKING ME FOR?
THAT'S YOUR BUSI-NESS.
THAT'S TRUE.
THANKS.
LATER...
...I HAPPENED TO SEE HIM TALKING TO MAIDA.
SHE'S ALWAYS SO TIMID AROUND ME...
...BUT SHE SEEMED TOTALLY RELAXED WHEN SHE WAS TALKING TO NAKANISHI.
HIS OUTGOING PERSONALITY MUST HAVE PUT HER AT EASE.
BUT I DIDN'T LIKE SEEING THEM TOGETHER.

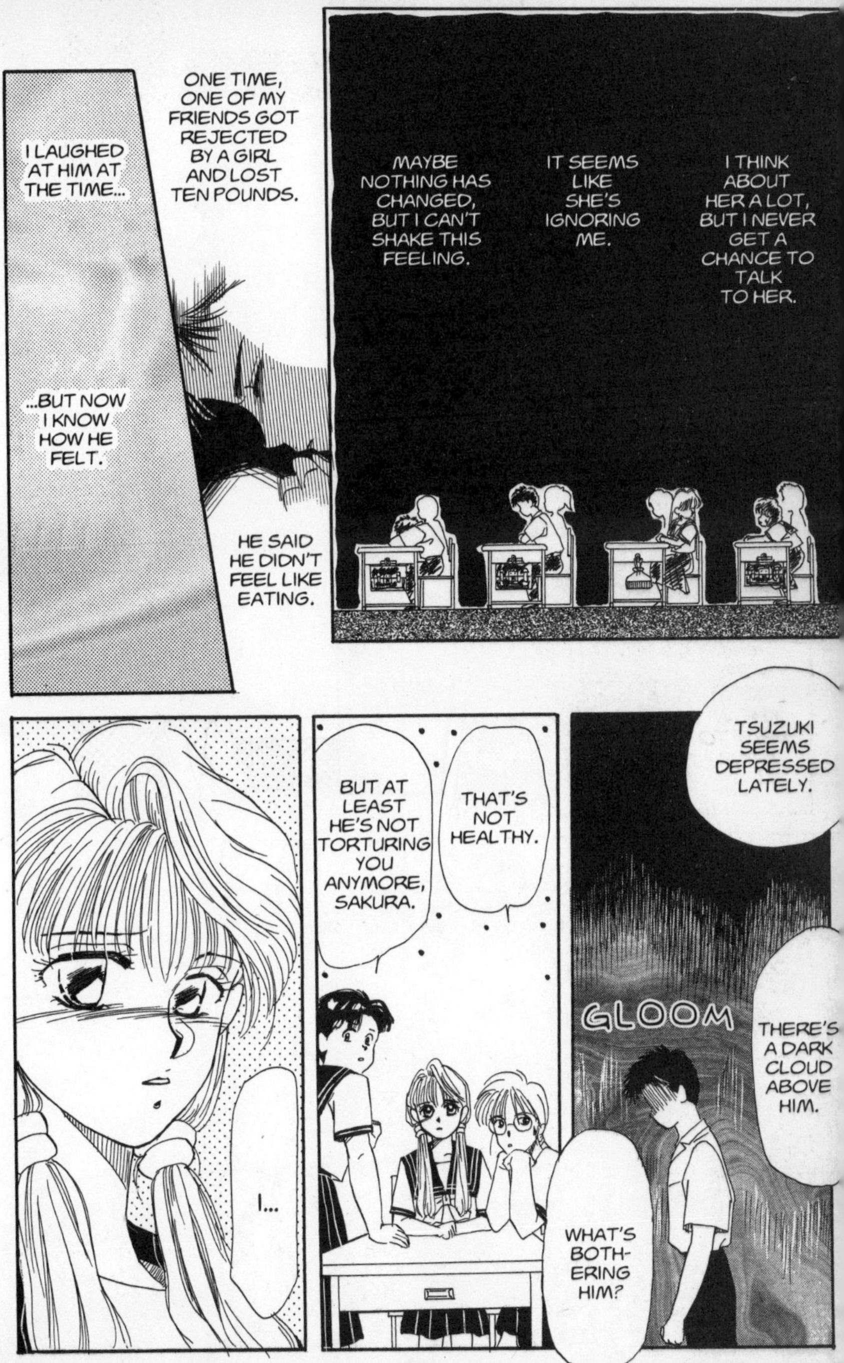
I THINK ABOUT HER A LOT, BUT I NEVER GET A CHANCE TO TALK TO HER.
IT SEEMS LIKE SHE'S IGNORING ME.
MAYBE NOTHING HAS CHANGED, BUT I CAN'T SHAKE THIS FEELING.
ONE TIME, ONE OF MY FRIENDS GOT REJECTED BY A GIRL AND LOST TEN POUNDS.
HE SAID HE DIDN'T FEEL LIKE EATING.
I LAUGHED AT HIM AT THE TIME...
...BUT NOW I KNOW HOW HE FELT.
TSUZUKI SEEMS DEPRESSED LATELY.
GLOOM
THERE'S A DARK CLOUD ABOVE HIM.
WHAT'S BOTH-ERING HIM?
THAT'S NOT HEALTHY.
BUT AT LEAST HE'S NOT TORTURING YOU ANYMORE, SAKURA.
I...

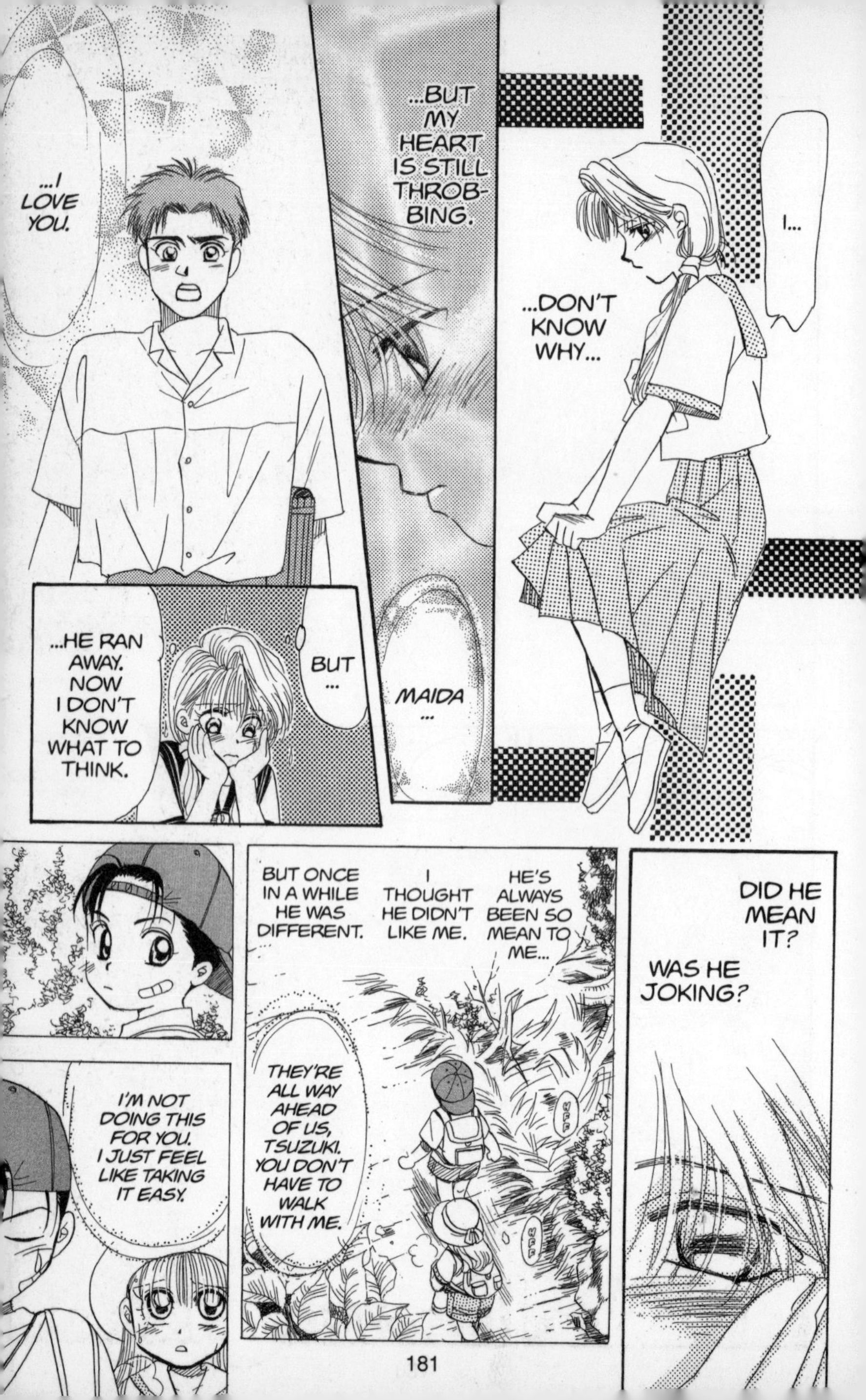
I...
...DON'T KNOW WHY...
...BUT MY HEART IS STILL THROBBING.
MAIDA...
...I LOVE YOU.
BUT...
...HE RAN AWAY. NOW I DON'T KNOW WHAT TO THINK.
DID HE MEAN IT?
WAS HE JOKING?
HE'S ALWAYS BEEN SO MEAN TO ME...
I THOUGHT HE DIDN'T LIKE ME.
BUT ONCE IN A WHILE HE WAS DIFFERENT...
THEY'RE ALL WAY AHEAD OF US, TSUZUKI. YOU DON'T HAVE TO WALK WITH ME.
I'M NOT DOING THIS FOR YOU. I JUST FEEL LIKE TAKING IT EASY.

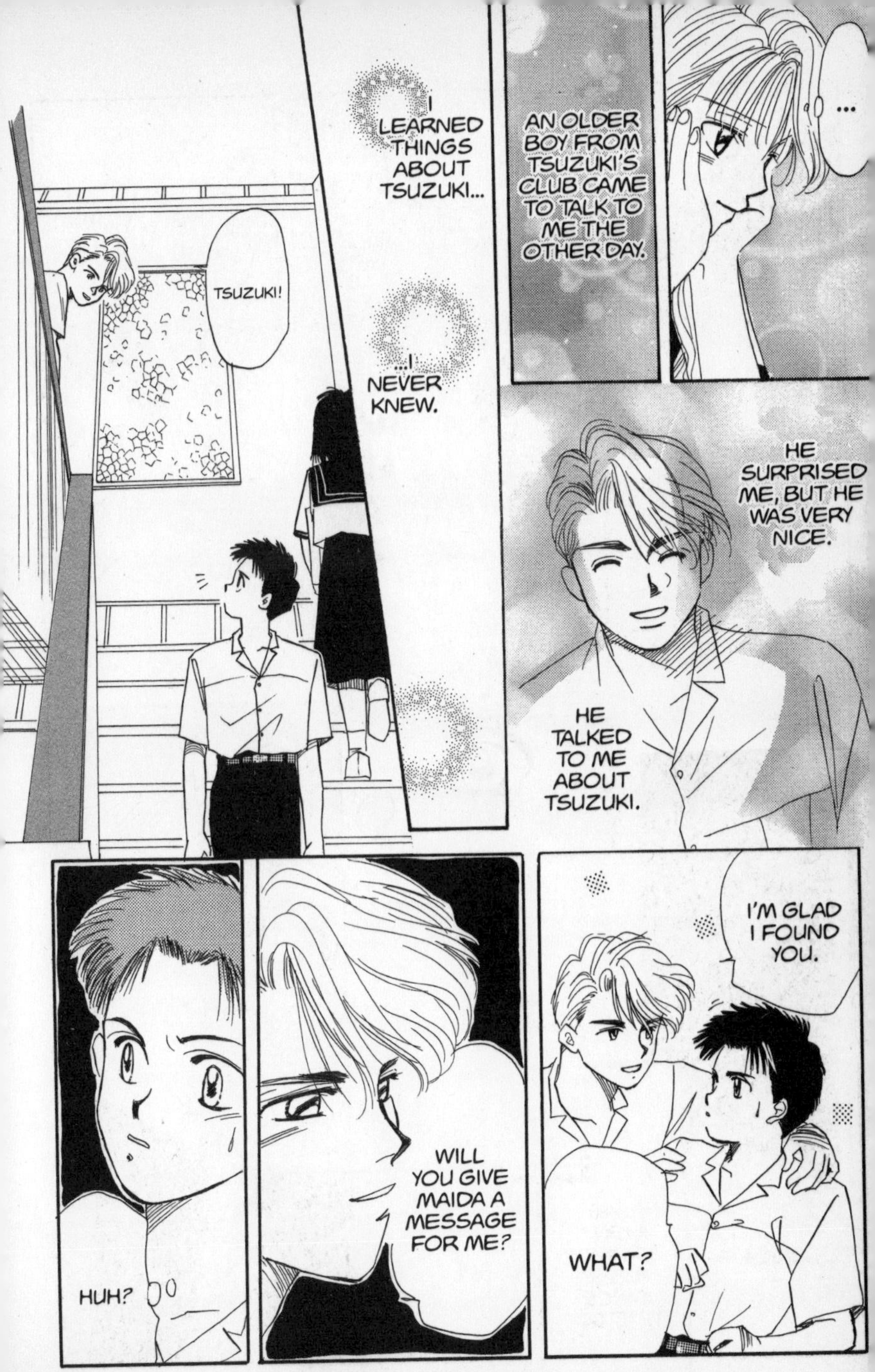
...
AN OLDER BOY FROM TSUZUKI'S CLUB CAME TO TALK TO ME THE OTHER DAY.
HE SURPRISED ME, BUT HE WAS VERY NICE.
HE TALKED TO ME ABOUT TSUZUKI.
I LEARNED THINGS ABOUT TSUZUKI...
...I NEVER KNEW.
TSUZUKI!
I'M GLAD I FOUND YOU.
WHAT?
WILL YOU GIVE MAIDA A MESSAGE FOR ME?
HUH?

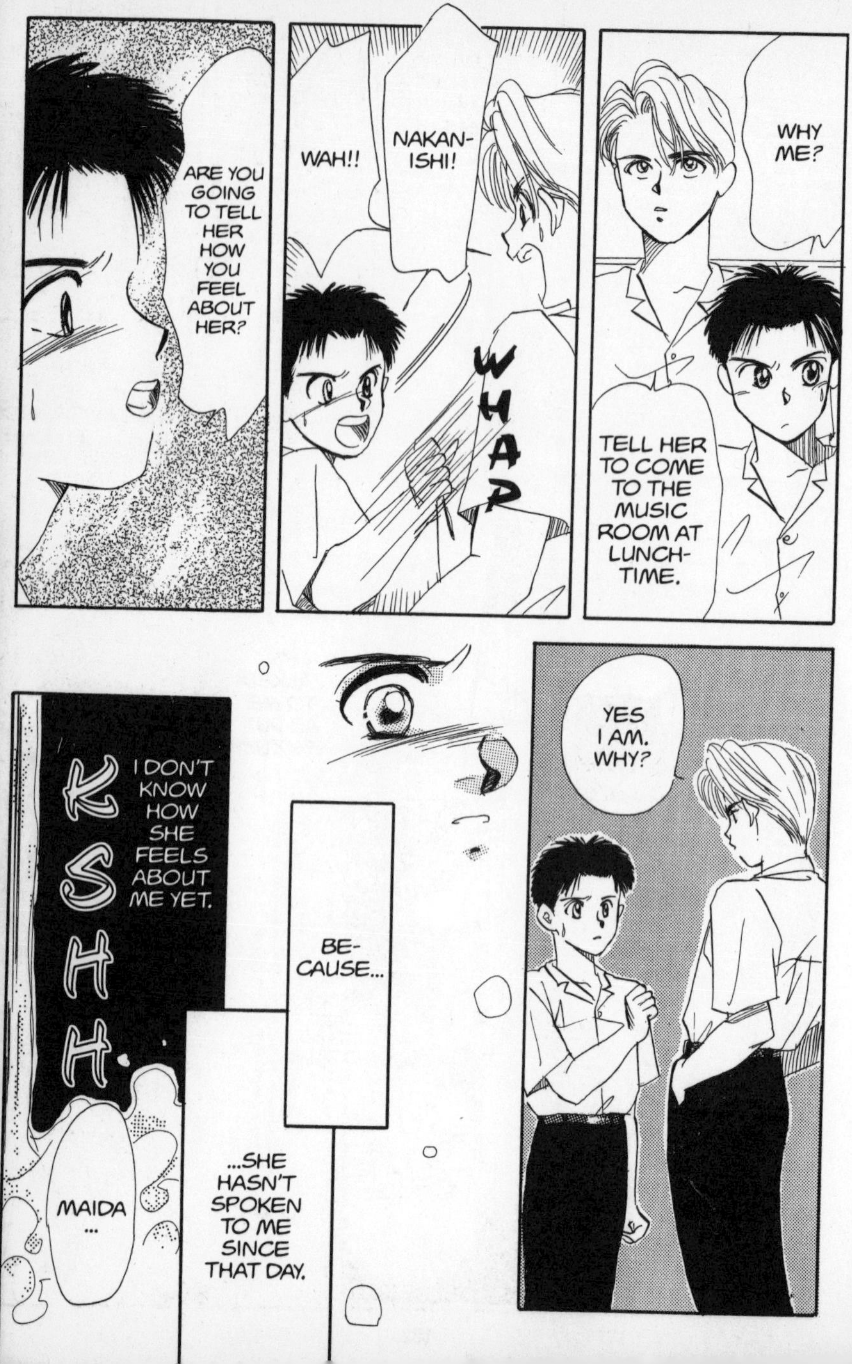
WHY ME?
TELL HER TO COME TO THE MUSIC ROOM AT LUNCH-TIME.
NAKAN-ISHI!
WAH!!
WHAP
ARE YOU GOING TO TELL HER HOW YOU FEEL ABOUT HER?
YES I AM. WHY?
BE-CAUSE...
...SHE HASN'T SPOKEN TO ME SINCE THAT DAY.
KSHHH
I DON'T KNOW HOW SHE FEELS ABOUT ME YET.
MAIDA ...

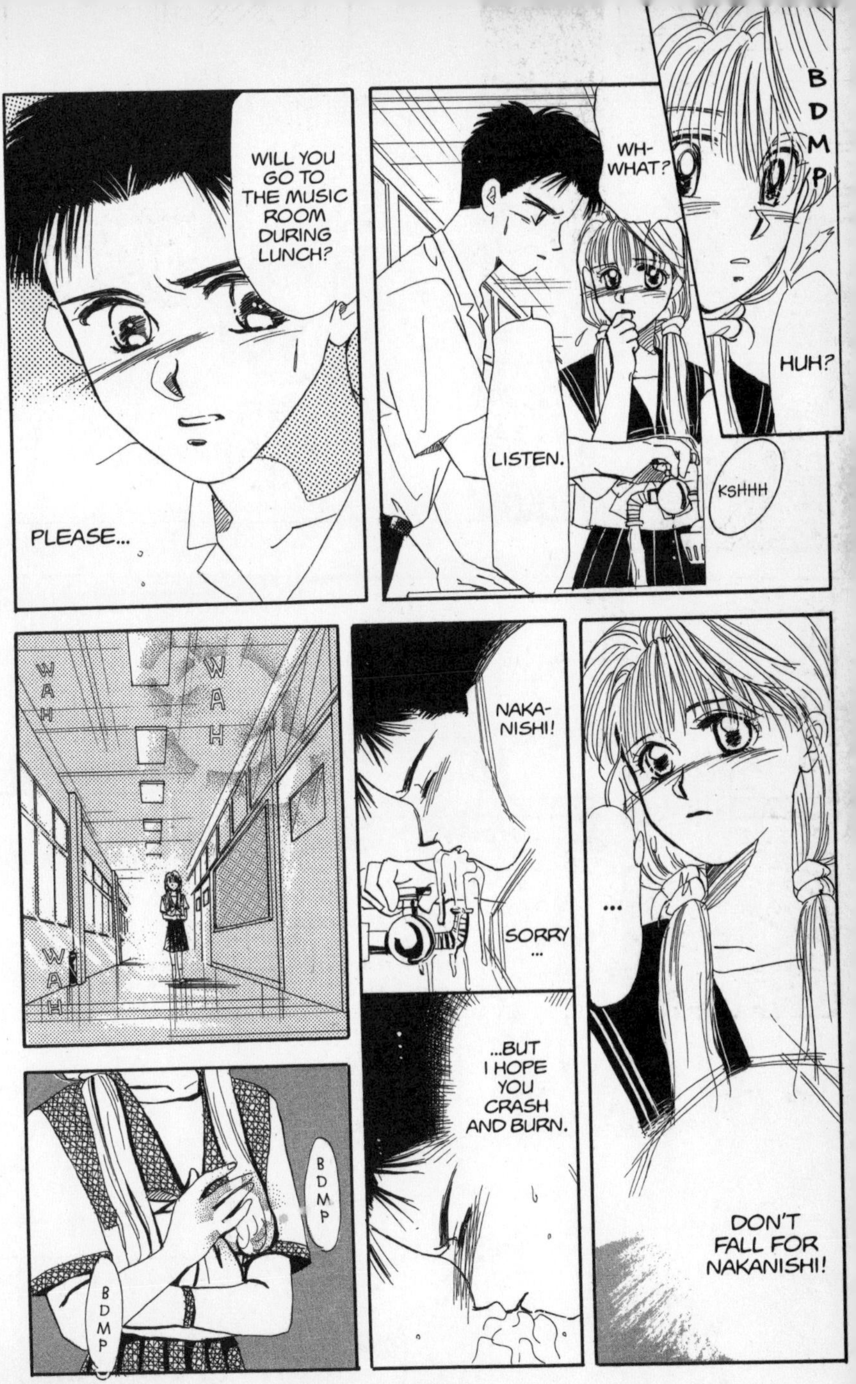
BDMP
HUH?
WH- WHAT?
KSHHH
LISTEN.
WILL YOU GO TO THE MUSIC ROOM DURING LUNCH?
PLEASE...
...
DON'T FALL FOR NAKANISHI!
NAKA- NISHI!
SORRY ...
...BUT I HOPE YOU CRASH AND BURN.
WAH
WAH
WAH
BDMP
BDMP

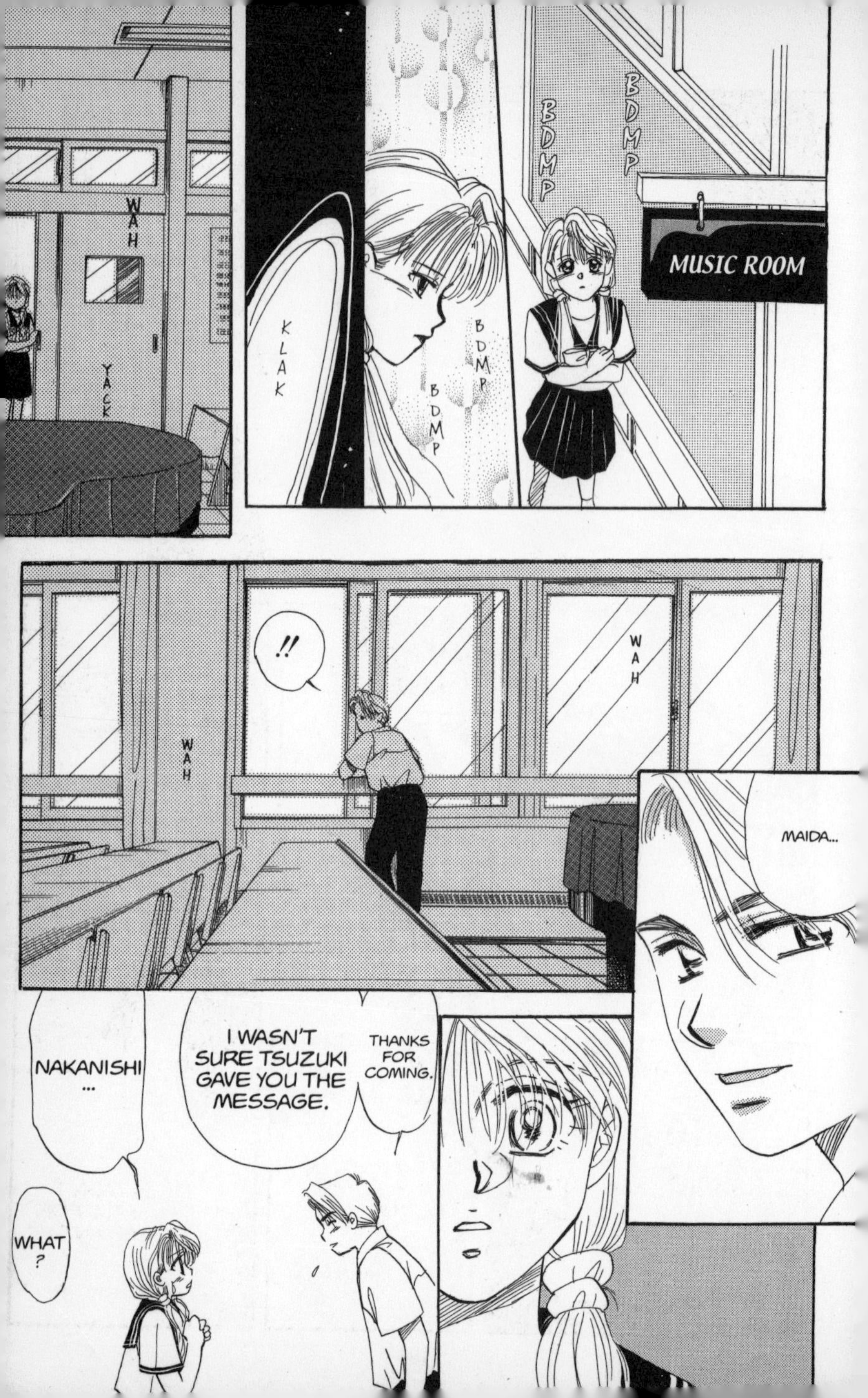
BDMP
BDMP
MUSIC ROOM
BDMP
BDMP
KLAK
WAH
YACK
!!
WAH
WAH
MAIDA...
THANKS FOR COMING.
I WASN'T SURE TSUZUKI GAVE YOU THE MESSAGE.
NAKANISHI ...
WHAT ?

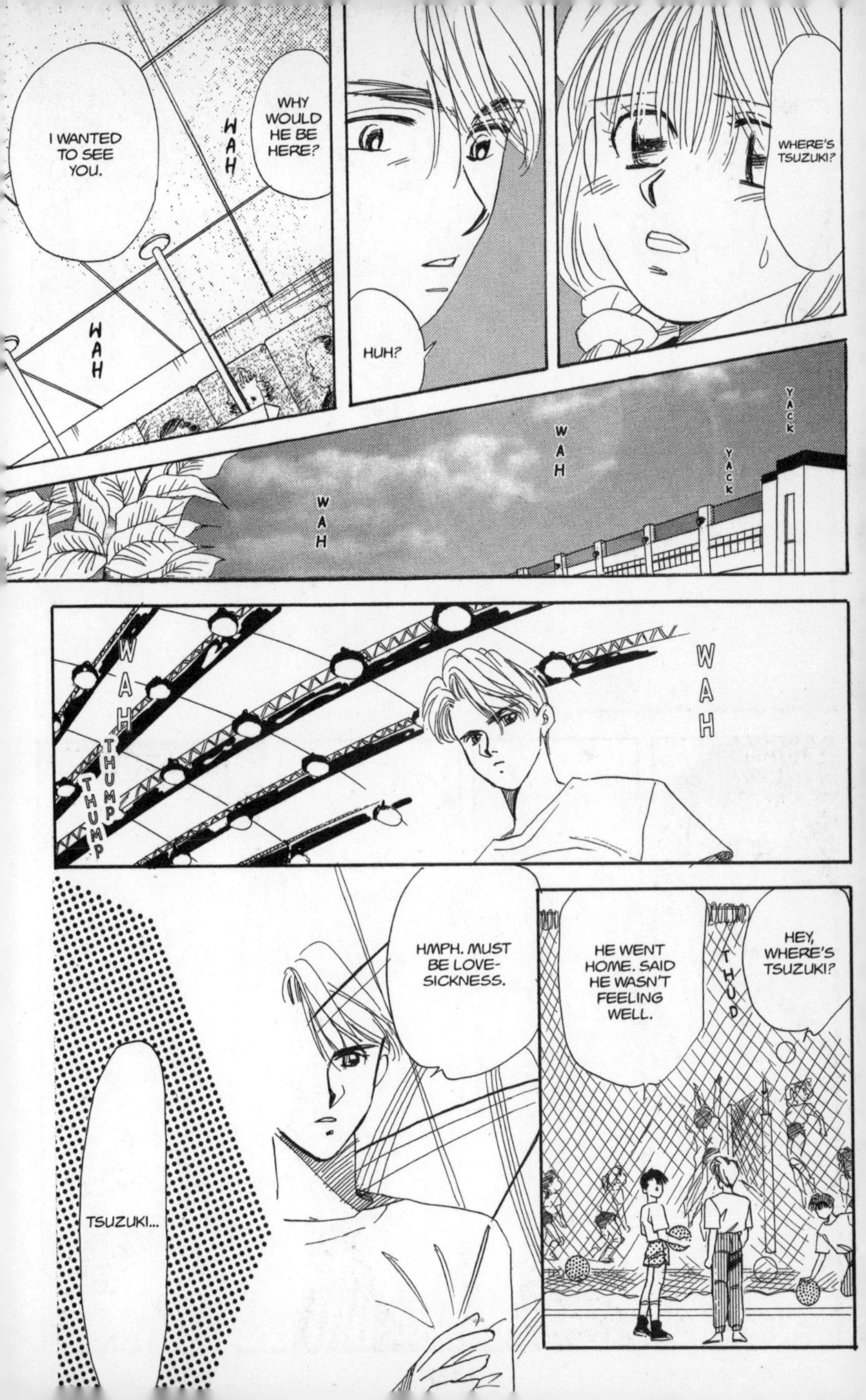
WHERE'S TSUZUKI?
HUH?
WHY WOULD HE BE HERE?
WAH
I WANTED TO SEE YOU.
WAH
YACK
YACK
WAH
WAH
WAH
WAH
THUMP
THUMP
HEY, WHERE'S TSUZUKI?
THUD
HE WENT HOME. SAID HE WASN'T FEELING WELL.
HMPH. MUST BE LOVE-SICKNESS.
TSUZUKI...

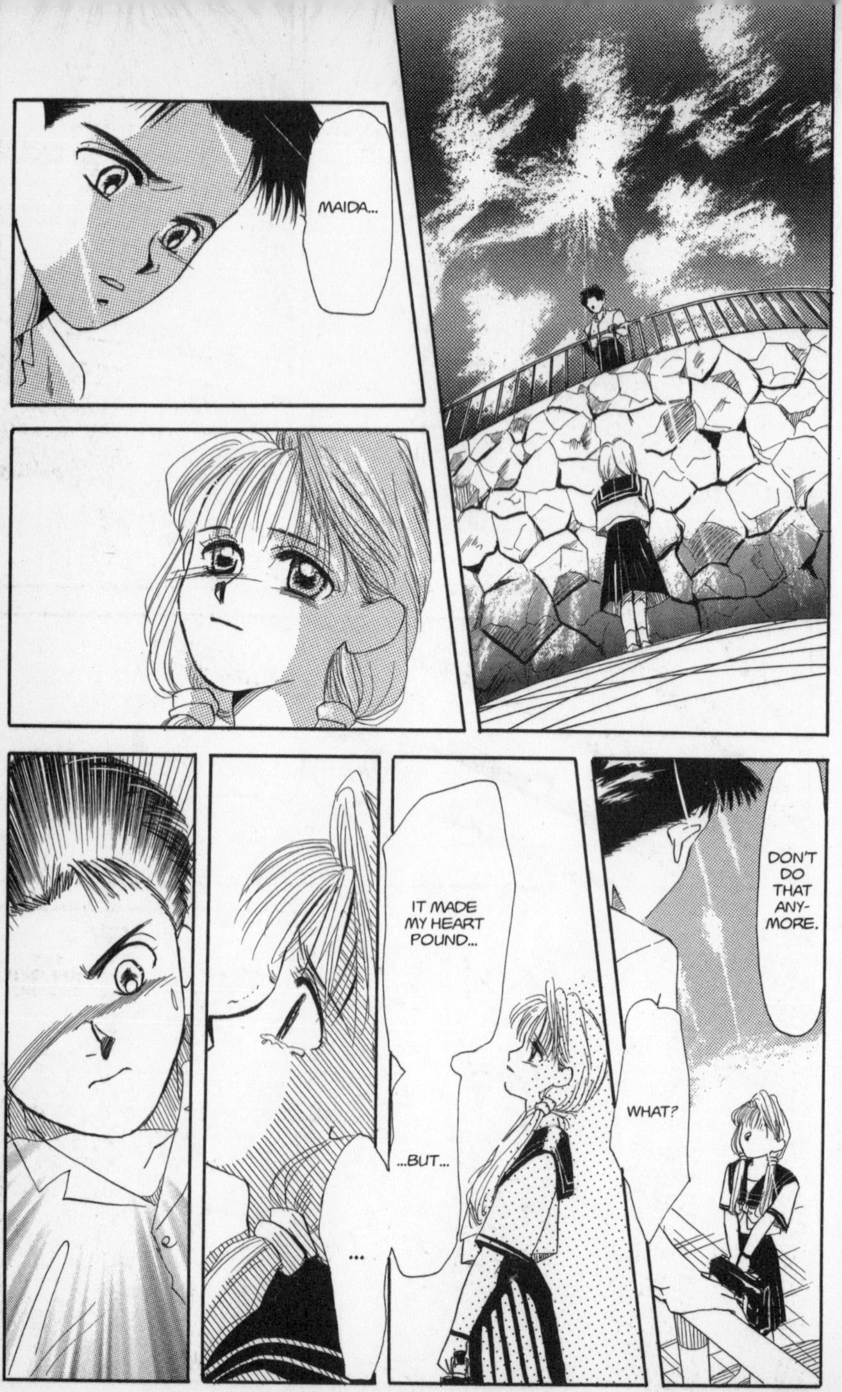
MAIDA...
DON'T DO THAT ANYMORE.
WHAT?
IT MADE MY HEART POUND...
...BUT...
...

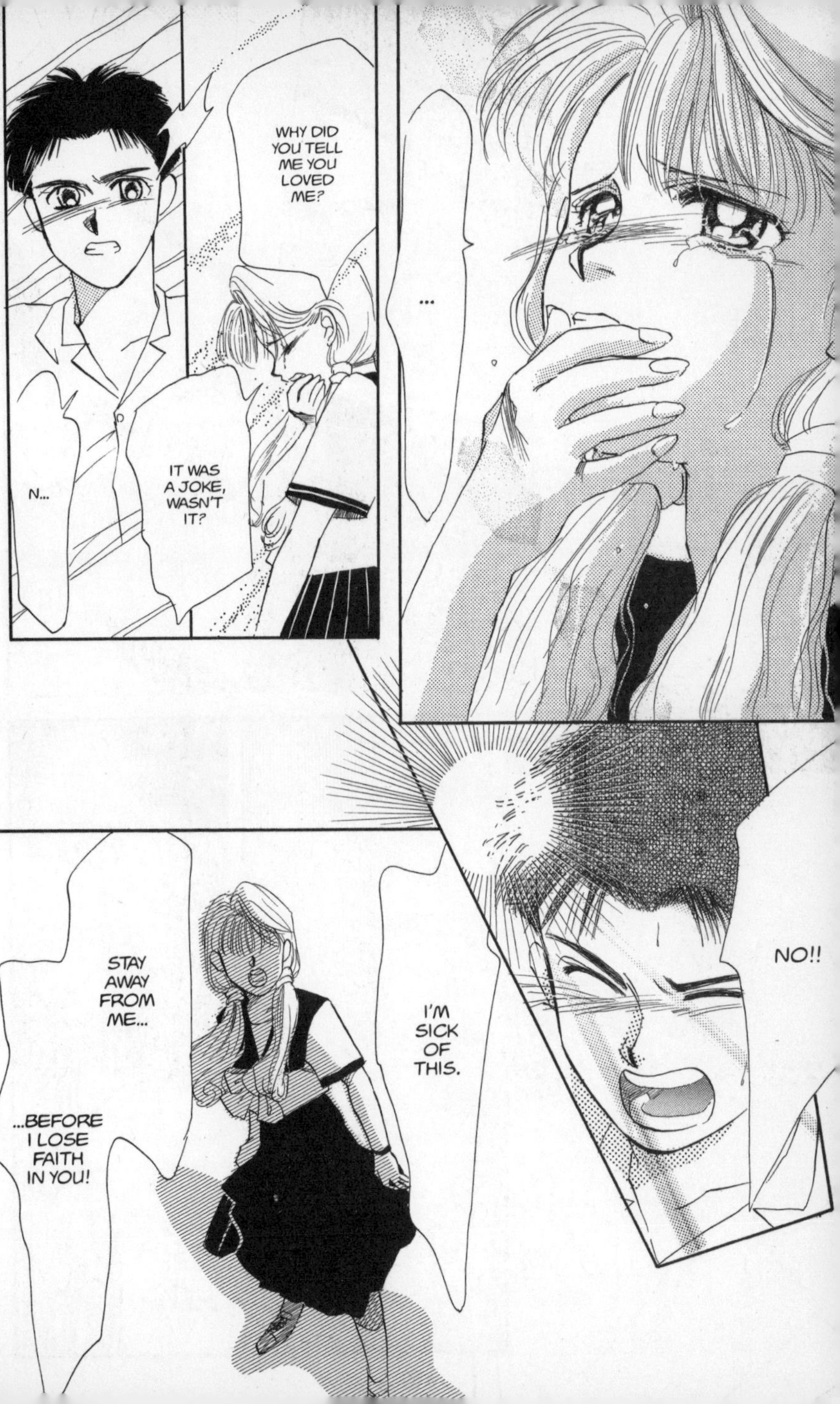
...
WHY DID YOU TELL ME YOU LOVED ME?
IT WAS A JOKE, WASN'T IT?
N...
NO!!
I'M SICK OF THIS.
STAY AWAY FROM ME...
...BEFORE I LOSE FAITH IN YOU!

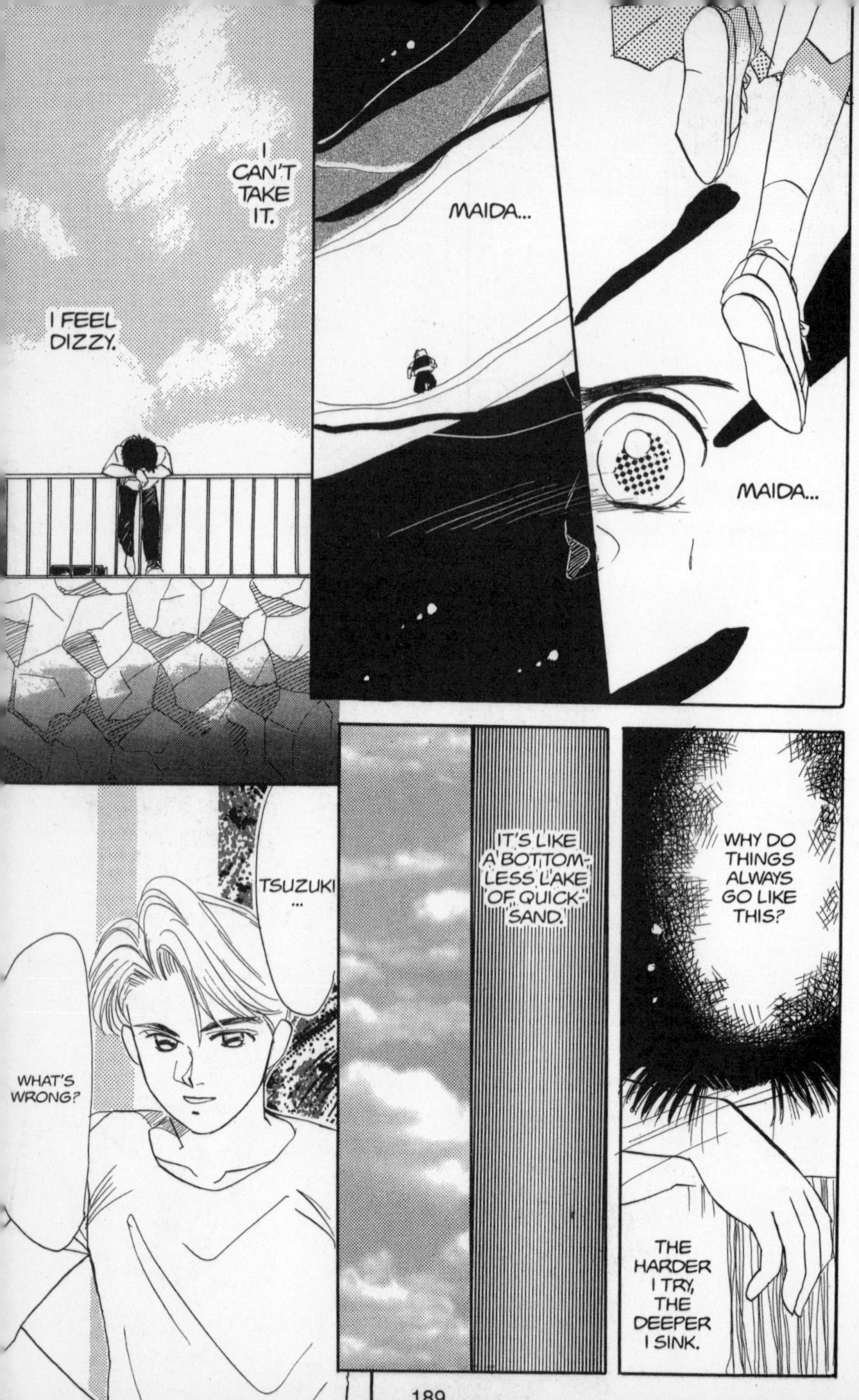
MAIDA...
MAIDA...
I CAN'T TAKE IT.
I FEEL DIZZY.
WHY DO THINGS ALWAYS GO LIKE THIS?
THE HARDER I TRY, THE DEEPER I SINK.
IT'S LIKE A BOTTOMLESS LAKE OF QUICKSAND.
TSUZUKI...
WHAT'S WRONG?

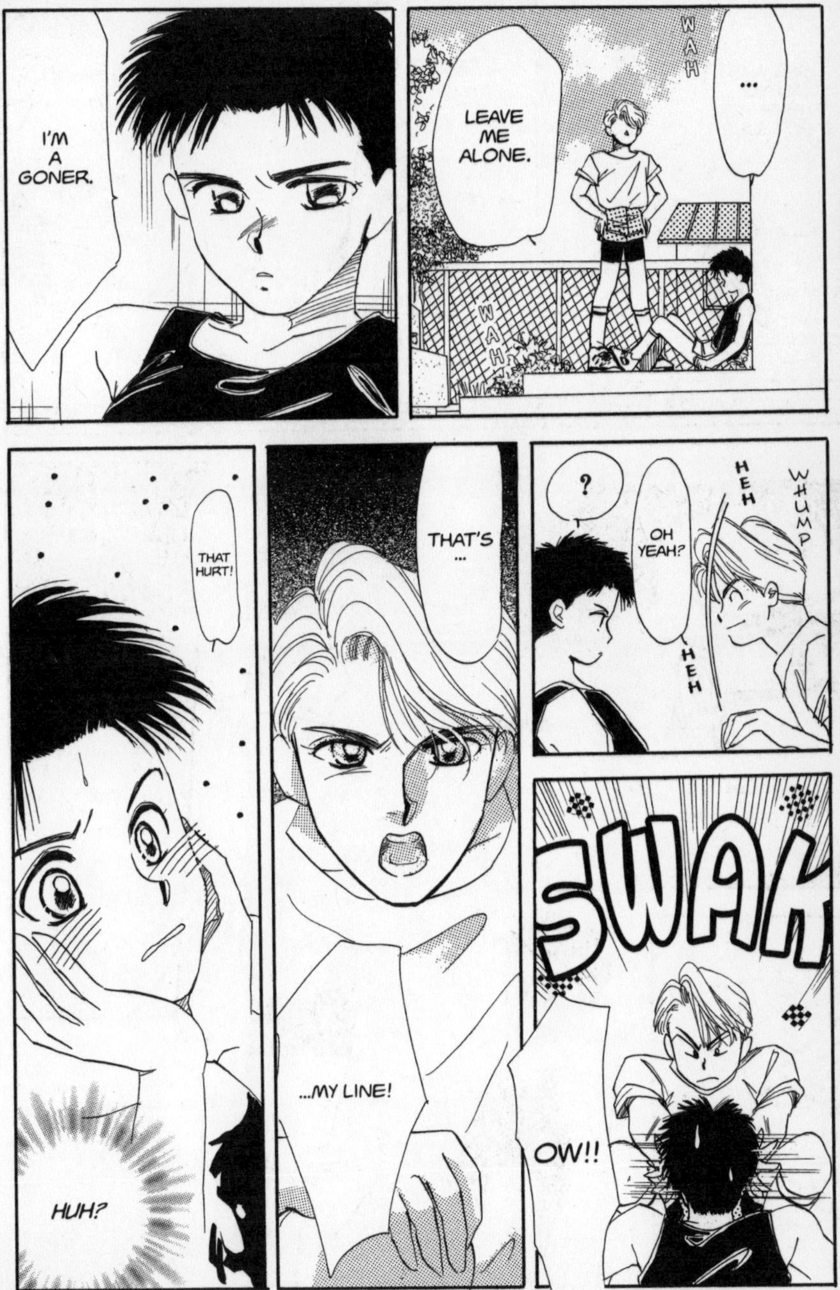
WAH
...
LEAVE ME ALONE.
WAH
I'M A GONER.
WHUMP
HEH
OH YEAH?
?
HEH
SWAK
OW!!
THAT'S ...
...MY LINE!
THAT HURT!
HUH?

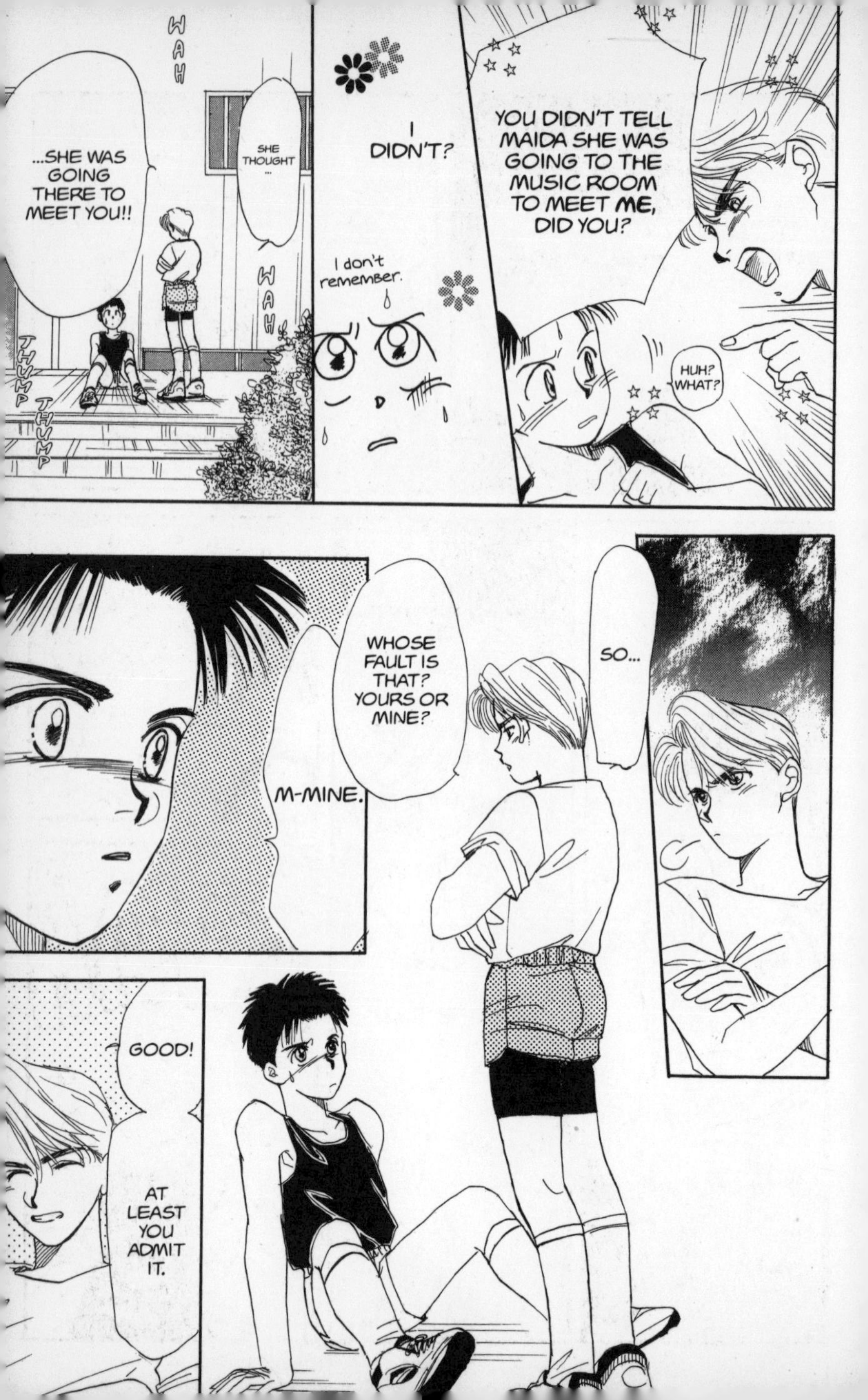
YOU DIDN'T TELL MAIDA SHE WAS GOING TO THE MUSIC ROOM TO MEET ME, DID YOU?
HUH? WHAT?
I DIDN'T?
I don't remember.
SHE THOUGHT...
...SHE WAS GOING THERE TO MEET YOU!!
WAH WAH
THUMP THUMP
SO...
WHOSE FAULT IS THAT? YOURS OR MINE?
M-MINE.
GOOD!
AT LEAST YOU ADMIT IT.

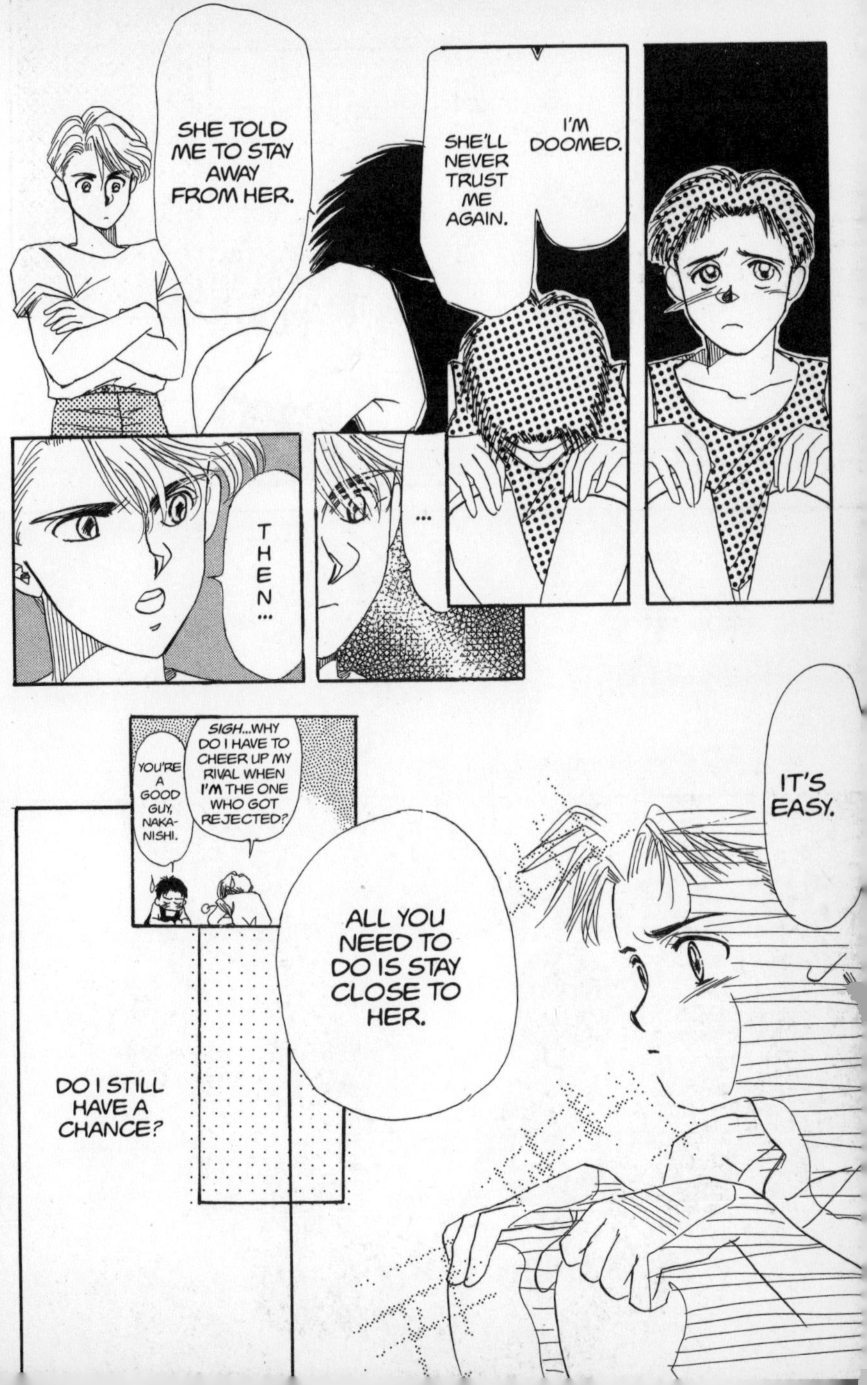
I'M DOOMED.
SHE'LL NEVER TRUST ME AGAIN.
SHE TOLD ME TO STAY AWAY FROM HER.
...
THEN...
IT'S EASY.
ALL YOU NEED TO DO IS STAY CLOSE TO HER.
SIGH...WHY DO I HAVE TO CHEER UP MY RIVAL WHEN I'M THE ONE WHO GOT REJECTED?
YOU'RE A GOOD GUY, NAKA-NISHI.
DO I STILL HAVE A CHANCE?

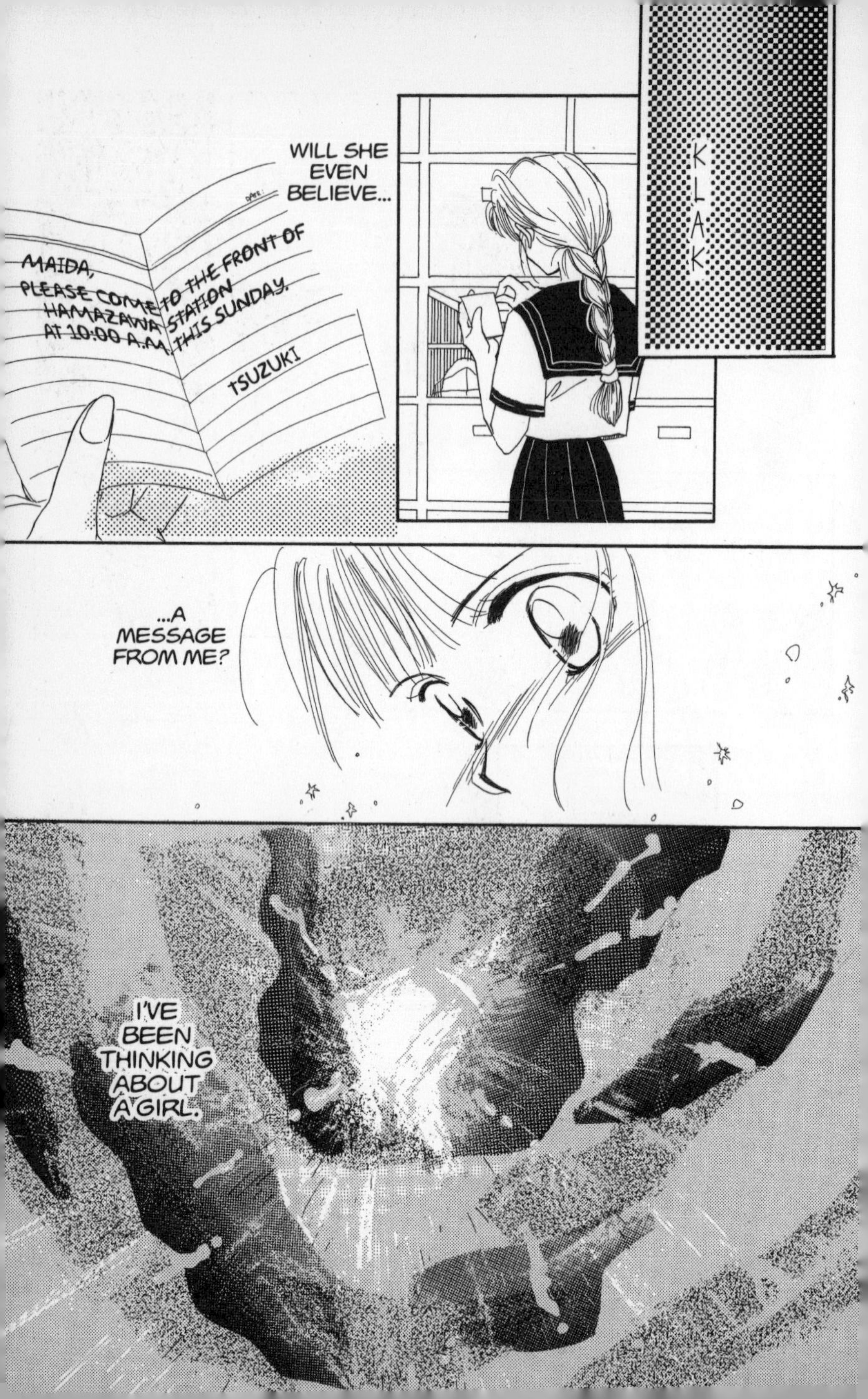
KLAK
WILL SHE EVEN BELIEVE...
MAIDA,
PLEASE COME TO THE FRONT OF HAMAZAWA STATION AT 10:00 A.M. THIS SUNDAY.
TSUZUKI
...A MESSAGE FROM ME?
I'VE BEEN THINKING ABOUT A GIRL.

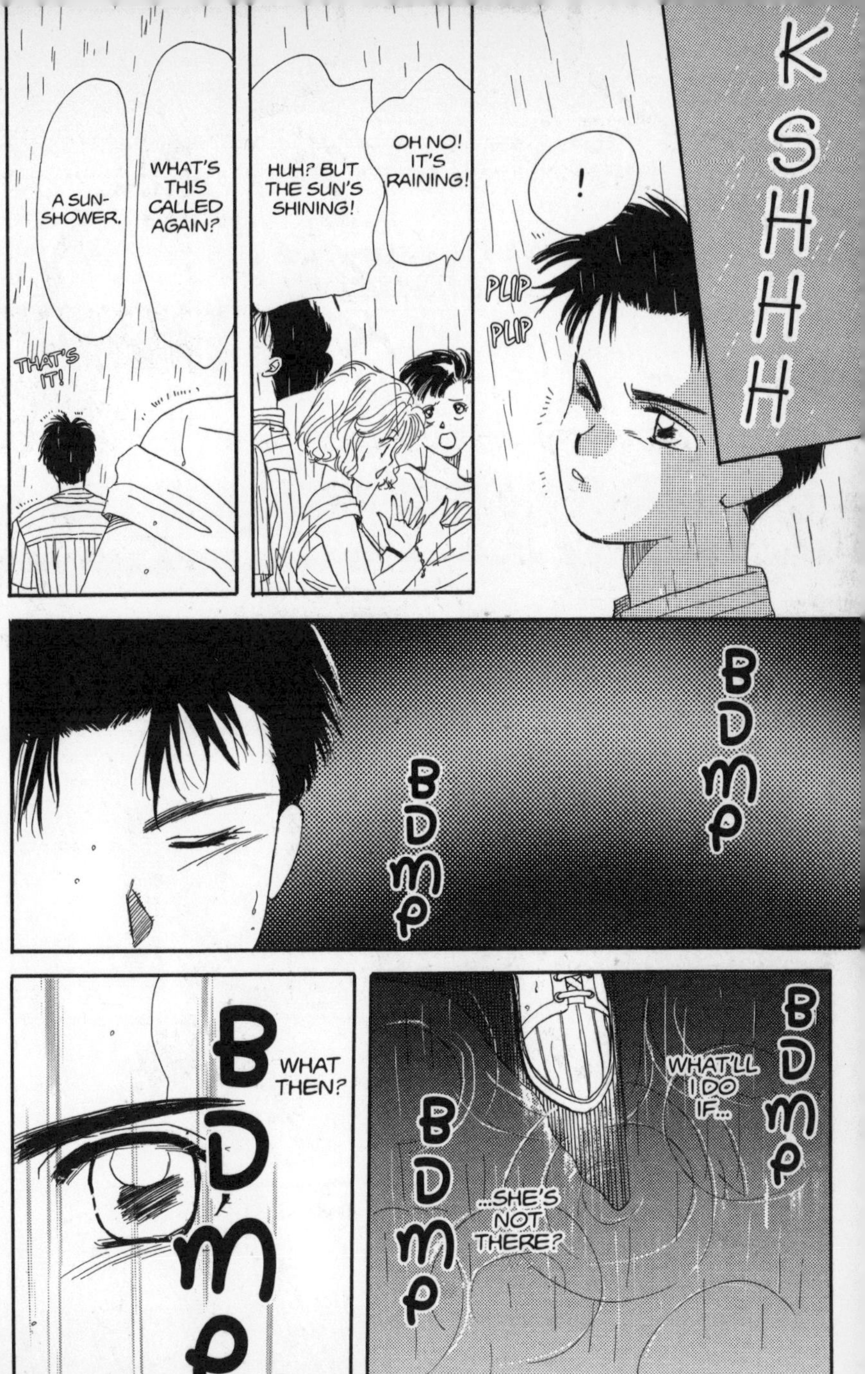
KSHHHH
!
PLIP
PLIP
OH NO! IT'S RAINING!
HUH? BUT THE SUN'S SHINING!
WHAT'S THIS CALLED AGAIN?
A SUN-SHOWER.
THAT'S IT!
BDUMP
BDUMP
BDUMP
WHAT'LL I DO IF...
...SHE'S NOT THERE?
BDUMP
WHAT THEN?
BDUMP

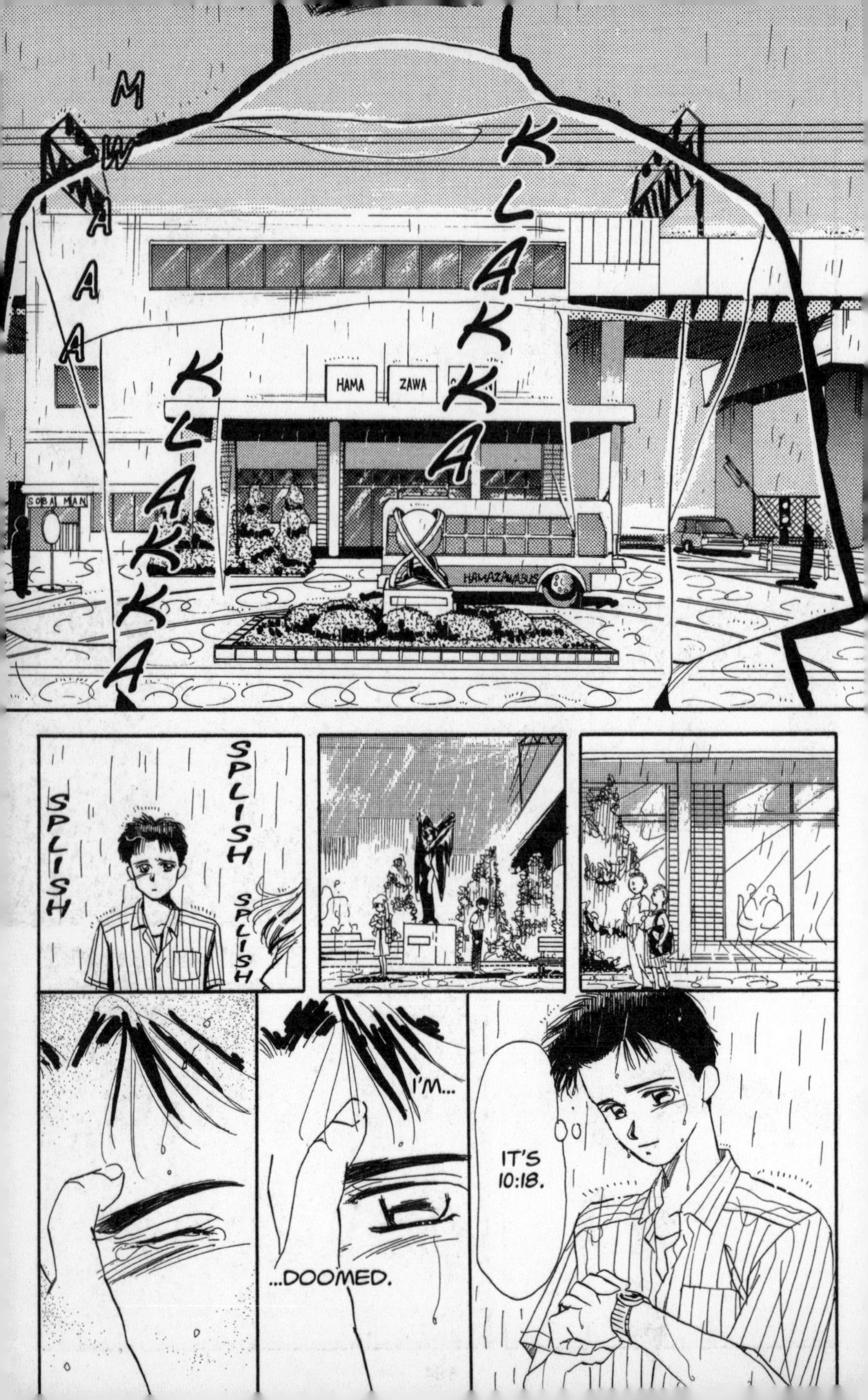
KLAKKA
HAMA ZAWA
KLAKKA
MWAAAA
SOBA MAN
SPLISH SPLISH
SPLISH
IT'S 10:18.
I'M...
...DOOMED.

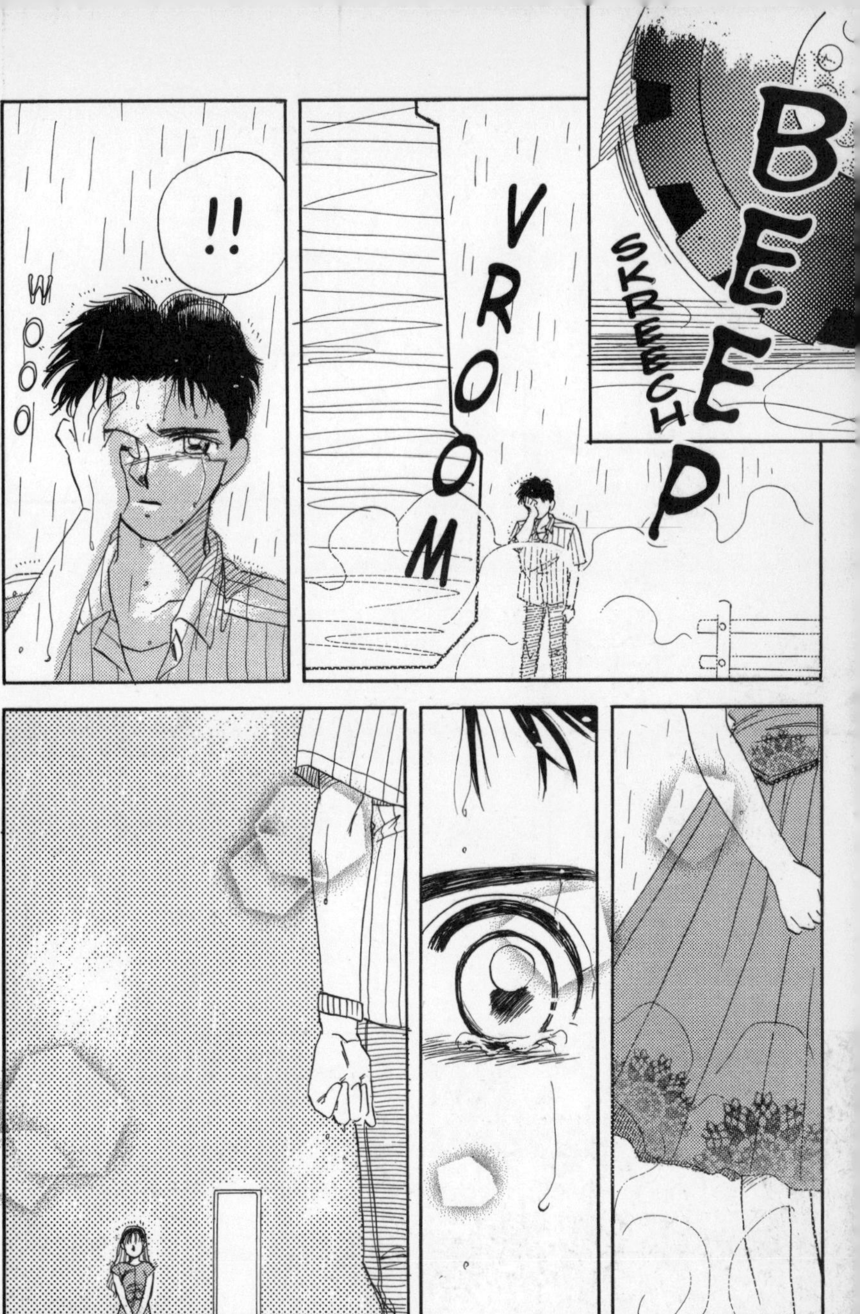
BEEEP
SKREECH
VROOM
!!
WOOO

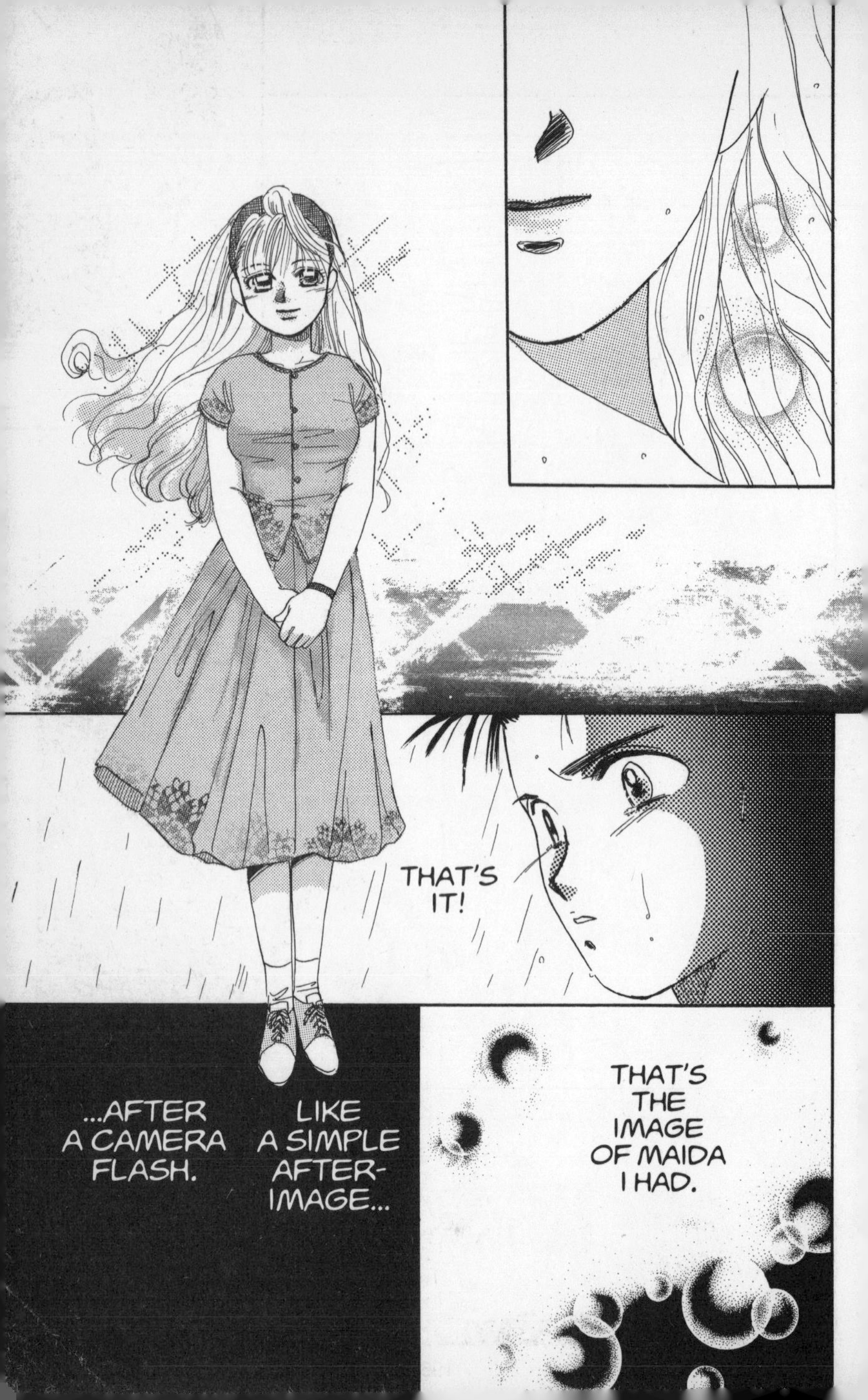
THAT'S IT!
THAT'S THE IMAGE OF MAIDA I HAD.
LIKE A SIMPLE AFTER-IMAGE...
...AFTER A CAMERA FLASH.

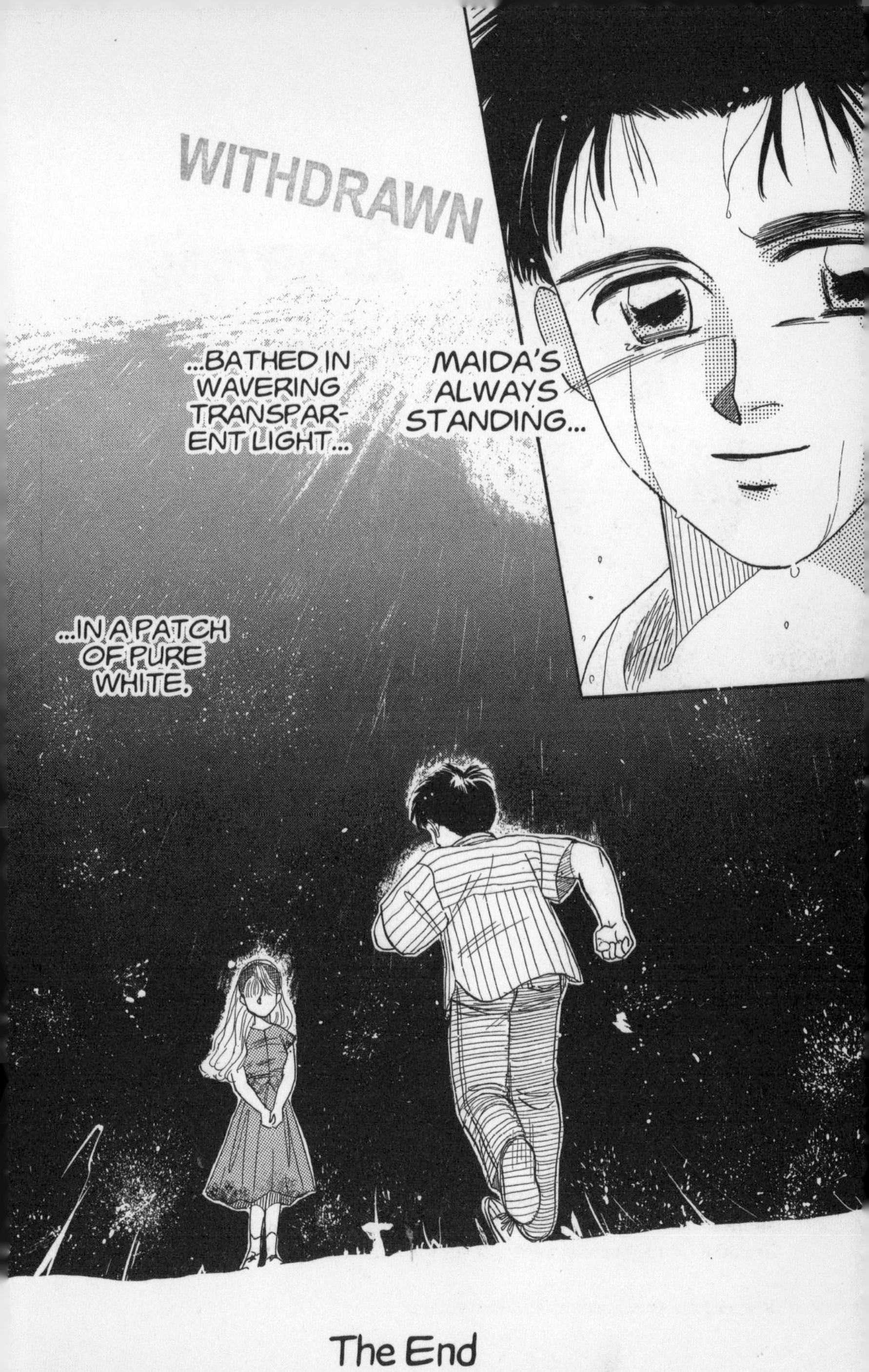
MAIDA'S ALWAYS STANDING...
...BATHED IN WAVERING TRANSPAR-ENT LIGHT...
...IN A PATCH OF PURE WHITE.

The End

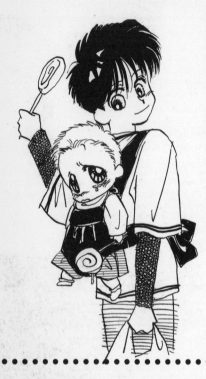

BABY & Me

Creator: Marimo Ragawa

SBM Title: *Baby & Me*

Date of Birth: September 21

Blood Type: B

Major Works: *Time Limit, Baby & Me, N.Y. N.Y.,* and *Shanimuni-Go* (Desperately—Go)

Marimo Ragawa first started submitting manga to a comic magazine when she was 12 years old. She kept up her submissions for four years, but to no avail. She decided to submit her work to the magazine *Hana to Yume*, where she received Top Prize in the Monthly Manga Contest as well as an honorable mention (Kasaku) in the magazine's Big Challenge contest. Her first manga was titled *Time Limit. Baby & Me* was honored with a Shogakukan Manga Award in 1995 and was spun off into an anime.

Ragawa's work showcases some very cute and expressive line work along with an incredible ability to depict complex emotions and relationships. Some of her other works include *N.Y. N.Y.* and the tennis manga *Shanimuni-Go*.

Ragawa has two brothers and two sisters.

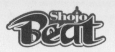

BABY & ME, Vol. 15
The Shojo Beat Manga Edition

STORY & ART BY
MARIMO RAGAWA

English Adaptation/Lance Caselman
Translation/JN Productions
Touch-up Art & Lettering/HudsonYards
Design/Yuki Ameda
Editor/Shaenon K. Garrity

Editor in Chief, Books/Alvin Lu
Editor in Chief, Magazines/Marc Weidenbaum
VP, Publishing Licensing/Rika Inouye
VP, Sales & Product Marketing/Gonzalo Ferreyra
VP, Creative/Linda Espinosa
Publisher/Hyoe Narita

Printed in Canada

Published by VIZ Media, LLC
P.O. Box 77010
San Francisco, CA 941

Shojo Beat Manga Edi
10 9 8 7 6 5 4 3 2
First printing, August 2

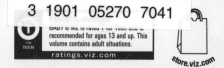

store.viz.com

VIZ
MEDIA